Public Relations in Schools

Fourth Edition

Theodore J. Kowalski

Kuntz Family Chair in Educational Administration
University of Dayton

PEARSON

Merrill
Prentice Hall

Upper Saddle River, New Jersey
Columbus, Ohio

Library of Congress Cataloging-in-Publication Data

Public relations in schools / [edited by] Theodore J. Kowalski.—4th ed.
    p. cm.
  Includes bibliographical references.
  ISBN 0-13-174797-5
1. Schools—Public relations. 2. Schools—Public relations—Case studies. 3. School
management and organization. 4. School management and organization—Case studies.
5. Community and school. 6. Community and school—Case studies.   I. Kowalski, Theodore J.
  LB2847.P82 2008
  659.2′9371—dc22

2006025318

Vice President and Executive Publisher: Jeffery W. Johnston
Executive Editor: Debra A. Stollenwerk
Production Editor: Alexandrina Benedicto Wolf
Production Coordination: Carlisle Publishers Services
Design Coordinator: Diane C. Lorenzo
Cover Designer: Jason Moore
Cover Image: Super Stock
Production Manager: Susan W. Hannahs
Director of Marketing: David Gesell
Senior Marketing Manager: Darcy Betts Prybella
Marketing Coordinator: Brian Mounts

This book was set in Goudy by Carlisle Publishers Services. It was printed and bound by R. R. Donnelley & Sons Company. The cover was printed by The Lehigh Press, Inc.

Pearson Education Ltd.
Pearson Education Singapore, Pte. Ltd.
Pearson Education Canada, Ltd.
Pearson Education—Japan

Pearson Education Australia Pty, Limited
Pearson Education North Asia Ltd.
Pearson Educación de Mexico, S.A. de C.V.
Pearson Education Malaysia, Pte. Ltd.

10 9 8 7 6 5 4 3 2 1
ISBN 0-13-174797-5

About the Authors

Theodore J. Kowalski is the Kuntz Family Chair in Educational Administration at the University of Dayton. A former teacher, principal, superintendent, and college of education dean, he is the author of 19 books and numerous research articles. His most recent books include *Case Studies on Educational Administration* (5th ed.) (2008), *Communication in School Administration: Leading Change in an Information Age* (2007), and *Data-Driven Decisions and School Leadership: Best Practices for School Improvement* (2008). In addition, he is editor of the *Journal of School Public Relations* and serves on the editorial boards of three other professional journals. He has delivered over 90 invited lectures at universities throughout the world and serves as a consultant to schools, universities, and businesses.

CONTRIBUTING AUTHORS

Robert H. Beach is Professor of Educational Planning and Doctoral Program Coordinator at Alabama State University. He has been an Assistant Dean at the University of Memphis, Professor at the University of Alabama, K–12 teacher and administrator, and Secretary/Treasurer of the International Society for Educational Planning. He is widely published, a Fulbright Scholar to Malawi in educational planning, and former Executive Director of the National Council of Professors of Educational Administration.

Lars Björk is the Director of the Institute for Educational Research and Associate Professor in the Department of Educational Leadership Studies at the University of Kentucky. He has coedited *Higher Education Research and Public Policy* (1988), *Minorities in Higher Education* (1994), *The New Superintendency: Advances in Research and Theories of School Management and Educational Policy* (2001), and *The Contemporary Superintendent: Preparation, Practice and Development* (2005). In addition, he has coauthored *The Study of the American Superintendency 2000: A Look at the Superintendent of Education in the New Millennium* (2000) and *The Superintendent as CEO: Standards-Based Performance* (2005).

Patti L. Chance is Associate Professor in the Department of Educational Leadership and Program Coordinator for PK–12 Education Leadership at the University of Nevada, Las Vegas. She has served as a building-level principal, assistant principal, and coordinator for

K–12 gifted education programs and has taught at the elementary, middle, and high school levels. Dr. Chance serves as the editor of *The Rural Educator*, a national refereed journal. In addition, she serves on editorial boards for several other national journals devoted to educational leadership and has published articles and chapters related to instructional supervision, educational administration preparation programs, and the application of organizational and leadership theory to the practice of education leadership. She is coauthor of *An Introduction to Educational Leadership and Organizational Behavior: Theory into Practice*, an introductory text for educational administration.

Nathan J. Daun-Barnett is a doctoral candidate in the Center for the Study of Higher and Postsecondary Education (CSHPE) at the University of Michigan, focusing on education policy affecting the transition from high school to college. Most recently, he has spent time exploring the process of creating change on college campuses with respect to college access and success. He has worked on a statewide project attempting to understand how communities and members of communities move from opinion to judgment on issues related to college access.

Thomas Glass is Professor of Leadership at the University of Memphis. He is coauthor of three recent books: *The Superintendent as CEO: Standards-Based Performance*; *The Study of the American School Superintendency 2000: A Look at the Superintendent of Education in the New Millennium*; and *The History of Educational Administration Viewed Through Its Textbooks*. He was the lead researcher of four national surveys of superintendents and board members sponsored by the Education Commission of the States in 2002 and 2003.

Glenn Graham is Professor of Educational Research at Wright State University. He and Gordon Wise founded the Center for School Tax Levies and Bond Issues at Wright State. They are the authors of the Phi Delta Kappa Fastback on passing tax levies and two books on the same topic published by the Ohio School Boards Association.

James F. McNamara is Professor at Texas A&M University, with graduate faculty appointments in the Departments of Educational Administration and Educational Psychology in the College of Education and the Department of Statistics in the College of Science. He is a noted authority on survey research methodology. His book *Surveys and Experiments in Educational Research* is used extensively by practitioners and graduate students.

Maryanne McNamara is a research associate and program evaluator in the Danforth Foundation School Leadership Program at Texas A&M University. She supervised student teachers at Texas A&M and was director of an alternative high school.

Doug Newsom is the coauthor of three textbooks: *Media Writing*; *This Is PR*; and *Public Relations Writing*. She is coeditor of a book of women's colloquium papers, *Silent Voices*. She is a professor at Texas Christian University in Fort Worth and a public relations practitioner. In 2005, Dr. Newsom received the Pathfinder Award for public relations research from the Institute for Public Relations Research.

Mary John O'Hair is Professor of Educational Leadership and the Vice Provost for School and Community Relations at the University of Oklahoma. She is founding director of the K–20 Center for Educational and Community Renewal (www.k20center.org), an international center designed to transform U.S. and global educational systems into high-achieving, technology-rich learning communities. She has published numerous books and articles. Her most recent book is *Network Learning for Educational Change*. Dr. O'Hair's research focuses on developing and sustaining interdisciplinary learning communities designed to improve teaching, learning, and leading in prekindergarten through graduate (K–20) education.

A. William Place teaches research, school public relations, and personnel courses at the University of Dayton. He received his baccalaureate and master's degrees from the University of Dayton and was a teacher, teacher association representative, and administrator for over 10 years before he received his Ph.D. in Educational Administration from The Ohio State University. He recently spent two years reconnecting with the field as a high school principal. He is a past president of the Mid-Western Educational Research Association and the 2005 School of Education and Allied Professions Teaching Award recipient.

Edward P. St. John is Algo D. Henderson Collegiate Professor of Education at the University of Michigan's Center for Higher and Postsecondary Education. His research focuses on the impact of public finance and educational policies on education opportunities in both K–12 and higher education. He is series editor for *Readings on Equal Education*. He has received the Robert P. Huff Golden Quill Award from the National Association of Student Financial Aid Administrators and the Leadership Award from the Association for the Study of Higher Education. He holds an Ed.D. from the Harvard University Graduate School of Education.

Angela Spaulding is Professor and Chair of the Educational Leadership program at West Texas A&M University–Canyon, where she also coordinates the educational leadership study abroad program and teaches courses in leadership. She has over 90 professional publications and presentations and has been awarded approximately $4 million in research grants. She is the recipient of the WTAMU Outstanding Professor Award. Her research interests include topics emerging from leadership and group dynamics, communication, conflict management, and micropolitics. She has been an early childhood classroom teacher and administrator.

Gordon Wise is Professor Emeritus of Marketing at Wright State University. He and Glenn Graham founded the Center for School Tax Levies and Bond Issues at Wright State. They are the authors of the Phi Delta Kappa Fastback on passing levies and two books on the same topic published by the Ohio School Boards Association.

Brief Contents

Contents

Chapter 3   **Public Opinions and Political Contexts**   **50**
Edward P. St. John and Nathan J. Daun-Barnett

Chapter 4   **Legal and Ethical Aspects of Public Relations**   **73**
Theodore J. Kowalski

Part II   ORGANIZATIONAL CHARACTERISTICS
OF PUBLIC RELATIONS   97

Chapter 5   Social Dimensions of Public Relations   99
Patti L. Chance and Lars Björk

Chapter 6   Public Relations in a Communication Context   128
Angela Spaulding and Mary John O'Hair

Chapter 7   **Programming in Public Schools   159**
          Theodore J. Kowalski

Chapter 8   **Programming in Private and Nontraditional Public Schools   184**
          Theodore J. Kowalski

Part III ADMINISTRATIVE APPLICATIONS   211

Chapter 9 Building Effective Public Relations Plans 213
Robert H. Beach

Chapter 10 Community Relations 244
Theodore J. Kowalski

Note: Every effort has been made to provide accurate Internet information in this book. However, the Internet and information posted on it are constantly changing, so it is inevitable that some of the Internet addresses listed in this textbook will change.

Preface

Studying the relationship between schools and communities has long been part of the curriculum completed by aspiring administrators; however, exposure to this knowledge has not eradicated a disjunction between theory and practice. For example, most practitioners understand that they should cultivate symbiotic relationships with parents, but many of them fail to do so. This disunion between normative and actual practice has become especially troubling in a time when many schools have simultaneously gotten larger and more diverse—culturally, religiously, economically, and politically.

Administrators' attitudes toward working with parents and other stakeholders can be traced to several dispositive conditions. Once in practice, for example, administrators find that they must choose between two contradictory convictions about community involvement. One, which they studied in graduate school, posits that broad participation in public education policy and decision making is morally correct, politically sound, and educationally beneficial. The other, transmitted during socialization to the workplace, posits that external interventions and power sharing cause conflict and subsequently prevent managerial efficiency. Regrettably, the latter outlook often remains dominant as principals and superintendents respond to the political realities of their work.

In its formative years, educational administration was influenced by tenets of traditional management, designed for and applied to business and industry. The goal was to include bureaucratic values that discouraged community involvement because interventions from individuals and groups outside the organization produced conflict and reduced efficiency. The merits of applying this approach to public education were not challenged vigorously until the 1980s and 1990s. America's transition from a manufacturing-based society to an information-based society provided an infrastructure for rapid and frequent communication, and an expectation that this infrastructure would be employed by administrators to engage the public—especially in relation to school reform.

Given this social and political context of an information-base, reform-minded society, the need for administrators to adopt new values and beliefs toward communication and community participation appears to be axiomatic. Unfortunately, however, many school officials continue to be guided by traditional convictions that they are most effective when they insulate themselves from employees and the public. For these misguided practitioners, communication remains a one-way process they use to disseminate information to their chosen audiences as they deem necessary.

Communicative behavior has both symbolic and actual consequences. One-way approaches have not only hindered necessary organizational adaptations, but also reinforced convictions among policy elites that many administrators are either insecure about bringing all segments of the school's community together to engage in reform or philosophically opposed to doing so. Vital tasks, such as constructing a shared vision and implementing a strategic plan, require broad-based participation—both within and outside districts and schools. Responding to this necessity, this text focuses heavily on identifying and explaining communication alternatives in the context of modern technology, prevailing social conditions, and political demands for change.

Two other noteworthy conditions that inhibit effective school–community relations and meaningful school reform are given considerable attention in this book. The first is persisting misinterpretations of the concept of public relations. Unless administrators and the general public understand this concept and its vital role in organizational development, they are unlikely to support its core functions. Second, relationships between school officials and media representatives have often been counterproductive. In the aftermath of critical reform reports, administrators and school board members blamed reporters for sensationalizing public education's shortcomings and for purposefully ignoring its accomplishments. Consequently, at a time when both image building and relationship building are imperative, many education personnel have come to view themselves as victims of misinformation and the media as their enemy.

Clearly, the quest for school reform in an information-based society has redefined effective practice in school administration. Today's outstanding principals and superintendents are both competent managers and dynamic leaders. They are educators who value democratic processes, respect teachers as professional peers, and treat diversity as an asset. They understand that schools are most effective when they maintain a mutual relationship with the communities they serve. As they seek to lead and facilitate positive change, they use modern communication technology to access, disseminate, and exchange information. They model two-way, relational communication as an effective approach to identifying and solving problems.

PURPOSE OF THIS BOOK

The primary objective of this book is to examine the essential nature of public relations in schools amidst contemporary societal conditions. It examines its relation to life in an information age, practice in social institutions, the use of technology in school administration, and sustained demands for school improvement. The following features are relevant to this goal:

◆ A broad perspective of public relations is presented—one that integrates theory and knowledge in promoting two-way communication and extended uses of information.
◆ Public relations is defined as an essential and pervasive administrative function. Consequently, every administrator, regardless of assignment, should completely understand how communication and community relations affect organizational behavior and, ultimately, organizational effectiveness.

◆ The functions embedded in a comprehensive public relations program are vital to school reform. Current strategies—such as state deregulation, district decentralization, and school restructuring—depend on schools identifying real needs and making appropriate adaptations based on those needs. Functions nested in public relations are integral to this task.

◆ The book's content encourages professional reflection. The case studies that open each chapter and the questions, suggested activities, and suggested readings that conclude each chapter promote critical thinking and problem solving.

This edition is divided into three parts. Part I, Contemporary Perspectives, provides a foundation for understanding the applications of public relations in educational institutions. The topics addressed include

◆ Historical perspective and modern definitions;
◆ Analysis of contemporary social conditions and their effect on education;
◆ Role of public opinion in prevailing political contexts, especially in relation to school reform; and
◆ Legal and ethical aspects of communication activities.

Part II, Organizational Characteristics of Public Relations, focuses on the nature of districts and schools. Chapter 5 examines districts and schools as social institutions and focuses on the importance of communication. Chapter 6 examines dimensions of organizational communication and the importance of communication to conflict resolution. Chapters 7 and 8 explore applications of public relations in public, private, and nontraditional public schools.

Part III, Administrative Applications, is devoted to specific duties assumed by administrative personnel engaged in public relations activities. These duties include

◆ Planning,
◆ Establishing media relations,
◆ Collecting and analyzing data,
◆ Conducting funding campaigns,
◆ Responding to crisis situations, and
◆ Evaluating public relations activities.

NEW TO THIS EDITION

The fourth edition continues to be guided by two macro objectives: melding theory and practice, and studying school public relations within an information-based and reform-minded society. However, many new features have been added.

◆ *New and updated chapters.* A new chapter, (Chapter 10) focusing on how administrators and other school employees should relate to the public has been added. It discusses the need for positive relationships, common problems in community relationships, and ways to build mutually beneficial associations.

Chapter 14 has been revised extensively to reflect emerging knowledge about the role of communication in preventing and managing crisis situations.

- *Case studies.* Case studies now appear at the beginning of each chapter. This provides a practice-based situation to frame and increase the relevance of your learning experiences. New cases and questions have been added and some have been revised.
- *School reform.* Some school reform issues have been expanded and reformulated to reflect changing conditions. This was done for two reasons. First, reform initiatives such as charter schools and school choice have elevated the importance of public relations. Second, administrators in nontraditional public schools (i.e., those that must recruit students) face public relations challenges that are nearly identical to those encountered by private school administrators.
- *Technology.* Expanded coverage throughout the book has been given to promises and potential pitfalls of technology. The use of Web pages, e-mail, and information networks in public relations is discussed.
- *Teachers' roles.* Teachers play a lead role as potential school reform leaders and public relations agents. Therefore, the manner in which they interact and communicate with administrators, other teachers, students, parents, and others is given considerable attention.
- *Updated citations.* In response to emerging knowledge and changing conditions, approximately 150 citations and suggested readings have been updated and/or added.

ACKNOWLEDGMENTS

Many individuals contributed to this project; however, I am especially grateful to the following:

- Elizabeth Pearn, my office assistant, contributed in countless ways, including editing and communicating with contributing authors.
- Cheryl Marcus, Assistant to the President of Central State University, helped with research and literature reviews.
- Debbie Stollenwerk, my editor at Merrill/Prentice Hall, continuously provided guidance, encouragement, and inspiration.

I also thank my family for their understanding and moral support and the reviewers of this manuscript for their candid comments and suggestions: Deborah Alexander-Davis, Tennessee Technological University and Tusculum College; Tony Armenta, Southeastern Louisiana University; David C. Bloomfield, Brooklyn College, City University of New York; Jerry Cole, Lincoln Memorial University; Karen B. Lieuallen, Marian College; and Kathy Laboard Brown, The Citadel.

PART I
Contemporary Perspectives

CHAPTER

School Public Relations
A New Agenda
Theodore J. Kowalski

CASE STUDY: THE NEW SUPERINTENDENT'S PUBLIC RELATIONS PLAN

When Janet Ferriter became superintendent of the Boswell School District, it marked the first time this farming community had employed a female in an administrative position. The district's five school board members selected her because she was energetic, enthusiastic, and self-confident. Above all, they were impressed by her commitment to a democratic leadership style. During her employment interview, for example, Dr. Ferriter said that the relationship between the school district and the community should be based on mutual trust and shared responsibility. She added that both district employees and other community residents should have input into school improvement and policy decisions.

At the time Dr. Ferriter interviewed for the Boswell superintendency, she assumed residents in this farming community were highly involved with the public schools. The school board members neither confirmed nor dispelled this assumption. But after beginning her new position, she learned that district residents depended on the school board members to represent their interests. There were no advisory committees or school councils, and only parents of students appeared to have direct contact with teachers and administrators. Moreover, the school board members appeared to be very comfortable with a political context in which they made all the important decisions, working with the superintendent.

Dr. Ferriter also learned that only a limited amount of information about the district was made available to residents. Media coverage was very limited. Two reporters, one from a newspaper and one from a radio station, regularly attended school board meetings. However, the media outlets that employed them were located in the county seat, a small city approximately 25 miles from Boswell. Other than summaries of school board meetings and coverage of athletic events, the school district rarely received media coverage. In addition, neither the district nor individual schools published newsletters or maintained Web pages. There were no information packets available to inform current or new residents about the public schools.

Dr. Ferriter also observed that communication among district personnel was largely informal. One principal commented to her, "This is a small town. Before an administrator has the time to prepare and send a memo or e-mail to employees, they already know what you are going to say. The grapevine in this school district is large and healthy."

Based on a discussion she had with the school board prior to her employment, Dr. Ferriter assumed that the school board was unaware of the limited amount of communication that had been occurring between school personnel and the community. However, when she shared this information with the board members, they were not surprised. The board president commented, "Everyone in this district is pretty satisfied with the schools. Our taxes are reasonable and students do well."

Dr. Ferriter reacted by pointing out that conditions in the state were changing. Local school districts were now required to engage in outcome-based assessments, and superintendents were urged to broaden community involvement in school improvement efforts. She also argued that even in the best of times, public schools should maintain active and ongoing relationships with community residents. She concluded by telling the board members that she intended to develop a plan for improving communication, both among district employees and between district employees and community residents. The board president, Roger Jackson, encouraged her to move forward, and the other board members did not disagree.

Over the next six months, Dr. Ferriter, with assistance from the district's three principals, developed a public relations (PR) plan. Its primary goals were to improve communication and to increase community participation in the schools. The following specific initiatives were included:

- ◆ A public relations advisory committee, consisting of three teachers, two administrators, and three district residents, would be formed. The committee's primary responsibilities would be to oversee implementation of the PR plan, to evaluate the plan's success, and to recommend improvements for the plan.
- ◆ Both the superintendent, on behalf of the district, and the principals, on behalf of the three schools, would ensure that newsletters would be published at least four times a year.
- ◆ The superintendent would oversee the development of a district Web page.
- ◆ Formal communication channels would be identified so that district employees would know how they were expected to communicate with each other and with the community.
- ◆ Efforts would be made to increase media coverage. The goal would be to initiate at least one positive story about the schools each month.
- ◆ District officials would conduct an opinion survey among district residents annually to obtain information relevant to state assessment and future school improvement projects.
- ◆ The PR committee's chairperson would make bimonthly progress reports to the school board.

The superintendent projected that first-year implementation costs would be $70,000.

The PR plan was sent to the school board in late April with a cover letter from Dr. Ferriter indicating that she would recommend approval of the plan at the May school board meeting. After receiving the plan, Mr. Jackson called Dr. Ferriter and suggested that she remove the plan from the May board meeting agenda because several board members had already voiced concerns about it. He added that if the item was not removed from the agenda, a motion to table the matter was probably the best outcome she could expect.

The superintendent was surprised and disappointed. She explained that delaying approval would jeopardize implementation, since funds would have to be appropriated in the budget for the next fiscal year and that document would have to be completed by mid-June. Before concluding the conversation, Mr. Jackson suggested that the item remain on the agenda so that it could be discussed publicly.

After the superintendent presented the plan at the board meeting, Mr. Jackson asked for a motion, indicating that a motion was necessary to proceed to discussion. One of the board members made the motion to accept the superintendent's recommendation, but quickly added that he was doing so simply to allow discussion.

After the motion was seconded, Mr. Jackson was the first board member to speak. "This plan includes good ideas and I appreciate the work Dr. Ferriter and the principals did developing it. Nevertheless, I did not anticipate that a public relations plan would cost so much. I'm not sure the taxpayers want to see us spending $70,000 on public relations."

Wilbur Stines, a farmer and the elder statesman on the board, spoke next. He concurred with the board president's comment and then added another objection. "In addition to my opposition to spending money on public relations, I have to tell you that people here are pretty happy with our schools—and to this point, they're pretty pleased with your leadership. Even if we had unlimited funds, and we don't, I would probably be against spending money on trying to make ourselves look good. We're not a business."

Dr. Ferriter sat silently, hoping that at least one of the board members would speak positively about the plan. She looked at Ella Chambers, the only woman on the school board. Mrs. Chambers owned a restaurant in Boswell, and she had developed a personal friendship with the superintendent. Recognizing that the superintendent was seeking support, she spoke next. "Janice, I think the ideas expressed in the plan are great, but I don't think there is much chance that the board will approve spending $70,000 for public relations. Many of our constituents, rightly or wrongly, are not demanding to be involved more directly. They expect us to represent their interests, and I'm fearful that if this plan was approved, not much would change."

The two remaining board members did not seek recognition, but Dr. Ferriter sensed that they agreed with the comments made by their fellow board members. She then responded. "This plan has two important goals—improving communication and increasing community involvement. When I arrived in Boswell last July, I studied what had occurred in these two areas. Based on my observations, improvement was needed in both areas. I indicated to you that I would be developing a plan to improve relationships. I know the cost seems high, but we cannot develop a Web page, put out newsletters, and support committees without resources."

Mrs. Chambers then asked to be recognized. "Roger, I move to table this matter for at least four months. Since it is apparent that the funds requested are not going to be in the next budget, we should take our time and study Dr. Ferriter's plan more carefully. I would like to see a Web page and school newsletters, and maybe we can find ways to fund some parts of this plan." Her motion to table was approved unanimously.

After the board meeting ended, Dr. Ferriter sat alone in her office, asking herself if she had taken the right approach in pursuing approval of the plan. Had she misread the school board? Had the school board misled her about their support for community involvement? Should she have been more aggressive in presenting the plan? Should she have tried to persuade board members to support it by meeting with them individually? Should she abandon the idea? As she left her office and got in her car to drive home, she had not answered any of these questions.

As the case study demonstrates, PR is arguably one of the most recognized, but least understood dimensions of organizational administration. It has been an American institution (Cutlip, 1995), and its status as a coherent discipline dates back to the beginning of the last century (Sitrick, 1998). Many burgeoning corporations adopted aspects of PR in an effort to develop relationships with customers who were spread across various publics (i.e., demographic groups such as farmers or housewives).

During the first few decades of the twentieth century, school administrators, and especially those working in city school systems, also faced the challenge of building relationships with multiple publics. In the case of public education, this challenge was framed by the political nature of policy making; that is, interest groups within larger school districts often competed to advance their interests through education policy. Not having studied PR, many administrators in these districts emulated the behavior of business executives (Callahan, 1964), but they did so without adequately recognizing that organizational mission affects PR applications. Professors of educational administration did, however, recognizing this fact and began to articulate the need to adapt PR to practice in their profession. The first school PR course was taught at the University of Michigan in 1925, and the first textbook on this subject was published two years later (Maher, 1997).

Today, the modern practice of school PR is intended to do more than apply persuasion techniques. Accessing information in a timely manner, exchanging information, empowering decision makers, identifying and solving organizational problems, and serving the community's interests exemplify objectives that have evolved over the last 50 years. One purpose of this book is to examine past, present, and future practices in school PR. Another is to demonstrate why this process has become indispensable to effective leadership and management of districts and schools.

This initial chapter provides a foundation for understanding PR; it has three objectives. First, differing perspectives of PR are examined, and examples and non-examples of the concept are provided. Second, PR applications are discussed in relation to meaning, goals, barriers, and increased importance. The final portion of the chapter explores four essential themes related to PR applications. The first two, *school reform* and *practice in an information-based society*, describe the context in which PR is applied; the last two, *communication* and *reflective practice*, pertain to administrator knowledge, skills, and dispositions.

PERSPECTIVES OF PUBLIC RELATIONS

Many principals and superintendents are still confronted with the following question: *Why should schools and districts spend money on and devote time to PR?* This appears to be a reasoned query, especially to persons who believe that the primary intent of PR is to manipulate public opinion and feelings. These lingering doubts about the program's necessity continue to be a major barrier to PR implementation, and as such, they help prevent district and school leaders from developing levels of communication and relationships essential to school improvement. More precisely, information management and communication, two central components of modern PR, are indispensable to organizational development (Kowalski, 2005)—and organizational development is indispensable to organizational renewal (Hoy & Miskel, 2005).

Generally speaking, PR is a social science—though some consider it an art as well (Cutlip, 1995). As a profession, PR practice has not been controlled as have other professions, such as law, medicine, and architecture: professions that require practitioners to complete a prescribed course of study and then obtain a license to practice (Seitel, 1992). This does not mean, however, that PR is not a coherent discipline; scholars conduct both theoretical and action research, and practitioners have access to the professional knowledge base produced by these inquiries (Sitrick, 1998). Many universities, in fact, offer undergraduate and graduate degrees in this specialization.

Unfortunately, the term *public relations* has many connotations, especially for those who have not studied the discipline. Even within the literature, PR has been described at varying times as a concept, a profession, a process, and even a goal. Further, PR's intended meaning is often linked to organizational context. For example, PR programs in large manufacturing companies may have missions, processes, and goals substantially different from those associated with school PR programs. Persons studying the history of PR (e.g., Cutlip, 1995; Dilenschneider, 1996) have concluded that both connotations and contexts make it virtually impossible for one definition to describe practice across organizations. This deduction, however, has not dampened the curiosity of scholars and practitioners who continue to ask "What is public relations?" (Gordon, 1997). The persistent exploration of this query has produced multiple definitions, and collectively, they reveal a process that has gotten progressively broader and more complex. An accurate understanding of PR and subsequently of school PR begins with a review of definitions.

Erroneous Perspectives

A first step to comprehending PR is to examine popular misrepresentations. The most distorted image of modern practice is that it entails nothing more than press agentry. Press agents are specialists whose work is typically confined to publicity functions; they concentrate on disseminating carefully crafted messages intended to benefit their clients (either individuals or corporations).

Another common error is viewing PR as a synonym for *advertising* or *marketing*. Advertising, like press agentry, entails the preparation of carefully controlled messages and their transmission to the public. In the case of advertising, the messages almost always are sent through purchased mechanisms (e.g., paid television or newspaper ads). Marketing, by comparison, involves the study of publics to determine the extent to which they need or desire a product or service. Although press agentry, advertising, and marketing are often integral PR components, especially in profit-seeking organizations, none of these functions standing alone is the equivalent of PR for at least two reasons. First, PR is broader than any of them. Second, many PR products are subject to media interpretation, meaning that they cannot be totally controlled by the issuer (Cohen, 1987). For example, one can control the content of a paid newspaper ad, but other aspects of PR, such as press releases, are subject to reporter interpretation.

Viewing PR as simply propaganda is yet another misinterpretation. Propaganda involves creating and spreading ideas, facts, or allegations in an effort to deliberately influence public opinion. Frequently, propagandists employ misinformation to manipulate opinions and actions, both in the organization and in society. Commonly, the propagandist's goal is either to enhance his or her organization's image or to destroy the image of competitor organizations. In part, the proclivity to equate PR with propaganda stems from historical depictions of PR used in business and industry. During the early decades of the last century, PR personnel often "played fast and loose with the truth" (Dilenschneider, 1996, p. xxi). In the current context of practice, propaganda is not considered to be an ethical practice for school administrators.

Lastly, some persons view PR as a synonym for *communication*. Commenting on this error, Haywood (1991) wrote, "Effective public relations is much more than communications: it should be more fundamental to the organization. Public relations should begin before the decision-making stage—when attitudes towards the issues are being developed by management and policies are being formulated" (p. 4). As Haywood suggests, PR is a comprehensive activity intended to influence leadership values and behaviors as well as to shape communication channels.

Multiple Definitions and Models

As noted, connotation and context largely explain why there are so many different PR definitions. In the face of multiple and often conflicting definitions, we may ask this: *Why should we care about PR definitions?* Gordon (1997) provided an answer when he wrote, "Many communication scholars agree that definitions are inherently rhetorical and that the formations of definitions are social processes that shape reality" (p. 58). Therefore, definitions have shaped and continue to shape our perceptions of PR.

All definitions fall into one of two categories. They are either *descriptive* or *normative*. Descriptive definitions seek to explain what actually occurs under the label of PR. These statements typically are general and refer to PR practices across organizations. Dilenschneider (1996), for instance, defined PR simply as "the art of influence." Crable and Vibbert (1986) described the process as a "multiphased function of communication management that is involved in researching, analyzing, affecting, and reevaluating the relationships between an organization and any aspect of its environment" (p. 5). The accuracy of descriptive definitions depends on objective observations, data collection, and interpretations. Often descriptive studies employ techniques such as interviews and focus groups, and the validity of these techniques can be attenuated by researcher bias (Austin & Pinkleton, 2001).

Normative definitions, on the other hand, identify goals describing how publics should be affected or how practitioners should behave (Grunig & Hunt, 1984). They are intended to influence practitioner values and beliefs and to delineate acceptable patterns of behavior. Normative definitions focus on desired practitioner behaviors (e.g., candidness, accessibility), desired outcomes (e.g., perceptions, attitudes), or both. In recent years, efforts to create a positive image for the PR function have included the formation of ideal behaviors to serve as a moral, ethical, and professional compass for practitioners.

Organizational goals in normative definitions are usually characterized by several recurring themes. *Intent* and *relationships between the organization and its many publics* are two of them. Some writers (e.g., Lovell, 1982) stress that PR's general purpose is to promote goodwill toward the organization; others (e.g., Lesly, 1983; McElreath, 1993) view PR as a management function intended to facilitate relationships and understanding between the organization and its ecosystems.

Although PR definitions have evolved to reflect the growing complexity of both the concept and its application, some of the earliest definitions still endure in the mainstream literature. Bernay's definition, constructed nearly 60 years ago, is one of them. This normative definition, analyzed by Cohen (1987), sets out three purposes:

- ◆ To *inform;*
- ◆ To *persuade*—that is, to modify attitudes and opinions; and
- ◆ To *integrate* the actions and attitudes of an organization with those of its publics and the actions and attitudes of its publics with those of the organization.

In 1978, when the First World Assembly of Public Relations Associations convened in Mexico City, the participants defined PR as "the art and social science of analyzing trends, predicting their consequences, counseling organizational leaders, and implementing planned programs of action which will serve both the organization and the public interest" (Newsom, Scott, & VanSlyke Turk, 1989, p. 6). This conceptualization treats PR as a core process in leadership and decision making.

Modern definitions and descriptions usually avoid mentioning the word *persuasion.* In large measure, the term is avoided because of a sensitivity to a Marxist worldview suggesting that anything other than a "two-way symmetrical model (in forms that attempt persuasion of others while disallowing reciprocal persuasion of self) is an agent of domination and, therefore, unethical" (Gordon, 1997, p. 62). Although there are other more acceptable perspectives of persuasion, writers (e.g., Dilenschneider, 1996) have preferred to substitute the word *influence.*

Some scholars have tried to clarify the meaning of PR by using key descriptors. Wilcox, Ault, and Agee (1992), for instance, suggested that students and practitioners focus on six recurring key words or phrases:

- ◆ Deliberate
- ◆ Planned
- ◆ Performance
- ◆ Public interest
- ◆ Two-way communication
- ◆ Management function

Most scholars writing about organizational administration (e.g., Yukl, 2006; Zaleznik, 1989) treat management and leadership as separate roles. The former typically connotes a process of implementing strategies and controlling resources (human and material) in order to achieve organizational objectives. The latter typically connotes functions that focus on determining organizational visions, objectives, and strategies. *School administration,* therefore, is a generic term, typically used to encompass both management and leadership (Kowalski, 2003). Table 1–1 contains an analysis of the key words that give meaning to PR.

Several writers believe that a nexus between activities and intended outcomes facilitates comprehension of this process. An example of this normative approach, developed by Sharpe, is shown in Figure 1–1. Environmental scanning, the last of the five behaviors in this illustration, is an integral element of strategic planning. Scanning refers to monitoring the organization's environment periodically to determine emerging needs and wants (Kowalski, 2006).

Our understanding of PR also is enhanced by looking at models. One of the most widely referenced sources for this purpose is Grunig's (1984) typology based on two factors,

TABLE 1–1
Key Words in Defining Public Relations

Key Word or Phrase	Meaning
Deliberate	PR does not occur by chance; it is a purposeful activity.
Planned	PR does not occur randomly; it is an organized activity.
Performance	PR is shaped and made effective by both policies and practices; process (i.e., how it is applied) is critically important.
Public interest	PR serves multiple publics, including those within districts and schools and those within the community.
Two-way communication	PR extends beyond the dissemination of information to include information exchanges.
Management function	PR involves the application of resources to achieve organizational goals.

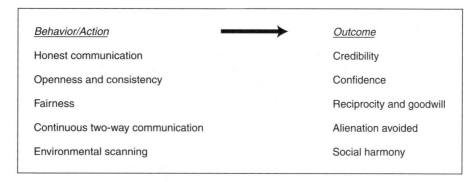

FIGURE 1–1
Sharpe's Five Links in Effective Programs (Source: Adapted from Seitel, 1992, p. 10.)

communication direction (pertaining to the flow of information) and *symmetry* (pertaining to the intended benefits). In combination, the two factors produce four PR models:

- ◆ *One-way asymmetrical.* This model is used to disseminate positive publicity and re-strict unfavorable information; it is a form of propaganda associated with press agen-try intended to benefit the organization. For example, a principal publishes a school newsletter that contains selected positive information about the school and him, but no information that would be beneficial to others. In addition, readers are not given an opportunity to respond or ask questions.
- ◆ *One-way symmetrical.* This model is used to disseminate accurate public information without volunteering negative information; it is more neutral than press agentry and is intended to benefit both the organization and society. For example, a principal publishes a newsletter that contains information beneficial to him and the readers (e.g., clarification of the discipline policies), but readers are not given an opportu-nity to respond or ask questions.
- ◆ *Two-way asymmetrical.* This model is used to persuade publics, but information about these publics is used to structure the communication to increase the probability

> **Constants** (elements found in virtually all definitions)
> - **Administrative function**—PR is managed and executed by administrators.
> - **Organizational context**—PR is delivered in an organizational context.
> - **Publics**—PR involves interactions within the organization and between the organization and its multiple publics.
>
> **Variables** (differences among definitions)
> - **Descriptive definitions**—The focus is on real processes and outcomes.
> - **Normative definitions**—The focus is on ideal processes and outcomes.

FIGURE 1–2
Constants and Variables in Public Relations Definitions

of influencing the behaviors of the publics. For example, a superintendent conducts a community interest survey before determining a strategy for passing a tax referendum to fund a new school building. There is an exchange of information, but the intended benefit is restricted to the school (i.e., determining how to be politically successful by capitalizing on support and countering opposition).

◆ *Two-way symmetrical.* This model is used for establishing mutual understanding and resolving conflict between the organization and its publics; it requires extensive knowledge and understanding of these publics and is intended to benefit both the organization and society (Dozier, 1995; Grunig, 1989). For example, a superintendent conducts a community interest survey before determining whether to pursue a tax referendum to fund a new school building. There is an exchange of information, and the superintendent wants to determine and then weigh whether community needs and values warrant moving forward with the project.

In modern PR practice, one-way symmetrical programs are considered the least desirable and two-way symmetrical programs the most desirable.

In summary, there are multiple PR perspectives that vary primarily in two ways: describing process versus outcomes and describing real behavior versus ideal behavior. All are addressed within a framework of three recurring themes: *administration, organization, and publics* (Gordon, 1997). That is, the PR concept is an administrative function occurring within an organization and involving contact with external publics (see Figure 1–2).

SCHOOL PUBLIC RELATIONS

School public relations refers to the application of PR in the context of organizations having the primary mission of delivering educational services. This includes public and private institutions at both the precollegiate and the collegiate levels. The largest subcategory within this organizational family includes public elementary and secondary schools. School PR is examined here with respect to meaning, goals, persistent barriers, and current importance.

Meaning

Awareness of the need to apply PR to public education evolved gradually during the first half of the last century (Harral, 1952). Historically, education writers and practitioners have preferred to refer to school PR as "community relations." Their intent was to avoid the negative connotations often associated with PR. For example, they did not want the public viewing school administrators as Madison Avenue persuasion specialists (West, 1985). This trepidation was well founded, since many taxpayers have considered PR to be "synonymous with words like cover-up, obfuscate, misinterpret, and lie" (Martinson, 1995, p. 85).

In this book, school PR is viewed as a positive construct that broadly encompasses communication functions within a district or school and communication functions between districts and schools and their multiple external publics. The process is intended to produce and maintain a positive organizational image, to ensure collaboration between school and community, and to ensure organizational effectiveness. Community relationships are seen as both a basic PR component and a primary objective for schools.

Definitions of school PR vary in focus and length. They usually allude to using information to influence perceptions and decision making (e.g., Knezevich, 1969; Saxe, 1984) and to enhancing the relationship between school and community through two-way communication (e.g., Jones, 1966; Lutz & Merz, 1992). Several authors have characterized school PR as both philosophy and process. Walling (1982), for instance, wrote that the concept incorporated values and beliefs about communication and embodied management techniques used by schools to communicate with their constituents.

The National School Public Relations Association (1986) defined educational PR as "a planned and systematic two-way process of communications between an educational organization and its internal and external publics designed to build morale, goodwill, understanding, and support for that organization" (p. 28). West (1985) offered this description: "Educational public relations is a systematically and continuously planned, executed, and evaluated program of interactive communication and human relations that employs paper, electronic, and people mediums to attain internal as well as external support for an educational institution" (p. 23). The focus on human relations in these two definitions is highly relevant because educational PR addresses how people feel about issues, services, and individual or organizational personalities. Alluding to this fact, Norris (1984) suggested that PR might be better understood if it was called "public relationship" because the process involves building connections with a great many different publics.

In summary, school PR is viewed as *an evolving social science and leadership process utilizing multimedia approaches designed to build goodwill, enhance the public's attitude toward the value of education, augment interaction and two-way symmetrical communication between schools and their ecosystems, provide vital and useful information to the public and employees, and play an integral role in planning and decision-making functions.* Its use is justified by three major propositions cogent to all governmental agencies:

1. A democratic government is best served by a free two-way flow of ideas and accurate information so citizens and their government can make informed choices.
2. A democratic government must report and be accountable to the citizens it serves.

3. Citizens, as taxpayers, have a right to government information—but with some exceptions (exceptions to disclosing information may be predicated on laws and administrative judgments about balancing public interests with citizens' rights) (Baker, 1997, p. 456).

School PR also is influenced by the philosophical dispositions of those who exercise power and control important education decisions—for example, governors, state legislators, and school boards.

Goals

Like any administrative function, PR should be guided by goals and objectives identified in an organizational PR plan—a document that helps ensure that goals remain focused and effective. Goals represent desired ends or purposes, and they are usually broad, long-term (i.e., extending beyond two or three years) philosophical statements providing a normative perspective. In addition to being in the PR plan, goals may be found in policy manuals, planning documents, and annual reports.

There can be, and often are, substantial differences between *stated* and *real* goals. For example, the policy manual in one school district states that the purposes of the PR program are to foster open communication and improve community relations, but in reality the program has focused exclusively on efforts to influence the taxpayers to support tax referenda.

Although the foci of a PR program may vary from institution to institution depending on contextual needs, several goals are pervasive for schools:

◆ *Improving the quality of education.* Every administrative, instructional, and support service provided by public education agencies, including PR, has as its ultimate goal the improvement of student learning. All PR activities should either produce or influence activities and outcomes that contribute to improved educational services (Armistead, 2000).

◆ *Encouraging open political communication.* Although public employees and taxpayers expect school officials to advocate their own ideas and recommendations, they want to be a part of open and fair debates about these ideas (Baker, 1997). Denied this opportunity, they may resort to covert political action that serves to divide the community into competing interest groups. Through effective PR programming, advocates of rival ideas should be able to express themselves by engaging in open and candid discourse (Martinson, 1999).

◆ *Enhancing the image of the school or district.* Imaging entails presenting a picture of an organization to its various publics. In the case of elementary and secondary education, the public's confidence has been diminished by a multitude of negative stories appearing in the news media (Peck & Carr, 1997). These reports, often based on conditions in the nation's most troubled schools, have had a cumulative effect of creating negative images because taxpayers often see public education on one giant bureaucracy (Kowalski, 2003). In truth, public schools are unique entities because their clientele, guiding philosophies, needs, problems, resources, instructional strategies, and institutional climates are not uniform. Imaging, therefore, should focus on establishing separate identities for districts and schools (Pfeiffer & Dunlap, 1988).

◆ *Building support for change.* Organizational development, including school improvement, requires change. Frequently, efforts to do things differently meet with resistance , both in the organization (e.g., opposition from teachers or students) and in the broader community environment (e.g., opposition from parents or pressure groups). Opposition can be based on misinformation, misunderstandings, and rumors, but even when publics understand the need for change, they may reject specific initiatives because they philosophically disagree with them. Consequently, when pursuing school improvement, administrators need to educate employees and the public and subsequently engage them in discourse to reconcile conflict emanating from opposing values and beliefs.

◆ *Managing information.* Traditionally, information has been viewed as a source of organizational power, especially for administrators who have had greater access to vital information and greater control over its distribution (Yukl, 2006). Accumulating power, however, is not the purpose of information management. In modern organizations, the process involves seeking and obtaining information—from employees, students, parents, governmental agencies, other educational institutions, and the community at large—and extends to storing, analyzing, and distributing information. Information management has quickly become a prerequisite for data-driven decision making.

◆ *Marketing programs.* The growing popularity of reform initiatives such as school choice, charter schools, and vouchers has prompted administrators to pay more attention to marketing. The primary characteristics of this function include (a) voluntary exchanges of values, (b) the identification of targeted audiences, and (c) sensitivity to consumers (Kotler, 1975). Hanson (2003) noted that educational marketing involves "developing or refining *specific* school programs in response to the needs and desires of specific target-markets (e.g., 'at risk' families, parents of pre-school children, voters)" (p. 235). Said another way, marketing is a mechanism for determining what the public needs and expects from its schools.

◆ *Establishing goodwill and a sense of ownership.* In the current political climate, there is a considerable level of dissatisfaction with public education (Kowalski, 2006). Taxpayers often see their relationship with local schools as one-sided; that is, they are forced to support schools financially, but receive little or nothing in return. Such negative attitudes are especially prevalent among taxpayers without students attending public schools. Recapturing goodwill and rekindling a sense of collective responsibility requires school officials to engage all publics in meaningful discourse—and in this vein, PR is an essential program.

◆ *Providing evaluation data.* Administrators have a responsibility to assess and evaluate the effectiveness of education programs. A PR program can facilitate these tasks by providing feedback from various publics. Data may be gathered formally or informally; written community surveys conducted by administrators and open telephone lines encouraging unsolicited comments exemplify common data-gathering methods. The topics of collecting and analyzing data are addressed in detail in Chapter 12.

To ensure that PR goals are pursued, administrators should develop performance objectives. These are specific statements containing behavioral criteria. They inform employees of expected behaviors, set benchmarks for performance, and provide a framework for summative and formative evaluations. In the case of expected behaviours, judgments are made about the amount of progress made toward goals and about the necessity of adding, deleting, or altering goals. Performance objectives should be sufficiently specific to communicate behavioral expectations and to provide a basis for evaluation, but not so specific that they restrict creativity or dehumanize administrative work. Examples of possible performance objectives and their relationship to goals are shown in Table 1–2.

Persistent Barriers

As noted earlier, implementing PR programs has not always been an easy assignment for district and school administrators. Connor and Lake (1988) identified three types of barriers to organizational change, and they are applicable to understanding resistance to school PR.

1. *Those related to understanding.* For example, individuals may not understand the true meaning of PR, or they may not understand why this process is necessary for districts and schools.
2. *Those related to accepting.* For example, individuals may philosophically reject the purposes of PR or its applications in districts and schools.
3. *Those related to acting.* For example, the district or school may have insufficient human and material resources to implement the program.

TABLE 1–2

Examples of Performance Objectives for Administrators

General Goal	Possible Performance Objectives
Enhancing learning	Establish partnerships; involve parents and other citizens on curriculum committees, textbook selection committees; enlist community members as volunteers.
Communicating politically	Manage conflict; hold open discussions to debate competing views; respect minority opinions; prepare communications for multiple publics.
Enhancing image	Celebrate accomplishments; highlight strengths; provide accurate and relevant information to the media and general public.
Supporting change	Engage the public in visioning and planning activities; hold open meetings to explain planned change; provide speakers for civic groups; educate the public about the need for change and the nature of recommended changes.
Managing information	Establish procedures for obtaining, analyzing, and storing data; create channels for accessing and distributing data; provide a mechanism for storing databases.
Marketing programs	Provide information about programs to the community on a regular basis; conduct periodic needs assessments to ascertain changing conditions.
Sharing responsibility	Create school councils that include citizen representatives; create advisory councils; invite employees and the public to suggest improvements; praise successful collaboration.
Obtaining evaluation data	Conduct employee, parent, and community surveys; encourage unsolicited comments; monitor the quantity and quality of complaints, concerns, and problems.

These barriers have a hierarchical relationship; that is, you must understand in order to accept, and you must understand and accept before you realize you are unable to act. This typology provides a useful diagnostic tool for administrators because it should help them to select appropriate actions to overcome resistance.

Current Importance

Experts believe that schools benefit from a well-conceived PR program even in the best of times because information management and communication are incessant core activities in any organization. In troubled times, the stakes are higher because the stability or status of schools is threatened. Whether this peril comes from within the schools or from the wider environment, administrators are expected to protect the well-being of the institution and the interests of its stakeholders.

In an information-based, reform-minded society, public schools are being exposed to greater levels of market competition; charter schools, vouchers, and home schooling are prime examples of concepts that threaten the future of traditional public schools. Under these conditions, organizational image, communication, marketing, and information management assume new levels of importance (Hanson, 2003). And as the future of education gets more uncertain, the PR function becomes more essential because maintaining institutional equilibrium (i.e., ensuring that schools are meeting community needs and wants) requires a greater quantity of change.

Two issues illustrate why PR is currently so important for schools. The first is the public's declining confidence in traditional education systems; the second is the need for school officials to engage various publics in discourse so that acceptable purposes, programs, and outcomes can be established (Lashway, 2002). Several education writers (e.g., Berliner & Biddle, 1995; Bracey, 1997) have pointed out that misconceptions about public education have been pervasive among education's chief critics. Commenting on the seemingly endless chain of reform ideas generated in the decade following the publishing of *A Nation at Risk* in 1983, Berliner (1993) observed that schools in this country were unfairly damaged by unsubstantiated claims that public education is expensive and wasteful, that students are lazy and unproductive, and that America's productivity has fallen as a result of inadequate education. Regrettably, rebuttals to these claims frequently have not changed public opinion, nor have they placed real needs in their proper context.

The public's concern with high school graduation rates during the 1990s illustrates how erroneous opinions often conceal real societal problems. At that time, many citizens believed that graduation rates were in decline when in fact they were increasing. In the mid-1990s, approximately 75 to 80% of all eligible students in this country were graduating from high school—a substantial increase over the 1950 rate of approximately 50% (Amundson, 1996). In addition to being incorrect, the conclusion about the decline of graduation rates distracted policy makers from framing the problem of school failure correctly. That is, policy makers failed to evaluate graduation rates in the context of prevailing social and economic conditions. Students who did not finish high school in the 1990s faced much more limited job prospects than did students in the 1950s (Schlechty, 1990). In essence, both the critics who incorrectly argued that graduation rates had declined and the educators who simply corrected the record failed to frame the real dilemma facing schools and society. Because dropping out of school was more consequential in the 1990s than it was in the 1950s, even an 80% graduation rate was not acceptable.

Although most administrators recognize that responding to criticism has become an inevitable part of their practice, they often are uncertain about the best strategy for doing it. This is true for the following reasons:

♦ The critics often have substantial credibility with the public, or they possess considerable political power. Elected officials, business leaders, and media representatives are prime examples. The critics often espouse positions that are politically popular. For example, they frequently blame schools for social problems, but avoid blaming society—even though pervasive problems such as poverty and child abuse unquestionably affect education outcomes negatively.

♦ The critics often believe that they are standing on the high moral ground; they pretend that their positions on school reform are unaffected by political and economic self-interests.

Amundson (1996) suggested that administrators have three choices when responding to criticism, including that offered by the media or detailed by journalists:

1. They could ignore the criticism. This alternative requires little risk or energy, but it usually fuels perceptions that administrators are indifferent or incompetent.
2. They could take a defensive posture. This alternative is precarious because simply refuting criticism creates the perception that administrators are denying the need for reform.
3. They could communicate openly and honestly. This alternative prompts administrators to educate the public and to enlist support and assistance in positive ways. It also is the only choice that allows administrators rather than the critics to manage the issues. Engaging the community in discussions about educational purposes, programs, and outcomes is the first step toward meaningful school renewal.

Dissatisfaction with student performance is not the only issue that has elevated the importance of PR in the past 50 years. The image of public education also has been damaged by incessant conflict between teachers' unions and school boards (Campbell, Corbally, & Nystrand, 1983). In addition, the populations in most school districts have become increasingly diverse (Kowalski, 2006), a factor spawning conflict and deep political divisions. As an example, conflict between the values of excellence and equity has often produced divergent and incompatible agendas for local districts. The range of contemporary conditions associated with a greater need for school PR is presented in Table 1–3.

UNDERLYING THEMES

Four themes frame present-day school PR practices (see Figure 1–3). They are the information age, school reform, communication, and reflective practice. These themes also provide a context for applying the information presented in the remainder of this book.

TABLE 1–3
Selected Contemporary Conditions Intensifying the Need for Public Relations

Condition	Ramifications
Public dissatisfaction	Economic and political support for public education suffer as negative images are reinforced.
Life in an information-based society	Accessing and using information rapidly is crucial to identifying and solving problems. An organization's competitiveness is partially determined by its information and communication systems.
Life in a pluralistic culture	Groups place conflicting demands on schools. School officials must be able to craft messages for targeted audiences; compromise becomes an important tool for resolving conflict.
Decentralization of governance	Efforts to reform schools from the bottom up lead to broader participation in critical organizational functions.
Lifelong learning	Learning is no longer considered a youth activity. Administrators are expected to provide learning opportunities for employees and adult patrons.
Demographic changes	The percentage of families having children in the public schools continues to decline. Building goodwill and support requires special efforts to reach taxpayers who have no direct link to the schools.
Expanded demands and shrinking resources	As demands for educational services increase, available resources either remain constant or decline. As a consequence, competition for scarce resources becomes more intense.
Market-driven reform ideas	Initiatives such as vouchers, choice, and charter schools require public schools to compete with other institutions for students.
Acceleration of change	The pace of change continues to accelerate. Organizational development entails continuous efforts to scan the environment, restate needs, and alter delivery systems.
Global economy	Expectations that schools will contribute to economic growth by adequately preparing students for the world of work are increasing.
Social and economic conditions	Because many public students are being reared in poverty conditions, greater pressures are being placed on public schools to provide medical, nutritional, psychological, and social services.
Funding concerns	As costs rise and demand for additional programs increases, administrators must spend more time competing for scarce tax dollars.
Philosophical ambiguity	School reform in the context of competing philosophies is extremely difficult. Administrators are expected to educate the public and to facilitate visioning and planning activities that involve a broad spectrum of the community.

Information Age

America's transition from a manufacturing-based society to an information-based society was predicted by noted futurist, Alvin Toffler (1970) as early as the late 1960s. A little more than a decade later, microcomputers began replacing typewriters in offices, homes, and schools. Shortly thereafter, the Internet was constructed, providing a distributed, fail-proof network that connected many of these computers. With the subsequent creation of the World Wide Web, the Internet became a global network. The phenomenal growth of

FIGURE 1–3
Themes Framing Contemporary Practice
in School Public Relations

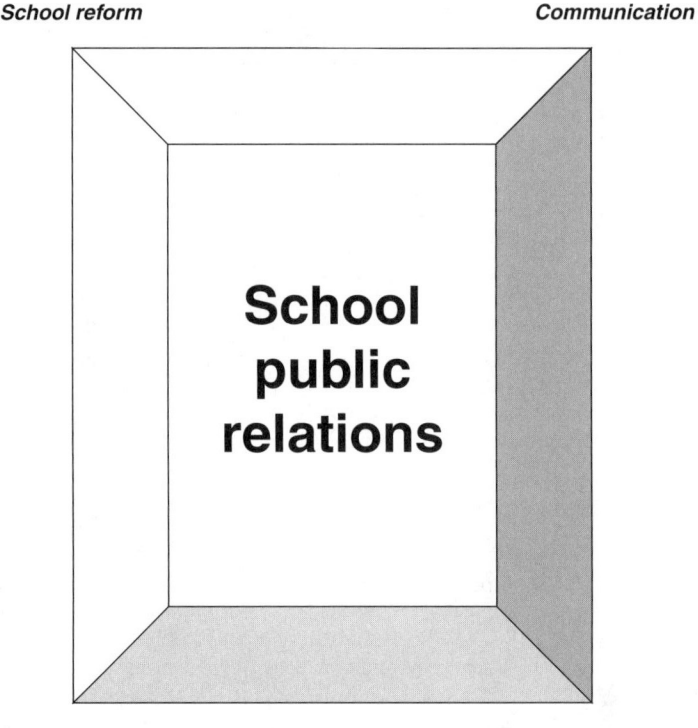

School reform   Communication

School
public
relations

Information age   Reflective practice

the Internet has been the major factor in the information revolution. In just one year, from 2001 to 2002, the number of U.S. citizens with access to the Internet increased from 158.9 million to 168.6 million—an astonishing 6.1% increase (Nielsen/Net Ratings, 2005).

By late 1970s, scholars had become confident that technology would improve access to information and increase the value of information in organizational management (Lipinski, 1978). West (1981) was one of the first authors to analyze these trends as they applied to school administration, and he concluded that technology would change normative standards of practice for principals and superintendents. Noting how previous efforts to generate high levels of interaction between school and community had routinely failed, he predicted that technology would allow practitioners to narrow gaps between communication theory and practice. The paradigm shift he envisioned centered on a combination of communication and techno-relations—the latter being a process utilizing electronic options devoid of physical contact. While extolling the possible virtues of technology, West (1985) cautioned that technology would not ensure school and community relations would improve. He concluded that creating positive relationships via technology depended on whether or not administrators would use such tools in a way that did not sacrifice human interaction for efficiency.

Today, state departments of education and virtually all districts and schools have Web pages offering the public access to information and an entry point for exchanging information with educators. And as citizens learned to use the Internet, they expanded their appetite for information and elevated their expectations of administrators as communicators (Kowalski, 2005). By the mid-1990s, technology had become so prevalent in education that many administrators were evaluated formally with respect to deploying it (Lare & Cimino, 1998). Even so, studies often found that experienced practitioners were slow to develop computer literacy skills. For example, Testerman, Algozzine, and Flowers (2002) found that assistant principals and graduate students aspiring to be principals had computer skills that exceeded those of practicing principals.

Technology enhances opportunities for administrators to satisfy an information-seeking public. In essence, the information age is characterized by the confluence of a rapidly increasing demand for information and the ability of organizational administrators to satisfy the demand. The potential for technology to affect school public relations is demonstrated by the following examples:

- Amassing and maintaining extensive databases that facilitate critical functions such as strategic planning and policy development
- Producing quality visual and printed materials rapidly and inexpensively
- Conducting videoconferences
- Providing information on demand
- Developing Web sites for districts and schools
- Using cable television to broadcast meetings and other school functions
- Personalizing messages to multiple publics and targeted audiences

School Reform

Over the past two centuries, there have been multiple educational reform movements, each trying to answer the same fundamental questions (Parker & Parker, 1995): What are the purposes of public education? Who should pay for this service? To what extent should public education solve societal problems? The current protracted effort to change schools that began circa 1980 is no exception.

In order to appreciate the present challenges facing administrators, one must understand how the current school reform movement has evolved. The first wave of changes occurred in the early to mid-1980s. Students were the primary targets, and making them do more of what they were already doing was the dominant strategy (Kowalski, 2003). Laws extending the length of the school year and the length of the school day and establishing high school graduation requirements are prime examples of policies adopted during this period. The same strategy of intensification mandates was used in the late 1980s, as teachers and administrators also drew the reformers' attention (Hanson, 1991). During this second wave, policy makers pressured schools of education to make their programs more rigorous, and they increased licensing standards, partly by requiring licensing examinations and partly by initiating new continuing education requirements.

By 1990, however, reformers faced the reality that getting tough with students and educators had produced only modest gains. In addition, their actions had only intensified the relevance of two gnawing queries: Could public schools simultaneously pursue excellence and equity? Could centralized "one size fits all" policies produce desired levels of improvement?

Many reformers either began searching outside mainstream education for solutions (e.g., proposing charter schools, choice, and vouchers) or focused on redesigning the organizational structure of existing schools (Kowalski, 2003).

The third and current wave of school reform has included a mix of economics, philosophy, politics, and pedagogy. The underlying purpose framed by two foundational beliefs: (1) Public schools will improve if they are forced to compete with other schools and (2) reform is more effective if it is tailored to the real student needs. Vouchers, charter schools, and home schooling are indicative of the first perspective, and state deregulation and district decentralization are indicative of the second perspective (Kowalski, 2003).

Both market-based concepts forcing competition and organizational concepts stressing individualization elevate the value of PR. Competition is driving administrators to engage in imaging and marketing. At the same time, there is a growing need to educate the members of the public and then engage them in visioning, planning, and evaluation activities. Discussing third-wave reforms, Wadsworth (1997) concluded that reaching public consensus on change requires an ongoing planning process, leaders who listen, diverse participants, choices, and productive communication. Studies of decentralization reforms carried out in Kentucky during the early 1990s found that communication between school and community was critical to forging a local reform agenda (Murray, 1993).

Communication

In this rapidly changing world, information and integrated communication programs are essential to both management and leadership functions (Caywood, 1997). Even so, the greater attention being given to organizational leadership has resulted in new behavioral expectations for administrators. Zaleznik (1989) observed, "Communication is important to both managers and leaders, but the modes differ. Managers communicate in signals, whereas leaders prefer clearly stated messages" (p. 24). Managers are less apt to use information directly; they rely more on sending symbolic messages to others. This approach is often impersonal and derives from the belief that information is supposed to be controlled by those with legitimate authority. Leaders, by comparison, are more likely to strive for harmony between the detached nature of management and the moral dimensions of dealing with people (Sergiovanni, 2006). Put another way, leaders treat information and communication as instruments of empowerment, allowing members of the school's community to collectively seek reform.

Scholars who have studied organizational change in business (e.g., Schein, 1999) and in schools (e.g., Fullan, 2001; Fullan & Stiegelbauer, 1991; Hall & Hord, 2001) conclude that new ideas are likely to be rejected if they are incongruous with deeply rooted assumptions shared by the people who will be affected. These shared beliefs, values, and norms constitute a school's culture—the glue that binds people in the school together (Hanson, 2003).

Historically, management literature has treated culture as a cause and communication as an effect. That is, communicative behaviors were viewed as manifestations of culture. More recently, enlightened communication scholars have viewed the relationship between culture and communication as reciprocal. Conrad (1994) wrote, "Cultures are communicative creations. They emerge and are sustained by the communicative acts of all employees, not just the conscious persuasive strategies of upper management. Cultures do not exist separately from people communicating with one another" (p. 27). Axley (1996) described the bond between culture and communication this way: "Communication gives rise to organizational culture, which gives rise to communication, which perpetuates culture" (p. 153). This association implies that communication cannot be understood sufficiently by reducing it to a loop of linear steps or by focusing research exclusively on the transmissions between senders and receivers (Katz & Kahn, 1978). Instead, communication should be seen as a process through which organizational members express their collective inclination to coordinate beliefs, behaviors, and attitudes. Put more simply, communication is the act that people use to give meaning to their organizational lives by sharing perceptions of reality (Kowalski, 1998, 2004). A negotiated order evolves from both internal and external interactions among individuals and groups, and this interplay occurs in the informal as well as the formal organization. When viewed from this social system perspective, communication is a process that shapes, transmits, and reinforces a socially constructed culture (Mohan, 1993).

If administrators are to lead others in reshaping school cultures, they must know how others perceive reality, and they must use this information to create mutual understandings about a school's purposes and practices. This objective is unlikely to be met, however, by administrators who either intentionally or unintentionally restrict the open debate of values, discourage conflict, or limit access to information (Deetz, 1992; Sarason, 1996). Nor is it likely to be met by administrators unable to communicate effectively across racial and economic lines (Walker-Dalhouse & Dalhouse, 2001).

Regrettably, managers in many organizations continue to treat information as power, and they restrict access to it as a means of protecting personal power (Burgess, 1996). Superintendents and principals who fall into this category are incapable of actualizing the primary function of transformational leadership—shaping and developing new norms in the school (Carlson, 1996). When an administrator appropriately recognizes that organization does not precede communication and becomes subsequently supported by the organization, he or she is more inclined to view organization as an effect of communication (Taylor, 1993). For example, structure and programs do not produce credibility and trust (essential characteristics of leaders who assume the role of change agent); rather, these qualities are created through human interactions. Unless leaders accurately evaluate the effects of communication on underlying assumptions, and unless they properly dissect the language of a school, they probably cannot determine the extent to which culture facilitates or obstructs change.

Clearly then, school PR is inextricably tied to the need for leaders to be effective communicators (Kowalski, 2004). Communication is both the backbone of a successful PR program (Newsom, Scott, & VanSlyke Turk, 1989) and an indispensable tool for organizational development (Hanson, 2003). Within districts and schools, the communication aspects of PR facilitate accurate understandings of culture and change; outside of districts and schools, they expand community involvement and political support for needed reform (Schlechty, 1997). As leadership becomes an increasingly important part of administration, PR and its core activities, information management and communication, become more central to best practice.

Reflective Practice

The concept of reflective practice is predicated on the fact that professional knowledge is different from scientific (or technical) knowledge (Sergiovanni, 2006). In his enlightening book *The Reflective Practitioner*, Schön (1983) observed that scientific knowledge is insufficient to resolve the problems encountered in most professions. Such technical knowledge consists of "theory and technique derived from systematic, preferably scientific knowledge" (p. 3). Technical rationality is the foundation for most professions where practice evolves from a positivist philosophy (Schön, 1987). A school administrator's practice, however, is neither totally rational nor highly predictable. Consequently, theory is a valuable, but fallible guide for practice. Administrators, like all other professionals, occasionally confront situations that do not fit the neat textbook examples studied in college. Yet some practitioners are neither flexible nor analytical, as evidenced by their routine application of theoretical constructs or systematic rules to problems, needs, and other challenges that are dynamic and context specific.

A problem's contextual variations are multifaceted; they may be environmental (i.e., conditions outside of the organization), organizational, or personal (i.e., conditions associated with individuals; Kowalski, 2004). Even slight contextual variations may diminish the effectiveness of technical knowledge. Consider, for example, a principal in a rural elementary school who found that using praise effectively motivated teachers to improve their performance. The principal had learned this technique while studying motivation theory in a graduate course on clinical supervision, and she had applied it successfully with three teachers in the rural school. Later in her career, after she became principal in an affluent suburban community, she employed the same motivational approach with another teacher. This time, however, she was dismayed to discover that it had actually angered the teacher and made him more resistant to improvement recommendations. What caused her tried-and-true approach to fail? Was it the difference between a rural and suburban setting? Was it the uniqueness of the suburban school teacher? Or did she do something differently in trying to motivate the fourth teacher? Unless the principal understands the importance of contextual variables and is able to analyze contextual variations, her technical knowledge has limited value, and failed efforts remain enigmatic and stressful.

Reflective practice is a concept used by professionals to deal with problems of practice, and especially those problems that defy textbook solutions. Given the nature of school administrative work, the process is anchored in a rationality that promotes reasonableness in learning through practice (Hoy, 1996). Reflection is an acquired skill that allows you to synthesize professional knowledge (what you think will occur) and experience (what actually occurs). The process is especially valuable when outcomes do not meet your expectations. For the reflective practitioner, unexpected results trigger both reflection-in-action and reflection-on-action; that is, he or she thinks about the causes of the unanticipated outcomes as they are occurring and later, after the heat of the moment has dissipated. The current event is compared with similar past experiences, and the similarities and differences in contextual variables are assessed and evaluated (Kowalski, 2003). More precisely, reflection can occur in three distinct time frames: during the period when an administrator is planning an action, during the period in which the action is taken, and during the period following the action (Reitzug & Cornett, 1991).

Imagine a superintendent who must inform the media that a teacher is being dismissed for incompetence. Before he releases the information, he may reflect on (a) his previous experiences with reporters, (b) the content of his intended message, (c) potential outlets for the message, (d) potential legal ramifications, and (e) implications for relations with the teachers union. When he actually communicates the message, questions by reporters may lead to further reflection. He may ask himself: How do I answer the questions? Should I give more information than I originally intended? After the message has been delivered, the third stage of reflection can occur as he contemplates the results and assesses the relationship between his actions and observed outcomes. Did things turn out as he had expected? If not, why not? This last stage is especially meaningful in augmenting the superintendent's professional knowledge base—that is, in determining if and how experience altered his professional convictions.

The open-ended case studies at the beginning of each chapter in this book provide opportunities for you to reflect. By assuming a decision-making role, you have opportunities to meld the professional knowledge contained in this book with your professional and personal experiences. In so doing, you will be able to plan and test alternative responses to the problems presented in the case studies.

SUMMARY

This chapter explored the meanings of PR. Multiple perspectives were reviewed, showing how definitions differ based on two primary foci: process versus outcomes and real versus normative behaviors. Virtually all PR descriptions, nevertheless, are framed by three recurring themes: *administration, organization, and publics* (Gordon, 1997). Public relations also was identified as both an art and a science, and it was broadly defined to include goodwill, public opinion, community interaction, two-way communication, employee relations, and planning and decision making.

School PR was defined in this chapter as *an evolving social science and leadership process utilizing multimedia approaches designed to build goodwill, enhance the public's attitude toward the value of education, augment interaction and two-way symmetrical communication between schools and their ecosystems, provide vital and useful information to the public and employees, and play an integral role in planning and decision-making functions.* The value of PR to modern school administration was premised on the following assumptions:

◆ The two-way flow of ideas and accurate information is essential to school improvement.
◆ School administrators are accountable to the public.
◆ The public has a right to information about schools.
◆ In a democratic society, the publics served by a school should participate in making critical decisions.

Also discussed were possible obstacles to school PR, which were broadly categorized as barriers to understanding, barriers to accepting, and barriers to acting. The current importance of school PR programs was linked to changes in the social, political, legal, and economic framework of American society. These evolving conditions have made key facets of PR (e.g., public opinion, information management, and communication) integral to leadership and school renewal.

Last, four themes pertaining to the application of school PR were summarized. They include an information-based society, school reform, communication, and reflection. The first two address contextual issues of practice; the last two address normative leadership behaviors.

QUESTIONS AND SUGGESTED ACTIVITIES

CASE STUDY

1. Using the three categories of barriers discussed in this chapter, what do you find to be the primary reason for the board's reluctance to approve the superintendent's recommendation?
2. Do you believe the board members are sincere when they say they support strong school-community relationships, but oppose the deployment of PR? Why or why not?
3. The PR plan was developed by the superintendent and principals. Would it have been beneficial to involve others in the planning process? If so, who?
4. If the school district already has a positive image, as claimed by the board members, is a PR plan really necessary? Why or why not?
5. What changes might make the plan acceptable to the board members? Should the superintendent drop the plan, seek a compromise, or fight for full approval?

CHAPTER

6. Definitions of PR and school PR are broadly categorized as descriptive or normative. What is the difference between these two types of definitions?
7. This chapter discussed barriers to implementing PR that are based on understanding, accepting, and acting. What is a barrier to accepting? What is a barrier to acting?
8. How has transition from a manufacturing era to an information age affected citizen expectations about exchanging information with their social institutions?
9. Technology provides tools for broadening communication, but if they are not used properly, these tools could be dehumanizing. Why?
10. Four models of PR based on symmetry and communication direction were discussed in this chapter. Which of them is most desirable for the modern school administration? Which is least desirable?
11. What is reflective practice? Why is the process relevant to applications of school PR?

SUGGESTED READINGS

Alsbury, T. (2003). Stop talking and do something: The changing role of superintendent involvement in school-community relations. *Journal of School Public Relations, 24*(1), 44–52.

Armistead, L. (2000). Public relations: Harness your school's power. *High School Magazine, 7*(6), 24–27.

Ashbaugh, C. R., & Kasten, K. (1993). Educating the reflective school leader. *Journal of School Leadership, 3*(2), 152–164.

Cannon, C. L., & Barham, F. E. (1993). Are you and your public polls apart? *Executive Educator,* *15*(10), 41–42.

Chappelow, M. A. (2003). New standards for educational public relations and communications professionals. *Journal of School Public Relations, 24*(1), 7–29.

Decker, L. E. (2001). Allies in education. *Principal Leadership, 2*(1), 42–46.

Eisentadt, D. (1994). After the ball: High-tech PR in the no-nonsense '90s. *Public Relations Quarterly, 39*(2), 23–25.

Flynn, P. D. (2002). School public relations and the principalship: An interview with Steven Mulvenon. *Journal of School Public Relations, 23*(1), 14–18.

Gordon, J. C. (1997). Interpreting definitions of public relations: Self-assessment and a symbolic interactionism-based alternative. *Public Relations Review, 23*(1), 57–66.

Holiday, A. E. (1994). The ultimate guide to school-community relations. *Journal of Educational Public Relations, 15*(4), 3–16.

Lashley, J. E. (1989). Attitude and communication build public relations. *NASSP Bulletin, 73*(513), 34–35.

Leverett, L. (1999). Connecting the disconnected. *School Administrator, 56*(8), 18–22.

Loveless, T. (1997). The structure of public confidence in education. *American Journal of Education, 105*(2), 127–159.

Martinson, D. (1995). School public relations: Do it right or don't do it at all! *Contemporary Education, 66*(2), 82–85.

Newsom, D. (2003). When "community relations" won't cut it: PR for public schools. *Journal of School Public Relations, 24*(1), 37–43.

Ramsey, S. A. (1993). Issues management and the use of technologies in public relations. *Public Relations Review, 19*(3), 261–275.

Sparks, S. D. (1993). Public relations: Is it dangerous to use the term? *Public Relations Quarterly, 38*(3), 27–28.

Sweetland, S. R., & Cybulski, T. G. (2002). School public relations and the principalship: An interview with Joseph Murphy. *Journal of School Public Relations, 23*(1), 7–13.

VanMeter, E. J. (1993). Setting new priorities: Enhancing the school-community relations program. *NASSP Bulletin, 77*(554), 22–27.

REFERENCES

Amundson, K. (1996). *Telling the truth about America's public schools.* Arlington, VA: American Association of School Administrators.

Armistead, L. (2000). Public relations: Harness your school's power. *High School Magazine, 7*(6), 24–27.

Austin, E. W., & Pinkleton, B. E.(2001). *Strategic public relations management: Planning and managing effective communications programs.* Mahwah, NJ: Lawrence Erlbaum Associates.

Axley, S. R. (1996). *Communication at work: Management and the communication-intensive organization.* Westport, CT: Quorum Books.

Baker, B. (1997). Public relations in government. In C. L. Caywood (Ed.), *The handbook of strategic public relations and integrated communication* (pp. 453–480). New York: McGraw-Hill.

Berliner, D. C. (1993). Education's present misleading myths undermine confidence in one of America's most cherished institutions. *Journal of Educational Public Relations, 15*(2), 4–11.

Berliner, D. C., & Biddle, B. J. (1995). *The manufactured crises: Myths, fraud and the attack on America's public schools.* Reading, MA: Addison-Wesley.

Bracey, G. (1997). *Setting the record straight: Responses to misconceptions about public education in the United States.* Alexandria, VA: Association for Supervision and Curriculum Development.

Burgess, J. C. (1996). *Corporate culture: Friend or foe of change?* Paper presented at the Academy of Human Resource Development, Minneapolis, MN.

Callahan, R. E. (1964). *The superintendent of schools: An historical analysis.* Final report of project S-212. Washington, DC: U.S. Office of Education, Department of Health, Education, and Welfare.

Campbell, R. F., Corbally, J. E., & Nystrand, R. O. (1983). *Introduction to educational administration* (6th ed.). Boston: Allyn & Bacon.

Carlson, R. V. (1996). *Reframing and reform: Perspectives on organization, leadership, and school change.* New York: Longman.

Caywood, C. L. (1997). The future of integrated communications and public relations. In C. L. Caywood (Ed.), *The handbook of strategic public relations and integrated communication* (pp. 564–566). New York: McGraw-Hill.

Cohen, P. M. (1987). *A public relations primer: Thinking and writing in context.* Upper Saddle River, NJ: Prentice Hall.

Connor, P., & Lake, L. (1988). *Managing organizational change.* New York: Praeger.

Conrad, C. (1994). *Strategic organizational communication: Toward the twenty-first century* (3rd ed.). Fort Worth, TX: Harcourt Brace College Publishers.

Crable, R. E., & Vibbert, S. L. (1986). *Public relations as communication management.* Edina, MN: Bellwether Press.

Cutlip, S. M. (1995). *Public relations history: From the 17th to the 20th century: The antecedents.* Hillsdale, NJ: Lawrence Erlbaum Associates.

Deetz, S. A. (1992). *Democracy in an age of corporate colonization: Developments in communication and the politics of everyday life.* Albany: State University of New York Press.

Dilenschneider, R. L. (1996). Public relations: An overview. In R. L. Dilenschneider (Ed.), *Public relations handbook* (pp. xix–xxix). Chicago: Dartnell Corp.

Dozier, D. M. (with L. A. Grunig & J. E. Grunig). (1995). *Manager's guide to excellence in public relations and communication management.* Mahwah, NJ: Lawrence Erlbaum Associates.

Fullan, M. (2001). *Leading in a culture of change.* San Francisco: Jossey-Bass.

Fullan, M., & Stiegelbauer, S. (1991). *The new meaning of educational change* (2nd ed.). New York: Teachers College Press.

Gordon, J. C. (1997). Interpreting definitions of public relations: Self-assessment and a symbolic interactionism-based alternative. *Public Relations Review, 23*(1), 57–66.

Grunig, J. E. (1984). Organizations, environments, and models of public relations. *Public Relations Research & Education, 1,* 6–29.

Grunig, J. E. (1989). Symmetrical presuppositions as a framework for public relations theory. In C. H. Botan (Ed.), *Public relations theory* (pp. 17–44). Hillsdale, NJ: Lawrence Erlbaum Associates.

Grunig, J. E., & Hunt, T. (1984). *Managing public relations.* New York: Holt, Rinehart & Winston.

Hall, G. E., & Hord, S. M. (2001). *Implementing change: Patterns, principles, and problems.* Boston: Allyn & Bacon.

Hanson, E. M. (1991). Educational restructuring in the USA: Movements of the 1980s. *Journal of Educational Administration, 29*(4), 30–38.

Hanson, E. M. (2003). *Educational administration and organizational behavior* (5th ed.). Boston: Allyn & Bacon.

Harral, S. (1952). *Tested public relations for schools.* Norman: University of Oklahoma Press.

Haywood, R. (1991). *All about public relations* (2nd ed.). New York: McGraw-Hill.

Hoy, W. K. (1996). Science and theory in the practice of educational administration: A pragmatic perspective. *Educational Administration Quarterly, 32*(3), 366–378.

Hoy, W. K., & Miskel, C. G. (2005). *Educational administration: Theory, research, and practice* (8th ed.). New York: McGraw-Hill.

Jones, J. J. (1966). *School public relations.* New York: Center for Applied Research in Education.

Katz, D., & Kahn, R. (1978). *The social psychology of organizations* (2nd ed.). New York: John Wiley.

Knezevich, S. J. (1969). *Administration of public education* (2nd ed.). New York: Harper & Row.

Kotler, P. (1975). *Marketing for nonprofit organizations.* Upper Saddle River, NJ: Prentice Hall.

Kowalski, T. J. (1998). The role of communication in providing leadership for school restructuring. *Mid-western Educational Researcher, 11*(1), 32–40.

Kowalski, T. J. (2003). *Contemporary school administration* (2nd ed.). Boston: Allyn & Bacon.

Kowalski, T. J. (2004). Case studies on educational administration (4th ed.). Boston: Allyn & Bacon.

Kowalski, T. J. (2005). Evolution of the school superintendent as communicator. *Communication Education, 54*(2), 101–117.

Kowalski, T. J. (2006). The school superintendent: Theory, practice, and cases (2nd ed.). Thousand Oaks, CA: Sage.

Lare, D., & Cimino, E. (1998). Not by print alone. *American School Board Journal, 185*(12), 40–41.

Lashway, L. (2002). The accountability challenge. *Principal, 81*(3), 14–16.

Lesly, P. (1983). The nature and role of public relations. In P. Lesly (Ed.), *Lesly's public relations handbook* (3rd ed., pp. 3–13). Upper Saddle River, NJ: Prentice Hall.

Lipinski, A. J. (1978). Communicating the future. *Futures, 10*(2), 126–127.

Lovell, R. P. (1982). *Inside public relations.* Boston: Allyn & Bacon.

Lutz, F. W., & Merz, C. (1992). *The politics of school/community relations.* New York: Teachers College Press.

Maher, J. W. (1997). *The development of a model public relations syllabus for professors of educational administration.* Unpublished doctoral dissertation, Texas A & M University, College Station.

Martinson, D. L. (1995). School public relations: Do it right or don't do it at all. *Contemporary Education, 66*(2), 82–85.

Martinson, D. L. (1999). School public relations: The public isn't always right. *NASSP Bulletin, 83*(609), 103–109.

McElreath, M. P. (1993). *Managing systematic and ethical public relations.* Madison, WI: WCB Brown & Benchmark.

Mohan, M. L. (1993). *Organizational communication and cultural vision: Approaches and analysis.* Albany: State University of New York Press.

Murray, G. J. (1993). KERA and community linkages. *Equity & Excellence in Education, 26*(3), 65–68.

National School Public Relations Association. (1986). *School public relations: The complete book.* Arlington, VA: Author.

Newsom, D., Scott, A., & VanSlyke Turk, J. (1989). *This is PR: The realities of public relations* (4th ed.). Belmont, CA: Wadsworth.

Nielsen/Net Ratings. (2005). *Global Internet population grows four percent year-over-year.* Retrieved October 5, 2005, from http://www.nielsen-netratings.com/pr/pr_030220_hk.pdf#search5'Internet%20and%20access%20and%20percent%20and%20population'

Norris, J. S. (1984). *Public relations.* Upper Saddle River, NJ: Prentice Hall.

Parker, F., & Parker, B. J. (1995). A historical perspective on school reform. *Educational Forum, 59*(3), 278–287.

Peck, K. L., & Carr, A. A. (1997). Restoring public confidence in schools through systems thinking. *International Journal of Educational Reform, 6*(3), 316–323.

Pfeiffer, I. L., & Dunlap, J. B. (1988). Advertising practices to improve school–community relations. *NASSP Bulletin, 72*(506), 14–17.

Reitzug, U. C., & Cornett, J. W. (1991). Teacher and administrator thought: Implications for administrator training. *Planning & Changing, 21*(3), 181–192.

Sarason, S. B. (1996). *Revisiting the culture of the school and the problem of change.* New York: Teachers College Press.

Saxe, R. W. (1984). *School–community relations in transition.* Berkeley, CA: McCutchan.

Schein, E. H. (1999). *The corporate culture survival guide: Sense and nonsense about culture change.* San Francisco: Jossey-Bass.

Schlechty, P. C. (1990). *Schools for the 21st century: Leadership imperatives for educational reform.* San Francisco: Jossey-Bass.

Schlechty, P. C. (1997). *Inventing better schools: An action plan for educational reform.* San Francisco: Jossey-Bass.

Schön, D. A. (1983). *The reflective practitioner.* New York: Basic Books.

Schön, D. A. (1987). *Educating the reflective practitioner.* San Francisco: Jossey-Bass.

Seitel, F. P. (1992). *The practice of public relations* (5th ed.). New York: Macmillan.

Sergiovanni, T. J. (2006). *The principalship: A reflective practice perspective* (5th ed.). Boston: Allyn & Bacon.

Sitrick, M. (1998). *Spin: Turning the power of the press to your advantage.* Washington, DC: Regnery Publishers.

Taylor, J. R. (1993). *Rethinking the theory of organizational communication: How to read an organization.* Norwood, NJ: Ablex.

Testerman, J. C., Algozzine, B., & Flowers, C. P. (2002). Basic technology compentencies of educational administrators. *Contemporary Education, 7*(2), 58–61.

Toffler, A. (1970). *Future shock.* New York: Random House.

Wadsworth, D. (1997). Building a strategy for successful public engagement. *Phi Delta Kappan, 78*(10), 749–752.

Walker-Dalhouse, D., & Dalhouse, A. D. (2001). Parent-school relations: Communicating more effectively with African American parents. *Young Children, 56*(4), 75–80.

Walling, D. R. (1982). *Complete book of school public relations: An administrator's manual and guide.* Upper Saddle River, NJ: Prentice Hall.

West, P. T. (1981). Imagery and change in the twenty-first century. *Theory into Practice, 20*(4), 229–236.

West, P. T. (1985). *Educational public relations.* Beverly Hills, CA: Sage.

Wilcox, D., Ault, P., & Agee, W. (1992). *Public relations: Strategies and tactics* (3rd ed.). New York: HarperCollins.

Yukl, G. (2006). *Leadership in organizations* (5th ed.).Upper Saddle River, NJ: Prentice Hall.

Zaleznik, A. (1989). *The managerial mystique: Restoring leadership in business.* New York: Harper & Row.

CHAPTER 2

Changes in Society and Schools

Thomas Glass

CASE STUDY: UNFORESEEN COMMUNITY UNREST

The need for community is universal. A sense of belonging, continuity, of being connected to others and to ideas and values that make our lives meaningful and significant. . . .

Thomas Sergiovanni (1994, p. xiii)

The Smithfield School District is growing rapidly and is located about 20 miles from the farthest suburb of a large midwestern city. Smithfield is the county seat of Washington County, which is mostly rural with rich cornfields and stock farms. A frequently heard joke in Smithfield is that the county has 10 times as many pigs as people.

In the past 10 years, many new families have moved to Smithfield from the metropolitan area. Many of these families have built new homes, and others have bought the large Victorian houses lining several wide streets shaded by 100-year-old oak trees. Almost all the newcomers are white-collar professionals who commute to high-technology workplaces in the nearby suburban communities. They have selected Smithfield because of the desire to live in a *real* community with a Main Street, courthouse, and dollar overtime parking tickets. More than several of the newcomers have commented that Smithfield is close to being Mayberry, USA.

The Smithfield School District comprises three elementary schools, a middle school, and a high school featuring one of the best vocational-agricultural programs in the state. All of the school buildings were built in the 1950s and 1960s, and very little recent remodeling has occurred. Historically, about 25% of Smithfield's high school graduates have gone on to college or university. Most of the graduates not going on to postsecondary education have remained in Smithfield to work in several nearby factories, on farms, or in nearby small towns. Prior to the influx of outsiders, the population of Smithfield had been steady for three or four generations.

In the past several years, the children of the new families have been so numerous that each of the school buildings has become seriously overcrowded. Last year the district employed a consulting firm to do a demographic study, which found the district to be on the verge of an even larger influx of new students. The board of education in turn employed an architect to determine the costs of building a new elementary school and putting additions on all the existing schools. A $30 million building bond referendum was held several months ago and failed by a margin of 2 to 1.

A self-appointed volunteer committee of newcomer parents had spearheaded community efforts to pass the referendum. The board of education, the minority of members composed of native Smithfield residents, was not overly active in speaking to community groups, having coffee sessions, or distributing campaign materials. One board member opposed and actually voted against the referendum. His reason was that the bonds would raise taxes to a level that was unfair for many senior citizens living on fixed incomes. Tax rates in Smithfield are very high because currently only 30% of the assessed valuation is based on farm and commercial properties; the remaining portion of the assessed valuation comes from homes. Only about 20% of the district's revenues come from the state. The dissenting board member was quoted in the local newspaper as not questioning the need for the new school space, but he just couldn't see how the local citizens could pay for it.

The board, however, was shocked at the size of the "no" vote, since no one had predicted that the referendum would fail by such a wide margin. The referendum committee had distributed thousands of pieces of literature, held dozens of coffee sessions, and conducted an extensive telephone campaign. The committee's efforts were not countered overtly by organized opposition.

At the first board meeting following the referendum defeat, the board decided to ask consultants from the college of education of a nearby state university to conduct a public opinion poll followed by a series of focus groups. The purpose of the studies was to discover why the referendum failed. Issues considered included: Did the aggressive behavior of the newcomers in trying to get new and technologically updated schools antagonize the long-time Smithfield residents? Were there just too many Smithfield residents who could not afford to have their property taxes go up? Is there a division in Smithfield, between the traditional values of the long-time residents and the emerging values of the white-collar-professional newcomers? What are the signs of such a division of values in the community? What effect is this division having on the school district? What should the school district do? Should it wait several years until the number of newcomers exceed that of Smithfield natives and then have a referendum?

About three months later the consultants reported the findings of the public opinion poll and the series of focus groups. Overall, all segments of the community in general actually supported the school district. However, many nonparents complained that they knew nothing about the building needs of the district and did not even know how well students were doing academically in the present buildings, despite the requirements of the No Child Left Behind Act (NCLB) and the district report card.

A large number of parents residing all their lives in Smithfield questioned the need to increase tax rates to build space for computer technology. A focus group session with local businesspeople was dominated by questions and comments about how the cost of the contemplated buildings was arrived at by the architects. Another focus group session with senior citizens brought forth a collective opinion that taxes were too high and should be raised only with very good justification. They did not feel the district and the board had provided a strong justification to support the referendum.

Problems confronting educational leaders are a complex mix of political, social, and economic topics that exist in schools and in society. For example, employee unionization and the development of technology exemplify internal developments; a loss of community and the decline of the traditional family structure are evolving external conditions. These matters are central to the practice of administration because they reflect the reality that society and the public schools are inextricably intertwined. Despite this fact, school administrators for much of the twentieth century were guided by management principles that considered democratic administration inefficient.

Today, however, the practice of school administration is focused on both leadership and management. Principals and superintendents are not only expected to manage resources, but also counted on to facilitate key decisions about institutional directions. This broader role obligates them to have a deeper understanding of society, organizational behavior, and communication; it also requires them to use information to identify and solve problems that prevent schools from making necessary improvements.

This chapter explores several topics that are axial to the relationship between society and schools. They are broadly divided into two parts: those relating to society and those relating more directly to schools. These conditions provide the context for contemporary applications of school public relations.

SOCIETAL CHANGE

The demographic profile of the typical public school student has changed considerably in the last 50 years. As an example, the population in many cities and towns has become increasingly diverse. In addition, more children are now living in poverty, more come from one-parent families, and more come to school with emotional, physical, and psychological problems. Despite such realities, some would-be reformers continue to blame only the public schools for the nation's educational problems. Moreover, these critics contend that districts and schools should be able to reform and be more productive without additional political and economic support. Such denials of the social and economic dimensions of public education serve to limit reasonable reform efforts, and they perpetuate the myth that schools are basically detached from society.

Community and Government

No period in history has witnessed such dramatic and sweeping changes in the basic context of society as the second half of the twentieth century. In the early 1900s, American communities were nearly all rural, with many being so tiny and isolated that families had to depend on one another for essentials. These small and detached communities were usually without electricity, telephones, paved roads, automobiles, and regular mail delivery. For the most part, these communities remained static from the first decades of the nineteenth century to the Industrial Revolution.

Today, by contrast, most Americans live in urban or suburban settings that have been shaped substantially by the industrial and technological products of the twentieth century— products such as automobiles, trains, airplanes, radio, television, computers, and biotechnology. In the twenty-first century, even fewer American households are located in rural communities, and many families remaining in these settings are apt to face the harsh realities of poverty if they are living in such areas, as the Mississippi delta, Appalachia, the Rio Grande valley, or any of the Native American reservations.

A loss of community has been apparent in all types of cities and towns, ranging from America's great cities to its affluent suburbs. Consider contemporary conditions in relation to those that existed just several decades ago. The feeling of belonging—not only to a nuclear family group, but also to a community-wide extended family—is no longer a positive social experience for America's children. In today's typical suburban environment, neighbors do not have *interlocking* relationships. Few families have social ties that bind them to other families in their neighborhoods; neighbors usually do not attend the same church, belong to the same clubs, shop at the same stores, share the same recreational activities, or work for the same employer. Often the only common social experience in suburbia is public education, and reform-related ideas such as vouchers and charter schools may eradicate this unifying characteristic for families and children.

The decline of *community* between and within social institutions, such as the church and the extended family, has resulted in significant changes in local government and schooling. Although the erosion of community life has had subtle effects on most schools, its impact on American politics has been visible and pronounced. Consider, for example, the traditional small, rural community. In the first half of the twentieth century, political participation was usually inclusive, allowing citizens to voice opinions and to participate directly in community decisions. Today, this form of participative democracy is found only in select parts of the country—for example, in sectors of rural New England.

Factors such as substantial population growth and a loss of community have contributed to the development of *representative* democracy. Consequently, a few officials may represent thousands or hundreds of thousands of citizens. This growing social distance between politicians and citizens is perhaps one of the most serious challenges facing contemporary American democracy and the local control of public education. At a time when many citizens suffer from a detachment from community life, they also feel increasingly alienated from their government. This is certainly reflected in voter apathy in state, local, and school board elections.

Community and Schools

Creation of secure and nurturing communities should be a key goal for America in the twenty-first century, since it can hardly be argued that children in vibrant and cohesive communities do not do well in school. Even though the critics of education are correct in asserting that the nation's children are much of its future, they are incorrect in suggesting that only schools determine whether children become productive citizens. Seldom do large numbers of students achieve academically when they live in environments saturated with crime, poverty, and social upheaval. Children, more so than others, need strong and purposeful communities providing them human and social capital (Annie E. Casey Foundation [Casey Foundation], 2004). This fact is especially evident when one correctly defines educational success broadly, rather than basing success solely on a single criterion, such as standardized test scores.

Current economic and political trends are creating a bipolar nation in which the rich and poor are increasingly separated. Instead of recognizing the obvious relationship between human capital level and social and economic attainment, many critics of public education have demanded that schools become the economic leveling force in society (Thernstrom & Thernstrom, 2003). In essence, the critics ignore the fact that living in poverty seriously restricts a student's ability to learn through denial of experiences closely associated with school learning. These "deprived" students are at a great disadvantage in finding a place in the workforce.

Whether America's schools can meet myriad challenges in the twenty-first century depends on the nation's political and educational leaders. Both groups must envision and pursue reform that addresses multiculturalism and poverty, and they must do so in a manner that integrates the community and school. At the beginning of the twenty-first century, 23% of the nation's schoolchildren were attending school in 1 of the 100 largest urban districts (National Center for Education Statistics [NCES], 2005a, p. 34). Nearly half of these children lived in families sufficiently impoverished to qualify them for a free or reduced-price lunch (NCES, 2005a, p. 2). Nationally, in 2001, approximately 17% of children lived in three-member families earning less than $15,000 annually (Annie E. Casey Foundation, 2004, p. 42). Thirty-five percent of female-headed families received child support payments, and 14% of children lived in households where no family member was fully employed (Annie E. Casey Foundation, 2004, pp. 90–91).

Those who study contemporary American communities constantly note that the vanishing extended family, the destruction of social networks, and the lack of participative democracy have had a negative effect on social institutions such as the school. Until the nation's political leaders reach consensus on how to socially balance economics in America, and until the critics of education accept the fact that both schools and communities need to be reformed, the increasing number of poor children will probably not receive quality schooling. If larger numbers of children living in poverty are not successfully prepared for adulthood, the cities and towns in which they live can be expected to continue their decline. It is likely that social reform is the most expedient path to successful educational improvement.

The Changing Family

The foundation of the American school system comprises both the community and the family. The community provides a broad base of support, and the family provides the day-to-day interaction with the school. The quality of community support and the family resources a student brings to school influence whether the school and the students are successful. In 2003, approximately 4 of every 10 public school students were members of an identifiable minority group. A majority of these students lived in families with minimal fiscal resources (NCES, 2005b, p. 2). Most lived in communities with few resources to support after-school social and learning activities.

As communities changed in the 1990s, so did family groups. In 1995, 25% of the nation's children under the age of 18 lived in single-parent households; in 1970, only 11% did so. For African-American children, the percentage living in single-parent homes during the mid-1990s was an alarming 60%; for Hispanic children, it was 29%; and for white children, it was only 11% (Thernstrom & Thernstrom, 2003).

Poverty is also a major concern. Consider the following statistics:

◆ In 1995, one out of five American children under the age of 18 was a member of a poverty-level family. In 2001, 28% of children lived in poverty (Casey Foundation, 2004, p. 169). Over 40% of impoverished children in 2004 lived in "extreme poverty" (Anyon, 2005, pp. 65–66).
◆ In 2003, 34% of public school students qualified for a free or reduced-price lunch (NCES, 2005b, p. 7).

◆ African-American and Hispanic children were in 1995 and still are more than twice as likely as white children to live in poverty (Annie E. Casey Foundation, 2006, p. 28).

◆ In 1995, 42% of African-American and 39% of Hispanic children lived in families classified as being below the national poverty level. (Annie E. Casey Foundation, 2006, pp. 28–29).

◆ A majority of African-American children resided in large urban school districts that were the primary targets of school reform in the 1990s. Many of these districts, such as those in Los Angeles, Chicago, and Boston, have shown some achievement gains, but in general, millions of minority children living in impoverished families still fall well below national averages on standardized tests (Symonds, 2005).

◆ A disproportionate number of minority students constitute the 13% of American students participating in special education programs (NCES, 2005).

High school dropout rates in urban school districts such as three in Chicago are nearly 50%. Many thousands of urban adolescents join street gangs and participate in criminal activity (Symonds, 2005). Many more thousands of dropouts have no jobs or have jobs that pay minimal wages, perhaps in the fast-food industry.

Many social researchers claim that a new *social underclass,* separate from the traditionally defined *lower class,* developed during the 1990s (Jencks & Peterson, 1991). Sociologists such as Wilson (1997) claim that many millions of Americans lack the job and social skills to ever function successfully (to hold a job) in society. This creation of an underclass in addition to the traditional lower class further illustrates the drift of American society into the "haves" and "have nots," clearly visible today in both urban and rural America.

The primary importance of the rapid growth of an *economic underclass* to schools is that a significant percentage of those in this category are students (Jencks & Phillips, 1998). This is especially relevant because underclass families provide children very few financial, emotional, and educational resources. Lower-income families always have struggled to provide resources to their children that would allow them to successfully compete against peers from higher-income families. Today, however, their numbers have swelled, and now millions of underclass families are unable to provide adequately for their children (Mayer, 1997). Most troublesome is the fact that this condition exists at a time when political conservatives continually lead efforts to reduce all forms of social welfare—even those that provide bare essentials such as food and clothing. In the inner cities, an intricate mix of economic and social issues affects the condition of the family. Wilson (1997), for example, concluded that many urban males avoid marriage and family responsibilities for both social and economic reasons.

Accompanying an increase in the number of children living in poverty and in single-parent households have been changes in the ways that Americans parent their children. Some recent studies highlight the popular media claim that average American parents talk or interact with their child only 17 waking hours per week. Add to this the influence of television watching, Internet browsing, organized activities (many school sponsored), and peer group clustering outside the home (e.g., at shopping malls), and it becomes readily apparent that traditional family activities are becoming rare. Consequently, many children do not learn how to be productive family members or members of any functional social group.

Just as American society is bifurcated along social and economic lines, so is it divided on the basis of parenting. Americans born after 1970 fall into one of two groups: those who grew up with a father and those who did not. Many in the former group benefited from the psychological, social, educational, and moral assistance provided by a male parent; most in the latter group had to depend entirely on a female parent who often worked outside the home. The decline of patrimony is due largely to the devaluation of nuclear family life. Those who have studied this problem conclude that the depreciation of fatherhood is a ticking social time bomb. For example, children from fatherless homes have been found to be both less productive in school and responsible for a high percentage of criminal behavior (Blankenhorn, 1995).

Few contemporary families fit the image of the traditional American family—one that consists of a working father, a stay-at-home mother, and two or three children. As a result, many children do not eat family meals, attend church activities, visit relatives, and engage in family recreation. The Norman Rockwell family portrait of what the family *should* be like is representative of the time in which it was painted. Family structure is important because it has a profound influence on preparing children to learn, supporting their learning activities, and providing a moral compass for social behavior. It also influences what public schools are able to do.

For much of the last half of the twentieth century, for example, educators were asked to assume many of the traditional responsibilities previously held by the family and church. Sex education, alcohol and drug education, character education, health education, and preschool education are just a few examples of evolving responsibilities that take teachers and administrators away from teaching the core subjects that form the basis for current high-stakes testing programs mandated by nearly every state.

Educational achievement also is affected by the extent to which children have their needs met within the family unit. Some social psychologists have noted that parenting practices have changed subtly over the past few decades. Some families are generally classified as *child centered*, meaning that their resources are focused on the needs of children. Most middle-class American families are in this group. Many other families, however, are viewed as being *adult centered*. In this category, priority is given to using available resources to satisfy adult needs. Parents in these typically lower-class or underclass families have great difficulty just obtaining day-to-day necessities (e.g., food, shelter, and clothing). Children in these families are commonly pushed to the rear; they are not provided structure, behavioral expectations, health care, and skills needed to be successful in school (Jencks & Phillips, 1998). Often these families are dysfunctional, producing physically challenged, emotionally abused, and cognitively delayed children.

Although educators have long recognized the nexus between poverty and achievement, they have been less cognizant of research that links educational achievement to parenting style and even peer group values (Steinberg, 1996). Some studies, for instance, indicate that children, regardless of ethnic or economic or family background, parented in either an *authoritative* or a *responsive* style typically do much better in school than children raised in either an *autocratic* or a *laissez-faire* parenting mode (Steinberg, 1996). In other words, these studies conclude that positive parenting can often overcome some of the debilities of poverty and discrimination.

CHANGES IN SCHOOLS

Contrary to popular thought, many changes made in public education during the last half of the twentieth century continue into the twenty-first century. Most, however, were the products of fated interactions between schools and society, rather than the products of purposeful planning. Consider the following examples:

- ◆ *Altered political environments.* Politics arguably has been a part of public education since the inception of this institution; the process has been intensified significantly in the last 50 years. As a result, school administrators are often caught between competing interests. The unionization of teachers and other employees provides an excellent example; a superintendent is expected to represent the interests of taxpayers and the school board while maintaining positive relationships with employees.

- ◆ *Intervention of the courts.* Litigation has become a common means for resolving serious conflict in education. Consequently, the role of the courts in setting policy has become greater. Through decisions involving taxation, district spending, student discipline, and personnel administration, the nation's judicial system has played a prominent role in shaping current policy and regulations. A significant law-related issue has been school safety. Incidents of in-school shootings and violence have resulted in a daily police presence at many schools. A near national obsession with security has created a quasi-lockdown environment in many schools, with locked doors, security badges, and metal detectors.

- ◆ *Scientific developments.* Since the early 1980s, schools have had to spend immense sums of money for technology. The inclusion of the computer in instructional environments has had a dramatic effect on the teaching-learning process. The computer has altered social relationships between students and family members. Heavy use of computer technology coupled with television viewing has changed the time for "human" interactions with peers as well as with parents and siblings. A successful life in the workplace and the community requires certain social and communication skills traditionally taught in the home and school. A precursor of the unraveling of society in the twenty-first century could well be the turning inward of youth to a solitary world of electronic technology. Even though this technology may well be interactive, the absence of face-to-face human communication will do little to create positive relationships between individuals and societal groups.

Alterations such as these reshape the institutional context for school administration. Thus, the practitioner needs to understand both the nature of this institution and how its structure continues to evolve.

The Unique Position of Public Education

The local school district is one of the very few remaining political institutions unprotected from direct citizen influence. For example, angry taxpayers can usually voice their discontent directly to board members, and their grievances are more likely to generate attention and action. This condition is especially noteworthy in multicultural settings, where two conditions contribute to conflict and political interventions:

1. Citizens often vehemently disagree with each other over the role of school prayer, sex education, the teaching of reading, evolution, bilingual programs, and how much public money is to be spent supporting public education (Howell, 2005).
2. Board members often are elected because of support from racial, ethnic, or political groups. Accordingly, they are politically responsive to the agendas of these groups (McAdams, 2006).

In many states, a school-related referendum is the only opportunity citizens have to participate directly in tax decisions. Theoretically, decisions on the public economy are to be made by representatives of the community, who are expected to make decisions in the best interests of all who are affected (Fowler, 2004). But unlike decisions made by Congress, state legislatures, or even large-city councils, those promulgated by school boards are usually subject to the personal interests of stakeholders. This is because school board members typically represent smaller constituencies. Further, the percentage of households having school-age children in many communities, both suburban and rural, is approximately 30% (NCES, 2005b, p. 4). Taxpayers not having school-age children are prone to vote against proposed tax increases, but they are also becoming increasingly active in trying to influence school board members and fellow citizens on fiscal and related policy matters. About the only districts in which parents remain a significant percentage of taxpayers are those in the inner cities. In these settings, inadequate resources are often associated with opposition to higher taxes from large property owners and low voter participation in school referenda.

Even though local school boards have become increasingly vulnerable to political interventions, this concept of local government appears secure (Hochschild, 2005); their legitimate function has changed very little since 1920. Some role modifications, however, appear likely to happen in the first decades of the twenty-first century. Increasing levels of cultural diversity and increased political interventions such as NCLB are prompting a reconsideration of primary responsibilities. For example, school board members may be more effective if they devote their time and energy to functions such as visioning and planning programs to effect higher test scores.

As representatives of the community, school board members are probably in the best position to bring different factions together to reach consensus about the purposes of public education. Focusing more on policy and less on the day-to-day operations, however, will require most board members to spend less time with fiscal management and parental concerns. In this vein, local boards will hopefully function more as policy boards. By capitalizing on their access to participative democracy, they could be the glue that unifies and holds together diverse communities. The evolution of local boards from political to policy entities heightens the need for accurate and timely communication between the school and its wider environment (McAdams, 2006).

Condition of the Public Schools

The most apparent changes that have occurred recently in schools relate to people (students, employees) and programs (curricula, scope of extracurricular activities). Not only students are far more diverse than they were just several decades ago, but also their educational needs have been revised by America's transition to an information age. Although today's students will live and work in an ever-changing world, their educational experiences often do not reflect this fact. For example, too many schools still place far more emphasis on rote learning than they do on teaching children to access and use information to solve problems.

Enrollment in America's elementary and secondary schools is expected to increase well into the twenty-first century. In 1995, there were 36.8 million public school children, and in 2002, some 48.2 million attended 91,380 schools in 14,229 regular districts (NCES, 2005b). The U.S. Department of Education projects that by 2007 that number will swell to over 50 million. The previous peak level of school enrollment was in 1971, when 51.5 million children attended America's schools (NCES, 1997, p. 11). Already, early in the twenty-first century, nearly 40% of students belong to minority groups. If current forecasts are correct, a large number of these approximately 18 million minority children will not live in homes where English is the primary language (NCES, 2005b, p .27). Perhaps half of Hispanic children do not speak sufficient English to function in school. The nation's schools in 2003 enrolled over 4 million students in programs teaching English language skills. (NCES, 2005b). Many urban and suburban districts (e.g., those in Seattle, San Francisco, and New York) already report that as many as 40 to 50 different languages are spoken by their students and parents.

Statistics about minority enrollments are important for at least three reasons. First, there is a high correlation between students dropping out of school and their abilities to speak English. Second, the issue of bilingual education has become another political football for educators; a referendum in the 1990s prohibiting bilingual instruction in California and the subsequent reaction by many educators exemplify the tensions created by this issue. Third, administrators in multicultural districts may have to adjust their practices in order to communicate with their various publics. This not only means communicating in several languages, but also entails adjusting to cultural differences associated with communication.

Immigrant Students

The number of immigrant students has been accelerating for more than a decade. Students from Hispanic countries, Asia, and the Middle East constitute a growing percentage in urban schools. Some of these students adapt well to American schooling, whereas others do not. For example, immigrant students from countries where their schooling was interrupted or spasmodic may encounter academic problems. Many Mexican-American students suffer great difficulties with English language acquisition, accentuated by living in poverty environments. Immigrant students needing personalized assistance in both content knowledge and language development often do not receive those services in the schools they attend (Ruiz-de-Velasco, 2000).

In 2000, the U.S. Census Bureau reported that 81.6% of Americans below the age of 25 possessed a high school diploma or certificate (Balfanz, & Legters, 2004). This statistic includes dropout rates that run nearly 50% in many urban school districts, such as those in Chicago, Cleveland, New York, and Los Angeles. A question is raised about state-reported graduation rates that exceed 90% when the NCES reported in 2003 that of ll.3 million students registered in the 100 largest districts, 517,000 received a high school diploma (NCES, 2005b, p. 45). Assuming that seniors would account for at least 20% of the 11.3 million, the number graduating should have been about 2 million.

These statistics, however, do not reveal the extent to which students are being adequately prepared for entering the world of work or higher education. No Child Left Behind data from 2004 provide a glimpse of this problem in states such as Mississippi and Tennessee, which report approximately three-fourths of their students "proficient" in meeting state standards. On the National Assessment of Education Progress (NAEP) tests, the scores for these states were 18 and 21 percent, respectively (Uzzell, 2005, p. 29). This glaring discrepancy points out that hundreds of thousands of children are far behind "national standards," even though their states report them to be "proficient."

In the very near future, high schools in many urban areas may be overcrowded due to increased enrollments, more stringent graduation requirements, curricular revisions, and higher levels of individualized instruction. Unfortunately, many urban and rural high schools are located in outdated buildings, and with the exception of technology-based subjects, their curricula have changed very little in the past 50 years. Thus, if these schools are to succeed, taxpayer costs will have to increase—often dramatically—in order to build new facilities and provide smaller class sizes.

Evolving Purposes

Even though a majority of children live and attend schools in an increasingly urbanized America, most school districts are still small in enrollment and located in other than urban environments. More than 70% of the nation's 14,229 districts enroll less than 3,000 students. More than 4,000 districts have fewer than 500 students (NCES, 2003, p. 18). The presence of so many small districts is one reason why an urban nation still has an educational system organized primarily to serve a rural society. Summer vacations and a five-hour school day are both vestiges of an agrarian society in which children worked on the summer harvest and did chores before and after school.

A little-discussed challenge facing America's public education system in the twenty-first century is how to restructure schools to make them more reflective of community life in a technological, urban society. The literature in the late twentieth century abounded with reform initiatives, many of which promised to improve the image of schools. Few, however, advocated a totally new paradigm of public education. Instead of concentrating on meaningful restructuring of existing institutions, many critics have promoted options that essentially bypass public schools (Tyack & Cuban, 1995). American public opinion, however, runs counter to the wishes of reform advocates desiring to move to alternative systems. In 2004, 72% of parents responding to the Phi Delta Kappa (PDK) Public Opinion Poll indicated that it would be better to reform the current public school system. Respondents felt the same way in the 1972 PDK Poll (Center for Education Policy [CEP], 2005, pp. 5–6).

The advocacy for charter schools, for example, is rooted in the belief that competition will force public schools to improve without massive infusions of new resources. There were 2,575 charter schools sponsored by 1,241 districts in 2003 (NCES, 2005, p. 25). The number continues to grow due to local and state political frustration with the "failing," high-cost, bureaucratic public schools that are not willing to reform.

Since the 1980s, state legislatures have responded to demands for reform by promulgating intensification mandates. This has often been done without much thought about the systemic consequences for the educational system or students. In many high schools, for instance, 70 to 80% of scheduled sections are in core subjects such as mathematics, English, and science. Electives such as music, art, and home economics have been pushed to the background so that university-bound students can take advanced placement classes. Large numbers of high school students are taking four or five units of science and mathematics. It is not unusual to find high schools with underutilized elective subject classrooms and overcrowded core subject classrooms.

In the twenty-first century, the gap between rich and poor may also be described as a gap between those Americans with and those Americans without access to technology. This is why the technology issue is critical to schools serving children from low-income families. In a world dominated by technology, greater value may be placed on technology-related skills than on diplomas and degrees.

Whether or not the public schools fully enter the technology world depends largely on adequate funding from taxpayers, the private sector, or other governmental sources. Many districts are already charging students technology fees, trying to obtain technology equipment through school–corporate partnerships, and lobbying for additional technology funds. Unfortunately, many schools spend valuable instructional time on yearly technology fund-raising events.

Many schools are currently faced with the hard choice of reducing programs, increasing class sizes, or deferring facility maintenance to free up money to buy technology equipment. Only about half of the nation's schools can boast of having a computer for every four students. Even fewer schools can say that all of its teachers are computer literate and integrate technology in their teaching every day.

Probably a large majority of middle-class students have greater access to technology at home than in their classroom and school. There has been little effort to "connect" home-based technology with that at school. Students word process and search the Internet for information needed in assigned papers, but seldom go past that point in integrating technology and instruction with home-based resources.

Unfortunately, public schools in the future will be either technology rich or technology poor. Technology-rich schools will offer students distinct advantages that will be manifested in higher standardized test scores, access to the best colleges and universities, and higher income in adulthood. Students in the technology-poor schools, by contrast, will struggle to be competitive (Trotter, 2002).

Intensification mandates and the utilization of technology are but two forces creating uncertainty about public education and instability within schools. Most experts agree that the challenges presented by these conditions are more likely to be resolved locally. This is why decentralization has become so popular. In the 1990s, a national small-school movement, spearheaded by the Gates Foundation, sought to "downsize" secondary schools to the point where they might become viable learning communities. Research on secondary school size has consistently shown improved test scores for minority students enrolled in smaller schools (Lee & Smith, 1997).

Accompanying the movement toward smaller schools have been efforts in many states to consolidate smaller and sometimes larger districts out of existence. However, research has shown that typical district consolidations result in larger schools that lose their previous small-school advantages, including community identity and participation (Berry, 2005, pp. 76–77).

Meaningful restructuring of schools should be anchored in some reasonable consensus about purpose, and such a consensus is more likely to be achieved within local communities. In this context, school administrators are expected to engage the broad community in fundamental discussions about the purposes of education and the means for achieving those purposes. Both communication and the exchange of information are essential.

ADDRESSING THE RELATIONSHIP BETWEEN SOCIETY AND SCHOOLS

The restructuring of public education should be based on both the needs of society and the potentialities of schools. This contention is largely responsible for a shift in thinking about school reform from centralized, coercive change models to decentralized, cultural models. More precisely, current reform efforts are focusing more directly on improving schools one at a time. This strategy is predicated on the belief that cooperation between community and school creates the most positive environment for achieving lasting changes, especially in foundational areas such as values and beliefs. In this context, school public relations can be an essential tool for rebuilding bridges to the community. Restoring or renewing community support is now a vital function for boards, superintendents, principals, and teachers as the far-reaching provisions of NCLB demand an immense accountability and at times community support for the schools.

School districts now must report to the community the number of students making adequate yearly progress, students' proficiency levels on state-mandated standards, the number of students requiring tutoring, graduation rates, and plans to address areas for improvement identified by the state. Those districts with schools needing improvement will likely need additional fiscal resources to serve at-risk minority children, who very often qualify for Title I and special education services.

The community role in NCLB has been underplayed, but as the legislation is more fully implemented, its intrusion into local control and its mandate of additional educational services will severely strain the ability of districts to increase local funding. State governments are well aware of these difficulties as many appear to look for ways to reduce the number of districts needing improvement (CEP, 2005).

USING PUBLIC OPINION

General data about societal change are essential, but insufficient to bring about effective practice. The modern administrator also needs to consistently monitor public thinking in the community. Writers such as Mathews (1996) have concluded that schools suffer because they have drifted far away from their publics. For example, far too many administrators do not personalize their contacts with parents; in far too many districts, decisions about community and student needs are made by a relatively small number of high-ranking school officials. Regrettably, only a handful of districts engage in the formal process of assessing public opinion, and some of these do so only when faced with a direct need for public support (e.g., on referenda on school construction or other tax increases).

It is unlikely that administrators can mount a successful public relations program connecting the schools with community groups unless they know

- ◆ The public's level of knowledge about the district,
- ◆ The public's attitudes toward the district's effectiveness, and
- ◆ The public's needs and wants.

Because communities vary substantially, administrators cannot assume that national or even state data are correct for their districts and schools. Nor can they be confident that data collected five or six years ago remain accurate. In most communities, public opinions are fluid and are influenced by evolving political, economic, and social issues. Finally, public opinions cannot be adequately assessed through casual contacts or informal polling. This is true for at least four reasons:

1. Communities are divided between parent taxpayers and nonparent taxpayers. The latter constitute a majority in virtually all districts—in some districts, nonparents may constitute 80% of the taxpayers. Although many districts do a reasonably good job of providing information to parents, most do very little to communicate with nonparents. Nonparents are most likely to have limited accurate information and to view the schools as being nonbeneficial to them. Asking only parents about an issue may result in a distorted picture of reality.

2. Most communication between the school and its patrons is one-sided. That is, school officials disseminate selected information, but make no attempt to gather or receive information. Thus, many patrons are not accustomed to communicating with school officials, and they may be more guarded and less than candid in casual conversations than in formal surveys.

3. Informal approaches to assessing public opinion tend to be sporadic; public opinion should be collected systematically at reasonable time intervals to ensure accuracy.

4. Most communities are culturally diverse. Values and opinions may differ significantly from one group to another. Informal approaches to assessing public opinion tend to ignore certain groups.

Potential problems such as these indicate that public opinion should be studied formally, periodically, and inclusively. Collecting public opinion data should be a frequent district activity, not one that is undertaken only when a crisis occurs. Chapter 13 in this book is devoted to collecting and analyzing data for this purpose.

SUMMARY

The fracturing of the American family has resulted in two distinct political positions on public education. One group contends that schools must do more. That is, schools should furnish many of the services heretofore provided by the family. The reasoning underlying this position is that children will not reach their academic potential unless they are reasonably prepared to learn. Coming to school hungry or being abused at home places a child at serious risk of not being successful in school. The concept of full-service schools (schools that are prepared to meet all the needs of the child, including medical, dental, social, and nutritional needs) exemplifies this position.

By contrast, others, such as the religious right and fiscal conservatives, envision reform as entailing higher expectations, higher standards, and a return to teaching the basics. These individuals oppose an expanded role for public education, either because they fear that moral or religious instruction will not be part of this expanded mission or because they view the expanded mission as just another ploy to allocate more money to public schools. They also believe that more governmental intervention is counterproductive to refocusing responsibilities on local communities, families, and individuals.

These two very different positions exemplify the difficulty of trying to change education through centralized mandates such as NCLB. The most reasonable opportunity to reconcile competing values and beliefs exists at the community level. Thus, administrators need to rekindle a close relationship between schools and their neighborhoods; they need to facilitate, rather than dictate; and they need to be respectful of public opinion.

QUESTIONS AND SUGGESTED ACTIVITIES

CASE STUDY

1. If you were the superintendent of schools in Smithfield, what actions would you recommend to the board of education after the referendum defeat?
2. If you were the superintendent of schools in Smithfield, what actions would you recommend to the board of education prior to the next bond referendum?
3. If you were one of the Smithfield board members, what information would you feel you needed before voting to have another referendum?
4. What information should be communicated to district parent groups about the failed referendum?
5. To what extent are changing demographics causing political strife in the district?
6. What might be the focus of a community information campaign sponsored by the district in upcoming months? Do citizens need to know more about test scores, compliance with NCLB, and community activities carried out by students?
7. What types of community involvement activities might result in parent and nonparent support at the polls in future referenda?

CHAPTER

8. Do public schools differ from other governmental agencies with respect to dealing with patrons? If so, how?
9. What factors are contributing to the decline of the traditional American family? How can the school minimize the negative factors?
10. How might students be affected by not living in a "traditional" family?
11. What is the concept of a true community school? What is the underlying reason for creating such schools?

12. What conditions have contributed to an increasing level of cultural diversity in many districts?
13. To what extent does cultural diversity affect communication needs in a school district?
14. To what extent do parents and other taxpayers communicate with administrators in your school district? What basis do you have for your answer?
15. Is it possible for public schools to compensate for social and economic problems faced by many students? Why or why not?
16. Does your district have a well-developed system of keeping in touch with the community?
17. Has your district developed a strategy of intervention for children who are at risk of academic failure?
18. How well does your district work and collaborate with social agencies, political entities, and the private sector? How might this collaboration be improved?
19. What are the differences between centralized and decentralized approaches to governance? Which is more congruous with the intention of having close relationships between school and community?

SUGGESTED READINGS

Blankenhorn, D. (1995). *Fatherless America: Confronting our most urgent social problem.* New York: Harper.

Blau, J. (1992). *The visible poor: Homelessness in the United States.* New York: Oxford University Press.

Etzioni, A. (1993). *The spirit of community: Rights, responsibilities, and the communitarian agenda.* New York: Crown.

Hill, P., & Celio, M. (1998). *Fixing urban schools.* Washington, DC: Brookings Institution.

Howell, W. G. (Ed.). (2005). *Besieged: School boards and the future of education politics.* Washington, DC: Brookings Institution.

Jencks, C., & Phillips, M. (Eds.). (1998). *The black-white test score gap.* Washington, DC: Brookings Institution.

Mathews, D. (1996). *Is there a public for public schools?* Dayton, OH: Kettering Foundation.

Mayer, S. E. (1997). *What money can't buy: Family income and children's life chances.* Cambridge: Harvard University Press.

McAdams, D. R. (2006). *What school boards can do: Reform governance for urban schools.* New York: Teachers College Press.

Ogbu, J. U. (2003). *Black American students in an affluent suburb.* Mahwa: Lawrence Erlbaum Associates.

Orfield, G., & Ashkinaze, C. (1991). *The closing door: Conservative policy and black opportunity.* Chicago: University of Chicago Press.

Sergiovanni, T. J. (1994). *Building community in schools.* San Francisco: Jossey-Bass.

Steinberg, L. (1996). *Beyond the classroom: Why school reform has failed and what parents need to do.* New York: Simon & Schuster.

Thernstrom, A., & Thernstrom, S. (2003). *No excuses: Closing the racial gap in learning.* New York: Simon & Schuster.

Tyack, D. (2003). *Seeking common ground: Public schools in a diverse society.* Cambridge: Harvard University Press.

Wilson, W. J. (1997). *When work disappears: The world of the new urban poor.* New York: Alfred Knopf.

REFERENCES

Annie E. Casey Foundation. (2004). *Kids count data book.* Baltimore, MD: Author.

Annie E. Casey Foundation. (2006). *Kids count data book.* Baltimore, MD: Author.

Anyon, J. (2005). What "counts" as educational policy? Notes toward a new paradigm. *Harvard Educational Review, 75*(1), 65–68.

Balfanz, R., & Legters, N. (2004). *Locating the dropout crisis: Which high schools produce the nation's dropouts?* Report 70. Baltimore: Johns Hopkins University.

Berry, C. R. (2005). School district consolidation and student outcomes: Does size matter? In W. Howell (Ed.), *Besieged: School boards and the future of education politics* (pp. 56–81). Washington, DC: Brookings Institution.

Blankenhorn, D. (1995). *Fatherless America: Confronting our most urgent social problem.* New York: Harper.

Center for Education Policy. (2005). *Identifying school districts for improvement and, corrective action under the No Child Left Behind Act.* Washington DC: Author.

Fowler, F. (2004). *Policy studies for educational leaders.* Upper Saddle River, NJ: Prentice Hall.

Hochschild, J. L. (2005). What school boards can and cannot (or will not) accomplish. In W. Howell (Ed.), *Besieged: School boards and the future of education politics* (pp. 324–339). Washington, DC: Brookings Institution.

Howell, W. G. (Ed.). (2005). *Besieged: School boards and the future of education politics.* Washington, DC: Brookings Institution.

Jencks, C., & Peterson, P. E. (Eds.). (1991). *The urban underclass.* Washington, DC: Brookings Institution.

Jencks, C., & Phillips, M. (1998). Black-white test score gap: An introduction. In C. Jencks & M. Phillips (Eds.), *The black-white test score gap* (pp. 1–54). Washington, DC: Brookings Institution.

Lee, V. E., & Smith, J. B. (1997). High school size: Which works best and for whom? *Educational Evaluation & Policy Analysis, 19*(3), 205–227.

Mathews, D. (1996). *Is there a public for public schools?* Dayton, OH: Kettering Foundation.

Mayer, S. E. (1997). *What money can't buy: Family income and children's life chances.* Cambridge: Harvard University Press.

McAdams, D. R. (2006). *What school boards can do: Reform governance for urban schools.* New York: Teachers College Press.

National Center for Education Statistics (NCES). (1997). *The social context of education.* Washington, DC: U.S. Department of Education.

National Center for Education Statistics (NCES). (2003). *Overview of public elementary and secondary schools and districts: School year 2001–2002.* Washington, DC: U.S. Department of Education.

National Center for Education Statistics (NCES). (2005a). *Characteristics of the 100 largest public elementary and secondary school districts in the United States: 2002–03.* Washington, DC: U.S. Department of Education.

National Center for Education Statistics (NCES). (2005b). *Public elementary and secondary students, staff, schools, and school districts: 2002–03 school year.* Washington, DC: U.S. Department of Education.

Ruiz-de-Velasco, J. (2000). *Overlooked and underserved: Immigrant students in U.S. secondary schools.* Washington, DC: Urban Institute.

Sergiovanni, T. J. (1994). *Building community in schools.* San Francisco: Jossey-Bass.

Steinberg, L. (1996). *Beyond the classroom: Why school reform has failed and what parents need to do.* New York: Simon & Schuster.

Symonds, W. C. (2005, November 21). America the uneducated. *Business Week,* 120–122.

Thernstrom, A., & Thernstrom, S. (2003). *No excuses: Closing the racial gap in learning.* New York: Simon & Schuster.

Trotter, A. (2002). Electronic learning goes to school [Special issue]. *Education Week, 18*(12), 22–26.

Tyack, D., & Cuban, L. (1995). *Tinkering toward utopia: A century of public school reform.* Cambridge: Harvard University Press.

Uzzell, L. A. (2005, September). Cheat sheets: No Child Left Behind has taught our nation's schools one thing: How to lie. *American Spectator, 38*(7), 26–30.

Wilson, W. J. (1997). *When work disappears: The world of the new urban poor.* New York: Alfred Knopf.

CHAPTER 3

Public Opinions and Political Contexts

Edward P. St. John

Nathan J. Daun-Barnett

CASE STUDY: SETTING THE STAGE FOR HIGH SCHOOL

Reform: The New Superintendent's PR Plan

James Goldberg was the new superintendent of The City School District (TCSD), in a city of 450,000. After two decades of reform efforts, the school district had seen some improvement in test scores in reading and math in its elementary and middle schools. While Goldberg knew the school board was impressed by this modest improvement, he was also aware that the improved scores corresponded with modest increases in the rates of retention and referrals to special education in TCSD over the past decade. He was also concerned because less than half of the ninth graders who started high school in TCSD actually graduated—which was a decline over previous years.

When Goldberg accepted the position, he understood that the board was interested in improving high school graduation rates and college enrollment rates. During his first three months in office, he interviewed local groups to build an understanding of how he might go about crafting a strategy for improving both high school graduation rates and college enrollment rates. Reviewing what he had learned so far, he recognized that opinions varied greatly and that the political context within which he had to work in some ways constrained the choices he could make.

The State had established itself as a leader in school reform. During this process, four significant changes were made in an effort to improve high school completion and college enrollment: (1) passage of state legislation requiring a more rigorous core curriculum for high school graduation; (2) implementation of a scholarship program for all students eligible for free and reduced-price lunch; (3) creation of a statewide community college system; and (4) passage of state legislation supporting charter schools.

The first reform—more rigorous high school graduation requirements—was instituted in an attempt to ensure that more students were adequately prepared for college-level work. The requirements call for more courses in the core subjects of math, science, English, foreign language, and social studies and at more rigorous levels (e.g., three years of math at least through trigonometry). Along with higher standards, The State added an exam in the eleventh grade that students had to pass to earn their diploma.

The second reform, the scholarship program, was developed to offset the fact that otherwise qualified students were not able to attend college due to cost. Students signed up in eighth grade and took a pledge to prepare for college, remain drug free, and apply for both college and federal student aid. If students who had taken this "scholars pledge" actually filled out the federal aid application and applied to any college in The State, they would have their tuition paid. Goldberg recognized that far fewer students were signing up for the program in The City than were eligible, and he saw this as an opportunity.

The third reform was the creation of a statewide community college system. Most states already had well-established, publicly funded two-year colleges, but this was a new development for The State. A number of two-year technical schools were reformulated as community colleges, with the expectation that students could either begin there and transfer to four-year institutions or earn a two-year degree or certificate.

Fourth, The State had passed a charter school law in 2002, which allowed school districts and colleges to offer "charters" to newly formed schools. Across The State, some suburban districts had experimented with charters prior to 2002, but TCSD had not done so. After 2002, TSCD opened several charter elementary schools, and parents were generally enthusiastic regarding the early results. Taken together, these four reform initiatives reflected the complex policy environment within which Superintendent Goldberg was to work.

As a new superintendent, Goldberg realized that he had some goodwill available. He was of mixed race—African-American mother and white Jewish father—and could muster local political support, which made it easier to communicate with some groups more than others. He found the school board was conflicted even though it had supported a number of reform strategies over the past decade. Some of the more seasoned members of the board wanted to give older reforms a chance to work, but a couple of new members were pushing for charters, especially for high school.

There were branch campuses of two state universities and a community college in The City. The Technical University branch campus had a strong engineering program, and many of its students either found jobs directly with an associate's degree or transferred to the main campus downstate. The other branch campus was locally oriented, but did not have a good graduation rate. In addition, it was focused on building programs for working students, who were typically of nontraditional age, rather than on building bridges with local high schools. The City Community College had only recently achieved two-year-college status, having previously been a technical college. It was focused on building a strong two-year liberal arts transfer program. When Goldberg met with faculty leaders and administrators at the three local colleges, he sensed a great deal of goodwill. All three campuses had something to offer to the conversation, but none of them had any experience collaborating effectively with local high schools.

Goldberg also recognized that any meaningful and sustainable change would require additional financial resources. The State had a large Points of Light Foundation (POLF) that had funded a state initiative to improve college access, which included supplemental funding for The State's scholarship program. Goldberg had a meeting scheduled with the president of POLF next week.

There were 12 public high schools of varying sizes in TCSD. The district's teachers union was well organized, especially in the elementary and middle schools. To Goldberg, the high schools seemed chaotic. Most teachers seemed to resent the high school graduation exam. They were torn between teaching for the exam and building sound preparatory programs—and the two goals did not seem especially well aligned. There was conflict about priorities for high school reform in the schools and with the union. At the same time, the parents' level of support was much higher than that of the teachers for both more rigorous standards and testing. The combination of teacher resistance and parental support created a challenging political context for Superintendent Goldberg.

Goldberg had reached the point of reflecting on possible approaches to high school reform. He hoped to interest the local universities in partnerships with the local high schools and perhaps even the local middle schools. He also hoped to develop a strategy for improving participation in the scholarship program. His biggest question was how to begin the process: Should he appoint a commission, start a community conversation, or take direct control as a veteran of urban high schools? He knew there was support for any of these strategies, and it was time for him to act. He also knew that he had to proceed both swiftly and cautiously; while everyone expected him to act quickly, he recognized that resistance could increase without nimble political maneuvering.

Increasingly, senior school administrators are confronted by two conflicting sets of beliefs about schools when they enter the public forum, especially with respect to the role of accountability. The opinions about education held by most educators are increasingly divergent from the opinions about education held by the citizens in their communities, including parents (Ridenour & St. John, 2003). For the past two decades, about half of the voting public has favored school choice, while most teachers resist the idea. More critically, testing and accountability have enjoyed substantial public support, but many teachers find these methods too intrusive.

This conflicted environment represents a shift from the progressive period of the late nineteenth century and most of the twentieth century. During most of the twentieth century, there was a high level of congruence between the beliefs of most citizens and the beliefs of most educators about the value of a common public education (St. John & Parsons, 2004). Most teachers were attracted to their profession by its social orientation (Smart, 1989), and there was a broad consensus about the value of public education. However, with the emergence of major initiatives for charter schools and other school-choice schemes in the past two decades, the old value of a common public system of schooling may no longer be a goal of the general public. Although taxpayers appear to be shifting toward a position of limited support for public schools, educators expect unqualified support.

The 1990s were a period of conflicted political beliefs about education, with a greater emphasis placed on public accountability. The methodology of using test scores to hold schools accountable was solidified in the No Child Left Behind (NCLB) Act. Now the National Governors Association (NGA) (Kazis, Conklin, & Pennington, 2004) and other groups (Kazis, Vargas, & Hoffman, 2004) are calling for high school reforms that could introduce new curricula and new accountability schemes into high school education.

This chapter examines the interrelationship between public opinion and the policy context for educational improvement and reform. First, it reviews trends in public opinions about education policy issues and compares them to educators' opinions about similar issues. Then it examines how the context for education policy decisions has changed over the past few decades. Finally, it considers different ways of viewing the interrelationship between public opinion and policy decisions within school districts and school buildings. All these issues help to place public relations in the context of current political conditions.

PUBLIC OPINIONS

Education holds a unique place in the hearts and minds of the members of the American public. They place a great deal of emphasis on the role of education in shaping students for participation in a civic society and in preparing them as future workers, and they recognize by and large that the more education you have, the more economically successful you are likely to be. However, there are two "publics"—parents and community residents are one, and teachers are the other—that may share a common set of goals for education, but disagree with respect to how the goals are to be achieved.

Two educational issues in particular have dominated public policy discussions in recent years: school choice and accountability. Both issues are central to the most recent iteration of the Elementary and Secondary Education Act—No Child Left Behind—which mandates testing, public reporting of outcomes, and school accountability for those outcomes. School-choice alternatives are promoted as consequences for failing to achieve the goals of the legislation—which ultimately requires that all students achieve at the same high level within the next 10 years.

The General Public

For more than 30 years Phi Delta Kappa, in conjunction with the Gallup Poll, has been surveying public attitudes regarding the state of K–12 education. The survey is useful to educational policy makers as it provides two ways to gauge people's perceptions regarding educational reform efforts. First, it demonstrates if attitudes change over time, which is clearly illustrated in questions about how much people know about No Child Left Behind. Second, it is timely in the sense that as new issues arise, a body of questions typically addresses that reform. The following summary of public attitudes draws largely on these polls.

School Choice.   Parents have a choice of at least two primary types of education for their children beyond home schooling—public schools and private schools. The first and in some respects the most contentious attempt to provide school choice in recent years has been the movement toward voucher programs. A voucher is simply an allocation of a certain dollar amount to a student to use for any school, public or private. Both Milwaukee and Cleveland have implemented citywide, publicly supported voucher programs, and recently, the U.S. Supreme Court upheld the Cleveland voucher program as constitutional (Friedan, 2002). While the programs vary with respect to where vouchers can be used and how much they are worth, they have been seen largely by conservative voters and politicians as a viable option for parents and children who are dissatisfied with their educational experience in the public schools. Private versions of voucher programs have been piloted as well, but on a smaller scale and with fewer dollars per student. Consider Table 3–1, which summarizes public opinion on the use of vouchers.

TABLE 3–1

Do You Favor or Oppose Choosing a Private School at Public Expense?

	National		Public School Parents	
Year	2000	2004	2000	2004
Favor	45%	42%	47%	46%
Oppose	52%	56%	51%	52%
Don't know	3%	2%	2%	2%

Source: Rose & Gallup, 2000, 2004.

While parents of public school children are slightly more in favor of vouchers than the general public, both continue to oppose their usage overall. These numbers have remained remarkably consistent over the years for both groups, but it should also be recognized that when the issue is cast in the context of whether to improve public schools or offer vouchers, nearly 70% of respondents would focus on improving public schools. In 2004, respondents were asked what type of school they would send their children to if they were given a voucher, and their responses depended on how much of the cost was covered. When the entire amount was covered, two-thirds of parents would send their children to a private school, whereas if only half was covered, 50% would remain in public schools (Rose & Gallup, 2004).

Charter schools are the second form of choice that has become popular in recent years. Charter schools are typically public institutions that are given the same allocation of money per student as other public schools and are granted greater latitude with respect to the administration of the school, including the hiring of teachers and the crafting of the curriculum. Charter schools have been particularly popular in Arizona and are increasing in other areas across the country as well. Table 3–2 provides a summary of opinions regarding charter schools.

On one level, the public has decidedly mixed opinions on the issue of charter schools, with nearly equal percentages in favor and in opposition. However, a substantial percentage of respondents indicate that they do not know what to think about charter schools. This might be the result of regional differences, where people who reside in areas with no charter options have no opinion, or it could be that the option itself is confusing. People are less equivocal, however, on two issues regarding charter schools. More than 75% believe that charter schools should be held to the same accountability standards as public schools, and between 65 and 70% would oppose charter schools if the result was less money for public schools (Rose & Gallup, 2002).

Accountability and Public Education. For more than 20 years, since the National Commission on Educational Excellence issued its report *A Nation at Risk* (National Commission on Excellence in Education, 1983), public policy has focused a great deal of attention on measures of accountability. In general terms, the focus has shifted from what is put into schools to the outputs or what students learn. In most cases, testing has served as the cornerstone of accountability efforts, and frequently, the same tests are used to hold students, teachers, schools, and districts accountable. Table 3–3 illustrates people's opinions on testing.

TABLE 3–2

Do You Favor or Oppose the Idea of Charter Schools?

	National	Public School Parents
Favor	44%	44%
Oppose	43%	44%
Don't know	13%	12%

Source: Rose & Gallup, 2002.

TABLE 3–3

Is There Too Much Emphasis on Achievement Tests in Your Community?

	National		Public School Parents	
	2000	2004	2000	2004
Too much	30%	32%	34%	36%
Not enough	23%	22%	19%	20%
Right amount	43%	40%	46%	43%
Don't know	4%	6%	1%	1%

Source: Rose & Gallup, 2000, 2004.

TABLE 3–4

Should One of the Measures of a Teacher's Ability Be Based on How Well Students Perform on Tests?

	National	Public School Parents
Favor	49%	49%
Oppose	47%	49%
Don't know	4%	2%

Source: Rose & Gallup, 2002.

The greatest percentage of people believes that there is an appropriate amount of testing in schools, whereas a smaller portion indicates that there is too much testing. The majority (52%) believe that all high school students should be required to pass a high school exam, and more than two-thirds believe that the primary purpose of testing is to tailor instruction.

Members of the public are split on whether the same tests should be used to assess a teacher's performance (see Table 3–4). As one might imagine, teachers feel very differently about this issue.

Teachers

In the 1990s, Phi Delta Kappa and Gallup polled teachers about their attitudes toward public schools. The last iteration of that survey took place in 1999, so a more recent poll conducted by the Educational Testing Service (ETS) provides the foundation for this section. It happens that the results reported here are similar to the patterns present in 1999. In 2005, Hart and Winston (2005) conducted a survey of parents, students, high school teachers, and K–12 administrators for ETS. Their results do not map specifically onto the public poll results described earlier, but they do provide a sense of where parents and teachers differ on No Child Left Behind and accountability.

School Choice.   In the age of No Child Left Behind, issues of choice have been less commonly explored in public opinion surveys. However, the 1999 Phi Delta Kappa/Gallup Poll of teachers reports strongly differing views between teachers and the public on the implementation of voucher programs. While 47% of the public at that time favored vouchers, only 17% of teachers felt the same way. On the question of opening public school services to home-schooled children, almost three-quarters of the public approved, while only 42% of teachers favored the idea.

Accountability.   The hallmark of No Child Left Behind is the strict accountability structure designed to penalize teachers and schools for failing to bring all students up to the same set of standards. The following results from the ETS poll illustrate how parents and teachers differ on this issue. The first question is whether people have a favorable opinion of NCLB (see Table 3–5). When this question was first asked by Phi Delta Kappa/Gallup (Rose & Gallup, 2003), more than two-thirds of respondents indicated that they did not know enough about the law to say. Fortunately, that has changed considerably over time.

In 2005, 15% were unable to answer this question about NCLB, but that is a considerable improvement in two years. Teachers, on the other hand, feel much better prepared to answer this question and clearly are not in favor of the law. While 46% of the public had at least a favorable opinion of NCLB, only 19% of teachers felt the same. In fact, 50% found the law very unfavorable, indicating that there is a considerable difference of opinion between teachers and parents on this issue.

Another point of contention between parents and teachers with respect to accountability is the degree to which teachers and schools should be held accountable using the same tests designed to assess students. Table 3–6 shows that parents are more than 2 to 1 in favor of using the same standard for all. At the heart of teacher opposition to this item is the belief that each student must be met where he or she is educationally and that one

TABLE 3–5
Do You Have a Favorable Opinion of the No Child Left Behind Legislation?

	K–12 Parents	High School Teachers
Very favorable	23%	2%
Somewhat favorable	23%	17%
Somewhat unfavorable	20%	25%
Very unfavorable	19%	50%
Unsure	15%	5%

Source: Hart & Winston, 2005.

TABLE 3–6
Should All Students, Teachers, and Schools Be Held to the Same Standard of Performance?

	K–12 Parents	High School Teachers
Favor	59%	26%
Oppose	30%	60%
Unsure	11%	14%

Source: Hart & Winston, 2005.

standard does not allow for this. However, unlike the item regarding NCLB, teachers are less sure on this item than parents (14% versus 11%).

In conclusion, educators and the public disagree substantially about the two issues central to more recent educational reform efforts: school choice and accountability. It is important to recognize opinions of teachers and parents on these issues for what they are: positions reflecting personal investment in education. Parents are interested in whether their sons and daughters succeed in school and whether they are prepared for work or college, as well as how their tax dollars are spent. Teachers are invested in the success of students generally, but they have become targets of accountability measures, which may temper any enthusiasm they might have for the spirit of NCLB. They also suggest that a single standard fails to recognize the current realities students, teachers, and schools face. Neither set of opinions alone should be relied on to make policy, but both should suggest where support and resistance are likely to arise.

POLITICAL CONTEXTS

When building an understanding of the significance of these dominant public views on educational policy issues, it is important to consider how the political context for education has changed in recent decades. During most of the twentieth century, there was broad public support for expanding educational opportunity, first by building schools and school systems and then by enhancing those systems to provide equitable opportunity for students with diverse backgrounds and diverse learning needs. Throughout this progressive period, the notion of expanding educational opportunity was considered integral to the political consensus among diverse publics in support of social and economic development. Those who supported economic development generally supported educational investment because it provided labor for industry. Those who supported social goals valued educational investment because it provided a means for upward mobility. The broad political contexts in which public opinion was forged shifted over time, but the balance was maintained, at least until the 1990s.

Themes Underlying Public Support of Schools

Throughout the century of progressive school development, the consensus between supporters of economic and social goals held together. Even Catholic voters remained part of a broad consensus because they were willing to make a choice—those who wanted to send their children to religious schools paid tuition, whereas those who wanted to send their children to common public schools did so. However, a shift in public opinion, and especially a growing number favoring tuition vouchers, represents a major change in political contexts. The old political consensus on the support of public education was constructed around four themes related to local community control, comprehensive education, equal opportunity, and educational excellence. A broad consensus among the public and educators emerged on each of these issues in the twentieth century.

Foundation Theme 1:   Local community involvement and control are essential to the general public's support of education.

From the colonial period forward, local communities created and operated schools. Even before the common school movement started in the mid–nineteenth century, communities imposed taxes to support schools (Marsden, 1994). With the emergence of common schools, these older schools were organized into local districts. In spite of the development of a nearly national curriculum over the last 100 years, the value of local community control remains central for those who continue to support public schools. After more than a century of incremental centralization, the core belief that the primary locus of control resides with parents and the community continues to influence policy decisions in school districts across the country. This continues to be a foundational belief about public education in spite of shifting public attitudes about educational issues. Consider the following description of an event in El Paso, Texas:

> The community organizing efforts among the Alliance Schools in El Paso helped to establish the constituency that took decisive action to stop administrators from firing a principal and closing a school that the community considered particularly successful. When almost 500 parents, community members, and teachers filed into a board meeting, board members quickly reinstated the principal and shelved the plans to close the school. (Hatch, 1998, p. 17)

The school site remains the basic unit of educational enterprise, and local collaboration among educators, parents, and community members provides the foundation for public support. These linkages help explain why members of the general public consistently rate their own schools better than they rate schools nationally (Rose & Gallup, 2004). When this public support for local schools is disturbed, schools and school systems become conflicted. Conversely, public support for education can probably be strengthened through public relations strategies that promote local collaboration.

Foundation Theme 2:   By providing comprehensive education, public schools broadened their base of public support.

A second theme underlying the public school consensus in the early twentieth century was the educational policy focusing on building comprehensive schools. Around 1920, states began to play a larger role in the financing of local schools. This support was coupled with increasing levels of control that became visible in areas such as extended school years and longer school days. For example, state requirements that schools provide more comprehensive high school opportunities led to the consolidation of districts through the middle part of the twentieth century; the number of school districts declined nationally from 127,649 in 1932 to 15,690 in 1983 (Burrup, Brimley, & Garfield, 1988). However, the number of districts declined by less than 10% since 1983 (the National Education Association, 1998, reported 14,461 districts in the United States).

The idea that the role of public schools is to provide a comprehensive education for all students has become part of the common public school ideal. Indeed, the comprehensive mission of schools—to meet the learning needs of all students—remains a core belief among public school advocates. Most advocates of public schools, however, stop short of endorsing full market-oriented, school-choice models because they fear that the most needy students would remain in public schools, whereas most others would opt for alternative forms of education. More precisely, private schools would skim off the wealthier and higher-ability students (e.g., Kozol, 1991). In the context of the current political environment, experts question the future of the "comprehensive ideal" (Wraga, 1992).

It is the comprehensive ideal, the belief that schools can meet the learning needs of all students, that is perhaps most challenged by the new emphasis on school choice. The ability to provide a comprehensive array of services in school systems has been linked to consolidation, especially to the creation of districts and schools of sufficient size to provide choices within school buildings. The new challenges raise questions about how to provide educational choice—within comprehensive public schools and systems or through other means.

Foundation Theme 3: The goal of equal educational opportunity provides a rationale for meeting the learning needs of students from diverse communities.

The emphasis on equalizing educational opportunity emerged in the 1960s as an extension of the historical goal of expanding the opportunity for an adequate education. Litigants in state school-finance cases argued that state systems had great inequities across school districts. Since the passage of the Elementary and Secondary Education Act '(ESEA)' of 1965, the federal government has played a substantial role in equalizing opportunity. It has supported compensatory education for students with educational and financial need under Title I, as well as special education. Federal programs supplemented the capacity of schools to meet the needs of all students, and the ESEA mandated that parents be involved in school-site governance of Title I starting in 1965. Over time, federal requirements for parent involvement have been strengthened through requirements that parents of special education students approve individualized education programs (U.S. Department of Education, 1997).

The courts also have had a substantial influence on the equal opportunity goal. Starting with *Serano v. Priest,* school advocates litigated for more adequate and equitable funding among districts in a given state. More recent litigation has raised questions about the adequacy of state funding in Kentucky and Ohio (Education Data Partnership, 2006). Periodic legal challenges serve to remind educational policy makers about the difficulty of balancing diverse public interests in the ongoing development of state education systems.

Litigation over school desegregation has also pushed districts in the direction of equalizing learning opportunities for all students. More specifically, it has added to the comprehensive nature of public schools by establishing the expectation that schools meet the learning needs of all students. Interestingly, desegregation plans that included magnet schools were early experiments with school choice (Willie, 1991). Through the 1970s, the expanded role of government in public education did not erode the old consensus. However, efficiency also began to emerge as a policy issue. Steadily rising costs for public education spawned cries for accountability, since many educators made no attempt to link increases in fiscal support with improvement in outcomes.

Unrest about the costs of government began to emerge in the mid-1970s. In 1976, Jimmy Carter was elected president on a platform of controlling government spending. He ushered in zero-based budgeting, which increased the emphasis on conducting cost-benefit analyses of educational programs. At the same time, he supported the creation of the U.S.

Department of Education. The strategy for the Education Consolidation and Improvement Act, which consolidated federal programs and gave block grants to school districts, was formulated in this period of transition (Turnbull, 1981).

The movement toward federal block grants stimulated the return of decisions about the direction of education programs back to state and local communities, where decisions about what to fund could more appropriately be made. However, a new wave of reductions in services was also ushered in during this period, raising questions about whose needs were being met in the educational system. The anti–affirmative-action movement, now evident in many parts of the country, raises further questions about the distribution of resources within schools and school districts. Thus, although educational opportunity remains central to educational policy, the mechanisms used to support equal opportunity have become more controversial within local communities.

Foundation Theme 4: Parent involvement remains both an aim of public policy and an essential core element of local support of schools.

For the past few decades, the dominant conception of parent involvement has been a hierarchical model developed by Epstein (1988). As refined (Epstein & Dauber, 1991), this model includes

1. Basic obligations of parents (for health and safety, as well as positive home conditions),
2. Basic obligations of schools (for communications with parents about schooling and student progress),
3. Involvement of parents at schools (as volunteers),
4. Involvement of parents at home (in learning activities at home and in school), and
5. Involvement of parents in decision making as child advocates and in participatory roles.

This conception of parent involvement is highly compatible with the notion that schools control the agenda and parent involvement meets the interest of schools. However, in the new context of growing public concern about school quality and choice, this conception does not capture the need to involve parents in deeper and more fundamental ways. In recent research on family involvement in restructuring schools, a new form of family involvement appears to be emerging: "When parents are welcomed into restructuring, their experience becomes an integral part of the process. They also begin to take personal ownership for the efforts they make to change their schools. And as schools begin to change, to become more welcoming and involving places for parents as well as children, they also become schools of choice, places where parents choose to enroll their children" (St. John, Griffith, & Allen-Haynes, 1997, p. 71).

Thus, the process of involving parents in local discourses about educational improvement in essence engages them in a genuine dialogue with educators about critical educational issues. This interaction potentially changes the political context for policy development. The success of this strategy depends on how parents are treated. Will they be treated as political pawns or as partners in restructuring?

The Shaky Foundations of Public Support for Education

With the emergence of excellence as a new theme in educational policy, the older foundations of public support for education are now uncertain. The review of public opinion confirms that the older goals of public education—including support for local schools and equal opportunity—remain as important to the general public as they do to educators. The passage of NCLB symbolizes solidification of legal mandates for accountability, but there is no sign that teachers believe this approach is the best means of improving education. Public support for accountability and school choice has created a deeply conflicted policy context, with new divisions between the values of the general public and those of the educators.

Emergent Themes in a Conflicted Political Context

The school-choice and public accountability efforts have become central to the educational policy environment in most states. The U.S. Supreme Court decision rendered in June of 2002 has opened the door for states to pass laws permitting vouchers (Walsh, 2002). In addition, NCLB has solidified the use of testing and accountability in K–12 education. Below, emergent policy themes are examined.

Emerging Theme 1: The excellence movement ushered in a renewed commitment to quality improvement in public education.

The excellence movement in education was a by-product of political maneuvers by Secretary of Education Terrell Bell. As President Ronald Reagan's first secretary of education, Bell fended off the administration's efforts to eliminate the recently established Department of Education. He defined a new federal role in providing educational leadership (Bell, 1982) and initiated a study group that published *A Nation at Risk*. This report focused public attention on the growing populations of students who were at risk of dropping out of school.

In the aftermath of reports criticizing the effectiveness of public schools, most citizens accepted the argument that the quality of these institutions had declined. Thus, doubts about education grew steadily after 1983. By the end of that decade, a new generation of conservative educational leaders had totally shifted the debates about the government's role in education. Finn (1990), for example, argued that the focus of public policy should shift from equalizing inputs (money to education) to improving outcomes, especially student achievement. There is little doubt that the public is now primarily concerned about quality, and consequently, the focus of educational policy has shifted to new indices, especially test scores. Recent polls indicate that public support of standards and standardized testing remains high (Rose & Gallup, 2004).

Emerging Theme 2: Achievement tests are generally accepted by taxpayers as a mechanism for accountability in education.

In the past two decades, new developments in the use of standardized achievement tests have influenced public attitudes about education (First, 1992). In this environment, the public has been oriented toward using test scores as a means of comparing schools. All too frequently, test score data have been used to emphasize the problems rather than strengths of school systems. For instance, the press usually ignores research findings that indicate American schools maintain their competitive position internationally (Atkin & Black, 1997; Mislevy, 1995; Wadsworth, 1998). Negative public perceptions of the quality of public education are complicated by two related developments:

1. Testing and curriculum tend to be tightly linked. As a consequence of the national testing movement, there is a clear movement toward a national curriculum (Stedman & Riddle, 1992).
2. The comparison of test scores across school districts usually focuses public attention on the education problems of inner-city schools.

Criticisms of schools in the popular press draw attention to achievement scores in inner-city schools, which in turn causes administrators in inner-city schools to tighten their control over curriculum. The proclivity to respond to concerns about test scores by controlling curriculum is enhanced by textbook companies that seek to link achievement solely with school-based experiences. This has influenced a standardization of curriculum that limits the ability of schools to respond to students' learning needs in diverse ways. Ironically, the movement toward a national system of testing has constrained the capacity of schools to respond to the interests of their local communities, especially in urban schools (Miron & St. John, 2004). The number of curricular choices within many schools has dwindled, as the national standards for curricular content have expanded.

Emerging Theme 3:   Comprehensive school restructuring has emerged as a widely accepted means of improving problem schools.

Negative perceptions of public education, and especially of inner-city schools, have generated myriad restructuring methodologies that focus on making fundamental changes. The goal of many of these methods is to improve education in schools that serve students who are at risk of failure because of their family and social circumstances. The test-driven reform movement has not served these children (or the schools that teach them) well. Three methods have been systematically pilot tested in urban settings across the country:

1. Comer's School Development Process (Comer, Haynes, Joyner, & Ben-Avie, 1996)—which was pilot tested originally in the New Haven, Connecticut, schools and expanded to urban systems in Detroit, New Orleans, and other cities— combines systematic curriculum reform with community development methods.
2. Slavin's Success for All (Slavin & Madden, 1989)—pilot tested originally in Baltimore, Maryland, and expanded to urban centers across the United States—has a well-developed process of intervening to improve reading achievement.
3. Levin's Accelerated Schools Project (Finnan, St. John, McCarthy, & Solvacek 1996; Hopfenberg, Levin, & Associates, 1993)—pilot tested in the San Francisco Bay area and expanded to more than 1,000 schools nationally—provides a systematic process focusing on the use of inquiry to address challenges confronting school communities.

In 1998, these and other restructuring methods were approved for use in a new federal program that infuses millions of dollars into inner-city schools. Each program includes an emphasis on involving parents in the school restructuring process, suggesting that there will be a sustained push to require parental involvement in systematic, comprehensive school improvement efforts. Attempts to reform inner-city schools reinforce the importance of local commitment and community involvement in education improvement, and these are values that historically have been integral to public schools.

Although independent research on the effects of comprehensive school reform has been limited, there is some evidence that it could facilitate improvement in urban schools (St. John, Manset-Williamson, et al., 2004). Comprehensive reforms are associated with reductions in retention and referral to special education, as well as enabling more children to pass standardized tests. Thus, they could keep more children in the educational mainstream and improve achievement. However, not all comprehensive reforms work equally well in all settings. Schools should carefully study reform options before choosing a comprehensive reform or a reading reform model (St. John, Loescher, & Bardzell, 2003).

Emerging Theme 4:   High school reform has become a major concern as most states have begun to focus on improving the college enrollment rates of high school graduates.

Doubling the number of low-income students who enroll in college has become a major theme in public policy. Many national studies have illustrated that completion of advanced math courses in high school is correlated with college enrollment and completion (Adelman, 1995; Choy, 2002; National Center for Education Statistics, 1997, 2001). Based in part on this research, the NGA has promoted high school reform as a means of improving college access (Kazis, Conklin & Pennington, 2004), an approach consistent with national calls for high school reform (Kazis, Vargas, & Hoffman, 2004).

Many new high school reforms have been rationalized based on these new initiatives, including introducing high school exit exams, implementing new math standards, and increasing math requirements for high school graduation. Research that examines the effects of these reform policies reveals a positive association with test scores, but a negative relationship with high school graduation rates (St. John & Musoba, in Press). In addition, cross-sectional analyses of national data from College Board surveys indicate that funding for instruction explains more variance in Scholastic Aptitude Test scores than do state education policies, such as math requirements and exit exams (Musoba, 2006). On the other hand, programs that provide financial guarantees to students have been shown to have a positive association with high school graduation and college enrollment (St. John, Chung, et al., 2004). However, financial strategies, including student grants, have not been explicitly considered by NGA and most other groups promoting high school reform.

Given these ambiguities, it is likely that high school reform will be a contested issue for the next decade or so. School districts, states, and colleges face critical decisions about how to encourage both high school graduation and college access. Most states now rationalize education reforms as means of improving economic development, a pattern that helps explain the emphasis now being placed on high school reform.

POLITICAL CONTEXTS AND PUBLIC OPINION

How should educators view the emerging political context for public schools? Educators increasingly need to reflect on their communication with parents and other groups about educational issues. In past decades, when there was a broader consensus about the goals of public education, it was less necessary to engage in such reflection. Today, educators who want to facilitate and lead local efforts to improve schools must recognize the various views held by diverse constituents. This new relationship between educators and the public can be viewed in three ways (St. John et al., 1997).

An Instrumental View

When school policies are set at the district and state levels, then schools are being treated instrumentally. Instrumental action has been defined as being implementation oriented, as having little relationship to strategic choices about goals and actions (Habermas, 1984, 1987). In school districts with tight control, educators feel as though they are being treated instrumentally, as though they have little influence over the policies that shape their roles as teachers (St. John et al., 1997). To the extent that the new political context exerts pressures on schools to implement a standard curriculum, teachers and principals may feel a loss of power. That is, they may see themselves as instruments of externally constructed policies.

How do parents perceive the effects of these tightly regulated school contexts? Very frequently, they feel alienated: They show up to receive report cards—if they show up at all (St. John et al., 1997). In tightly regulated schools, parents and other community members often resort to agitation to address their interests (Miron, 1996), much like the example in El Paso described previously. In this view, collective political action constitutes an alternative community groups can use to contend with schools that are highly regulated by government agencies and their managers.

When there was a broader consensus about educational policy, teachers and administrators simply assumed that they knew what was best for students, schools, and districts. But as more policy issues were contested, and as parents became more active in expressing their values and beliefs about the goals for education and their goals for their children, educators discovered that they could neither dictate decisions nor take parental support for granted.

A Strategic View

One of the central aims of the excellence movement is to build a decision capacity within schools through the development of school-site plans formulated by school-site councils. When these processes take hold and are used to engage educators and parents in a conversation about the direction of the schools, then the loci of strategic action shift, at least in part, from the central offices to the schools. The process of setting strategic goals and moving toward those goals can be characterized as strategic action (Habermas, 1984, 1987).

To the extent that schools develop and pursue their own goals, they increase their chances of becoming more distinctive. The strategic decision process allows parents to influence decisions in schools and to take actions that influence schools in ways they think are best for their children (St. John et al., 1997). This type of environment can be more compatible with the new choice environment advocated by many reformers. However, this idealized strategic environment can be difficult to actualize, especially given the divergent visions of educators and parents. One of the limitations of the strategic model as it applies to education is that it assumes a high degree of goal compatibility between schools and central offices, schools and educators, and schools and families.

Since the initial passage of the ESEA in the mid-1960s, there has been a growing government mandate for parental involvement. Yet parents often feel excluded from decision processes, even when there are mechanisms that support their involvement (Igo, 1997; St. John et al., 1997). Therefore, the strategic planning processes—including the local site-based planning now required for schools in many states—do not seem to have substantially improved this situation.

A Communicative View

Communicative action focuses on building understanding, rather than on achieving goals per se (Habermas, 1984, 1987). In one study of restructuring schools, the following characteristics were associated with a communicative approach to educational leadership:

1. Publicly testing personal hypotheses about the causes of problems,
2. Wrestling internally with the morally problematic aspect of educational practice (that is, critical reflection), and
3. Helping and encouraging the development of others (St. John et al., 1997, pp. 10–11).

When these concepts are applied to the current discourse between schools and their various publics, one discovers that a radically different leadership attitude is needed. First, it is difficult for leaders who believe in control to be open about their framing assumptions, their personal hypotheses about the causes of problems. However, when dealing with parents and educators, critical reflection is necessary to generate and sustain open discussions. Candid, two-way communication, especially the exchange of ideals that could radically alter the organization of public schools, is foundational to school reform.

These exchanges between educators and parents need to get beneath the surface of claims and counterclaims about the goals of education. Educators need to seek an understanding of why parents are advocating for new directions, just as parents need to understand the educational and social values that underlie the arguments of educators. When both groups have a chance to explore their points of view, a new common understanding can emerge.

Second, the notion that educators should wrestle internally with the morally problematic aspects of educational practice is widely advocated (Foster, 1986; Miron, 1996), but infrequently practiced when difficult issues are being debated. In the current conflict between liberal and conservative ideologies about education, the problematic aspects of the espoused positions seldom get fully addressed. Claims are frequently made about the reasons for opposing or resisting any particular policy initiative. For example, if one believes that vouchers would skim the best students out of public schools, then it could be difficult to hear the voices of disillusioned parents who have little hope for their children in schools as they are currently constructed. Alternately, school-choice advocates need to wrestle with the problems associated with their claims that it would cost less to finance vouchers, as the advocates of California's voucher initiative discovered. Underfunding education—spreading fewer dollars across more students (which would result if vouchers really did go to students in private schools and total public spending on education was reduced)—could create even worse circumstances for children in at-risk situations than the present system. In other words, when administrators and other educators wrestle internally with the moral aspects of the positions they hold, it is easier for them to listen to others.

Finally, the notion that educational leaders should be supportive of the professional development of teachers has long been recognized in the education literature (Bull & Buechler, 1996; St. John, Loescher, & Bardzell, 2003). However, it is frequently difficult for educators and other professionals to act in ways that are consistent with the espoused value of empowering other professionals (Argyris, 1993; Argyris, Putnam, & Smith, 1985). Further, this argument is not frequently extended to include parents, since it relates to their involvement in schools. In research on communicative action in schools, it is becoming apparent that educational leaders need to use open discourse as a means of encouraging teachers and parents to state and publicly test their views (St. John et al., 1997).

Questions about how learning communities can create more open discourses about education remain critical, however. There are many calls for open public forums on the purposes of education (Carr, 1995; Sokoloff, 1997). Also, parent groups seem very concerned about their own involvement in school decisions (Igo, 1997; Storer, Licklider, & Cychosz, 1996). If these new public forums limit their topics to public schools, without opening the dialogue to broader questions about private school choice, then a growing percentage of taxpayers may feel alienated. Whether educators will enter into open dialogue about the critical issues that divide them from the general public—the measurement of outcomes and the opening of school choice—remains a vital question.

Educational leaders may need to create forums where diverse and divergent views can be examined and evaluated in ways that not only support the development and improvement of educational systems, but also provide a forum for creating a local agenda for educational improvement. The real moral challenge, viewed from a postconventional frame (Habermas, 1991), is to build an understanding within local communities about why existing patterns have emerged in the first place. The most complex questions pertain to ways of reformulating policy when local public attitudes are divergent from the plans developed by educational systems.

SUMMARY

When trends in the opinions held by the public are examined and contrasted to those in the views commonly held by educators, several incongruencies become apparent. These new areas of disagreement are complicated by a rapidly changing policy context. First, the general public seems increasingly supportive of using tuition subsidies for open choice about public and private schools, whereas educators are less supportive of extending choice schemes to private schools (Ridenour & St. John, 2003). However, even though a considerable portion of the population now supports tuition subsidies for students attending private schools, there is not a clear public mandate to move in this new direction. Indeed, less than half of the population supports this strategy in the latest poll, even though a slightly larger percentage favors this option than opposes it. Further, the United States has a strong history of integration and equal opportunity across race and ethnic groups; an ethic that would seem to extend to schools that accept tuition vouchers (Eckes & Rapp, 2006). In contrast, educators support more limited choice schemes that extend the opportunity to families to choose among public schools. Thus, there is contested terrain that could complicate the efforts of educational leaders to build support for their educational plans.

Second, achievement tests and their use in the policy arena have emerged as an area of disagreement among educators, parents, and the public (Ridenour & St. John, 2003). The majority of the public would like to see more testing. In contrast, educators are more concerned about the uses of test information in the public forum. Indeed, many experts have expressed concerns that members of the public do not understand how to interpret test scores; thus as a result, they use scores improperly to compare schools with respect to effectiveness or to make comparisons with other countries. Further, educators are much less convinced that the new testing movement is actually helping schools to improve.

The policy context is also contested. States and the federal government are increasingly focusing their reform efforts on restructuring and implementing choice schemes, as well as on refining their approaches to testing student achievement. All these reform efforts complicate local school planning and policy development because they conflict with the attitudes held by educators in public school systems. Indeed, the current policy context reflects public attitudes more than it reflects educators' attitudes, and many educators hold beliefs that are in conflict with the policies that now govern public education. After nearly two decades of public investment in new approaches to testing, educators remain unconvinced of their value. Therefore, there is reason to question how educators will view the new initiatives to increase choice and restructure schools and whether they will embrace these new initiatives as opportunities for innovation or continue to resist them after they have been legislated.

There is also an embedded conflict between school choice and the methods being used for school accountability. The emphasis on testing and standards constrains change in public schools, inhibiting adaptation to choice schemes (Ridenour & St. John, 2003; St. John & Ridenour, 2002). Public schools are often caught between two contradictory forces, one forcing student-centered changes, the other inhibiting these changes.

The new policy context presents a challenging situation for administrators who are concerned about public relations in education. In this new policy environment, public relations will involve more than disseminating information about the goals established through district planning processes. Schools need better information about the expectations of parents and taxpayers so they can communicate with these groups about opportunities that exist within schools. Public relations may also involve creating new forums within school communities to discuss the new challenges facing education.

QUESTIONS AND SUGGESTED ACTIVITIES

CASE STUDY

1. How do state and local policy developments described in The City School District case relate to national trends in public opinion?
2. How do the actions of the teachers union in TCSD reflect the opinions of teachers in national polls?
3. How are recent changes in the national policy context reflected in The City School District case?
4. How did TCSD Superintendent Goldberg design his strategies for high school reform in this political context?
5. Should a public forum be created in The City to discuss the conflicting notions of educational improvement?
6. How should school-restructuring methodologies, such as charter school initiatives, be coordinated with efforts to improve high schools in The City?
7. How did educators in The City respond to the scholarship program? What roles could this program play in the high school reform process in TCSD?
8. How could parents be involved in the planning processes for high school restructuring? For charter schools?
9. How are the themes that underlie the support of public education evident in the case?
10. How are the emerging themes of the new policy context evident in the case?
11. How might a forum be created to encourage discussion about the high school reform initiatives in The City?

CHAPTER

12. How do the opinions of educators and voters compare and contrast?
13. How are the opinions about education policy held by parents reflected in the new political context?
14. How do changes over time in public policy for education relate to the opinions about education held by taxpayers?
15. How does the popular reform concept of school-based management relate to the instrumental, strategic, and communicative views discussed in this chapter?
16. What are some of the tensions between the values of educational excellence and educational equality?

SUGGESTED READINGS

Carr, B. (1995). Communication failure can threaten progress. *Journal of Educational Relations*, 16(4), 18–22.

Comer, J. P., Haynes, N. M., Joyner, E. T., & Ben-Avie, M. (Eds.). (1996). *Rallying the whole village: The Comer process for reforming schools*. New York: Teachers College Press.

First, P. F. (1992). *Educational policy for school administrators*. Boston: Allyn & Bacon.

Howe, H., II. (1996). The continuing question: Will public schools make it in America? *School Administrator*, 53(5), 14–17.

Miron, L. F., & St. John, E. P. (Eds.). (2004). *Reinterpreting urban school reform: A critical-empirical review*. Albany: State University of New York Press.

St. John, E. P. (2006). *Education and the public interest: School reform, public finance, and access to higher education*. Dordrecht, Netherlands: Springer.

REFERENCES

Adelman, C. (1995). *The new college course map and transcript files: Changes in course-taking and achievement, 1972–1993*. Washington, DC: National Center for Education Statistics.

Argyris, C. (1993). *Knowledge for action: A guide to overcoming barriers to organizational change*. San Francisco: Jossey-Bass.

Argyris, C., Putnam, R., & Smith, D. (1985). *Action science: Methods and skills for research and intervention*. San Francisco: Jossey-Bass.

Atkin, J. M., & Black, P. (1997). Policy perils of international comparisons. *Phi Delta Kappan, 79*(1), 22–28.

Bell, T. H. (1982, November). The federal role in education. *Harvard Educational Review, 52*(4), 375–380.

Bull, B., & Buechler, M. (1996). *Learning together: Professional development for better schools*. Bloomington: Indiana Education Policy Center.

Burrup, P. E., Brimley, J. V., & Garfield, R. R. (1988). *Financing education in a climate of change*. Newton, MA: Allyn & Bacon.

Carr, B. (1995). Communication failure can threaten progress. *Journal of Educational Relations, 16*(4), 18–22.

Choy, S. P. (2002). *Access & persistence: Findings from 10 years of longitudinal research on students*. Washington, DC: American Council on Education.

Comer, J. P., Haynes, N. M., Joyner, E. T., & Ben-Avie, M. (Eds.). (1996). *Rallying the whole village: The Comer process for reforming schools*. New York: Teachers College Press.

Eckes, S., & Rapp, K. (2006). Charter school research: Trends and implications, In E. P. St. John (Ed.), *Reading on equal education*, Vol. 21 (pp. 3–36). New York: AMS Press.

Education Data Partnership. (2006). *Serrano V. Priest and funding equity*. Retrieved July 25, 2006 from http://www.ed-data.k12.ca.US/Articles/Articles. Asp?title=Serrano.

Epstein, J. L. (1988). How do we improve programs of parent involvement? *Educational Horizons, 91*(3), 58–59.

Epstein, J. L., & Dauber, S. L. (1991). School programs and teacher practices of parent involvement in inner-city elementary schools. *Elementary School Journal, 91*(3), 289–305.

Finn, C. E. (1990). The biggest reform of all. *Phi Delta Kappan, 72*(1), 584–592.

Finnan, C., St. John, E. P., McCarthy, J., & Slovacek S. P., (Eds.). (1996). *Accelerated schools in action: Lessons from the field*. Thousand Oaks, CA: Corwin Press.

First, P. F. (1992). *Educational policy for school administrators*. Boston: Allyn & Bacon.

Foster, W. (1986). *Paradigms and promises: New approaches to educational administration*. Buffalo, NY: Prometheus Books.

Friedan, T. (2002). *Supreme Court affirms school voucher program*. CNN Law Center. Retrieved January 23, 2006 from http://archives/cnn.com/2002/LAW/06/27/scouts.school.vouchers/.

Habermas, J. (1984). *The theory of communicative action: Vol. 1. Reason and the rationalization of society*. Boston: Beacon Press.

Habermas, J. (1987). *The theory of communicative action: Vol. 2. Lifeworld and system: A critique of functionalist reason*. Boston: Beacon Press.

Habermas, J. (1991). *Moral consciousness and communicative action*. Cambridge, MA: MIT Press.

Hart, P. D., & Winston, D. (2005). *Ready for the real world: Americans speak on high school reform*. Princeton, NJ: Educational Testing Service.

Hatch, T. (1998). How community action contributes to achievement. *Educational Leadership*, 55(8), 16–19.

Hopfenberg, W. S., Levin, H. M., & Associates. (1993). *Accelerated schools resource guide*. San Francisco: Jossey-Bass.

Igo, S. (1997). Continuing a commitment. *Phi Delta Kappan*, 78(10), 771–773.

Kazis, R., Conklin, K., & Pennington, H. (2004). How states can promote secondary and postsecondary success in tough economic times. In R. Kazis, J. Vargas, & N. Hoffman, (Eds.), *Double the numbers: Increasing postsecondary credentials for underrepresented youth* (pp. 265–270). Cambridge: Harvard University Press.

Kazis, R., Vargas, J., & Hoffman, N. (Eds.). (2004). *Double the numbers: Increasing postsecondary credentials for underrepresented youth*. Cambridge: Harvard University Press.

Kozol, J. (1991). *Savage inequalities*. New York: Harper.

Marsden, G. M. (1994). *The soul of the American university*. New York: Oxford University Press.

Miron, L. F. (1996). *The social construction of urban schooling: Situating the crisis*. Cresskill, NJ: Hampton Press.

Miron, L. F., & St. John, E. P. (Eds.). (2004). *Reinterpreting urban school reform: Have urban schools failed or has the reform movement failed urban schools?* Albany: State Unnecessarily of New York Press.

Mislevy, R. J. (1995). What can we learn from international assessments? *Educational Evaluation & Policy Analysis*, 17(4), 419–437.

Musoba, G. D. (2006). Accountability versus adequate funding; which policies influence adequate preparation for college. In E. P. St. John (Ed.), *Reading on equal education*, Vol. 21 (pp. 79–132). New York: AMS Press.

National Center for Education Statistics. (1997). *Confronting the odds: Students at risk and the pipeline to higher education* (NCES 98-094, by L. J. Horn). Washington, DC: Author.

National Center for Education Statistics. (2001). *Bridging the gap: Academic preparation and postsecondary success of first-generation students* (NCES 2001-153, by E. C. Warburton & R. Bugarin). Washington, DC: Author.

National Commission on Excellence in Education. (1983). *A nation at risk: The imperative for educational reform*. Washington, DC: U.S. Government Printing Office.

Ridenour, C. S., & St. John, E. P. (2003). Private scholarships and school choice: Innovations or class reproduction? In L. F. Miron & E. P. St. John (Eds.), *Reinterpreting urban school reform: Have urban schools failed, or has the reform movement failed urban schools?* (pp. 177–206). Albany: State University of New York Press.

Rose, L., & Gallup, A. M. (2000). The 32nd annual Phi Delta Kappan/Gallup Poll of the public attitudes toward public schools. *Phi Delta Kappan*, 82(1), 41–58.

Rose, L., & Gallup, A. M. (2002). The 34th Annual Phi Delta Kappan/Gallup Poll of the public attitudes toward public schools. *Phi Delta Kappan*, 84(1), 41–58.

Rose, L., & Gallup, A. M. (2003). The 35th Annual Phi Delta Kappan/Gallup Poll of the public attitudes toward public schools. *Phi Delta Kappan*, 84(1), 41–58.

Rose, L., & Gallup, A. M. (2004). The 36th Annual Phi Delta Kappan/Gallup Poll of the public attitudes toward public schools. *Phi Delta Kappan*, 86(1), 41–58.

St. John, E. P., Chung, C. G., Musoba, G. D., & Simmons, A. B. (2004). Financial access: The impact of state financial strategies. In E. P. St. John (Ed.), *Readings on equal education: Vol. 19. Public policy and college access: Investigating the federal and state roles in equalizing postsecondary opportunity* (pp. 109–129). New York: AMS Press.

St. John, E. P., Griffith, A. I., & Allen-Haynes, L. (1997). *Families in schools: A chorus of voices in restructuring.* Portsmouth, NH: Heinemann.

St. John, E. P., Loescher, S. A., & Bardzell, J. S. (2003). *Improving early reading in grades 1–5: A resource guide for programs that work.* Thousand Oaks, CA: Corwin Press.

St. John, E. P., Manset-Williamson, G., Chung, C. G., Simmons, A. B., Loescher, S. A., Hossler, C. A., et al. (2004). Research-based reading reforms: The impact of state-funded interventions on educational outcomes in urban elementary schools. In L. F. Miron & E. P. St. John (Eds.), *Reinterpreting urban school reform: Have urban schools failed or has the reform movement failed urban schools?* Albany: State University of New York: Press.

St. John, E. P., & Musoba, G. D, (in Press). Acaden Access. In E. W. St. John (Ed.), *Education and public interest: School reform, public finance, and access to higher education,* (pp. 57–82). Dordrecnt, Netherlands: Springer.

St. John, E. P., & Parsons, M. D. (Eds.). (2004). *Public funding of higher education: Changing contexts and new rationales.* Baltimore, MD: Johns Hopkins University Press.

St. John, E. P., & Ridenour, C. S. (2002). School leadership in a market setting: The influence of private scholarship on educational leadership in urban schools. *Leadership & Policy in Schools 1*(4), 317–344.

Slavin, R. E., & Madden, N. A. (1989). What works for students at risk: A research synthesis. *Educational Leadership, 46*(5), 4–13.

Smart, J. C. (1989). Life history influences on Holland vocational type development. *Journal of Vocational Behavior, 29,* 216–225.

Sokoloff, H. (1997). Convening the community: Why schools must invite the public to join the dialogue on public education. *American School Board Journal, 184*(11), 25–27.

Stedman, J. B., & Riddle, W. C. (1992). *National educational goals for federal policy issues: Action by the 102d Congress.* Washington, DC: Congressional Research Service.

Storer, J. H., Licklider, B., & Cychosz, C. M. (1996). Perceptions of educators and parents—Where they disagree causes conflict. *Journal of Educational Relations, 17*(4), 2–5.

Turnbull, B. J. (1981). Issues for a new administration: The federal role in education. *American Journal of Education, 89*(4), 396–427.

U.S. Department of Education (1997). *Individuals with Disabilities Act of 1997.* Retrieved July 27, 2006, from http://www.ed.gov/offices/OSERS/Policy/IDEA/the_law.html.

Wadsworth, D. (1998). Prevailing perceptions of public schools. *American School Board Journal, 185*(5), 41–42.

Walsh, M. (2002). Charting the new landscape of school choice: Justices settle case, nettle policy debate. *Education Week, 21*(42), 1, 18–21.

Willie, C. V. (1991). Controlled choice: An alternative desegregation plan for minorities who feel betrayed. *Education & Urban Society, 23*(2), 200–207.

Wraga, W. G. (1992). School choice and the comprehensive ideal. *Journal of Curriculum & Supervision, 8*(1), 28–42.

CHAPTER

4

Legal and Ethical Aspects of Public Relations

Theodore J. Kowalski

CASE STUDY: MAYNARD CONSTRUCTS A SCHOOL WEB PAGE

Last year Maynard Richards, age 31, became principal of Silver Creek Elementary School, located in a rural area of South Dakota. This was his first assignment as an administrator; previously, he had taught fifth grade for seven years in neighboring Minnesota. Silver Creek was one of two schools in the East Chadwick School District—the other school being East Chadwick junior-senior high school.

As he was pursuing the position in South Dakota, Maynard was surprised to discover that Silver Creek Elementary School did not have its own Web page (neither did the junior-senior high school). During his interview, he told the superintendent, Dr. Margaret Weigand, that he had the expertise to create Web pages and made a commitment to develop one for Silver Creek if he became principal.

After beginning his new job, Maynard searched the Internet looking for good ideas that he could use. He eventually focused on two elementary school Web pages, one from suburban Chicago (Warren G. Harding Elementary School) and the other from southeastern Iowa (Bush City Elementary School). After weighing the merits of both, he decided to adopt the format used on the Illinois Web page. Maynard then basically copied the entire design, including all the graphics, from the Warren G. Harding Elementary School Web page. Before doing so, however, he looked carefully for any indication that this material was copyrighted. Finding none, he concluded that the material was in the public domain and he was free to use it. Therefore, he simply changed names, titles, links, and so forth as necessary.

The Silver Creek Web page drew praise from school board members, parents, and Dr. Weigand. The superintendent even offered to provide Maynard a $1,000 stipend if he would help develop a Web page for the district's junior-senior high school during the following summer.

Approximately two months later, however, both Maynard and Dr. Weigand received identical letters via registered mail from an attorney representing the school district that included Warren G. Harding Elementary School. The letter indicated that the unapproved use of the layout and graphics on the Silver Creek Elementary School Web page violated copyright laws. The attorney requested both the superintendent and the principal to provide a detailed response to the charge within 30 days; he then indicated that their failure to do so would result in his filing a lawsuit seeking damages on behalf of his client.

Dr. Weigand immediately called Maynard and inquired about the accuracy of the charge. Maynard explained that there was no evidence showing that the other Web page was copyrighted. The superintendent then called the attorney representing the East Chadwick School District. After a brief discussion, he told Dr. Weigand that Maynard probably had violated copyright laws and that financial damages were certainly a possibility. He recommended that the district remove the Web page immediately and make an apology to the appropriate officials in Illinois so that litigation might be avoided.

Effective public relations (PR) requires more than good intentions. As the case study demonstrates, not understanding the legal dimensions of mass communication can result in serious problems for school administrators. Over the last decade, many superintendents and principals have taken advantage of the Internet as a medium for communicating with school publics. Though their efforts are laudable, their decisions have occasionally resulted in legal or ethical problems.

Court decisions over the past four decades have set in motion social changes that have fundamentally altered the relationship between schools and the communities they serve. Supreme Court decisions concerning school desegregation, the role of religion in public schools, the rights and freedoms of teachers and students, sexual harassment, race discrimination, gender discrimination, the rights of individuals with disabilities, and the teaching of values have had important and lasting ramifications for the larger society. Many legal and education scholars have commented on the expanding judicial role in setting or altering education policy (Yudolf, Kirp, Levin, & Moran, 2002). Tyack, James, and Benavot (1987), for example, documented the dramatic increase in litigation and the heavy reliance on the courts to set education policy after World War II. Kirp and Jensen (1986) labeled the expanded role of the judiciary the "legalization" of education. More recently, the school administration profession has focused more directly on ethical and moral issues (Kowalski, 2003). This attention has extended to school public relations, an area of practice where communication and data management create concerns regarding the use of information and the treatment of stakeholders.

This chapter first examines the legal dimensions of school public relations. This assessment includes an overview of the quantity and quality of litigation, liability and constitutional torts, and copyright issues. Then the chapter addresses the ethical dimensions of PR, including applications to school administration and applications to school public relations.

LIABILITY TORTS

Studies that have analyzed judicial decisions uniformly report that the amount of education-related litigation greatly increased in the United States from the 1960s to the mid-1970s and then decreased modestly from 1977 to 1987—mainly because of a decrease in new desegregation lawsuits. Despite this slight downturn, litigation rates remain at historically high levels (Alexander & Alexander, 2001; Zirkel, 1997). Imber and Thompson (1991) estimated that in the early 1990s, one lawsuit was filed every year against a school in the United States for every 3,500 students attending public schools. The significant increase in litigation has had direct and indirect implications for school public relations. For example, lawsuits related to the rights of individuals with disabilities, negligence, and equity in funding have required administrators to provide both explanations and education for stakeholders. More directly, however, information management and communication, integral PR functions, present the possibility of lawsuits.

A school district's greatest exposure to lawsuits in relation to school public relations lies in the category of tort law. In attempting to build and maintain effective relationships with relevant publics, school administrators seek to increase community participation and the exchange of information. Though these efforts are clearly beneficial, if not absolutely necessary, they increase legal risk.

In an action based in tort against a school district (or school), the injured party seeks a judgment holding the school district or a school employee responsible for the consequence of a wrongdoing. Tort law imposes liability on schools for injury or harm to individuals using the school, including students, parents, and outsiders injured at school. By allowing compensation for such injuries, tort law in effect requires schools to take appropriate steps to provide a safe and orderly environment. There are three major categories of tort law: negligence, intentional torts (including defamation), and strict liability. The categories of negligence and intentional torts are especially relevant to school public relations.

Negligence

The most prevalent tort action involving schools and school personnel is negligence. Negligence may be defined as conduct falling below an established standard fixed and imposed on the parties by the law, common or statutory, that results in injury (Keeton, Dobbs, Keeton, & Owen, 1984, p. 288). Negligence encompasses all human behavior. The test commonly used to determine negligence is based on a construct created by the courts, a hypothetical person who "has never existed on land or sea: the reasonable man of ordinary prudence" (p. 174). The "reasonable" person conducts himself or herself in an ideal manner; he or she is a community standard. Although the reasonable person operates as a community model, his or her conduct varies appropriately based on the circumstances surrounding that conduct at any given time. In a negligence lawsuit, the question becomes this: Would the reasonable person have been expected to foresee and, as a result, to have been able to take action to prevent the injury that occurred? An affirmative answer to the question suggests that the defendant in a negligence action was negligent.

There are four elements in a cause of action for negligence:

1. There must be a duty of care between the plaintiff and the defendant.
2. There must be a breach of the duty of care by the defendant.
3. The defendant's breach of duty must have been the proximate cause of the resultant injury to the plaintiff.
4. The plaintiff must have suffered actual loss or damage as a result of the injury. (For liability to be proven, all four elements must be shown by the plaintiff.)

In the realm of PR, administrators and other employees typically encourage stakeholders to visit and make use of school facilities. School personnel have a duty to maintain school buildings and grounds and school equipment to ensure that they are in proper and safe condition. A school district will be held liable to an injured person if it is shown that school officials knew or should have known of an unreasonably dangerous or hazardous condition at the school and failed to take steps to eliminate the danger. Courts impose a high standard for the proper maintenance of school facilities and equipment, and concomitantly, the judiciary has looked favorably on schools that have developed preventive maintenance programs that provide for regular facility and equipment inspection.

Within the general framework of negligence tort liability as discussed here, most states have developed special liability rules concerning owners and possessors of property and buildings and their duty toward occupiers of the property (premises liability). Individuals who enter upon the property of another are legally classified according to the level of duty owed them as trespassers, licensees, or invitees. A trespasser is an individual who enters upon the property of another without a privilege to do so or without consent from the possessor. A licensee is a person who enters upon the property of another with permission (express or implied). An invitee is an individual who is invited (express or implied) to enter and remain on the premises of another for a particular reason. Invitees include individuals on premises as members of the public for purposes for which the property is held open to the public (American Law Institute, 1986).

Traditionally, most individuals, other than students, parents, and employees, entering a school are considered to be licensees. Examples include community groups and organizations using the school facility for meeting purposes. A school district owes a licensee only one duty: to warn him or her of concealed dangerous conditions of which the school district has actual knowledge. A school district owes a greater degree of care to an invitee than it does to a licensee. School districts that make facilities available to groups and individuals run the risk of creating invitees out of groups traditionally characterized as licensees. A school district owes an invitee a duty to exercise reasonable care for his or her safety and to take reasonable steps, including regular inspection of the premises, to make sure the premises are safe for the invitee. This heightened duty to invitees means in practical terms that school employees must, among other things, be vigilant in mopping and drying slippery floors, in removing dangerous snow and ice from entrances and sidewalks, in adequately lighting halls and parking lots, and in providing or increasing security measures when attacks on school invitees are foreseeable. These precautions are generally met when school is in session, but they become problematic at other times when community groups are allowed to use the facilities.

Due care and adequate supervision depend largely on the circumstances surrounding an injury. The traditional standard of care and supervision applicable in most situations is the level of care and supervision an ordinary, reasonably prudent person would exercise under the circumstances. However, when supervising students during school functions, school personnel are held to a higher standard of care and supervision than is the ordinary, reasonably prudent person. In general, school district liability for injuries sustained by individuals other than students will be decided within the general and special (premises liability) tort liability framework.

Crime committed in the nation's schools emerged as a major concern during the 1990s. By the end of that decade, students, ages 12 through 18, were victims of about 880,000 nonfatal violent crimes while at school (National Center for Education Statistics, 2001). School authorities have a legal obligation to maintain safe and violence-free environments. The duty to provide adequate supervision and security extends to parents and citizens invited to school. School officials should go on the offensive and take proper precautionary action if assaults on school personnel, students, and members of the community using the school are reasonably foreseeable. These safety measures might include warning the public, increasing on-campus security, providing crowd control at sporting events, regulating access to buildings, and installing metal detectors and surveillance cameras (in the worst situations). The legal reasoning applied in school violence cases appears to be grounded in whether or not a school could reasonably have foreseen the violence and prevented the injury under all the circumstances of the case.

A 1998 case illustrates a school's duty to maintain a safe environment. A student's mother brought an action against a school district and school officials, arising from the death of her son, who was attacked and stabbed in a classroom. The mother contended that despite previous student violence at the school, nothing had been done to implement security or safeguards beyond hanging a "No Trespassing" sign near the front door. The court agreed and found that the school district was not immune from a negligence suit where it had neither adopted nor implemented any security policy, procedure, or safeguards (*Brum v. Town of Dartmouth*, 1998).

Many school districts involve adults as *volunteers*. For example, senior citizens often serve as readers in primary classrooms and assist in the cafeteria and media center. Such activities enhance PR, but they also expose the school to liability. School officials are expected to take reasonable precautions in relation to volunteers. Some school districts have adopted behavioral expectations and require background checks for persons who volunteer regularly. In a New Jersey case, a volunteer instructor during a school board–sponsored swimming program sexually molested an 8-year-old student in a swimming pool. The parents of the child sued the school district. The court adopted the "deliberate indifference" standard to evaluate the action of the school board and the swimming program coordinator to screen volunteers. The court ruled in favor of the school board because it had developed and followed its official policy of screening volunteers (*C. P. v. Piscataway Township Board of Education*, 1996).

Several *defenses against negligence-related liability* are available to educators. The most common are (a) contributory negligence, (b) assumption of the risk, and (c) governmental immunity (Alexander & Alexander, 2001). In order to prove *contributory negligence*, a school district must demonstrate that the plaintiff (the party filing the suit) failed to exercise reasonable care for his or her own safety and that failure contributed to the plaintiff's own injury. Contributory negligence is a potent defense for educators because, if established, this defense totally excuses a school district from liability. Because of the harshness of the "complete bar to recovery" rule of contributory negligence, the majority of states have adopted the defense of *comparative negligence*, which permits damages to be apportioned according to the assessed degrees of fault of all parties. However, in some states where comparative negligence has replaced contributory negligence, the comparative fault provisions do not apply to tort claims brought against government entities, including school districts (Cambron-McCabe, McCarthy, & Thomas, 2004).

Another defense available to schools is the defense of *assumption of the risk*. It involves a plaintiff's consent or voluntary acceptance (express or implied) of a specific risk or danger of which the plaintiff has actual knowledge. Assumption of the risk operates to relieve a school district of liability even if the school district has created the risk of danger. The doctrine of assumption of the risk has been frequently and successfully raised in sports injury cases. For example, the defense has been deployed successfully in lawsuits regarding injuries sustained at school-sponsored sporting events (e.g., when a spectator is struck by a foul ball at a baseball game or a spectator is hit in the eye by an errant tennis ball) (Korpela, 1971).

Prior to the 1970s, litigation against public schools and most government entities was limited or entirely prohibited by the doctrine of *governmental immunity*. In the United States, this legal concept is based largely on English common law, exemplified by the ancient maxim that "the king can do no wrong." The prevailing doctrine in the United States has been that both the state and the federal governments are immune for torts committed by their officers and employees unless the government consents to such liability. The *doctrine of sovereign immunity* was traditionally extended to school districts in most states for injuries to individuals that were caused by the negligent acts of government employees. Governmental immunity for school districts in tort actions still exists under common law, even though judicial actions have partially eroded the vitality of this doctrine in most states (Cambron-McCabe, McCarthy, & Thomas, 2004).

In many states where governmental immunity does not protect school districts from tort liability, state legislatures have enacted laws that limit damages that can be awarded to an injured party as a result of governmental negligence. Some states have statutes (tort claim acts) that require compliance as a prerequisite to recovery of damages. By engaging in risk management, administrators can transfer risk from the school district and its employees to an insurance company. Drake and Roe (2003) suggested that school districts purchase all-risk property insurance, comprehensive liability insurance, and errors and omissions liability insurance for teachers, administrators, and school board members.

Protection for educators against personal liability varies across the states. For tort liability purposes, state laws typically distinguish between *ministerial functions* and *discretionary functions*. The former involve compliance with mandates of legal authority not requiring the exercise of judgment (e.g., following state child abuse laws); the latter involve the exercise of professional judgment, formulation of school policy, setting of goals, and planning. States often permit immunity for torts in relation to discretionary acts, but hold school personnel responsible for ministerial acts (e.g., failing to report child abuse as required by a state law).

Defamation

The tort that most directly touches aspects of school public relations is defamation. This law involves communication and pertains to an injury or invasion of a person's interest in his or her good reputation, name, and character by a false and defamatory communication concerning the person (American Law Institute, 1986). Defamation also can be an offense against a legal entity other than a person, for example, against a corporation (Moore, 1999). The offense can occur in written form (*libel*) or in verbal form (*slander*).

In seeking to keep the community informed of programs, needs, and problems, school officials may use various communication methods and channels. Public relations is supposed to be a two-way, symmetrical process; therefore, school officials and personnel are encouraged to exchange information with various stakeholders rather openly and almost continuously. At this level of communicative interaction, misinformation, propaganda, and false statements often occur.

Cases involving alleged defamatory communication among parents, students, citizens, and school authorities and related to school matters have been litigated, but proving defamation is quite difficult. Two defenses are possible: an *absolute privilege* and a *conditional privilege*. The former completely excuses what may be considered a defamatory statement. Statements made in the performance of legislative, judicial, or executive duties and in official proceedings are usually covered by this defense (American Law Institute, 1986). Accordingly, statements made by school board members and superintendents in the course of evaluating school personnel are often protected by an absolute privilege (Reutter, 1985).

A conditional (or qualified) privilege excuses defamatory speech made in good faith and without malice. This legal concept, used extensively to defend school officials and employees, arises from common law and is pertinent to communications between parties sharing an interest or duty. The judiciary, noting the public's interest in education, has extended the qualified privilege to teachers engaged in evaluating students and to school administrators engaged in evaluating teachers and other employees (Reutter, 1985). This defense also is available to parents in relation to communication with school personnel about teacher performance and other matters directly bearing on the welfare of their children at school.

The Supreme Court in *New York Times v. Sullivan* (1964) ruled that the First Amendment requires that a "public official" who files a defamation suit against critics (for example, individuals or the press) of his or her "official conduct" show that the defamatory statements were made with "actual malice" and that the defendant(s) made the statements with knowledge of their falsity or with reckless disregard of whether they were true or false. The courts have been divided on the issue of whether school administrators and teachers who have been defamed are public officials within the meaning of *Sullivan*. While the judicial trend has been toward not considering administrators and teachers as public officials, school board members, superintendents, and principals have been considered public figures (Alexander & Alexander, 2001). When viewed as private citizens, teachers need only prove that defamatory statements made against them are untruthful.

In disseminating information about the school to the community through the mass media, the *Sullivan* (1964) ruling concerning defamatory communication is applicable. In the aftermath of *Sullivan*, defamation liability is extremely difficult to prove against the media when the defamatory communication concerns a public figure or official. This in no way, however, obviates the need for school officials to practice honest, well-researched journalism.

CONSTITUTIONAL TORTS

Many PR issues are relevant to constitutional law. Examples include issues pertaining to (a) student discipline; (b) freedom of speech, religion, assembly, and the press; (c) voting rights; and (d) invasion of privacy, due process, and equal protection. School officials or employees who interfere with the federal constitutional rights of individuals may be liable to the party injured in an action known as a constitutional tort. Constitutional torts protect and secure individual rights under the U.S. Constitution from being restricted by state laws. The number of constitutional tort actions brought against schools has increased dramatically over time. The legal authority for maintaining a constitutional tort against a school district is found in the *Civil Rights Act of 1871*, which was codified in the federal laws as Title 42 of the U.S. Code shortly after the Civil War. Congress intended that awards under this law would deter the deprivation of the constitutional rights of newly freed African-American citizens.

The provision of Title 42 most often used by plaintiffs to bring constitutional tort actions against school districts is *42 U.S.C. § 1983*. Section 1983 provides in part:

> Every person who, under color of any statute, ordinance, regulation, custom or usage, of any state or Territory, subjects or causes to be subjected any citizen of the United States or other person within the jurisdiction thereof to the deprivation of any rights, privileges, or immunities secured by the Constitution and laws shall be liable to the party injured in an action at law.

In *Monell v. Department of Social Services of New York* (1978), the U.S. Supreme Court held that Section 1983 suits could be brought against government units, including school boards. However, the Court held that government bodies cannot be held liable under Section 1983 on a respondant superior theory, whereby employers are liable for the acts of their employees. Therefore, school districts are liable under Section 1983 for a constitutional wrong committed by an employee only when the employee's action represents well-established custom or official policy of the school district.

In *Wood v. Strickland* (1975), a case involving student discipline, the U.S. Supreme Court held that individuals, including school board members, could be held liable for committing constitutional torts. Before *Wood v. Strickland*, school employees had been completely immune from Section 1983 actions. However, in this case, the Court granted school employees "good faith immunity." The Court said that a school board member or school employee loses the immunity and may be liable for damages under Section 1983 if "he knew or reasonably should have known that the action he took within his sphere of official responsibility would violate the constitutional rights of the students affected" (*Wood*, p. 322). In *Harlow v. Fitzgerald* (1982), the Court explained that as long as a school employee's action does not "violate clearly established statutory or constitutional rights of which a reasonable person would have known" (p. 818), he or she will not be held liable under Section 1983.

The number of student-initiated Section 1983 lawsuits against schools and school personnel dramatically increased during the 1990s (Alexander & Alexander, 2001). Many of the cases involved charges of sexual misconduct, peer-to-peer sexual harassment, enforcement of "zero tolerance" policies, and student-to-student violence that purportedly was not prevented by school officials.

Political Speech

As described in Chapter 1, an effective PR program requires ongoing communication between school personnel and external publics. In this vein, there are certain to be times when administrators, teachers, and other employees express views on matters related to the schools that differ from the official positions taken by the school board and superintendent. Although the employees are likely to view their comments as constructive and necessary, board members and the superintendent may have a different perspective. In these situations, the right of an employee to criticize becomes an intricate issue.

Prior to the 1960s, public employment, including that of teachers, was considered a privilege, rather than a right. Accordingly, teachers were expected to limit and give away their First Amendment rights to their employers. However, during the 1960s, with the public's attention focused on individual rights, the courts determined that the "privilege doctrine" was inappropriate, and the relationship between teachers and school boards began to change (Alexander & Alexander, 2001). The U.S. Supreme Court in *Pickering v. Board of Education of Township High School District 205* (1968) established the legal principle that public school teachers have the First Amendment right of freedom of expression. In *Pickering*, a school board terminated the employment of a teacher for writing a letter to a local newspaper criticizing the school superintendent and school board for spending public funds on athletic programs without informing the district's taxpayers of their decisions; the letter was published. The Court applied a "balance of interests" test and ruled in favor of the teacher. In so doing, the Court recognized the right of teachers as citizens to express their views on matters of public concern. A teacher's right of speech and expression, however, is not unlimited. If comments seriously damage the relationship between employer and employee or are deliberately or recklessly false or seriously impede the educational mission of the school, then the exercise of such speech may be grounds for dismissal. However, the burden of proving any of these matters rests with the employer (i.e., the school district).

Where an educator's First Amendment right is at issue, the judiciary uses a three-step analysis.

1. The court must determine if the teacher's speech is constitutionally protected. Here the court determines whether the statements made by the teacher, taken as a whole, are on a matter of public concern.
2. The court must ascertain whether the school board's dismissal was motivated by the teacher's exercise of his or her First Amendment rights.
3. The school district must be given an opportunity to demonstrate that it would have taken the same action in the absence of the teacher's constitutionally protected conduct.

A federal district court used this three-step analysis to determine that a school district's policy prohibiting criticism from staff members other than to the person being criticized, the principal, or the superintendent or at a school board meeting was unconstitutional. As written, the policy prohibited speech that numerous courts had already determined was protected. The court found that this policy failed to narrowly define criticism and that the *Webster's Dictionary* definition of criticism included activity that the school admittedly did not seek to prohibit; therefore, the policy did not provide employees with fair warning as to what could and could not be said (*Westbrook v. Teton County School District*, 1996).

Privacy Rights

Increased community participation usually results in a better understanding of community concerns and values, but such involvement also can result in legal problems. Certainly, public schools belong to the community, but ownership does not imply that the community's standards (e.g., values and moral principles) can be imposed unilaterally at the expense of individual constitutional rights. Even so, the courts historically have recognized the role of community values and attitudes in relation to teacher employment.

Though the U.S. Constitution does not expressly mention privacy, the U.S. Supreme Court has interpreted the Constitution to include a fundamental right of privacy. A teacher's conduct outside the classroom may be the basis for cancellation of his or her contract or disciplinary action. The problem in cases involving protection of personal privacy is to arrive at a balance among the privacy interests of the teacher, community morals, and the school's interest in maintaining an appropriate educational environment. Teachers have been discharged from public school employment for matters arising in their private lives that conflict with community sentiment.

Four separate torts have been associated with an invasion of privacy. According to Moore (1999), they include

1. Appropriation—illegally using a person's name or likeness for benefit or advantage of another,
2. Intrusion—illegally violating an individual's physical solitude or seclusion,
3. Public disclosure—illegally revealing objectionable private facts about an individual, and
4. Damaging publicity—illegally placing an individual in a false light in the public eye.

Though any of these torts may be applicable to districts and schools, those related to objectionable facts and damaging publicity are especially noteworthy.

States commonly have tenure laws that variously set forth grounds for terminating teachers. Immorality is one common reason for dismissal that often leads to conflict between privacy rights and community values. In an often-cited case involving allegations of teacher immorality, the Pennsylvania Supreme Court defined immorality as "not essentially confined to a deviation from sex morality; it may be such a course of conduct as offends the morals of the community and is a bad example to the youth whose ideals a teacher is supposed to foster and to evaluate" (*Horosko v. Mount Pleasant Township School District*, 1939, p. 868). Indeed, there have been a number of cases in which the dismissal of tenured teachers or principals for immoral behavior has been upheld even though sexual behavior was not involved (e.g., purposefully telling untruths about a school superintendent and cheating on employment-related examinations) (Kowalski & Benway, 1979).

In 1974, on the basis of widespread allegations of abuse and misuse of student records, Congress enacted the *Family Educational Rights and Privacy Act* (FERPA, commonly referred to as the *Buckley Amendment*). The handling of student records by school officials was criticized on several grounds, including the release of information to third parties such as police, news media, social service agencies, and vendors without the consent of parents; failure to provide parents with access to records; and maintenance of inaccurate records. In response, Congress passed legislation that provided substantive and procedural safeguards for the privacy rights of students and their parents. FERPA grants parents and students, 18 years of age or older, a legal right of access to such records. Within a reasonable period of time from their request, parents must be allowed to inspect and review (and make copies at their own expense) all records directly related to their child. In no event may the school stall for more than 45 days from the parent's initial request for records. With respect to inaccurate records, FERPA provides parents with an avenue to amend records, and if not satisfied, parents may request an impartial hearing on the issue. Parents may also file complaints concerning violations of FERPA with the U.S. Department of Education. Schools found not in compliance with FERPA face the ultimate sanction of losing federal aid (LaMorte, 1996).

FERPA mandates that most data contained in student records be kept confidential. Personally identifiable information contained in school records may be released only with written consent from the student's parents. The most common exception to rules regarding confidentiality is that student records may be made available to school officials, including teachers within the school district where the child attends school, who have legitimate educational interest in the student. Schools must keep a record of individuals and agencies that are given access to the records of a student. Under FERPA, public schools may release general information to the public, including a student's name, address, telephone listing, date and place of birth, major field of study, participation in activities and sports, dates of attendance, and degrees and awards received.

In addition to the privacy rights protected by FERPA, the *Individuals with Disabilities Education Act* (IDEA) contains specific confidentiality requirements covering the records of students with disabilities. Moreover, most states have enacted legislation according confidentiality rights in records containing personal information kept by state agencies, including public schools. In some instances, state privacy statutes grant more privacy rights to students than does FERPA. The U.S. Supreme Court recently weighed in on a FERPA issue. The Court determined that the practice of students grading other students' papers does not violate FERPA. The Court emphasized it was answering the narrow question of whether peer grading violates FERPA (*Owasso v. Falvo*, 2002).

Religion and Public Schools

The relationship between religion and the public schools is an extremely important, delicate, and controversial issue in the context of PR. Wide-ranging issues of community concern such as prayer, Bible reading, the distribution of religious materials, student-initiated devotional meetings on school property, and the use of school facilities by religious groups are among the thorniest church-state separation issues.

The First Amendment of the U.S. Constitution provides that "Congress shall make no law respecting an establishment of religion or prohibiting the free exercise thereof." The majority of church-state cases involving public education arise under this Establishment Clause. In most church-state cases since 1970, the U.S. Supreme Court has applied a three-part test derived from the Court's ruling in *Lemon v. Kurtzman* (1971). Although the so-called *Lemon Test* has been criticized by some respected jurists, the Court has not eliminated the test from Establishment Clause adjudication. This test includes the following standards:

1. The governmental action or statute must have a secular purpose.
2. Its primary effect must neither advance nor inhibit religion.
3. The governmental action must avoid excessive governmental entanglement with religion.

In two landmark decisions in the early 1960s, the U.S. Supreme Court struck down school-sponsored Bible reading and daily prayers. The decisions were and continue to be controversial and unpopular with certain segments of the public. Supported by popular opinion, almost half of the states enacted legislation permitting some form of prayer (e.g., silent meditation or voluntary prayer) in public schools. In *Wallace v. Jaffree* (1985), the Court found an Alabama statute calling for a daily one-minute period of silence for meditation or prayer to violate the First Amendment. However, the Court suggested that a statute authorizing a moment of silence for meditation or prayer during the school day might pass constitutional muster if the state legislature's intent in passing the law was not motivated by a religious purpose. In 1997, the Eleventh Circuit Court of Appeals said that public schools may begin each day with a state-mandated moment of silence (*Bown v. Gwinnett*, 1997). However, the U.S. Supreme Court held that a school district's policy of permitting an invocation over the loudspeaker before football games, by an individual elected by the student body, violated the Establishment Clause (*Santa Fe Independent School District v. Doe*, 2000).

Graduation exercises also have become a subject of legal controversy. A national debate over having prayers at graduation erupted after the U.S. Supreme Court, in *Lee v. Weisman* (1992), struck down school-arranged, clergy-led invocations and benedictions. The prayers contested in *Lee* were designated nondenominational and given by a local rabbi who was invited by the school principal. The Court found the active participation of school authorities in organizing the prayer, the students' susceptibility to peer pressure, and the importance of graduation ceremonies to students (resulting in coercive pressure to attend) coalesced to create a violation of the Establishment Clause. However, the Court left unresolved the constitutionality of student-organized and student-led prayers at graduation. Indeed, in 1993, the U.S. Supreme Court declined to review a Fifth Circuit decision that let stand a Texas policy permitting student-initiated invocations and benedictions at high school graduation ceremonies (*Jones v. Clear Creek Independent School District*, 1992). The Eleventh Circuit subsequently held that a school district's policy of permitting a graduating student, elected by classmates, to deliver an unrestricted message of her choice at the beginning and/or closing of the graduation ceremonies did not on its fare violate the Establishment Clause (*Adler v. Duval County School Board*, 2001).

Students, community groups, and organizations often request the use of school facilities for religious purposes. Legal precedent for such requests have been established by several cases. In 1990, the U.S. Supreme Court upheld the constitutionality of the *Equal Access Act* (passed by Congress in 1984), which permits student-initiated religious groups to meet on school premises during noninstructional time. In deciding *Board of Education of West-side Community Schools v. Mergens* (1990), the Court found that a public high school with at least one noncurriculum-related student group must recognize a wide array of groups, regardless of the philosophical, political, or religious content of their members' speech.

In *Lamb's Chapel v. Center Moriches School District* (1993), the U.S. Supreme Court held that a school board's refusal to permit a church access to school facilities, after hours, to show a film series on family and child-rearing issues was unconstitutional. A close analysis of the case reveals that the Court ruled narrowly on the issue of public access to school facilities for religious purposes.

The U.S. Supreme Court also upheld the right of an outside adult-led group to actively preach and provide religious instruction to elementary school students on school grounds immediately after the school day. The Court affirmed the right of the religious club to be on school grounds on the same basis as any other club or activity (*Good News Club v. Milford Central School District*, 2001).

One other volatile church-state separation issue involves the distribution of religious literature by students on school property. Beginning in the late 1980s, most courts have held that students have a free speech right to distribute religious materials on school property. Schools maintain the right to set reasonable rules regarding the time, place, and manner of distribution of religious literature on school premises (*Harless v. Darr*, 1996; *Peck v. Upshur County Board of Education*, 1998).

Community Values and Curriculum

Curricular decisions also can ignite legal disputes that affect school-community relations. The role of the community in shaping the public school curriculum has long been recognized (e.g., Tyler, 1949). Primarily after 1970, and especially during the 1990s, parents and interest groups aligned with myriad causes attempted to influence the content of programs provided by public schools. According to the Office for Intellectual Freedom, there were close to 5,000 challenges to materials in schools or school libraries between 1990 and 2000. Approximately 1,140 challenges were made to "sexually explicit" material and 1,013 to material considered to use "offensive language" (Office for Intellectual Freedom, 2002).

The Seventh Circuit upheld a school board in a case where parents attempted to prevent the elementary school from using the *Impressions* reading series as the main supplemental program in grades K–5. Parents contended that the reading series violated the First Amendment by promoting wizards, witches, and other creatures with supernatural powers, thus indoctrinating children in anti-Christian values. The court reiterated that schools have broad discretion in curriculum matters and that courts should interfere only where constitutional rights are directly implicated. The court rejected the notion that stories with witches, goblins, and Halloween violated the Establishment Clause, holding instead that Halloween is an American tradition and is a purely secular affair (*Fleischfresser v. Directors of School District 200*, 1994).

During the 1990s, outcome-based education (OBE) became another contentious curriculum issue. Though many educators viewed the instructional paradigm as an effective approach for individualizing education and emphasizing outputs over inputs, thousands of parents objected to OBE either on the grounds that its effectiveness was unknown or on the grounds that it promoted values inconsistent with their religious convictions (Zlatos, 1993).

Courts have granted school boards and administrators broad discretion to determine curricular matters. However, such discretion is not absolute because the courts also consider the constitutional rights of students, teachers, and parents. Most state legislatures have granted primary responsibility for public school education to local school boards, which generally have considerable power in regulating the instructional program. Though local school authorities have broad powers concerning curriculum, textbooks, and other educational matters, the U.S. Supreme Court made it clear in *Board of Education, Island Trees Union Free School District No. 26 v. Pica* (1982) that books may not be removed from a school library by school officials if they are motivated by an intent to suppress or deny access to ideas with which they disagree. At the same time, the Court maintained that school boards could remove books from a school library if motivated by the "pervasive vulgarity of the book," its "educational unsuitability," or its "bad taste" or "irrelevance," or by age and grade inappropriateness. Alexander and Alexander (2001) warn that the direction of the courts in the 1990s on issues related to the curriculum

> appear[s] to place less emphasis on a broadly conceived standard that secures the expansion of knowledge preventing the "casting of a pall of orthodoxy" and allows more flexibility in allowing curriculum decisions to be made on the basis of local school board judgment and possibly, local political pressure. (p. 289)

Copyright

The dissemination of information about districts and schools via print, audio, and visual media activities is an integral part of PR. In preparing such materials, school administrators need to know and understand copyright law. Copyright protects the ownership and use of original works of authorship and provides the creator of an original work control over many activities, including the right to reproduce, distribute, display, perform, adapt, and translate the work (17 U.S.C. §§ 101 *et seq.*).

When the U.S. Congress passed the *Copyright Act of 1976*, substantially amending the *Copyright Act of 1909*, the concept of copyright became more comprehensive and complex. Federal protection now applies to any original work, fixed in any tangible form of expression. Registration of the copyright with the U.S. Copyright Office is not a condition of a valid copyright; however, registration is a prerequisite to filing a copyright infringement action. Copyright law extends to such items as literary works, computer programs, multimedia works and lyrics, dramatic works, graphic and sculptural works, sound recordings, and audiovisual works. Significantly, copyright does not cover ideas, procedures, and concepts (17 U.S.C. §§ 101, 102).

The 1976 copyright law places some limitations on the exclusive rights enjoyed by copyright owners. Section 107 of the act sets forth the "fair use" doctrine, a component that is particularly relevant to educators. This doctrine states in pertinent part that "the fair use of a copyrighted work, including such use by reproduction for purposes such as: criticism, comment, new reporting, teaching (including multiple copies for classroom use), scholarship or research is not an infringement of copyright" (17 U.S.C. § 107). Further guidelines for educators regarding the reproduction of multiple copies of copyrighted works for educational purposes (cited by courts) are found in *Classroom Guidelines of the Fair Use Doctrine* (1976). These guidelines represent part of the legislative history of the 1976 act, but are not considered part of the law. They permit educators to make multiple copies (not to exceed in any event more than one copy per pupil in a course) for classroom discussion, provided that the copying meets the tests of brevity and spontaneity and the cumulative effect test and that all copies contain a notice of copyright. It is clear that the copying of anthologies containing substantial portions of copyrighted books or articles without the permission of the copyright owner even for educational purposes violates the fair use doctrine (*Basic Books v. Kinko's Graphics Corp.*, 1991). Many persons wrongly assume that they can use up to 10% of any document without consent; in truth, there is no specified amount "either [in] statute or in case law" (Moore, 1999, p. 523). Often publishers state their standard for fair use either in books or other publications or on their Web page.

Computer software also may be protected under the copyright law. The owner of a copy of a computer program may make copies of the program only when the new copy is created as an essential step in using the program in conjunction with a machine or when the new copy is for archival purposes only. All archival copies of the program must be destroyed when the program is no longer used (17 U.S.C. §§ 117, 2002). It is clearly illegal for a school to load a copy of a program on one machine and "boot" that copy into the fixed memory of its microcomputers. The state of the law in the area of computer software is complex and rapidly evolving. School districts are well advised to inform teachers and students of the changing law regarding the use of copyrighted software.

The Internet has become a major instructional tool in schools all across America. The Internet and the World Wide Web have generated an array of additional copyright concerns. Daniel (1998) summarized copyright law as it impacts Internet use by schools, and he suggested that the following provisions be included in acceptable use policies:

1. Students may use computing facilities for educational purposes only. Acceptable use of the Internet refers to activities that support teaching and learning.
2. Students must observe standard copyright restrictions, which are the same as for printed materials.
3. Students may not send or receive copyrighted material without permission.
4. The unauthorized installation, use, storage, or distribution of copyrighted software or materials on a school district computer is prohibited.

Moore (1999) identified several major *defenses to copyright infringement*. One is called innocent infringement, and it is used typically by a person who uses copyrighted material without permission on the basis of a good-faith assumption that the work is not copyrighted because a copyright notice is not visible. Other defenses center on the nature of consent (e.g., there is a dispute between plaintiff and defendant regarding the consent agreement) and expiration of copyright (e.g., there is a dispute between plaintiff and defendant regarding the legality of the copyright at the time the material was used). As shown in the case study at the beginning of this chapter, copyright issues, and especially those involving cyberspace, are not always clear. For example, using artwork, organizational plans, and content from another person's or organization's Web page without permission can result in a serious legal problem. The safe alternative is to obtain written consent from the copyright holder and consult with legal counsel for the school district regarding your actions.

ETHICS

Ethics are commonly described as a set of nonlegal rules (i.e., rules outside the legal system) that guide human relationships. What is generally called professional ethics is actually the consensus of experts on the human responsibilities and obligations involved in a given profession. References to ethics suggest that the term relates to moral action, human character, and a sense of duty; that it pertains to what is fair, equitable, good, and professionally right, conforming to professional standards of conduct.

The distinction between illegal and unethical behavior is exemplified by copyright violation and *plagiarism*. The former, already discussed, involves the use of protected intellectual property without permission and outside the fair use standard. The latter involves stealing and passing off the ideas or words of another as one's own. For example, assume a student plagiarizes by copying a term paper that he or she bought from a college student. If the copied term paper is copyrighted, then the student has broken the law and the ethical code of the school. In this case, he or she could receive a conviction and be expelled or suspended from school. If the term paper was not copyrighted, the student can still be expelled or suspended for breaking the school's code of conduct.

Ethics in School Administration

During the past several decades, American educators have shown a growing interest in, and a genuine concern for, ethical and moral practice. Textbooks on ethics in school administration, the inclusion of ethics courses in educational administration preparation programs, and a proliferation of scholarly articles devoted to exploring ethics are evidence of this heightened awareness (Kowalski, 2003, 2006; Rebore, 2001; Strike, Haller, & Soltis, 1988). Crowson (1989) observed that to a "large degree all [educational] administrative decisions are rooted in moral codes and cultural values, thus all decisions have an ethical component" (p. 418). On a more political plane, Pratt and Shin (1997) pointed out that reputation management or credibility enhancement is a key element in generating public support.

The line separating legal and ethical issues in school administration is neither crisp nor clear. Incident-specific legal issues related to teacher dismissal, values inoculation, freedom of the press, student discipline, the Internet, parental rights, copyright infringement, student and teacher privacy rights, student and teacher free speech rights, compliance with federal and state laws and regulations, and teacher evaluation also pose ethical questions (Moore, 1999). In addition, policy and governance matters relate to ethical and moral choices.

Starratt (1991) contends that the educational program "is supposed to serve moral purposes (the nurturing of the human, social and intellectual growth of the youngsters)" (p. 187). Summarizing the role of ethics in school administration, Reitzug (1994) adds that administrator dispositions toward ethics affect the entire school. As an example, principals often determine which ethical issues they will analyze, and their choices influence school culture and character.

One of the most cited ethical typologies for school administrators was developed by Starratt (1991). His framework includes three perspectives for identifying, evaluating, and making ethical decisions: the ethic of critique, the ethic of justice, and the ethic of caring.

1. *Ethic of critique*. An examination of the structural (managerial) issues involved in educational administration, such as bias in the workplace, is central to this ethic. Primary issues include the use of power, subordination, and discrimination.
2. *Ethic of justice*. This ethic is concerned with values such as individual rights, the common good, and democratic participation in school governance.
3. *Ethic of caring*. This ethic emphasizes human connection and relationships. The ethic of caring provides a perspective for dealing with a school's internal and external constituencies, and as such, it is especially pertinent to public relations.

The Josephson Institute for the Advancement of Ethics (Josephson, 2002), an organization that provides materials and workshops for school administrators, identifies six pillars of character in relation to making ethical decisions:

1. Trustworthiness (including honesty, integrity, reliability, and loyalty),
2. Respect (including civility, courtesy, and decency; dignity and autonomy; tolerance and acceptance),
3. Responsibility (including accountability, pursuit of excellence, and self-restraint),

4. Fairness (including impartiality and equity),
5. Caring (including compassion and respect), and
6. Citizenship (including democratic principles).

Public Relations

The search for the meaning and the practice of ethics in any profession generally begins with an examination of the profession's *code of ethics*. An ethics code is a set of standards and guidelines aimed at promoting the ideals of social responsibility within the context of a profession. From the standpoint of school administration generally and PR specifically, it is important to note that most of the professional mass communications organizations have ethical codes. Compliance with these codes is generally voluntary. Both the Public Relations Society of America (PRSA) and the National School Public Relations Association (NSPRA) have established ethical principles for communication professionals.

The PRSA's Member Code of Ethics was last revised in 2000. A core component of this document is the member statement of professional values, which includes the following six values:

1. Advocacy—standards related to serving as an advocate for his or her employer;
2. Honesty—standards pertaining to being accurate and truthful;
3. Expertise—standards pertaining to acquiring and responsibly using specialized knowledge;
4. Independence—standards pertaining to providing objective counsel;
5. Loyalty—standards relate to fulfilling obligations to employers and society; and
6. Fairness—standards related to fairly treating all parties and allowing the expression of free speech. (PRSA, 2006)

The entire code, which includes a preamble, code provisions, and member pledge, is available on the PRSA Web page at http://www.prsa.org/_About/ethics/preamble.asp?ident=eth3.

NSPRA adopted its code of ethics in 1981. This document stipulates that PR specialists working with schools should:

◆ Be guided constantly by pursuit of the public interest through truth, accuracy, good taste, and fairness; follow good judgment in releasing information; not intentionally disseminate misinformation or confidential data; avoid actions, which lessen personal, professional, or organizational reputation.

◆ Give primary loyalty to one's employing organization, insisting on the right to give advisory counsel in accordance with sound PR ideas and practices; cooperate with other groups while avoiding conflicts with primary responsibilities; object to untenable policies or activities.

◆ Be aware of personal influence, but avoid making promises or granting unprofessional advantage to others; refrain from accepting special considerations for influences on organizational decisions; avoid unauthorized use of organizational facilities, resources, or professional services for personal gain or for promotion of the candidacy of aspirants to elected offices; forego derogatory acts or utterances against other professionals.

◆ Recognize that effectiveness is dependent on integrity and regard for ideals of the profession; do not misrepresent professional qualifications; give credit for ideas and words borrowed from others; cooperate with professional colleagues to uphold and enforce this ethics code. (NSPRA, 2006)

The document then notes that members are expected to sever relationships with organizations or individuals if these relationships require conduct that violates the organization's ethical codes.

Baker and Martinson (2002) argued that effective PR practice is both ethical and proactive. They identified five principles that guide ethical persuasion:

1. Truthfulness—avoiding lies and half truths,
2. Authenticity—questioning motives involved with persuasion,
3. Respect—respecting individuals in the targeted audiences,
4. Equity—being fair, and
5. Social responsibility—considering the broader social interest.

The issue of social responsibility has become central to PR professionals. In this regard, PR experts, such as Seitel, argue that all organizations, including private enterprises, have a responsibility to their communities. This includes contributions such as maintaining a healthful environment, providing jobs for people of color, and generally enhancing the quality of life (Stone, 2005).

Kruckeberg (2000) argued that ethics in PR need to move from being treated as tactical statements to being treated as strategic statements. That is, practitioners must think strategically about their behavior and their organization; this perspective has a moral connotation. In this vein, Kruckeberg also focuses on social responsibility:

1. In sum, consideration of strategic ethics requires that public relations practitioners look more broadly, more strategically, at their role as interpreters and ethicists and social policymakers in guiding organizational behavior and take strategic responsibility in influencing and reconciling public perceptions of their organizations within a global context. (p. 39)

With respect to education, this means that administrators engaging in PR need to be guided by a commitment to making schools moral institutions that serve society and improve the quality of community.

SUMMARY

Public relations practice is shaped by the law, both in policy making and in application. School administrators interact with internal and external publics in different forms and through various activities, and the law applies to PR in ways that reflect those differences. In general, legal problems are broadly categorized as liability and constitutional torts.

Ethics also play an important role in school public relations. In a communicative context, school administrators shape information, determine the extent to which they share information, and decide how they will use information. All of these decisions have ethical and moral dimensions (Kowalski & Petersen, 2007). More recently, PR and school administration scholars have emphasized the issue of social responsibility. When PR is viewed in a social context, ethics extend beyond individual compliance with accepted behavioral standards; practitioners are expected to contribute to making their organizations moral and to ensuring that their organizations improve society and the quality of life for all citizens (Kruckeberg, 2000).

QUESTIONS AND SUGGESTED ACTIVITIES

CASE STUDY

1. What is copyright law?
2. How does copyright law affect school Web pages?
3. What errors did Maynard make in constructing the Web page for his school?
4. What could have prevented these errors?
5. What defenses are available to Maynard if he becomes a defendant in a lawsuit?
6. To what extent is Dr. Weigand legally and professionally responsible for the problem?

CHAPTER

7. What interests do the courts balance in cases involving a teacher dismissal?
8. What is defamation?
9. What is the difference between conditional and qualified immunity?
10. What is the difference between libel and slander?
11. Assume that a high school principal writes an article in the school newspaper explaining that he recommended the dismissal of an English teacher because she consistently used unacceptable language in the classroom. To support his decision, he adds information about the teacher's background, including the fact she had been arrested for shoplifting when she was a sophomore in college. Discuss whether including this information violated the dismissed teacher's privacy right.
12. Since public schools are government agencies, is social responsibility a greater issue for them than it is for executives in private corporations? Discuss the issues that are pertinent to answering this question.

SUGGESTED READINGS

Baker, L. (1993). *The credibility factor: Putting ethics to work in public relations.* Homewood, IL: Business One Irwin.

Champion, W. T. (1993). *Sports law in a nutshell.* St. Paul, MN: West Publishing.

Chappelow, M. A. (2002). New standards for the school public relations profession. *Journal of School Public Relations, 23*(3), 197–212.

Chappelow, M. A. (2003). Standards for educational public relations and communications professionals. *Journal of School Public Relations, 4*(1), 7–29.

Dayton, J. (1998). Free speech, the Internet, and educational institutions: An analysis of *Reno v. ACLU. Education Law Reporter, 123,* 997–1011.

Grossman, H. G. (1998). *Achieving educational equity.* Springfield, IL: Thomas.

Harvey, C. (1997). Liberal indoctrination and the problem of community. *Synthese, 111,* 115–130.

Henderson, E. (2003). Advice for retaining legal counsel: Guidelines for superintendent and board members. *Journal of School Public Relations, 24*(3), 199–211.

Hogan, J. C. (1985). *The schools, the courts, and the public interest* (2nd ed.). Lexington, MA: Lexington Brooks.

Hutchinson, L. L. (2002). Teaching ethics across the public relations curriculum. *Public Relations Review, 28*(3), 301–309.

Kowalski, T. J. (2002). Reactions to the new standards for school public relations specialists. *Journal of School Public Relations, 23*(4), 296–312.

Kowalski, T. J., & Benway, M. (1979). Dismissal for immorality. *Education Digest, 45*(1), 39–42.

Kowalski, T. J., & Petersen, G. J. (2007). *Communication in school administration: Leading change in an information age.* Lanham, MD: Rowman & Littlefield.

Shapiro, J., & Stefkovich, J. (2001). *Ethical leadership and decision making in education.* Mahwah, NJ: Lawrence Erlbaum Associates.

Smolla, R. V. (1991). *Law of defamation.* New York: Clark Boardman.

Webber, N. (2004). Images and copyright. *School Arts: The Art Education Magazine for Teachers, 103*(9), 68.

Weston, A. (1997). *A practical companion to ethics.* New York: Oxford University Press.

REFERENCES

Adler v. Duval County School Board, 250 F.3d 1330 (11th Cir. 2001).

Alexander, K., & Alexander, D. (2001). *American public school law* (5th ed.). Belmont, CA: West-Wadsworth Publishing.

American Law Institute. (1986). *Restatement of torts* (2nd ed.). St. Paul, MN: American Law Institute Publishers.

Baker, S., & Martinson, D. L. (2002). Out of the red-light district: Five principles for ethically proactive public relations. *Public Relations Quarterly, 47*(3), 15–19.

Basic Books v. Kinko's Graphics Corp., 754 F. Supp. 1522 (S.D.N.Y. 1991).

Board of Education, Island Trees Union Free School District No. 26 v. Pica, 457 U.S. 853 (1982).

Board of Education of Westside Community Schools v. Mergens, 496 U.S. 226 (1990).

Bown v. Gwinnett, 112 F.3d 1464 (11th Cir. 1997).

Brum v. Town of Dartmouth, 690 N.E.2d 844 (Mass. Ct. App. 1998).

Cambron-McCabe, N. H., McCarthy, M. M., & Thomas, S. B. (2004). *Public school law: Teachers' and students' rights* (5th ed.). Boston: Allyn & Bacon.

Civil Rights Act of 1871, 42 U.S.C. § 1983.

Classroom Guidelines of the Fair Use Doctrine, H.R. 94-1476, 94th Cong., 2d sess. (1976).

Copyright Act of 1976, 17 U.S.C. §§ 101, *et seq.*

C. P. v. Piscataway Township Board of Education, 681 A.2d 105 (N.J. Super. A.D. 1996).

Crowson, R. (1989). Managerial ethics in educational administration: The rational choice approach. *Urban Education, 23*(4), 412–485.

Daniel, P. (1998). Copyright law, fair use and the Internet: Information for administrators and other educational officials. *Education Law Reporter, 122,* 899–911.

Drake, T. L., & Roe, W. (2003). *The principalship* (6th ed.). Old Tappan, NJ: Pearson Publishing.

Fleischfresser v. Directors of School District 200, 15 F.3d 680 (7th Cir. 1994).

Good News Club v. Milford Central School District, 533 U.S. 98 (2001).

Harless v. Darr, 937 F. Supp. 1351 (S.D. Ind. 1996).

Harlow v. Fitzgerald, 457 U.S. 800 (1982).

Horosko v. Mount Pleasant Township School District, 6 A.2d 866 (Pa. 1939).

Imber, M., & Thompson, G. (1991). Developing a typology of litigation in education and determining the frequency of each category. *Educational Administration Quarterly, 27*(2), 225–244.

Jones v. Clear Creek Independent School District, 977 F.2d 963 (5th Cir. 1992).

Josephson, M. (2002). *Making ethical decisions.* Los Angeles: Josephson Institute for the Advancement of Ethics.

Keeton, P., Dobbs, D., Keeton, R., & Owen, D. (1984). *Prosser and Keeton on the law of torts* (5th ed.). St. Paul, MN: West Publishing.

Kirp, D., & Jensen, N. (1986). *School days, rule days.* Philadelphia: Falmer.

Korpela, A. E. (1971). *American law review* (Vol. 35). San Francisco: Lawyers Co-operative Publishing.

Kowalski, T. J. (2003). *Contemporary school administration: An introduction* (2nd ed.). Boston: Allyn & Bacon.

Kowalski, T. J. (2006). *The school superintendent: Theory, practice, and cases* (2nd ed.). Thousand Oaks, CA: Sage.

Kowalski, T. J., & Benway, M. (1979). Dismissal for immorality. *Education Digest, 45*(1), 39–42.

Kowalski, T. J., & Petersen, G. J. (2007). *Communication in school administration: Leading change in an information age.* Lanham, MD: Rowman & Littlefield.

Kruckeberg, D. (2000). The public relations practitioner's role in practicing strategic ethics. *Public Relations Quarterly, 45*(3), 35–39.

Lamb's Chapel v. Center Moriches School District, 508 U.S. 384 (1993).

LaMorte, M. W. (1996). *School law: Cases and concepts* (5th ed.). Boston: Allyn & Bacon.

Lee v. Weisman, 505 U.S. 577 (1992).

Lemon v. Kurtzman, 403 U.S. 602 (1971).

Monell v. Department of Social Services of New York, 436 U.S. 658 (1978).

Moore, R. L. (1999). *Mass communication law and ethics* (2nd ed.). Mahwah, NJ: Lawrence Erlbaum Associates.

National Center for Education Statistics. (2001). *Indicators of school crime and safety.* Washington, DC: Author.

National School Public Relations Association. (2006). *NSPRA code of ethics.* Retrieved January 20, 2006, from http://www.nspra.org.

New York Times v. Sullivan, 476 U.S. 254 (1964).

Office for Intellectual Freedom, American Library Association. (2002). *The 100 most frequently challenged books of 1990–2000.* Retrieved June 12, 2002, from http://www.ala.org/bbooks/bbw database.html.

Owasso v. Falvo, 534 U.S. 426 (2002).

Peck v. Upshur County Board of Education, 155 F.3d 274 4th Cir. (1998).

Pickering v. Board of Education of Township High School District 205, 391 U.S. 563 (1968).

Pratt, C., & Shin, T. (1997). Ethical implications of corporate communications. In C. L. Caywood (Ed.), *The handbook of strategic public relations and integrated communications* (pp. 255–273). New York: McGraw-Hill.

Public Relations Society of America (PRSA). (2006). *PRSA member statement of professional values.* Retrieved January 20, 2006, from http://www.prsa.org/_About/ethics/preamble.asp?ident=eth3.

Rebore, R. (2001). *The ethics of educational leadership.* Upper Saddle River, NJ: Merrill/Prentice Hall.

Reitzug, U. C. (1994). Diversity, power and influence: Multiple perspectives on the ethics of school leadership. *Journal of School Leadership, 4*(2), 197–222.

Reutter, E. E. (1985). *The law of public education* (3rd ed.). Mineola, NY: Foundation Press.

Santa Fe Independent School District v. Doe, 530 U.S. 290 (2000).

Starratt, R. J. (1991). Building an ethical school: A theory for practice in educational leadership. *Educational Administration Quarterly, 27*(2), 185–202.

Stone, J. D. (2005). Public relations and public responsibility. *Public Relations Quarterly, 50*(1), 31–34.

Strike, K., Haller, M., & Soltis, J. (1988). *Ethics of school administration*. New York: Teachers College Press.

Tyack, D., James, T., & Benavot, A. (1987). *Law and the shaping of public education*. Madison: University of Wisconsin Press.

Tyler, R. (1949). *Basic principles of curriculum and instruction*. Chicago: University of Chicago Press.

Wallace v. Jaffree, 472 U.S. 38 (1985).

Westbrook v. Teton County School District, 918 F. Supp. 1475 (D. Wyo. 1996).

Wood v. Strickland, 420 U.S. 308 (1975).

Yudolf, M., Kirp, D., Levin, B., & Moran, R. (2002). *Educational policy and the law* (4th ed.). Belmont, CA: Wadsworth Group/Thomas Learning.

Zirkel, P. A. (1997). "The explosion" in education litigation: An update. *Education Law Reporter, 114*, 341–350.

Zlatos, B. (1993). Outcome based outrage. *Executive Educator, 15*(9), 12–20.

PART II
Organizational Characteristics of Public Relations

CHAPTER 5

Social Dimensions of Public Relations

Patti L. Chance and Lars Björk

CASE STUDY: THE DYNAMICS OF DISTRICT-LEVEL SYSTEMIC REFORM

Madison County School District is a moderately growing, high-wealth district because golf resorts and retirees have raised the per capita income level to seventh out of 100 counties in the state. Although it is one of the wealthiest districts in the state, it also has one of the lowest tax rates. Out of 117 school districts in the state, it ranked as one of the highest in receiving state funds and one of the lowest in receiving local support. Overall, it ranked 69th in the state with a per pupil expenditure of approximately $6,200 per student. However, outside its two major municipalities, it is very rural and less affluent and has one of the fastest-growing Hispanic populations in the state. The Madison County School District has about 11,000 students, of which 74% are Caucasian, 22% are African-American, and 4% are Hispanic. Income levels of families vary widely across the county. Districtwide, 37% of students qualify for free or reduced-price lunches, but that ranges from school to school, from as low as 14% to as high as 80%.

Superintendent Jim Hawkins is the fourth superintendent in Madison County during the past 50 years. Two superintendents that preceded him had long tenures in office, with one serving for 35 years and the other 12 years. The only "outsider" hired, other than the current superintendent, lasted 18 months. When he arrived in Madison County, Hawkins learned that the county commission and the board of education had adopted a local accountability agreement three years before. The Madison County Commission, a politically and financially conservative body, wanted some way to assess the appropriateness of school district requests for funding. The local accountability agreement stated that the four core criteria for comparing the success of Madison County schools in educating children to other counties in the state would include SAT scores, the dropout rate, the proficiency level of students as a district, and the State Accountability status, which classifies schools as having expected exemplary growth or as being a low-performing school. The agreement also established a five-year averaging model. During the first five-year period, Madison County's ranking out of the state's 117 districts went from 47 to 53 and then to 44. Superintendent Hawkins was hired by the Madison County Board of Education at the end of the second year of this five-year period. He raised expectations for students, implemented a data-driven assessment system for schools, began annual performance reviews of administrators, and placed an emphasis on increasing academic performance of all students. During the last two years of the five-year period, the district improved its ranking, moving to 27 and then to 22. The most recent estimates rank Madison County around 15th in the state. Madison County presently is considered a high-performing, large district ranking in the top 10% of the state's schools. Although the district's efforts to improve learning for all students met board and county commission expectations and strengthened community support for schools, Superintendent Hawkins understood that continued progress, particularly for students who performed less well academically, could not be achieved without systemic reform.

Jim Hawkins believed that having greater program discretion, financial flexibility, shared governance, and decision making at the school level and forging partnerships with other education systems would lay a foundation for better serving all students.

Hawkins and John Demarest, president of Greenhills Community College, informally talked about ways they could collaborate to expand education opportunities for Madison County high school students. Both the Madison County Board of Education and the Board of Trustees of Greenhills Community College endorsed the notion of collaboration and asked that they explore how the two education systems could create partnerships. As a consequence, they developed "Strategic Moment for Madison County," a 12-point white paper outlining possible collaboration in technology and several other joint program ventures.

As these programs were being developed, it was discovered that state regulations governing public education and community colleges inhibited innovation. For example, state regulations prohibited any student less than 16 years old from taking classes at a community college. In the natural course of events, the question was raised as to whether or not the state could grant waivers to allow community colleges and school systems flexibility in pursuing creative education programs. Subsequent meetings with staff at the Office of Charter Schools and the Public Policy Forum failed to answer questions or generate support for flexibility.

Hawkins and Demarest approached their state legislative delegation, including two Democratic senators and a Republican member of the house, and proposed pursuing deregulation to gain greater program and operating flexibility. In a remarkable act of solidarity, all three agreed that the notion of increasing flexibility for the district was worthwhile and encouraged them to proceed. During the next month and a half, they looked at several possible approaches to increasing flexibility, including drafting a legislative bill. A number of different drafts were developed and shared with a number of stakeholders. The first two drafts used the term *Charter School District* to refer to the initiative. In addition, the Democratic senator drafted a Senate Blank Bill as a way of having that legislation "on the table" for consideration during the legislative session. This Blank Bill allowed Madison County to move forward with drafting legislation. Drafts of the proposed Bill were shared with many people, including members of the state legislative delegation, a member of the State Board of Education who lives in Madison County, and a representative of the state education association, which acts on behalf of about 30% of the teachers in Madison County.

The superintendent reviewed and adopted a number of recommendations that shaped the language of the Bill, including changing the title of the Bill from "Charter School District" to "First in America." The term *Charter School District* had provoked considerable negative reaction across the state and had generated political opposition to the initiative. In addition, language in the Bill established a process by which the Madison County Board of Education could petition the state superintendent of education for consideration and approval of any waivers for deregulation. Essentially, the language allowed the state superintendent to approve a request for waiver and pass it on to the State Board of Education for consideration; if no action was taken within 60 days, the request would automatically be approved. Third, the district would receive "lump sum" funding.

Throughout the spring, as language of the Bill was refined, the superintendent continued to solicit input from various sources and correct rumors about and misinterpretations of the intent of the initiative. The state education association openly voiced its opposition to the proposed legislation and planning process. The senior Democratic senator, who had advised school district officials during the previous several months, called Superintendent Hawkins and told him that he could not support the Bill unless there was greater school and community support for the initiative. In addition, he advised the superintendent that he was referring the Bill to the Education Oversight Committee, a move that would allow consideration during the "short" legislative session.

Board members who encouraged the initiative also supported it by approving the proposed project during the board's April meeting with a 7-to-1 vote. Many board members were instrumental in this systemic reform effort and remained supportive and involved in the process. During April, as information about the project was being shared with district staff, it was evident that many people were not familiar with or were opposed to the charter district concept and had negative reactions to it. Local newspapers reported on reactions to certain aspects of the initiative that fueled continued controversy and rumors. Over a period of a week, a well-orchestrated campaign flooded both state senators' offices with hundreds of e-mails and telephone calls against this piece of legislation. Throughout this period, the Madison County Board of Education remained steadfast in its support of the superintendent and the continuation of the planning and development process.

In an effort to correct misinformation being circulated and maintain an open process, Superintendent Hawkins visited every school in the district during the last five weeks of school, explained the school improvement initiative, and asked for feedback. More than 72% of voting staff indicated a desire to move forward with the project. A similar series of community meetings on the topic was held in each of the district's three regions. These meetings attracted members of the business community, as well as representatives from the Chamber of Commerce, Kiwanis, and Rotary Club. Informal votes taken at these meetings generated an 80% positive vote to continue the planning and development effort.

Strong support for the project in the schools and community convinced the superintendent to establish a yearlong planning process designed along the lines of the process proposed in the draft legislation. He created a district Planning and Framework Team to guide the process. Its task was to organize a large-scale planning effort to ensure deliberations would be conducted in an open and inclusive environment in which schools and community citizens could establish a clear understanding of expectations for the schools and provide direction for accomplishing future goals. Invitations to participate in the planning process were published in the local newspaper and aired on the radio station, and an open invitation to participate was personally extended by Superintendent Hawkins at community meetings. No community member was denied the opportunity to serve on this team. In addition, he asked for a teacher representative from each school, invited representation from support staff, and included 11 of the district's 22 principals. It was a large-scale effort, the intent of which was to involve as many people in the planning process as possible.

The initial meeting of the Planning and Framework Team convened approximately 120 individuals, including teachers, support staff members, community citizens, state representatives, and state and national experts. Two meetings were held in the fall—one in September and one in November. The first one helped set the stage for the yearlong planning process. The November meeting began the process of delineating tasks. Eleven teams and subteams were established in specific areas, including technology; high school model, learning environment, and school/class size; school and instructional time; curriculum, testing, and accountability; exceptional needs children and preschool programs; human resources; parental and community engagement; governance issues; and funding. Each team was appointed based on expressed interest and representation from stakeholder groups, including parents, community members, staff members, teachers, and principals. District staff chaired or co-chaired the teams and were assured they would be given the time to commit to the effort. The Planning and Framework Team, acting as a body of the whole, charged each group with the task of using the intervening three and a half months to prepare feedback and recommendations to the group as to how they might improve the system.

On March 18, the Planning and Framework Team convened a meeting during which all the teams and subteams made preliminary reports, discussed findings, and formulated future plans. An analysis of these preliminary recommendations indicated that the vast majority of the recommendations did not need enabling legislation or waivers from the state. The district had the authority to move forward and implement these reforms. It was decided that before the next meeting planned for April 19, teacher representatives would be asked to share the 64 recommendations with colleagues at their respective schools. During this intervening period, Superintendent Hawkins conducted another round of regional community meetings to share recommendations. Over 600 concerns and questions were generated and answered in writing by the Planning and Framework Team. The objective of the April 19 meeting was to vote on each recommendation and to decide whether the district should continue to examine its viability or eliminate it from future work. The superintendent reiterated that a vote to continue discussion was not a final vote to adopt the proposed recommendation. It was only a vote as to whether or not the Planning and Framework Team should continue considering its relative merits.

During the April 19 meeting, six to eight teacher representatives indicated they felt very uncomfortable about voting on these recommendations insofar as they had received written answers to their questions only several days prior to the meeting and had little opportunity to poll the sentiments of their colleagues. In keeping with the spirit of the planning process, Superintendent Hawkins gave teacher representatives an opportunity to caucus so they could discuss the issue, ensuring that everyone felt comfortable before moving forward. They spent over half an hour caucusing and came back with a number of recommendations, including having the principal at each school call a meeting dedicated to discussing concerns and questions about the 64 "First in America" recommendations. The teacher representatives would review each recommendation, and then the school faculty would vote on each. A composite school vote would be compiled for each recommendation and representatives would be obligated to vote in accordance with the wishes of their respective schools. In addition, it was agreed that a vote of 50% plus one vote constituted consensus to move forward on any recommendation. Voting would be by secret ballot; however, composite data by recommendation and by school would be available to anyone, thus ensuring an open process. In addition, a series of regional community meetings was planned. Using the same process, community sentiment for each recommendation was recorded, which guided voting by their representatives. Furthermore, it was agreed to convene the Planning and Framework Team on May 21 to finally vote on each of the 64 recommendations. Members of the Planning and Framework Team who were unable to attend the May 21 meeting were mailed copies of the recommendations with paper ballots.

An examination of the voting pattern provides considerable insight into school and community responses to the comprehensive planning process and the complexity of school and community relations. When teacher representatives polled their colleagues in their respective schools to ascertain how they should vote at the May 21 meeting, they found considerable variation in support for proposed recommendations. Two schools rejected all recommendations and four others approved less than 10. Most, however, voted to accept nearly all of them. Superintendent Hawkins said, "That's a dramatic statement for schools relative to their overall nonsupport of this initiative." A final count of school-based teacher voting indicated that they approved only 27 of the 64 recommendations for further planning and development. Some recommendations that teachers did not support included host academies (schools within schools), smaller school size, smaller class size, expanded opportunities for elementary education, more guidance counselors, alternative schedules, choice within district schools, year-round schools, 11-month contracts that would increase their salaries and provide opportunities for staff development, technology training for teachers, collaboration with Greenhills Community College for academic programs and staff development, and school funding. In addition, governance recommendations creating parent councils, staff leadership teams, and increased decision-making authority in each school did not pass. It is evident that teachers did not support major systemic reforms in the schools.

Members of the Planning and Framework Team were evenly divided between school and community representatives. The team included school counselors, principals, and noninstructional support staff, as well as teacher and community representatives. On May 21, a meeting was convened to vote on the recommendations. Of the original 103 members of the Planning and Framework Team who participated throughout the year, 89 attended the meeting or returned a paper ballot. Approximately 17 individuals that were originally part of the process were considered "interested parties"; however, they did not have voting privileges. A tally of the votes indicated that 56 out of the 64 recommendations received consensus (50% plus one vote) and were advanced to the next planning and development stage.

The issue of how to allow schools greater flexibility to innovate was brought to the attention of the Madison County Board of Education by Superintendent Hawkins. Rather than inhibiting change, board members joined with Superintendent Hawkins in engaging the local community and school staff in defining the role of schools in the community and how they could increase opportunities for all children and enhance their academic performance. The comprehensive community planning process was highly successful; however, teachers, those most directly responsible for school improvement, were reluctant to change.

This case study illustrates the dynamics of social systems. Superintendent Hawkins attempted systemic change in the educational paradigm in Madison County School District. Why did this systemic reform effort meet with such strong opposition, even after Superintendent Hawkins had successfully led the Madison County School District to substantial improvement in student achievement and even though he had widespread community and board support?

Understanding the dynamics of social systems is key to answering this question. Although Superintendent Hawkins kept stakeholders informed and engaged the community in planning for reform, many resisted systemic change. In terms of public relations (PR), communication appeared to be open. However, systems theory provides a larger concept from which to frame communication. In order to fully understand a system's feedback or communication loop, one must also know the system's deeply held cultural values and beliefs. These are the system's paradigms, which, according to Caine and Caine (1997), consist of "all those deeply held beliefs and ideas that shape our grasp of reality" (p. 12). Senge (1990) referred to paradigms as "mental models." As this case ended, teachers and other stakeholders had failed to make a paradigm shift.

The concept of schools as open social systems offers a framework for understanding the functions and purposes of planned, organized PR. Social systems theory helps explain the communication dynamics of organizations, which are fundamental to all PR efforts. This chapter focuses on three interrelated concepts relevant to the social dimensions of PR:

- ♦ Systems thinking as a conceptual framework for understanding PR within the context of organizational dynamics,
- ♦ The role of leadership in building and communicating a shared school-community vision, and
- ♦ Schools as communities that reflect the diversity of American culture and the leader's role in working with multiple stakeholders.

As this chapter explores the social and political dimensions of PR, it becomes evident that all communications—from school to community, from community to school, and internally within the school organization itself—affect the public's perceptions of schools. Moreover, this chapter provides a framework for understanding PR in the context of schools as open social systems that exist within a larger social-political context. Internal and external communication among school personnel and between them and stakeholders affects a school's image and readiness for change. Social systems theory explains complex political relationships between schools and the communities they serve, and it provides a framework for understanding how culture, values, and beliefs define community and educational systems.

SYSTEMS THINKING

During previous decades, schools were viewed as providing a unique service to society, and as a consequence, they were infrequently challenged and were provided adequate public resources (Tyack & Hansot, 1982). In this stable environment, conventional inward-looking management practices were built on notions of the corporate values of efficiency, scientific management, hierarchical organizational structures, apolitical perspectives, and professionalism (Björk, 2001; Rowan & Miskel, 1999). During the past several decades, however, changing demographic trends (Reyes, Wagstaff, & Fusarelli, 1999), the increasing political involvement of interest groups and the expanding role of the courts in shaping education policy (Björk & Lindle, 2001), fluctuating economic conditions, and contested values have altered the landscape of American education. Educators are being forced to look outward and develop a better understanding of the dynamic relationship between society and schools (Björk & Keedy, 2001a). In addition, it has become necessary for school leaders to develop "very different ways of thinking about the purposes of their work, and the skills and knowledge that go with these purposes" (Elmore, 2000, p. 35).

Changing school contexts pressed school leaders to increase political acuity (Björk & Keedy, 2001a; Carter & Cunningham, 1997); share decision making (Ogawa, Crowson, & Goldring, 1999); adopt distributed, instructional, and moral leadership practices (Björk, 1993; Sergiovanni, 1992; Spillane, Halverson, & Diamond, 1999; Starratt, 1996); know about school cultures and professional communities (Firestone & Louis, 1999); and interact with the political community (Björk & Keedy, 2001b). Thus, conventional ways of doing administration shifted from management and control by the few to leadership and consultation by the many.

The Concept of System

Systems theory emerged as a reaction to the unrealistic assumption that organizations and human behavior could be separated from external environmental forces (Hoy & Miskel, 2001). Classical organizational theories tend to be one-dimensional, view organizations as static, and embrace simplistic assumptions about organizational relationships. Systems theories, on the other hand, tend to be multidimensional, include complex assumptions about organizational relationships, and view organizations as continuously changing in pursuit of equilibrium with their external environment. The systems perspective advances the notion that organizations are dependent on their environment for survival. Thus, viewing them as closed systems is both artificial and limiting. It also suggests that it is equally unrealistic to view them as completely open, as they would be overwhelmed by inputs that would diminish their capacity to function. Darwin's notion of natural selection is often used to illustrate the idea that organizations, like organisms, are compelled to adapt to changes in their external environment or face extinction. This example may be better suited to private-sector organizations, which are compelled to struggle for survival, than to public monopolies such as schools and government agencies, which serve the public interest and thus have a guarantee of continuing support. Nevertheless, the idea that organizations need to be responsive to their respective clients is an important concept.

A common liability among schools and government agencies is the tendency to screen out information from their external environments that could improve their performance. School boards, shared governance, site-based management, and vouchers reflect attempts to ensure public accountability and enhance the responsiveness of schools to community and parent demands. Parsons (1967) underscored the importance of organizations maintaining connection with the community. In his discussion of a general theory of formal organizations, he acknowledged that no organization can exist in isolation and that it is interdependent with the larger social system from which it derives legitimacy, meaning, and support. The ecology of organizations is characterized as a symbiotic relationship in which organizations and society derive mutual benefits. With regard to public schools, this relationship is unambiguous: Society provides resources to schools in exchange for their producing numerate and literate citizens. The inability of schools to meet these expectations can jeopardize continuing public support and threaten their survival.

Systems are composed of interdependent parts that engage in ongoing relationships. These characteristics can be observed in a single school having graded classes, counselors, administrators, and office staffs; a district composed of many schools; or a district that is part of a state education system. Two basic concepts define a system. First, the notion of complex causality helps guard against adopting simplistic cause-and-effect relationships that can lead to inappropriate administrative decisions. Events are often influenced by multiple factors, and understanding complexity may lead to more-appropriate decisions. Second, the notion of subsystems suggests that an organization is composed of interdependent parts that must work in concert for it to survive and adapt. Thus, units within a school, district, or state education system are interdependent and as such should align with corresponding units at different levels in the system.

Systems theories of organizations have two distinct strands: (a) the notion of cybernetics advanced by Wiener (1948) and (b) general systems theory advanced by Bertalanffy (1951). Although management and social systems theories have been influenced by different social science traditions and have distinct analytical approaches, they share a number of important assumptions. Cybernetic and social systems theorists concur that because external organizational environments are often turbulent, unpredictable, and in a constant state of change, codifying events can help administrators understand complex relationships and make decisions that ensure organizational survival.

Wiener (1948), the father of cybernetics, employed a wide array of techniques to understand organizational complexity and environmental uncertainty. His work was directed toward improving organizational efficiency and decision-making processes and was focused on improving organizational efficiency (Shafritz & Ott, 2001). These efforts contributed to the development of systems analysis tools such as the Planning, Evaluation, Review Technique (PERT); Zero Based Budgeting System (ZBGS); Planning, Programming, Budgeting System (PPBS); and more recently, Total Quality Management (TQM) approaches. These systems rely on computer-based management information systems to identify problems, select optimum solutions, and adjust organizational activities.

Although the emergence of cybernetics and systems analysis techniques held considerable promise for understanding organizational dynamics, social scientists were troubled by the dominance of technology in understanding social process. Social systems perspectives were grounded in the seminal work of Mayo (1933), Roethlisberger and Dickson (1939), and Follett (1940). Biologist Bertalanffy (1951), considered the founder of general systems theory, discussed the importance of viewing a living organism as part of its larger natural environment. He saw organisms as being interdependent with other organisms and posited that any change in their environment or in any other organism with which they were interdependent would force them to adjust to survive. The notion of mutual interdependence contributed to formulating an approach to analyzing organizations as interdependent parts of the larger social system. Sociologists, anthropologists, political scientists, social psychologists, and scholars studying complex organizations assimilated this concept. They also made clear that in an orthodox sense, systems theory is not a theory, as it does not attempt to explain phenomena (Katz & Kahn, 1966). Rather, it is a heuristic theory that is limited to describing and categorizing events in an effort to understand complex relationships between organizations and their environments. Bertalanffy (1951) proposed a general systems model that had four basic components: input, process, output and feedback loops (see Figure 5–1).

Figure 5–1 illustrates how the general systems model can be applied in a school or district setting. The systems process involves (1) environmental *inputs* that identify demands and needs of the community, state policies, court decisions, resources, knowledge, goals, and shared societal values; (2) organizational *processes* that identify and convene internal and external experts to deliberate on the issue, build consensus, and determine actions needed to resolve the problem at hand; (3) *outputs* resulting from *processes* that change how an organization does work or the product delivered to meet the demand; and (4) formative and summative *feedback* that provides information to those in the organization. Formative feedback occurs as a normal part of program implementation that is directed toward improving operations. Summative feedback is evaluative in nature and examines the impact of the program in relation to its intended purposes at the end of a specified period of time (e.g., student performance on standardized tests at the end of the school year). Information transferred through feedback loops becomes new input into system deliberations. During the last half of the twentieth century, notions derived from systems dynamics influenced the work of political and social scientists interested in better understanding the relationship among organizations and environments, institutional behavior, and organizational learning.

Easton (1965) described the political system as a subsystem of the larger social order. He referred to his conceptualization of these interactions between the political system and the larger environment as political systems analysis. Subsequently, political and social scientists rationalized that schools are part of the political subsystem because board members are elected and make authoritative decisions regarding the allocation of resources (Campbell, Flemming, Newell, & Bennion, 1987). Their actions are legitimated by the

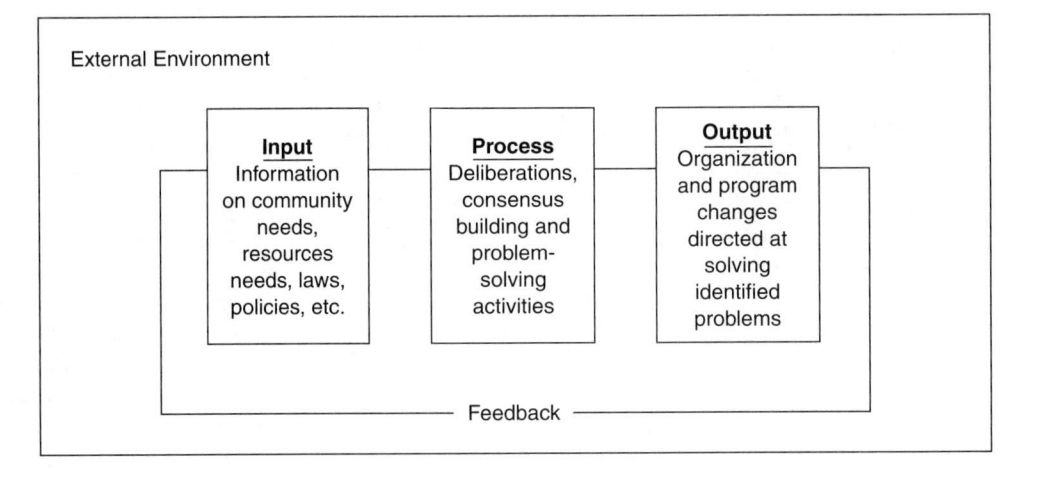

FIGURE 5–1
General Systems Model

larger community (Thompson, 1967) and persist in society as a means through which schools and society can adapt to change (Easton, 1965). Wirt and Kirst (1982, 2001), as well as Tyack and Hansot (1982), applied Easton's political analysis approach to understanding the relationship between education organizations and society. They persuasively argued that because school boards mediate inputs (demands and supports) from the external environment and convert them into appropriate outputs (action, program, or policy), schools are part of the political subsystem.

Campbell et al. (1987) extended the work of Easton (1965) and Wirt and Kirst (1982) in developing an open-systems view of school administration. This perspective provided a more definitive framework for using systems thinking to increase the effectiveness and efficiency of schools as organizations. Recently, Björk and Keedy (2001b) found that the relationship between school boards and superintendents often influences these processes, suggesting that school leaders are also part of the political process, not merely administrative functionaries. These findings make a compelling argument for the utility of systems thinking in understanding complex political relationships among communities, school boards, and district superintendents.

Getzels and Guba (1957) drew on systems thinking in discussing the relational nature of social systems in organizations. They noted that internal social systems have two classes of phenomena that are independent, yet interactive, and influence the behavior of organizational members. Social systems have two broad dimensions: (a) the institutional (nomothetic) and (b) the individual (idiographic) dimensions. The institutional (nomothetic) dimension represents the organization's ascribed roles and expectations that are embedded in formal structures and cultures. The individual (idiographic) dimension encompasses idiosyncratic personalities and the need-dispositions that motivate individuals. The social behavior of individuals in organizations emanates from the interplay between institutional expectations and individual need-dispositions.

In school organizations, formal offices and positions represent the nomothetic dimension. These formal positions are accompanied by role expectations that are typically defined in written job descriptions, as well as in group norms. Individuals (idiographic dimension) who hold these offices and positions have their own personalities and need-dispositions, which also influence how they carry out their duties. The mechanism through which the needs of the organization and individuals are accommodated or balanced is the work group. The dynamic interaction among individuals that compose work groups, the culture and climate of the organization, and individual personalities contribute to balancing institutional and individual needs and influence social behavior. Continuous monitoring provides feedback that helps school administrators ascertain the degree to which institutional and individual needs are met and whether an appropriate balance between the two is achieved within the work group. Understanding the relational nature of social systems can provide opportunities to influence goal achievement and staff satisfaction within the social system.

Argyris (1982) also acknowledged the relational nature of institutions and their environments and provided a normative prescription for enhancing organizational learning. He observed that although people in modern industrial societies learn from their individual actions, they are often unaware of dissonance between their theories of action and organizational contexts. He argued that significant changes in role behavior can be achieved through learning processes that focus on detecting and correcting errors; integrating knowledge, action, and reflection; and synthesizing independent learning accrued over time.

Argyris and Schön (1978) characterized adaptive behavior produced by identifying and correcting errors, or troubleshooting, as single-loop learning. Single-loop learning is described as initial feedback in the systems process and is suited to stable conditions, high levels of control, and a rational system of organizing. In these circumstances, fundamental operating assumptions are neither examined nor altered to achieve a change in behavior. Double-loop learning, on the other hand, is useful in complex situations in which basic assumptions governing behavior and action are examined to determine whether they are contributing to the problem (Argyris & Schön, 1978). They posit that through the integration of reiterative cycles of reflective inquiry and action, root causes of problems can be uncovered, organizational performance improved, and equilibrium with its external environment achieved.

Although the notion of organizational learning holds promise, Argyris (1982) also recognized that most people in modern societies are acculturated and predisposed by theories of action that are commonly referred to as accepted ways of doing things. Recognition that theories of action inhibit fundamental organizational change challenged the field to reconceptualize the notion of leadership in learning organizations.

Senge's (1990) pioneering analysis of learning organizations is an insightful attempt at using systems thinking and knowledge to create learning organizations and acknowledges that institutionalizing change takes time. He drew on the notion that organizations are interconnected systems (Katz & Kahn, 1966; Weick, 1976) and on the notions derived from systems dynamics in conceptualizing and redefining the work of organizational members as nonlinear interrelationships and processes, rather than as conventional, cause-and-effect linear processes. Thus, Senge's (1990) reality is composed of circles of causality in which actions change the future state of affairs of the organization.

Senge (1990) calls systems thinking the fifth discipline because it is the conceptual foundation for other disciplines including personal mastery, mental models, the building of a shared vision, and team learning. Taken as a whole, they contribute to a shift from seeing parts to seeing wholes, from viewing individuals as reactors to viewing individuals as active participants in organizational life, from seeing change as a snapshot in time to seeing change as a process, and from dwelling on the present to creating the future. He contends that success in creating and sustaining organizations where individuals are responsible for their learning is highly dependent on the nature of leadership and characterizes visionary leaders as designers, stewards, and teachers who help guide ongoing processes of questioning, testing assumptions, and learning. These leadership activities are intended to continuously expand the capacity of individuals to understand the complexity of their organization, clarify its purposes, and share mental models. Senge's (1990) concept of organizational learning offers organizations opportunities to anticipate and correct difficulties before they become problems. Over the past decade, empirical research has moved Senge's (1990) compelling theoretical description of schools as learning organizations from a hopeful literature into the realm of possibility (Leithwood, Jantzi, & Steinbach, 1998; Louis & Kruse, 1998).

Chaos theory offers a number of useful perspectives that can augment social systems thinking. It emerged out of wide-ranging interdisciplinary research in physics, chemistry, mathematics, meteorology, medicine, economics, and epidemiology and uses such terms as *nonlinear dynamics, dynamical systems theory,* and *dynamical systems methods* in referring to phenomena (Griffiths, Hart, & Blair, 1991). This body of work explores the relationship between order and disorder in an attempt to understand the nature of complex systems in which nonlinear problems are examined holistically.

Over the past several decades, two branches of chaos theory have emerged (Hayles, 1990). The first branch posits that chaos in a system facilitates rather than inhibits self-organization (Prigogine & Stengers, 1984). Those who hold to the "order out of chaos" perspective tend to focus on issues of being and becoming and are often criticized by the scientific community as being more philosophically oriented than empirically grounded. The second branch argues that chaos is not a system out of order and that events are not random, but are governed by deeply encoded structures called strange attractors (Gleick, 1987; Lorenz, 1963; Mandelbrott, 1983). The "strange attractor" group tends to focus on problems of practical interest and emphasizes the ability of chaotic systems to generate new information to help in self-renewal.

Griffiths, Hart, and Blair's (1991) analysis of the characteristics of chaos theory identified several concepts that can be applied to the field of educational administration. The *butterfly effect* heightens awareness that seemingly unrelated small events produce large consequences. Thus, school administrators are cautioned to pay attention to seemingly innocuous incidents, as they can grow into major problems. The impact of *random shocks* to a stable system is often small, and as a consequence, the system will regain equilibrium quickly. If the system is nonlinear, a small random shock can alter the system and inhibit it from returning to its original state. A *strange attractor* is a hidden element around which events revolve. Changes in the characteristics of the strange attractor can signal changes in the system's behavior and help predict where it will be in the future. Thus, school administrators should be aware of changes in recurring education or organizational themes, as they may signal a change in the school system. *Recursive symmetries* suggest that structural forms are replicated across different levels and alert school administrators to look for and align organizational functions across levels to enhance efficiency. *Feedback mechanisms* reflect a fundamental principle of systems thinking: Output is fed back into the system as new input that then causes it to change. For example, school administrators may use test scores in working with teachers to align the curriculum, develop course content, and change instructional practices. Chaos theory underscores the notion that turbulent and unpredictable environments are pervasive. It also acknowledges that systems have the capacity to reorganize and adapt to changing circumstances.

Wheatley (1996) characterized organizations as open, dynamic systems in which chaos and order are complementary elements in the ongoing self-renewal process. She posited that organizations must be understood holistically as well as relationally within the larger environment. Terms including *interdependence* and *interconnectivity* imply that relationships contribute to defining and redefining structures, work, and meaning over time. She persuasively argued that schools are living systems that possess the same capacity to adapt and survive that is common to all life and that these circumstances call for different ways of leading. Wheatley (1996) contended that leaders of dynamic social systems can neither predict nor control events, as is assumed by classical management theories. As a consequence, they must develop skills that complement organizational learning, change, and innovation. Leadership in self-regulating, learning organizations is the responsibility not of the few, but of the many. Thus, emphasis is placed on the quality of relationships, broad participation, and the building of staff capacity for innovation and continuous change. The flow of information is enhanced by ever-widening circles of exchange. The simultaneous flow of information across multiple and diverse levels in the organization also contributes to self-referent behavior, sense making, and clarity of purpose.

During the last several decades, the American public has persistently demanded that schools reform conventional practices to better align their work with the changing demographic, social, economic, political, and technological realities of society. Although some school administrators are threatened by these events, others recognize them as opportunities for change. Systems thinking provides a framework for understanding the relational nature of schools and society. Through an understanding of systems theories, educational leaders may better identify conflict among key elements of the system, assess the nature of problems, deliberate on their causes, build consensus for solutions, evaluate the relative effectiveness of corrective measures, change basic assumptions of schools and practice to improve organizational effectiveness, and achieve greater congruence with society (Hoy & Miskel, 2001).

Systems thinking is essential for education leaders' understanding of PR and the role it plays in change processes. The Public Relations Society of America (2002) offered the following comment about the role of PR: "Public relations helps our complex, pluralistic society to reach decisions and function more effectively by contributing to mutual understanding among groups and institutions. It serves to bring private and public policies into harmony" (http://www.prsa.org/_Resources/Profession/index.asp?ident=prof1).

Thus, at the heart of PR is the mediation of the complex flow of information between the school and its diverse stakeholders, as well as among its various internal subsystems. Systems thinking helps education leaders see PR as a continual, systematic process, rather than as a single activity.

DEVELOPING A SHARED SCHOOL-COMMUNITY VISION

One of the most viable methods that school administrators can use in working with a multitude of external and internal publics is creating a collaborative school-community vision. Much of what is commonly thought of as PR deals with a school's formal communication to its external environment, through such means as news releases, parent and community newsletters, and business partnerships. However, systems thinking helps us understand that such communication is only one part of a much more complex web of information flow. Because schools are open systems, there is a constant flow of information into and out of the school environment. Schools as open systems seek to maintain equilibrium with the social and political characteristics of the community. Indeed, the school is not separate from the external culture: It influences as well as responds to cultural change. Vision development is a way to provide a strong focus and sense of purpose for both the school and the community. A shared school-community vision provides a platform for facilitating school improvement and guiding education reform that complements, rather than clashing with, community values.

Defining a Vision

The concept of vision is not new, although it is often confused with a school's mission. In simplest terms, mission is what people are supposed to do in a school, whereas vision is what the school should look like at some future point in meeting its mission. Visions are, without exception, future oriented in wording and concept.

A vision has been variously described as "the development, transmission, and implementation of a desirable future" (Manasse, 1985, p. 150) and as a "journey from the known to the unknown . . . creating a montage of facts, hopes, dreams . . . and opportunities" (Hickman & Silva, 1984, p. 151). Zmuda, Kuklis, and Kline (2004) described a shared school vision as "a coherent picture of how the system will function when the core beliefs have been put into practice" (p. 58). At the core of all vision definitions is the notion that a vision shapes an organization or an institution as it moves toward a better future (Chance, 1992; Rutherford, 1985; Shieve & Shoenheit, 1987). The transformation of vision from a concept to action is the result of leadership. Starratt (1996) proposed that "vision embraces an ideal, a dream that is grounded in those fundamental meanings and values that feed a sense of human fulfillment." He further noted that "the compelling power of leadership flows from a shared vision" (p. 14).

Sergiovanni (1996) suggested that the role of the principal is vital in the vision process because "most of us are not accustomed to thinking in terms of vision" (p. 84). Carter and Cunningham (1997), in their work on the school superintendent, indicated that "the superintendent must lead the schools in developing a clear vision of curriculum, instruction, and student achievement connections" (p. 189). They expanded on the importance of the role of the superintendent by concluding that "successful superintendents recognize that the power of a clear vision . . . can be more effective than the power of authority" (p. 189).

Nanus (1992) noted that "vision attracts commitment and energizes people . . . vision establishes a standard of excellence . . . vision bridges the present and future" (pp. 16–17). DuFour and Eaker (1998) described the importance of vision in their work on professional learning communities. "The *sine qua non* of a learning community is shared understanding and common values. What separates a learning community from an ordinary school is its collective commitment to guiding principles that articulate what the people in the school believe and what they seek to create" (p. 25). Certainly, research and the leadership literature point to the need for an organizational vision. But how does this vision develop? Does it emanate from the leader, who dictates his/her vision in the form of an edict to subordinates and stakeholders in the organization? Vision that is imposed on an organization is often doomed to ultimate failure. The sense of disequilibrium created by such an act either leads to outright rejection of the vision or results in a type of creative insubordination.

Any approach to developing a vision should adopt a philosophy of inclusiveness instead of exclusiveness. The vision development process should be viewed as a collaborative effort among all stakeholders. In an educational setting, it is imperative to involve both those in the community and those in the school district. The creation of a shared school-community vision may be one of the most important PR activities in which a school administrator participates. A vision developed collaboratively opens lines of communication; it provides for constructive involvement of a widely representative group of the school's stakeholders and constituents; and it charts a path for the school district to follow into the future.

Building a Vision

How is a collaborative school-community vision built? It does not happen spontaneously or serendipitously. Vision building is a planned event, requiring strong leadership committed to building coalitions among all school stakeholders and community partners. Chance (1992) developed a five-stage process for vision development (see Table 5–1) that invites participation and collaboration and has been used successfully by school administrators. The most significant result of building a shared vision is the tremendous community support that it generates for the school district and the educational process. Through school-community vision building, everyone comes together in mutual agreement about the direction in which the school district should be moving. The feeling of goodwill between those in the school district and those in the community extends to issues such as school bond elections, curriculum design, school discipline, and parent-teacher conversations.

In the first component of the five-step vision development process, school district leaders identify and develop their personal educational visions. Leaders involved in this first stage include, but are not limited to, the superintendent, other central office personnel, site administrators, board members, and lead teachers. This initial step in the process provides an opportunity for reflection by asking those involved to recognize their personal values and beliefs while examining their professional careers. Upon the completion of self-reflection, school leaders are asked to think about the strengths and weaknesses of the school district. They are also asked to examine the school district's relationship with the external environment and reflect on how all the various interpersonal components of the school district (social system) work together in the educational process. Finally, they discuss with one another their concepts of an ideal school and identify the types of learning-related activities that would take place in these school environments. At this point, participants do not write or develop a vision; the initial step simply asks participants to reflect and share with one another. During this first stage, the leadership cadre forms a bond in preparation for leading other stakeholders through subsequent stages.

Step two of the vision process results in the development of an overall collaborative school-community vision. This step begins by inviting a variety of individuals who represent the diversity of the school district and its community to participate. Those invited at stage two may be community leaders, parents and nonparents, teachers, staff members, board members, district administrators, students, and representatives of all ethnic,

TABLE 5–1

Five-Stage Model for Vision Development

Stage	Description
1	Developing a personal vision
2	Developing a shared school vision
3	Communicating the vision
4	Actualizing the vision
5	Sustaining the vision

Source: Chance (1992).

political, and social groups, as well as those in the community who are educational critics. Depending on the size of the school district, the total number of participants can range from 40 to 300. It is important to be as inclusive as possible at this point.

The development of the organizational vision is the result of a multitiered effort that gradually moves from numerous small groups composed of 5 to 7 members to one large, democratically selected group of 10 to 15 members (see Figure 5–2). Members of the small groups representing the diversity of the school and the community respond to questions related to school district strengths and weaknesses, community support, community concerns, and the focus of the school district for the future. A consensus-building process is used, which allows group members to come to an agreement on a group response. Representatives from each initial small group are elected to move forward to form new groups with members from other groups. Consensus is again reached in these newly formed groups. The process continues in a similar manner until a final group of 10 to 15 members, representing initial stakeholder groups, is formed. At this point, a school vision is finalized. This shared school-community vision represents input and agreement from the diverse stakeholders who were involved in the initial stages of step two. The result of this process is a

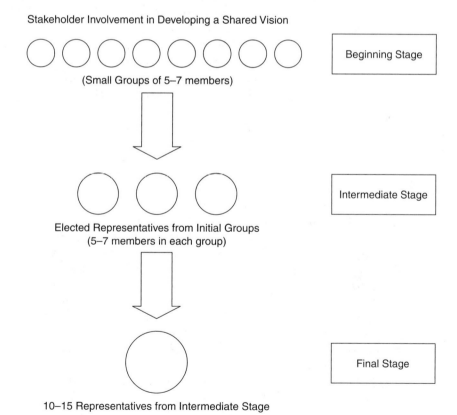

FIGURE 5–2

Stakeholder Involvement in Developing a Shared Vision

collaboratively formed school-community vision statement that reflects all the participants' appraisal of the school district and their ideas of what the school should be working toward in the future.

During this second phase, short- and long-term goals are also developed. Step two is a complex, time-consuming process, and it is important to allow the time necessary for the process to work. Too often, administrators and others are in a hurry to complete this step. It must be remembered that the process of group interaction and discussion is as important as the product, the vision statement. The process at this step represents a tremendous PR opportunity for the school district. It allows people to work together in a positive way for the good of the school district. The "fallout" of this step is long-lasting and should be capitalized on by the school's administrators. Think about it in this way: It is very seldom that stakeholders representing a variety of viewpoints are allowed to discuss the future direction of the school district. This sharing of ideas, concerns, and beliefs allows for a unification of school and community forces with a greater sense of collaboration and cooperation among stakeholders.

The next step is to communicate the vision and the newly developed short- and long-term goals to the internal and external publics. Effectively communicating the vision is vitally important. A PR program that addresses the vision and explains how the district plans to achieve or actualize it is crucial. Generally, a vision is best communicated by metaphorical statements, symbols, or models. Pronouncements representative of the vision, such as "Where Dreams Grow," "Excellence and Equity," and "Striving for Excellence," provide both impetus and direction for an organization. Communicating the vision is not an end unto itself. A vision without action is really useless and futile. Action is represented by the short- and long-term goals established through the vision process.

These short- and long-term goals represent step four, actualizing the vision. In addition to the goals, strategies should be developed that provide viable opportunities to measure progress toward the school district's goals. Without monitoring and evaluation, one will never be able to ascertain areas of needed focus and areas where success has occurred. The establishment of vision-monitoring teams at each school site is a useful way to determine how the actualization process is proceeding.

The school administrator can effectively utilize a PR approach to communicate the vision and district goals. An annual vision audit to the community provides a way to maintain the focus on the district's vision while documenting to stakeholders what the district has accomplished. Appointing those who have been involved in the vision development process as vision ambassadors to the community is another good way to engender support for the school district. The saying that those who create something will support it certainly holds true. Vision ambassadors who represent the diversity of the community become the "sales staff" for the school district's vision.

The final step in this five-step process is sustaining the vision. Schools are very busy places, and although they are often open to new ideas and approaches, follow-through can be inefficient because something new always comes along and diffuses the impetus toward goal attainment. That is why this final step is important. A constant and continual focus on the school district's vision is necessary. Before anything new is adopted by the school district, one question must be answered: Does it help the school achieve its vision? That question should be a guide for all decisions. There must be an ongoing opportunity by school leaders to reflect on and analyze the direction of the school district. Finally, there needs to be a concerted effort to create a visionary culture that becomes embedded in the school district's social system because organizations with a visionary culture "display a remarkable resiliency, an ability to bounce back from adversity" (Collins & Porras, 1994, p. 4). By staying focused on a school's shared vision, the system maintains equilibrium because the work of the school system represents values shared by the system's members.

The creation of a collaborative school-community vision is a potent PR force for school administrators. It opens lines of communication across all ethnic, social, political, and economic barriers. It provides a positive image of the school to all stakeholders because there is a clear focus on where the school district is going and how it plans to get there. The use of internal and external vision ambassadors assists in institutionalizing the vision into the school district so that all subsequent decisions and programs are evaluated on their ability to achieve the school district vision. A visionary culture is established that outlives the leadership of any one individual. All stakeholders, both inside and outside the organizational boundaries of the school district, share a responsibility to pursue the vision. The school district benefits from renewed support from a variety of stakeholders. The processes of building, communicating, and sustaining vision are in essence PR activities that result in a "win-win" situation for all stakeholders. And, of course, ultimately the real winners are the students who benefit from the collaboration of all stakeholders.

School administrators work with numerous stakeholders in both individual and group settings. In order to move toward a new organizational vision, a leader must be comfortable with some level of disequilibrium in the system. As stakeholders come together to examine and share their core beliefs, a vision evolves that will guide those involved in the system toward a new organizational paradigm. At the core of this process is a leader's ability to build collaborative teams. Collaborative teams, when properly developed, result in a level of expanded self-esteem for all education stakeholders, while building a strong degree of cooperation among various group members (Maeroff, 1993).

Building collaboration among stakeholders involves bringing together people from diverse cultural backgrounds and overcoming their differences. In discussing multicultural aspects of PR, Banks (2000) proposed that public relations is cultural because it "communicates across cultural borders" and "it is a cultural practice itself" (p. 29). Moreover, Banks pointed out that cultural boundaries are determined by a group's cohesive and homogeneous understanding of particular practices. Thus, even though a school's stakeholders may represent various cultures as defined by race, ethnicity, religion, gender, and so on, these groups may come together as one culture bound by their common understanding and lived experience of the school community.

Such collaboration and cultural blending are what school-community vision building is all about. The school leader who successfully builds collaboration among stakeholders is one who is knowledgeable about group dynamics and skilled in facilitating communication among diverse populations.

Groups and Collaborative Visioning

The following section introduces some fundamental concepts related to group dynamics and a leader's role in facilitating communication among group members in order to lead stakeholders toward a common vision. This is an essential, but often overlooked, function of PR and a key to understanding the social dimensions of PR.

As groups are formed to accomplish some school-related task, it is necessary to have as diverse a group as possible. This creates a strong support foundation for educational decisions (in the same manner the vision process does). A variegated group may be more difficult to work with, but its members will often have more useful aggregate knowledge and skills to accomplish the group's agenda. The effective development of work groups may be easier if one remembers that groups evolve through a series of developmental stages. According to group theorists, groups develop in a sequential, highly predictable manner. Groups, like social systems, have characteristics similar to living organisms. They come into being, evolve, change, and mature as a result of experience, opportunities, and knowledge.

The development and the functioning of each group also must be viewed in light of sociological differences. Each group member's sex, ethnicity, age, socioeconomic status, educational background, and beliefs and values contribute to the successful functioning or failure of each group. Additionally, considerations related to the school organization, the "ruralness" or "urbanness" of the community, personal and community aspirations, and the school administrator's ability to establish group parameters and expectations of performance affect the group's development and success.

When forming stakeholders work groups, school leaders should be cognizant of the multicultural dimensions of the community. Further, while each member of a group may represent a unique cultural aspect of the community, it is important to remember that cohesive work groups form their own cultural identity. Culture refers to the values, beliefs, norms, and ways of thinking of a group of people (Owens, 1995). Banks (2000) proposed that "a culture is as large or small as the group whose ways of constructing meaning about any salient practice are cohesively and homogeneously defined. It is the saliency of a particular practice that determines the cultural boundary of concern to the public relations communications" (p. 12). Thus, the intent of bringing together stakeholder groups should be to develop mutual agreement about important educational issues, practices, or decisions that will be supported by all stakeholders in the community. In essence, school leaders utilize stakeholder groups in an effort to seek common values that bind, rather than divide, the community.

One of the most important skills for a school administrator is knowledge of group developmental theories. For the purpose of this chapter, a classical and well-known theory of group development will be discussed. The theory put forth by Tuckman and Jensen (1977) concluded that all groups evolve through five distinct stages: forming, storming, norming, performing, and adjourning. All five stages are best utilized by a school administrator, as they relate to the group's task and changes in interpersonal relationships.

The first stage, *forming,* is associated with the creation of a new group and the feeling of discomfort that can result from such a situation. This initial period of caution, apprehension, and uneasiness is followed by a period of storming. *Storming,* the second stage, is best understood as a time when the group members begin to focus on their individual perceptions of the task and when they vie for influence and power. Conflict can come in several forms and, in the extreme, can destroy group productivity before the group reaches stage three.

The third stage is aptly called *norming.* This stage occurs when explicit and implicit norms are established. A sense of order is evidenced at this third stage, allowing for movement to the fourth stage, *performing*. At the performing stage, the group really begins to work; the group's focus is on the task at hand. Group membership and individuals' roles are well defined, and group norms are entrenched. Productivity is high, and there is an increased sense of camaraderie among group members.

The final stage, *adjourning*, takes place after the group has accomplished its task. Too often groups continue to meet, but their work is aimless, because there is nothing more to be done. If new tasks are not assigned, the group's function is complete, and the group should be disbanded. A group without a purpose or task is both ineffective and inefficient.

Community involvement in task forces and work groups helps school districts market educational concepts. Stakeholders who participate in such activities become savvy consumers of educational priorities and needs. School leaders should not consider school-community work groups as burdensome. Instead, such groups should be viewed as vehicles for school improvement and effective PR. Taken from this perspective, the school leader's role is to facilitate a group so that the group maintains a positive focus on a common goal. In designing groups, school leaders should keep in mind that a group will be effective only if each member perceives his/her association with the group as satisfying personal needs. Furthermore, leaders should consider diversity in group membership. The initial involvement of a diverse population whose members represent various interests creates a stronger foundation for organizational support of decisions or recommendations made by the group. The size of the group should also be considered. The larger the team, the more difficult it will be to maintain focus and facilitate communication. The task to be accomplished may affect the size of the group. Complex activities may require the involvement of greater numbers of people, and this large group may need to break into smaller subgroups to accomplish specific tasks.

After a group's initial formation, the leader should anticipate conflicts that may arise as the group enters the storming stage. It should be remembered that the variety of perspectives, knowledge, and experiences that individual members bring to the group serves to enhance productivity and improve the quality of desired outcomes, but it is inevitable that disagreements will arise due to these differences. A leader should prepare for this by seeking the assistance of all group members in setting ground rules that facilitate task completion. Ground rules should include agreement on attendance, promptness, participation, agendas, and group behavioral expectations. The explicit rules will facilitate the group's development of implicit norms, which characterizes a group's movement into the third stage.

The following are some implicit norms indicative of effective and productive group behavior:

- ◆ People are listened to and recognized.
- ◆ Members criticize ideas, but not individuals.
- ◆ Objectivity and honesty are valued by the team.

A leader can facilitate the development of positive norms, which promote a group's effectiveness, through modeling desired communication strategies and interpersonal behaviors. If team coordination and facilitation are delegated to group members, the leader should provide training and direction to these individuals.

With the parameters outlined above firmly established, the group should be ready to enter the performing stage. At this point, the group's task should be clarified and expected outcomes delineated. Questions to be considered at this stage might include these:

- ◆ What is the problem to be studied?
- ◆ What standards or criteria must be applied to the problem?
- ◆ What are the group's boundaries or limitations, especially related to time, money, and information to be provided?
- ◆ What is the authority of the group? Will the group make recommendations to administration, or will the group make final decisions that will be implemented? (Scholtes, 1988)

Not all groups work as well as expected. Often that is because the group is unable to move past the storming stage. It may also be related to the roles that individual group members choose. Roles are often a reflection of personality, the group task, and the level of commitment by an individual to the task at hand. Obviously, there are roles that facilitate group performance just as there are roles that hinder group productivity. A school administrator should foster the roles that assist with group output, while discouraging roles that are negative.

Following are some of the group's roles that the school administrator should support:

- ◆ Encourager—Praises and supports others
- ◆ Summarizer—Brings the group's ideas into focus
- ◆ Elaborator—Builds on the ideas of others
- ◆ Harmonizer—Mediates disagreements and seeks common ground
- ◆ Procedural Expert—Understands rules and policies of the organization
- ◆ Energizer—Motivates and moves the group forward

Roles to discourage include these:

- ◆ Blocker—Disagrees for the sake of disagreement
- ◆ Aggressor—Attacks group members, not their ideas
- ◆ Dominator—Tries to control and manipulate the group
- ◆ Withdrawer—Fails to participate and blames the group for this failure
- ◆ Recognition Seeker—Wants to talk of himself or herself and be the center of attention
- ◆ Special Interest Pleader—Has a personal agenda for the group

A leader can choose from many methods to facilitate the development of group roles that assist in the completion of group tasks. Obviously, one of the most important things school leaders must do is to be prepared for each and every meeting with the group. The strategy of using questions that keep the group's focus on productive behavior is perhaps one of the best approaches a school administrator can choose.

Questions can be asked in several different ways. They may be front-end loaded, where the individual's name is spoken first. They may be nebulous and not asked of any one individual. Also, they may be rear-end loaded, where the question is asked and then a person's name is called. Each approach to the question has both problems and strengths. Questions fall into several categories, but the following represent those most often used:

- ◆ Factual questions—Seek needed information
- ◆ Leading questions—Gather opinions and move people toward a particular conclusion

- ◆ Alternative questions—Most often elicit a yes or no response with follow-up questions as necessary
- ◆ Ambiguous questions—Can be interpreted in several ways and provoke critical thinking
- ◆ Provocative questions—Are designed to create an emotional response from the group

The types of questions used depend on both the situation and the particular need at a given time. Group focus, intensity, and productivity help determine the types of questions to be asked.

As one works with groups, conflict becomes inevitable. It certainly takes place at the storming stage of group development, but may also happen at the productive or performing stage. Although this chapter is not designed to discuss conflict resolution in detail, a brief mention of it is needed here. Conflict happens within all social systems and among all people. It is important for the administrator to be able to determine if the conflict is constructive or destructive. Constructive conflict offers an opportunity for group and system growth. It most often reflects differences in goals, methods, values, and group or organizational focus. Destructive conflict, on the other hand, is often the result of pettiness, jealousy, inordinate power struggles, and individual or group immaturity. Destructive conflict can destroy any group or social system. Conflict, in this setting, is analogous to system disequilibrium. The goal of vision development is to explore and reflect on the common values and beliefs that will serve to guide the organization toward its future.

As school administrators work with the multitude of social systems that compose their professional world, they must not allow conflict to destroy the school district's focus on its vision. If conflict is not successfully resolved or managed, the organization may cease to be productive. A school administrator needs to be able to listen, conceptualize, interpret, react or respond, and synthesize, among other skills, in order to end a conflict within the school setting. A sense of timing and a capacity to communicate effectively may be an administrator's best tools for resolving conflict.

In order to successfully carry out the goals and objectives of the school district or school site, the administrator must be able to work with a variety of individuals representing diverse beliefs and values. Much of this work takes place in groups. Therefore, knowledge of group developmental theories and how groups function is crucial. The ability to diagnose and successfully resolve conflict becomes an important tool in the school administrator's repertory. Group-related facilitation skills that ensure group and organizational productivity are vital to long-term success. Thus, an administrator's group leadership skills are needed assets for effective PR.

EVOLVING SYSTEMS: COMMUNITY DEVELOPMENT IN CYBERSPACE?

This chapter has presented PR in terms of understanding the dynamics of the school as a social-political system and in terms of building community among diverse stakeholders. Systems theories describe organizations as dynamic systems involving constant interactions among the formal and informal systems within the organization, as well as exchanges (feedback and input) between the organization and systems outside the organization.

Individuals and groups communicate through both formal structures, such as department- or grade-level meetings, and informal structures, such as conversations after school in the faculty workroom. In addition, a school organization receives information from the outside environment, as feedback or input, and produces output that is exported to the outside environment.

As new information technologies (specifically the Internet and World Wide Web) become commonplace, the lines of information access are increasing and becoming more complex. Building community in cyberspace is an aspect of PR that educational leaders must seriously consider. To what extent can cyberspace communication promote the development of school culture, where stakeholders share common values, beliefs, and ways of thinking? Computer-based information technologies, like other communication venues, can either promote or impede community building.

Advantages of computer-based information technology include greater access and interconnectivity among a variety of stakeholders instantaneously and without actually occupying the same space. Through Web pages, schools can provide information that is easier to update and less costly to disseminate than printed material. Schools can even offer interactive opportunities through electronic chat rooms, electronic surveys, threaded discussions, e-mail, and the like. On the other hand, the stakeholders most likely to utilize information-based technologies are those who are computer literate and who have ready access to the technology. It is probable that certain segments of a school's community will be left out of electronic communication, thus widening a gap that already exists between various subcultures, particularly those related to socioeconomic and age factors. However, Chance and Lee (2001) noted that change is ubiquitous in technology development, resulting in apparent spontaneous metamorphoses of systems. They further observed that technology allows for customization, a defining characteristic of the information age. Thus, there is a potential for information technology to play an increasing role in defining future educational cultures by allowing more involvement from a diverse array of stakeholders and by creating greater capacity to respond to individual needs of stakeholders.

Whereas information technology is a reality of modern life that is in effect transforming ways of conducting personal and professional business, it has yet to fully redefine our shared cultural experiences. The creation of a culture defined by the common construction of meaning and purpose requires full participation by and interaction among all stakeholders. Banks (2000) proposed that building community requires dialogue that promotes mutual disclosure, validation of others' viewpoints, and an authentic desire for shared endeavors. Thus, while new technologies offer invaluable vehicles for disseminating and receiving information, they cannot build community or develop a shared school-community vision to guide educational decision making. The fundamental building blocks of PR will continue to be personal communications that foster trust among stakeholders who share a common cultural bond surrounding educational issues.

SUMMARY

Systems theories provide a conceptual framework for understanding PR in educational settings. Public relations is a fundamental responsibility of education leadership. School administrators work in a highly complex system with a multitude of expectations from a variety of stakeholders. School leaders are accountable to a variety of publics and must balance the needs of various cultures within a pluralistic society. Thus, they must be system thinkers. An understanding of systems theories will aid school leaders in communicating, decision making, and problem solving for a complex organization.

While education leaders are public servants, they are also change agents. A clear, concise vision for the future, with well-established organizational goals and strategies to achieve them, is the most effective tool for organizational change and improvement. When everyone supports the direction of the organization, coalitions are built among a variety of stakeholders. A collaborative, productive work environment focused on the future is created when groups of people work together to achieve something greater than their individual needs and wants. The development of such a collaborative milieu among all the various internal and external publics requires education leaders who are able to facilitate various work groups and who exhibit an appreciation for the contributions of diverse members of the community. Ultimately, systems theories teach us that PR is a systematic process for bringing together various groups and institutions for a common goal.

QUESTIONS AND SUGGESTED ACTIVITIES

CASE STUDY

1. What external and internal factors (inputs) motivated the superintendent to pursue increased flexibility for the district and schools?
2. Assess the superintendent's strategy to involve school and community citizens in a comprehensive district planning and development effort. Compare his process with the shared community vision development process described in the chapter.
3. What risks did the superintendent take when he contacted Madison County's state senators and representative to discuss how the district could gain greater flexibility through deregulation and waivers?
4. What were the outcomes (outputs) of the district planning process?
5. Analyze the voting patterns (feedback) from teachers, staff, and community members at the May 21 meeting.
6. Discuss what teachers, administrators, staff, and community members learned from the comprehensive planning process and whether their respective assumptions about teaching, learning, and governance changed.
7. Based on an analysis of the votes taken at the regional community meetings, as well as the May 21 meeting, what strategies would you recommend the superintendent adopt to move the planning and development process forward to the next stage?
8. Discuss how the external and internal dynamics influenced the district and school reform initiatives. What happened (or did not happen) that interfered with change?
9. Discuss how steadfast support of the board of education may have positively influenced community support and continuation of the planning process.

CHAPTER

10. What are the major elements of general systems theory?
11. What are common characteristics across systems approaches developed in the social sciences and used in the field of educational administration?

12. How can these components contribute to understanding relations among school personnel and between school personnel and other stakeholders?
13. Why is educational vision important? Which is the more important element of visioning, process or product? Why?
14. Explain the relationship between facilitation of group processes and PR.

SUGGESTED READINGS

Argyris, C. (1982). *Reasoning, learning and action*. San Francisco: Jossey-Bass.

Björk, L., & Gurley, D. K. (2003). Superintendents as transformative leaders: Schools as learning communities and communities of learners. *Journal of Thought, 38*(4), 37–78.

Caine, R. N., & Caine, G. (1997). *Education on the edge of possibility*. Alexandria, VA: Association for Supervision and Curriculum Development.

Chance, E. W. (1992). *Visionary leadership in schools: Successful strategies for developing and implementing an educational vision*. Springfield, IL: Charles C. Thomas.

DuFour, R., & Eaker, R. (1998). *Professional learning communities at work: Best practices for enhancing student achievement*. Bloomington, IN: National Educational Service.

Easton, D. (1965). *A systems analysis of political life*. New York: Wiley.

Getzels, J., & Guba, E. (1957). Social behavior and the administrative process. *School Review, 65*, 423–441.

Griffiths, D., Hart, A., & Blair, B. (1991). Still another approach to administration: Chaos theory. *Educational Administration Quarterly, 27*(3), 430–451.

Leithwood, K., Jantzi, D., & Steinbach, R. (1998). Leadership and other conditions which foster organizational learning in schools. In K. Leithwood and K. S. Louis (Eds.), *Organizational learning in schools* (pp. 67–90). Lisse Netherlands: Swets & Zeitlinger.

Senge, P. (1990). *The fifth discipline: Mastering the five practices of the learning organization*. New York: Doubleday.

Shafritz, J., & Ott, J. (2001). *Classics of organizational theory* (5th ed.). Fort Worth, TX: Harcourt College Publishers.

Wheatley, M. (1996). *Leadership and the new science: Discovering order in a chaotic world*. San Francisco: Berrett-Koehler.

Wirt, F., & Kirst, M. (2001). *The political dynamics of American education* (2nd ed.). Berkeley, CA: McCutchan.

REFERENCES

Argyris, C. (1982). *Reasoning, learning and action*. San Francisco: Jossey-Bass.

Argyris, C., & Schön, D. A. (1978). *Organizational learning: A theory of action perspective*. Reading, MA: Addison Wesley.

Banks, S. P. (2000). *Multicultural public relations: A social-interpersonal approach* (2nd ed.). Ames: Iowa State University Press.

Bertalanffy, L., von. (1951). General systems theory: A new approach to unity of science. *Human Biology, 23*, 303–361.

Björk, L. (1993). Effective schools—effective superintendents: The emerging instructional leadership role. *Journal of School Leadership, 3*(3), 246–259.

Björk, L. (2001). The role of the central office in decentralization. In T. Kowalski (Ed.), *21st century challenges to educational administration* (pp. 286–319). Lanham, MD: Scarecrow Press.

Björk, L., & Keedy, J. (2001a). Changing social context of education in the United States: Social justice and the superintendency. *Journal of In-Service Education, 27*(3), 405–427.

Björk, L., & Keedy, J. (2001b). Politics and the superintendency in the USA: Restructuring in-service education. *Journal of In-Service Education, 27*(2), 275–302.

Björk, L., & Lindle, J. C. (2001). Superintendents and interest groups. *Educational Policy, 15*(1), 76–91.

Caine, R. N., & Caine, G. (1997). *Education on the edge of possibility.* Alexandria, VA: Association for Supervision and Curriculum Development.

Campbell, R., Flemming, T., Newell, L., & Bennion, J. (1987). *A history of thought and practice in educational administration.* New York: Teachers College Press.

Carter, G. R., & Cunningham, W. G. (1997). *The American school superintendent: Leading in an age of pressure.* San Francisco: Jossey-Bass.

Chance, E. W. (1992). *Visionary leadership in schools: Successful strategies for developing and implementing an educational vision.* Springfield, IL: Charles C. Thomas.

Chance, P. L., & Lee, K. (2001). Exploring technology, change, and chaos theory: Moving educational leadership preparation programs into the new millennium. In T. J. Kowalski (Ed.), *21st century challenges for school administrators* (pp. 189–202). Lanham, MD: Scarecrow Press.

Collins, J. C., & Porras, J. I. (1994). *Built to last: Successful habits of visionary companies.* New York: Harper & Row.

DuFour, R., & Eaker, R. (1998). *Professional learning communities at work: Best practices for enhancing student achievement.* Bloomington, IN: National Educational Service.

Easton, D. (1965). *A systems analysis of political life.* New York: Wiley.

Elmore, R. (2000). *Building a new structure for school leadership.* Washington, DC: Albert Shaker Institute.

Firestone, W., & Louis, K. (1999). School cultures. In J. Murphy & K. Louis (Eds.), *Handbook of research on educational administration* (2nd ed., pp. 297–336). San Francisco: Jossey-Bass.

Follett, M. P. (1940). *Dynamic administration: The collected papers of Mary Parker Follett* (H. C. Metcalf & L. Urwick, Eds.). New York: Harper & Brothers.

Getzels, J., & Guba, E. (1957). Social behavior and the administrative process. *School Review, 65,* 423–441.

Gleick, J. (1987). *Chaos: Making a new science.* New York: Penguin.

Griffiths, D., Hart, A., & Blair, B. (1991). Still another approach to administration: Chaos theory. *Educational Administration Quarterly, 27*(3), 430–451.

Hayles, N. (1990). *Chaos bound: Orderly disorder in contemporary literature and science.* Ithaca, NY: Cornell University Press.

Hickman, C. P., & Silva, M. (1984). *Creating excellence: Managing corporate culture, strategy and change in a new age.* New York: New American Library.

Hoy, W., & Miskel, C. (2001). *Educational administration: Theory, research and practice* (6th ed.). New York: McGraw-Hill.

Katz, D., & Kahn, R. (1966). *The social psychology of organizations.* New York: Wiley.

Leithwood, K., Jantzi, D., & Steinbach, R. (1998). Leadership and other conditions which foster organizational learning in schools. In K. Leithwood & K. S. Louis (Eds.), *Organizational learning in schools* (pp. 67–90). Lisse, Netherlands: Swets & Zeitlinger.

Lorenz, E. (1963). Deterministic non-periodic flow. *Journal of Atmospheric Sciences, 20,* 16–19.

Louis, K., & Kruse, S. (1998). Creating community in reform: Images of organizational learning in inner-city schools. In K. Leithwood & K. S. Louis (Eds.), *Organizational learning in schools* (pp. 17–45). Lisse, Netherlands: Swets & Zeitlinger.

Maeroff, G. I. (1993). Building teams to rebuild schools. *Phi Delta Kappan, 74*(7), 512–519.

Manasse, A. L. (1985). Vision and leadership: Paying attention to intention. *Peabody Journal of Education, 63*(1), 150–173.

Mandelbrott, B. (1983). *Fractal geometry of nature.* New York: Freeman.

Mayo, E. (1933). *The human problems of an industrial civilization.* New York: Viking.

Nanus, B. (1992). *Visionary leadership.* San Francisco: Jossey-Bass.

Ogawa, R. T., Crowson, R. L., & Goldring, E. B. (1999). Enduring dilemmas of school organization. In J. Murphy & K. S. Louis (Eds.), *The handbook of research on educational administration* (2nd ed., pp. 277–295). San Francisco: Jossey-Bass.

Owens, R. G. (1995). *Organizational behavior in education* (5th ed.). Boston: Allyn & Bacon.

Parsons, T. (1967). *Sociological theory and modern society.* New York: Free Press.

Prigogine, I., & Stengers, I. (1984). *Order out of chaos: Man's new dialogue with nature.* New York: Bantum.

Public Relations Society of America. (2002). *About public relations.* Retrieved June 25, 2002, from http://www.prsa.org/_Resources/Profession/index.asp?ident=prof1.

Reyes, P., Wagstaff, L., & Fusarelli, L. (1999). Delta forces: The changing fabric of American society and education. In J. Murphy & K. S. Louis (Eds.), *The handbook of research on educational administration* (2nd ed., pp. 183–201). San Francisco: Jossey-Bass.

Roethlisberger, F., & Dickson, W. (1939). *Management and the worker.* Cambridge: Harvard University Press.

Rowan, B., & Miskel, C. (1999). Institutional theory and the study of educational organizations. In J. Murphy & K. S. Louis (Eds.), *The handbook of research on educational administration* (2nd ed., pp. 359–383). San Francisco: Jossey-Bass.

Rutherford, W. L. (1985). School principals as effective leaders. *Phi Delta Kappan, 67*(1), 31–34.

Scholtes, P. R. (1988). *The team handbook: How to use teams to improve quality.* Madison, WI: Joiner Associates.

Senge, P. (1990). *The fifth discipline: Mastering the five practices of the learning organization.* New York: Doubleday.

Sergiovanni, T. J. (1992). *Moral leadership: Getting to the heart of school improvement.* San Francisco: Jossey-Bass.

Sergiovanni, T. J. (1996). *Leadership for the schoolhouse: How is it different? Why is it important?* San Francisco: Jossey-Bass.

Shafritz, J., & Ott, J. (2001). *Classics of organizational theory* (5th ed.). Fort Worth, TX: Harcourt College Publishers.

Shieve, L. T., & Shoenheit, M. B. (1987). Vision and the work of educational leaders. In L. T. Shieve & M. B. Shoenhiet (Eds.), *Leadership: Examining the elusive* (pp. 93–104). Washington, DC: Association for Supervision and Curriculum Development.

Spillane, J., Halverson, P., & Diamond, J. (1999). *Distributed leadership: Toward a theory of school leadership practice.* Paper presented at the annual meeting of the American Educational Research Association, Montreal.

Starratt, R. (1996). *Transforming educational administration: Meaning, community, and excellence.* New York: McGraw-Hill.

Thompson, J. (1967). *Organizations in action.* New York: McGraw-Hill.

Tuckman, B. W., & Jensen, M. A. C. (1977). Stages of small group development revisited. *Groups & Organizational Studies, 2*(4), 419–427.

Tyack, D. B., & Hansot, E. (1982). *Managers of virtue: Public school leadership in America.* New York: Basic Books.

Weick, K. (1976). Educational organizations as loosely coupled systems. *Administrative Science Quarterly, 21,* 1–19.

Wheatley, M. (1996). *Leadership and the new science: Discovering order in a chaotic world.* San Francisco: Berrett-Koehler.

Wiener, N. (1948). *Cybernetics.* Cambridge, MA: Technology Press.

Wirt, F., & Kirst, M. (1982). *The politics of education: Schools in conflict.* Berkeley, CA: McCutchan.

Wirt, F., & Kirst, M. (2001). *The political dynamics of American education* (2nd ed.). Berkeley, CA: McCutchan.

Zmuda, A., Kuklis, R., & Kline, R. (2004). *Transforming schools: Creating a culture of continuous improvement.* Alexandria, VA: Association for Supervision and Curriculum Development.

CHAPTER

Public Relations in a Communication Context

Angela Spaulding
Mary John O'Hair

CASE STUDY: GREENHILL SCHOOL DISTRICT

A Context of Ineffective Communication and Conflict

The Greenhill School District is a large, inner-city district located in what is known as the "slums" of a large industrial city. As required by a new state mandate, the Greenhill School District had initiated a competency-testing program for graduating seniors. According to the mandate, students are required to score in the 70th percentile on the test in order to participate in graduation ceremonies and to receive their certificate of graduation. Upon completion of the competency tests at Greenhill High School, it was discovered that one-fourth of the seniors had failed to reach the minimum passing percentile. Parents of the failing students were notified by letter and were informed that their child would need to attend summer school for remedial instruction. Following summer school, the students would be given an opportunity to retake the competency test.

Two days following the notification of test results, the school was inundated with complaint calls from parents whose students had failed the test. Finally, the school's administrative staff, who rarely heard from parents in the past, declined to take calls and sent home a memo restating the school's position: Students who failed the competency test would not be graduating,[1] regardless of the number of calls made to complain.

Memos were the usual way of communicating with parents of the Greenhill School District, and memos had earlier been sent home with students to explain the competency test. Interpersonal contact between parents and school staff was extremely rare. Parents never came to the school and were never invited unless it was to attend a sporting event. According to the administrative staff, it was useless to try to involve parents in school events and issues because parents lacked the knowledge to make useful contributions, were too busy just trying to keep food on the table and their children off the streets, and/or were indifferent and uncaring as to what went on at school.

Four days after the test results had been mailed, the superintendent of the Greenhill School District received a call from B. J. Halihan, attorney at law. Halihan stated that he represented a newly formed parent group called "Parents for Fair Educational Opportunities." According to Halihan, the parents who had formed this group had students at Greenhill High School who had failed the graduation competency test, but a large number of other parents who were sympathetic to the cause had also joined with the group. The parent group was attempting legal action against the district for educational negligence. In addition, parents were making an issue of the lack of communication from the school staff concerning the academic welfare of their children. Most parents stated that they had been unaware of the new competency test requirement.

A preliminary meeting was set up between the parent group and the school's administrative staff. In attendance was a representative from the state educational agency.

---

[1] The authors thank Professor Randy S. Averso, Department of Educational Leadership and Policy Studies at the University of Oklahoma, for his contributions to the revisions of this chapter.

During the meeting, Halihan, as lawyer for the parent group, quizzed the school's administrative staff on the accuracy and appropriateness of the competency test and the effectiveness of the district's teachers. He also criticized school communications, stating that parents were not made aware of the competency test until two days prior to the testing. Furthermore, according to Halihan, if memos were indeed sent out, the memos had not made it home to parents. He further criticized the school for not providing the type of assistance that students needed in order to pass the test. In his argument, Halihan was quick to point out that many of the students who had failed the graduation competency test had successfully passed all of their classes throughout the school year. He questioned the type of instruction provided by teachers, the type of curriculum used by the district, and the lack of, or shortage of, resource support provided by the school. In particular, Halihan mentioned the lack of equipment in the science and math labs; the shortage of desks, textbooks, and classroom space; poor lighting in the majority of classrooms; leaking roofs; and the outdated library.

The administrative staff was unprepared to deal with the accusations of the parent group. No record of the original memo sent to parents explaining the graduation competency test could be found. In the end, the school requested and was granted permission from the state educational agency to provide the failing students with tutorial assistance for three weeks in order to prepare the students to retake the test before the graduation deadline. Students who still did not pass the test would have to take a summer school session before taking the test again. Although not completely satisfied, the parent group agreed with the decision.

Whereas the meeting failed to provide evidence of educational negligence, the state agency did feel that the high school had serious problems that needed immediate attention. The state agency determined that in order to maintain its accreditation, the school had to develop and implement a plan that addressed all of the issues that the parent group had identified. The plan was to be developed through the use of professional learning communities with parental and community input. The agency further recommended a communication audit to determine the types, amounts, and implications of communication at Greenhill. It was the feeling of the agency that Greenhill lacked appropriate communication channels. According to the state agency, this lack of communication had resulted in a poisoned relationship between the school personnel and parents.

As noted in the case study above, professional learning communities are being recognized as a preferred method for resolving educational problems. Educational research continues to document the power of the professional learning community as a model for school improvement, and researchers are becoming increasingly specific when identifying the conditions necessary for professional learning communities to maximize successful teaching and learning for today's students (Eaker, DuFour, & DuFour, 2002; Hord, 1997; Huffman & Hipp, 2003; O'Hair, Reitzug, et al., 2005). Consistent with organizational theory, learning inevitably leads to change (Fullan, 2003; Lambert, 2003), and how school leaders manage learning and change is largely predicated on communication skills. This chapter provides a two-pronged approach to understanding the role of communication in public relations (PR). The first prong seeks to establish an understanding of the professional learning community conditions associated with high-achieving schools and the role of skillful communication in advancing these conditions. The second prong utilizes communication theory to provide a foundation for successful school communication, which consists of three core communication competencies:

Competency 1: Listening effectively

Competency 2: Defining and decoding nonverbal communication

Competency 3: Understanding and managing conflict

Operating from the assumption that schools seek to be high-achieving, it is necessary to clarify both the latest research on conditions associated with high-achieving schools and the vital role of skillful communication by school leaders in advancing these conditions. Of particular relevance is the increasing evidence of the positive effect of the professional learning community on student achievement (Atkinson, 2005; Newmann & Wehlage, 1995; Williams, 2005). The professional learning community model represents a school organizational shift from isolated classrooms and top-down decision making toward a shared vision developed and sustained through collaborative learning environments, the broad-based participation of diverse school stakeholders, and research-based decision making.

The current research on effective school visioning advocates moving from a leader-developed school vision that is sold to school stakeholders to a vision in which the leader facilitates identifying the values, beliefs, and individual visions of school stakeholders and merging them into an overarching shared vision for high achievement (Averso, 2003; Bernhardt, 2002; Tichy & Devanna, 1986; Yukl, 2002). In a professional learning community, participation in the process of developing a shared vision is broad-based. As American society moves into a highly technological and informational age, helping educators communicate to diverse groups of students and their parents becomes increasingly important. A school that communicates effectively will be able to establish effective intervention and PR programs that result in precrisis management. One of the most important lessons we can learn about American society is the fact that there is no "culture of one." Over the past decade, demographic changes have greatly affected notions of who is "majority" and who is "minority." Analyzing 2000 Census data, Brewer and Suchan (2001) found that diversity increased in all states in the country and that in parts of some states, it increased as much as 34%. Additionally, White European Americans are no longer a clear majority of the population, revealing the need for educators to respond commensurately in their PR and communications with their diverse communities.

Ours is a heterogeneous society, infused with many diverse cultures, each with its own collection of experiences, beliefs, values, attitudes, and notions of what is important. Many students live in cultural environments that are quite different from those of the school and the mainstream community. Only by reaching across the lines of ethnicity and multicultural differences can school systems hope to reach all the at-risk and troubled students. One way to accomplish this is through an acculturation process involving the successful implementation of a cultural awareness program that is capable of reaching across the communication barriers that currently exist in our schools and communities. "Knowledge entails developing a non-stereotyping, flexible understanding of cultural, social, and family dynamics of diverse groups, along with a comprehension of the critical sociopolitical, historical, and economic contexts in which people from diverse multicultural groups are embedded" (Sanchez, 1995).

School leaders commit to the use of inquiry and discourse as a way for the stakeholders to unpack the available research and data and to translate it into meaningful goals and objectives aligned to the shared vision (McLeod, 2004; O'Hair, McLaughlin, & Reitzug, 2000). A well-constructed vision can be valuable in guiding the inevitable change that occurs as educators incorporate new learning into their practices (Lambert, 2003; Yukl, 2002). The meaningful participation of the school community in defining the direction of the school also results in an enhanced culture of collective responsibility for all of the students. In increasingly diverse cultures, broadly inclusive participation can yield important gains in trust and typically resultant increases in student learning through parental support in the learning process (Henderson & Mapp, 2002; Putnam, 2000). The synergy generated through broad-based participation in creating a school's shared vision would diminish if it stopped there. In fact, professional learning communities culturally embed such participation. However, for the participation to be skillful, there must be an intentional effort on the part of the school leader(s) to provide professional development opportunities aimed at developing skillfulness. The combination of broad-based and skillful participation has been associated with high student achievement and is generally referred to as "building capacity" (Lambert, 1998). Developing knowledge and skills is not simply about acquiring existing skills and knowledge, but also about teachers and principals reflecting critically on their practice and fashioning new knowledge and beliefs about content, pedagogy, and learners (Darling-Hammond & McLaughlin, 1995).

The historical tradition of the one-room schoolhouse led by a teacher who then played a powerful, autonomous role as far as making decisions about teaching and learning appears even today in the isolated physical structure of schools. "The one-room schoolhouse is repeated every few yards, all the way down the hall" (Glickman, 1993, p. 19). Teachers continue to enter their classrooms, close their doors, and operate autonomously with the students in their classrooms. The lack of professional dialogue remains a significant impediment to the successful development of strategies to improve schools and make progress toward a shared school vision. This condition is, in part, due to the history of teachers having little to no say in decisions about teaching and learning across classrooms, grade levels, and departments. This reality was particularly evident in the era of legislative reforms in education seen in the 1980s. Schools were fraught with a barrage of top-down decisions by people external to classrooms and schools, from central office personnel to politicians (Darling-Hammond & Snyder, 1992). As schools moved into the 1990s, educators sought to base decisions about teaching and learning on school data. Unfortunately, traditional structures still continue to experience difficulty in enabling access to school information and data, often exacerbated by little or poor–quality access to technology and communication methods that would facilitate the analysis of such data and subsequent discourse about the implications of what the data reveal. The task of school leaders is to creatively impede the perpetuation of these traditions of isolation.

School leaders in restructured schools view communication skills as the skills most needed for success as schools move from a traditional, isolated stance to one fostering shared vision and collegiality (Fullan, 1991; O'Hair & Reitzug, 1997). Thurston, Clift, and

TABLE 6–1

Building Capacity Through Professional Development

Form of Professional Development	Examples
Direct instruction	Skill demonstration; modeling; simulated skill practice.
Job-embedded learning	Inquiry; discussion; evaluation; consultation; collaboration; problem solving. These are typically empowered through teachers sharing leadership roles (for example, teacher leader, peer coach, teacher researcher), structures (for example, problem-solving groups, decision-making teams, common planning periods, self-contained teams), and tasks (for example, leading an in-house workshop, journal writing, collaborative case analysis, grant writing, curriculum and assessment writing).
Coaching and mentoring	Coaching and mentoring involve reflecting, sharing, planning, and working together to develop mutual support between coach or mentor and learner in order to increase student achievement.
Networking	Loosely organized collection of educators from different schools who interact regularly to discuss and share practices around a particular focus or philosophy of teaching (for example, new technology standards, authentic instruction). They interact via in-person sharing meetings, cross-school or cross-classroom visitations, professional institutes, critical friends groups, and electronic forms of communication.

Schacht (1993), emphasizing the development of an educator's abilities to reflect and communicate, stated that "[c]ommunication will be crucial in establishing a school-wide commitment to a mission and in sharing the decision-making process" (p. 262). Table 6–1 summarizes how building capacity involves crafting opportunities and employing strategies to reduce isolation and foster generative learning, specifically through professional development that balances direct instruction, job-embedded learning, coaching/mentoring, and networking (O'Hair, Reitzug, et al., 2005).

It is important to note the ever-increasing role of technology in schools—and in professional learning communities specifically. It becomes increasingly obvious that skillful communication is at the heart of the various conditions of a professional learning community. Equally obvious is the amount of time required to support the roles, structures, and tasks. In a professional learning community, technology is viewed as one important tool that can conserve time and effort when collaborating, examining data, and generating learning opportunities. As schools continue to make remarkable advances in their technology connectedness, such communication aids as e-mail, graphic organizers of knowledge and information, videoconferencing technologies, blogs, portable technology devices, and servers that store and make information accessible to stakeholders are becoming increasingly available. Internet connectivity is a significant vehicle for advancing communication and participation options that build skillfulness aimed at improved student achievement. Studies are confirming that technology can be an effective tool for collaboration and for the development of professional learning communities, which increase student achievement (Atkinson, 2005).

As we look to the future, researchers envision that technology will greatly enhance collaborative learning and that teaching and research will be represented by network learning communities (Carroll, 2001). Carroll (2001) posits that this new environment will support three modes of learning: knowledge transmission, knowledge adaptation, and knowledge generation. Knowledge transmission, the mode that occurs in most schools today, basically supports the transmission of skills and knowledge from the old to the young. Knowledge adaptation occurs when new developments and circumstances necessitate a modification in existing knowledge, and this modification disrupts the traditional knowledge transmission mode of learning. The knowledge generation mode is rooted in the concept of intergenerational collaboration (everyone represents an active learner and contributor) to construct new knowledge. Technology will enable this mode to flourish, removing the barriers of place and transforming stakeholder roles, particularly those of teacher and student. Carroll suggests that teachers (he calls them "expert learners") will collaboratively develop differentiated learning plans *with* each student and orchestrate learning activities within the multitude of network sources made possible through technology. It would be a network of learning nodes, where each node represents a resource site to meet the goals of the plan. The node is not bound to either the traditional physical school classroom or the immediate community of teachers, but could be anyone at any place in the world who has the ability to advance the skill set needed by a learner. It becomes obvious that organizing and managing collaboration will be key among educators in a networked learning community.

The professional learning community model, represented by a shared vision developed and sustained through collaborative learning environments, broad-based participation of diverse school stakeholders, and research-based decision making, is clearly predicated on the communication skills of school leaders. Examining standards of school leadership, such as those of the Educational Leadership Constituent Council (ELCC), we see the critical role of communication (Wilmore, 2002). Embedded in the identified skills of a successful school leader is an ability to promote, articulate, steward, assess, and gain community support for the components of a high-achieving school. The professional learning community model is validated in the ELCC standards of school leadership. School leaders must be able to successfully manage school improvement through inclusive collaboration marked by broad-based, skillful sharing of leadership within the school community. They must also be committed to the use of research and quality professional development to drive best practices.

Recognizing the inevitable and crucial role of effective communications in successfully leading schools, we must examine the specific competencies that comprise effective communication. The role of the school leader includes an ability to justly and intentionally influence the use of research-based practices of high-achieving schools. In this quest, the leader will be in the position to build accurate knowledge and skills in the school community about what those practices are and how best to implement them. Unfortunately, communication skills are an often neglected part of an educator's formal and informal education. Generally, when one thinks of communication skills, the first image that comes to mind is that of speaking. Unless accused of poor listening or of being unobservant, educators tend to downplay the importance of listening and nonverbal communication. However, when a crisis exists, listening and observation skills may be more important than verbal skills, especially when an educator is trying to bridge the cultural gaps in any given classroom. "Although there has been a greater recognition of the need for training in multicultural competence across professions, many programs still conceptualize this training as more of an 'add-on'; that is, programs require only one or two courses for their particular professional specialty" (Sanchez, 1995).

Although speaking and writing can always improve, the communication skills needing the greatest attention from school principals include sharing information, seeking feedback, listening, exhibiting nonverbal awareness, and resolving conflict (McNulty & O'Hair, 1998). A study of 17 New York educators found the following communication skills to be vital for effective school change: reducing conflict, enhancing collaboration in interpersonal and group situations, and gathering feedback (Miles, 1993). Without adequately developed communication skills, school life and school PR are simply incomplete and ineffective. Operating in the context of a learning community, exchanges of thoughts and ideas are expected and encouraged. Understanding the skills needed to successfully benefit from such collaboration requires specific communication skills. In particular, as noted above, we will examine

Competency 1: Listening effectively

Competency 2: Defining and decoding nonverbal communication

Competency 3: Understanding and managing conflict

Knowledge of these skills will greatly advance the school leader's success in realizing a vision of a high-achieving school.

COMPETENCY 1: LISTENING EFFECTIVELY

Research studies have shown that about 75% of the interactions in a school building are one-on-one meetings (Dolan, 1996). These meetings involve students, faculty, parents, secretaries, and principals in classrooms, in hallways, during lunch, during class changes, and before and after school. To avoid miscommunication, a great deal of effort must be devoted to listening. In order to improve listening skills, one must first understand the barriers that impede the ability to listen.

Identifying Barriers to Effective Listening

What barriers affect the ability to listen? Golen (1990) identified a number of common listening barriers; they are presented in test form in Table 6–2.

Every "yes" answer indicates a barrier to listening abilities. Educators should take a serious inventory of their listening skills; otherwise, improvement is not possible.

Improving Listening Skills

As discussed earlier, successful school communication requires an understanding of the importance of effective listening and an understanding of the barriers to effective listening.

TABLE 6–2
Top-Ranked Barriers to Effective Listening

Listening Barrier	Yes	No
Do you listen primarily for details or facts?		
Do you become distracted by peripheral noises like those from office equipment, telephones, or other conversations?		
Do you daydream or become preoccupied with something else?		
Do you think of another topic or follow some thought prompted by what the speaker has said?		
Do you find that you have no interest in the speaker's subject?		
Do you concentrate on the speaker's mannerisms or delivery rather than on the message?		
Do you become impatient with the speaker?		
Do you disagree or argue outwardly or inwardly with the speaker?		
Do you try to outline everything mentally?		
Do you fake attention to the speaker?		
Do you jump to conclusions before the speaker has finished?		
Do you become emotional or excited when the speaker's views differ from yours?		
Do you cease to listen if the subject is complex or difficult?		
Do you allow your biases and prejudices to interfere with your thinking while listening?		
Do you pay attention only to the speaker's words, rather than to the speaker's feelings?		
Do you avoid eye contact while listening?		
Do you fail to put yourself in the speaker's shoes or to empathize?		
Do you refuse to relate to and benefit from the speaker's ideas?		
Do you refuse to give feedback?		

Listening Barrier	Yes	No
Do you refuse to paraphrase to clarify a point?		
Do you overreact to certain language, such as slang or profanity?		
Do you not listen because it takes too much time?		
Do you not read the speaker's nonverbal cues?		
	Total =	Total =

Source: Golen, 1990, 25–36. Copyright 1990 by S. Golen. Adapted with permission.

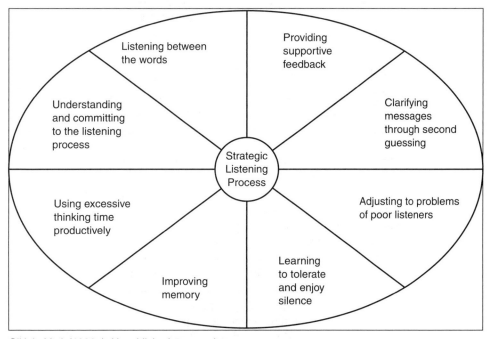

O'Hair, M. J. (1998a), Unpublished manuscript.

FIGURE 6–1
The Strategic Listening Process (Source: O'Hair, 1998a.)

Figure 6–1, a visual image of a listening process referred to as the strategic listening process, can be used to improve listening skills. Key components of this process are shown.

Understanding and Committing to the Listening Process

"Listening" comprises three elements: what is heard, what is understood, and what is remembered. Listening includes hearing or receiving aural stimuli from the environment;

connecting or processing the stimuli into meaningful messages; and storing messages for immediate or delayed retrieval. Listening occurs at different levels, depending on the message. For example, a simple request, such as "close the door" or "turn off the lights," generally requires basic processing and rarely the more complex task of reflective thinking. However, reflective listening requires the listener to understand the sender's personality, culture, and environment. As schools become increasingly diverse, reflective listening becomes more difficult and more necessary. Although the teaching force remains predominately white and female (91.8%), the student population is becoming more diverse in terms of race, class, language, and gender-role socialization patterns. By 2040, less than 50% of school-age children will be white (O'Hair, Friedrich, & Dixon, 2005).

Some listeners tune out during a meeting because of disagreement with the messages being communicated. However, listening, even under protest, is informative and crucial to school success. New ideas and concepts may be sparked at any given time, even under protest. Successful educators are committed to the listening process and rarely tune out conversations.

Listening Between the Words

Effective listening requires more than hearing words. In his 1988 campaign, President George Bush seized on the slogan: "Read my lips. No new taxes." The impact of the message was supported by his paralanguage or the *way* he said those six words. Later, when he broke his promise, this statement caused Bush and his advisers much embarrassment. Perhaps his critics and voters in general would not have remembered so vividly the original message if his paralanguage had not been so compelling.

Effective listeners must do more than merely read lips—or hear words. Effective listeners listen for deeper meanings. Listeners can miss 100% of the "feeling content" of spoken messages by not listening *between* and *beyond* the words. To understand deeper meanings in oral communication, educators must listen for the paralanguage elements of speech. Paralanguage refers to *how* something is said, rather than to *what* is said. More specifically, paralanguage involves aspects of verbal communication that are unrelated to the words used. For example, after a teacher has worked for weeks on a PTA program, her principal stops by her classroom and congratulates her on a job well done. However, the teacher notes that the principal's voice lacks enthusiasm and excitement, and she begins to question the principal's sincerity; she wonders what her principal really thought about the PTA program. Tone and loudness are two of the more obvious elements of paralanguage, but there are others that are more difficult to discern.

Improving Memory

Memory is crucial to the listening process because memory increases listening comprehension. After examining the purely informational level of listening, the majority of oral communication is ignored, misunderstood, or quickly forgotten. It makes little sense to hear, attend to, comprehend, and then fail to remember oral communication.

Memory is often thought of as "storage." The memory can store great amounts of information and is often examined through the temporal classifications of short- and long-term memory. Short-term memory (STM) involves pattern recognition by transfer from sensory storage to the form of memory described by memory researchers as "attention." Unfortunately, STM consists of a very brief unit of information, usually about 15 seconds, unless the unit is rehearsed, which allows for an extension of up to 60 seconds. The term *memory* commonly refers to long-term memory. However, long-term memory is rarely activated until at least 60 seconds after the presentation of a stimulus. Actual entry into long-term memory may depend on both rehearsal and organizational schemes. In other words, long-term memory requires a linkage between the new stimulus and the old information previously stored in memory. Storing and retrieving information that is unconnected and meaningless are extremely difficult.

Teaching individuals to develop visual images in listening situations results in a significant increase in comprehension and memory for both children and adults. The visual images produced while listening to a conference speaker or while watching a video can provide the framework for organizing and remembering key information.

Providing Supportive Feedback

Conversation with individuals who do not provide feedback—that is, who do not nod their is head or utter "uh-huhs"—is extremely uncomfortable. Under normal conversational conditions, it is extremely difficult to carry on a conversation with someone who is unresponsive. Without feedback, the sender does not know if the receiver is in agreement or disagreement with the message, is bored and ready to terminate the conversation, or is daydreaming and not properly hearing the message. Feedback is essential for strategic communication to occur.

Good listeners provide appropriate supportive feedback by

- Demonstrating interest in what the speaker says,
- Maintaining appropriate eye contact,
- Smiling and showing animation,
- Nodding occasionally in agreement,
- Leaning toward the speaker to demonstrate an attitude of interest and confidentiality,
- Using verbal reinforcers like "I see" and "yes,"
- Phrasing interpretations of the speaker's comments to verify understanding, and
- Consciously timing their verbal and nonverbal feedback to assist rather than hinder the speaker.

If listening is gaining meaning from situations involving the spoken word, then feedback is crucial in gaining meaning. Feedback helps the continuity of conversations, which in turn provides verbal and nonverbal cues that help inform the individual and guide him or her to an understanding of others' motivations, fears, and goals. Without feedback, listeners are deprived of this fundamental information.

Clarifying Messages Through Second-Guessing

It is common, while strategically listening, to be skeptical of the initial interpretation of the message received from a speaker. This skepticism is referred to as "second-guessing," or seeking the "truth" in a message. The theory of second-guessing expands the role of cognition in communication to help clarify the hearer's understanding of the truth behind the message. Second-guessing is a mental process through which listeners attempt to make better sense of what they believe to be a "biased" message. By reviewing and analyzing additional information pertinent to the original biased message, listeners gain a clearer picture of the true state of affairs, rather than a slanted and prejudiced view from only the sender of the message (Hewes & Graham, 1989).

Second-guessing is used only when a perceived need for accuracy in information exists. For example, a principal's superintendent tells him that the shared governance report that he has worked on for the last several weeks is "interesting and informative." The principal is not sure what the superintendent means by "interesting and informative." Does she mean literally "interesting and informative," or does she mean "not exactly what I wanted, but I know that you worked hard"? Rather than taking the comment at face value, the principal may have reason to doubt the message. At this point, the principal may decide that his superintendent's feelings about the project are not important, and he really does not need complete accuracy of the message; thus, he accepts the initial interpretation and stops analyzing the message further. However, if message accuracy is important to him, he might begin to second-guess. After second-guessing, he might request clarification from his superintendent to determine the superintendent's true feelings.

Second-guessing as a listening strategy can help redefine and clarify messages and can guide the listener to respond appropriately. The second-guessing process involves exploring alternative interpretations, prioritizing interpretations, and selecting the best interpretation. The reinterpretations are assumed to be closer to the truth than the initial face-value interpretation of the message, though it is still possible that upon reflection in the reinterpretation phase, an individual will return to the original interpretation.

Using Excess Thinking Time Productively

Most people do not realize the amount of excess thinking time that is available during listening. Speech speed is much slower than thought speed (approximately 90 to 200 words per minute versus 1,000 to 1,500 words per minute). The arduous speaker uses only a fraction of the listener's thought capacity. Thus, listeners have a great amount of "free time" while listening. The difference between good and poor listeners is that good listeners use excess thinking time to concentrate on the message, while poor listeners indulge in negative listening behaviors such as daydreaming. Few individuals can daydream without losing a great part of the speaker's message.

Effective listeners use excess thinking time to

- ◆ Outline the speaker's message mentally,
- ◆ Identify the speaker's purpose and determine how the speaker's points support that purpose,
- ◆ Organize listening by constantly summarizing previous points and identifying main points with key words or phrases,
- ◆ Evaluate the soundness of the speaker's logic,
- ◆ Paraphrase,
- ◆ Verify and integrate information presented with past knowledge and experience,

♦ Maintain eye contact in order to observe and interpret the speaker's nonverbal signals,

♦ Formulate questions to ask at appropriate moments in order to verify the accuracy of their understanding, and

♦ Provide encouraging verbal and nonverbal feedback.

Without constantly processing information received, listeners may experience daydreaming.

Learning to Tolerate and Enjoy Silence

How do you feel about silence? If there is a lull in conversation, do you immediately begin talking to fill the void? Unfortunately, many people feel uncomfortable with silence. Silence provides opportunity to reflect. It brings people face to face with themselves and often forces them to deal with issues they might otherwise avoid. Silence is essential to self-communication, which is vital to personal growth. Consider the following personal suggestions for learning to tolerate and even enjoy silence: (a) turn off the car stereo when driving to and from work; (b) plan to spend some quiet time at home, free from television, radio, or computer distractions; (c) when in conversation, encourage others to fully develop their ideas; (d) plan to have a silent day, in which reflecting and listening replace talking; and (e) think of someone whose words were previously ignored and make special time to "lend them an ear." Learning to tolerate and enjoy silence is an essential step in preparing for meaningful communication.

Adjusting to Poor Listeners

Poor listeners have a habit of interrupting speakers. To prevent this, verbally request that all interruptions or comments be held until the speaker has completed his or her communication. Interruptions prevent speakers from thoroughly developing and explaining key points and ideas. If interruptions occur, the speaker should return to the topic to adequately complete the discussion. Repetition is advantageous when communicating with poor listeners.

COMPETENCY 2: DEFINING AND DECODING NONVERBAL COMMUNICATION

Improving listening behavior is a difficult and time-consuming task. Careful attention to overcoming listening barriers and eliminating the silent enemy, a negative attitude toward listening, helps educators improve communication within and outside their school context. However, improving listening behavior alone will not provide educators with the communication competence required to develop and lead high-achieving learning communities. Understanding the nonverbal message is equally important in that task.

Nonverbal communication involves those behaviors that convey meaning without the use of language—that is, any behaviors that do not use words. The manner in which principals use their voices, faces, and bodies–and even how they arrange their offices—communicates meaning to their publics. Nonverbal behaviors can even unintentionally convey information. For example, feelings of dislike or disapproval may be expressed although there is no conscious attempt to do so.

As the school community becomes increasingly diverse, understanding nonverbal communication becomes vital for educators. Everything from lifestyles to products to technologies to the media is becoming more heterogeneous. This increased diversity produces complexity, which in turn means that schools need more and more data and know-how to function effectively. Awareness of nonverbal communication can help educators access essential information.

The verbal communication process is, by and large, controllable and intentional, but nonverbal behavior is often difficult to manage and control. Communication scholars consider nonverbal communication to be a double-edged sword (O'Hair, Friedrich, & Dixon, 2005). If used effectively, it can enhance one's ability to communicate with others. It can also damage one's ability to act constructively.

This section of the chapter examines nonverbal communication research over the past 30 years and focuses on those areas that are relevant to improving public relations through effective school communication. The major functions of nonverbal communication and the synthesis of these functions into the framework of visual communication skills are discussed.

Major Functions of Nonverbal Communication

Nonverbal communication serves a number of functions in a school context. Argyle (1988) identified four functions of nonverbal behavior. The first is to *express emotions*. Emotional expression is as important in school settings as it is in personal encounters. When school members (administrators, faculty, staff, students, parents) communicate excitement through their voices and gestures, it is possible to get a sense of their commitment to what they are saying. In addition, educators can have an idea of how faculty and staff feel about their duties and responsibilities by their posture or by their facial expressions. Without nonverbal behavior, the understanding of emotions would be difficult, and schools would have less knowledge of how others feel and respond to educational issues and challenges.

The second function of nonverbal communication is to *convey interpersonal attitudes*. When a parent enters the school office, a perceptive principal can often tell how the parent feels about the visit. If she says, "Hello," without much expression in her voice and without looking directly at anyone, she may simply be going through the motions expected of all humans. If, however, she smiles, turns, and looks directly at the principal, she is perceived to be genuine in her greeting.

The third function of nonverbal communication is to *present one's personality to others;* this is sometimes labeled the process of impression formation and management (Burgoon, Buller, & Woodall, 1989). Without tone of voice, gestures, facial expressions, and so forth, humans appear and sound mechanical and uncaring. As communicators, educators can obtain an accurate sense of what others are trying to transmit by knowing their personality, and nonverbal behavior can be a rich source of information about a person's character, disposition, and temperament. An awareness of others' personality characteristics allows principals to make and confirm predictions about the actions, plans, and behaviors of others. This makes communicating easier. For instance, a parent who talks loudly and positions himself directly in the principal's face could be perceived as aggressive and pushy. In contrast, a parent who avoids eye contact, talks softly, and uses few gestures may be perceived as shy and reluctant to confront others on issues. Without understanding culture, race, and gender expectations, it is difficult to accurately interpret nonverbal cues that convey another person's personality.

The fourth function of nonverbal communication is to *accompany verbal communication.* Nonverbal behavior can *reinforce* what is said verbally (smiling while stating satisfaction with a project); it can help *regulate* verbal behavior (breaking eye contact to signal that a conversation is over); it can *complement* oral communication (talking very slowly and deliberately to make an important point); it can *substitute* for verbal behavior (nodding, winking, or gesturing approval); and it can even *contradict* verbal language (stating pleasure at meeting someone without establishing eye contact; O'Hair & Ropo, 1994). When verbal and nonverbal messages contradict, the receiver of the message relies on nonverbal behaviors. Educators should carefully monitor their nonverbal behaviors to ensure that they reinforce, rather than contradict, verbal messages.

Framework of Visual Communication Skills

A *framework of visual communication skills* describes the essential components of nonverbal communication in business and educational settings (O'Hair & Spaulding, 1996). The framework has five major components: facial expression, eye and visual behavior, gestures and body movement, space, and dress (Figure 6–2). Each component is described and discussed here in relation to nonverbal communication in educational settings.

Facial Expression.   One of the most expressive channels of nonverbal communication is the face. Although only a few words are available to describe them (for example, frown, smile, sneer), there are in fact more than 1,000 different facial expressions (Ekman, Friesen, & Ellsworth, 1972). The challenge is to interpret these various expressions and to decode their messages. They are the most reliable signal for determining an individual's emotional state. A principal who pays close attention to facial expressions is likely to accurately judge an individual's true feelings.

Facial expressions also provide feedback as to how communication is being understood. For example, a teacher may *state* that she understands a particular assignment, but *looks* confused. A principal who is aware of facial expressions and uses feedback appropriately is alerted immediately to a potential problem. Facial expressions are beneficial in determining the real motivations and intentions of others. Often individuals try to change their facial expressions to deliberately mislead others about how they feel. Although facial expressions are important for principals to observe and analyze, this information alone is probably not enough to establish, with a high degree of accuracy, another's emotional state. According to the framework of visual communication skills, other nonverbal clues are needed.

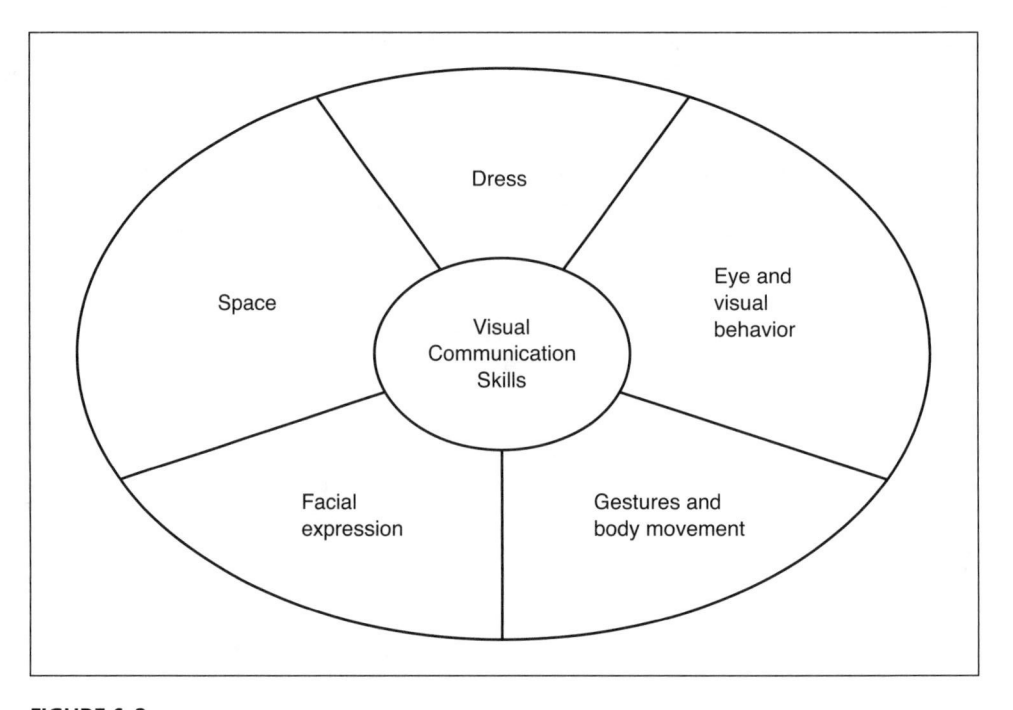

FIGURE 6–2
Framework of Visual Communication Skills (Source: O'Hair, 1998b.)

Eye and Visual Behavior. The eyes provide rich information. Because humans are becoming more and more visually oriented, the movement of the eyes and how they are focused on other people and objects provide a great deal of knowledge and insight.

Eye gaze indicates that one person is looking directly at another individual's face, particularly the eyes. *Eye contact* refers to mutual and simultaneous eye gaze between two people; that is, both people are looking directly into each other's eyes (Harper, Wiens, & Matarazzo, 1978; O'Hair & Ropo, 1994). With eye gaze, one person is searching for information about another. With eye contact, both individuals are committed to the communication process (O'Hair, Friedrich, & Dixon, 2005). Research on nonverbal communication through the eyes alerts educational leaders to the need to consider cultural, social, and gender differences and provides clues to communication avoidance.

Cultural, Social, and Gender Differences. Cultural differences in eye gaze and eye contact are well documented. The eyes are important in regulating the flow of communication among people. For example, when one person greets another, a certain sequence is generally followed: gaze, smile, eyebrow lift, quick head nod (Eibl-Eibesfeldt, 1972).

This behavior may seem to be one of those things known through common sense until educators realize that all parents, staff, and community members do not share the same nonverbal behaviors. The most distinguishing feature in the cross-cultural use of eye contact is the focus of the listener's eyes (Burgoon et al., 1989). Anglos are socialized to gaze directly at the speaker's face when they are listening; American Indians and African Americans often refuse to look directly into the eyes of any authority figure. In their culture, direct eye gaze with an authority figure is considered rude and inappropriate. Japanese Americans avoid eye contact when listening by focusing on the speaker's neck. Educators may damage professional relationships by being unaware of and insensitive to cultural differences.

A summary of research findings reveals other factors involving eye behavior and nonverbal communication:

- People tend to "match" the gaze duration of their conversational partner.
- Speech rate is higher when the speaker looks at the listener.
- Eye gaze increases when communicating positive information and decreases when communicating negative information.
- Smiling causes a decrease in eye gaze.
- In groups, there is a tendency to look more while speaking and look less while listening. (The opposite is true when only two people are talking.)
- People who gaze longer are better liked.
- Increased gazing causes favorable impressions when positive information is communicated and unfavorable impressions when negative information is revealed.
- Compared with high-status people, people with lower status (less power) look more when listening than when speaking.
- Females gaze more than males.
- Females are looked at more than males.
- Females are more uncomfortable when they are unable to see their conversational partner.

An awareness of cultural, social, and gender differences may prove helpful in understanding visual behavior and improving communication.

Communication Avoidance. Visual behavior is a good indicator of communication avoidance. It is important for educators to understand that certain meanings are to be found in both intentional and unintentional avoidance. In addition, educators must remember that there are several reasons why an individual may avoid eye contact. First, the individual may be unwilling to communicate. An individual may feel unprepared to answer a question, may be busy thinking about something else, or may even be unhappy with someone and, as a result, avoid eye contact. Emotional arousal may also reduce eye contact. As mentioned earlier, the face is an excellent source of clues for determining the emotional state of an individual. The eyes can provide that type of information as well. Sometimes adults avoid eye gaze to cover up emotional arousal such as despair, depression, and even stress. For example, consider the nonverbal behavior of a parent who feels embarrassed. The parent will probably divert his or her eyes to objects rather than looking directly at people. This is an effort to recover lost self-esteem (O'Hair & Ropo, 1994). Once the parent recovers, normal eye behavior will resume. A principal's awareness of nonverbal communication will allow the parent time to regain self-esteem and return willingly to the conversation. Understanding eye and visual behavior is important in understanding people and building the trust needed to develop productive relationships between educators and the public.

Gestures and Body Movement. Gestures and body movement, sometimes referred to as "kinetics," are another aspect of nonverbal communication. Individuals use gestures to complement what they say verbally. Communication problems occur whenever a person's gestures suggest a different meaning than the verbal message. As mentioned earlier, it is important for educators to remember that whenever a contradiction exists between the verbal and nonverbal messages, listeners believe and accept more readily the nonverbal message (Burgoon et al., 1989).

Emblems and *posture* are two types of body gestures. Emblems refer to gestures that take the place of words. All cultures have emblems. Some are universal in meaning (e.g., waving goodbye); others are not. Postures refer to the positions of the body. For example, postures include crossing one's legs, folding one's arms, slouching, and sitting on one's knees. Cultural awareness of nonverbal emblems and posture is a necessity.

Space. Often school leaders and the public respond and react differently to space. Space may be examined from two differing viewpoints: personal space and environmental space.

Personal Space. Proxemics, or the distance that exists between communicators, is referred to as *personal space*. School leaders must consider two aspects of personal space: first, the distance measured in feet and inches; and second, the perceived distance measured only by how comfortable people feel about the spatial distance between them and their communicating partners (O'Hair & Ropo, 1994). People differ according to their tolerance for personal space: Some individuals prefer very close communicating distances, and others require greater distances.

Hall (1973) developed a system for determining personal space preferences. Four zones in which all communication takes place consist of the intimate, the personal, the social, and the public. The intimate zone (skin contact to 18 inches) is not often observed in educational settings. It is usually reserved for family or other close persons. The personal zone (18 inches to 4 feet) is reserved for interactions that are personal or private. The social zone (4 to 12 feet) is used a great deal in educational committee meetings and small-group problem-solving sessions. The public zone (12 feet and beyond) is used in educational orientation sessions and assembly programs. If school leaders violate the rules of personal space as dictated by these zones, others may be offended or repulsed. Entering the intimate zone with a casual acquaintance can be misleading and troublesome. However, if school leaders choose to interact at distances that are greater than what the situation requires, they may be perceived as cold and aloof.

The culture, age, and gender of individuals may also affect personal space preferences. For example, many cultures display differences in spacing and touching distances. In general, adhering to the norms of the situation, culture, and degree of acquaintance is the best advice for educators in using personal space appropriately.

Environmental Space. This space refers to how individuals perceive, construct, and manipulate physical space in educational settings. Environmental space is important because people are influenced by what they see. Office arrangement, reception areas, decorations, wall hangings, colors, plants, and furniture are what school visitors see first when entering the building. Not only are first impressions of school personnel important to keep in mind when developing a school's professional image, but first impressions of the building, classrooms, cafeteria, and principal's office are important to consider as well.

The effective use of environmental space offers schools the "power of suggestion" in that principals can express to their school community through space arrangement that the school is student centered, professional, personable, effective, and accessible. For example, principals can communicate professionalism and accessibility through their office arrangement. The best office arrangement is one that puts the least distance and fewest barriers between communicators. The objective is to produce walkways, functional seating areas, and a relaxed meeting space. Making effective use of environmental space is a constant challenge for educators.

Dress. What others wear and their general appearance communicate a great deal about the wearer and the school organization. It has been found that human relationships are established, reconfirmed, or denied within the first four minutes of contact (Zunin & Zunin, 1972). Dress has much to do with the early stereotyping and misconceptions. Acceptable dress may reduce inaccurate perceptions and improve first impressions. What is "acceptable" may vary based on the community, climate, geographical location, and fashion trends.

Accurately decoding the nonverbal communication of others and being aware of one's own nonverbal behavior can help educators project a positive, caring image to the public. Providing the human touch in school public relations involves understanding the personalities, emotions, and feelings of others. Awareness of nonverbal communication provides educators with an in-depth analysis of human behavior often otherwise overlooked.

COMPETENCY 3: UNDERSTANDING AND MANAGING CONFLICT

No longer does the old flying-by-the-seat-of-the-pants approach to conflict work, if it ever truly did. Now, more than ever, schools must proactively plan for conflict because it is an undeniable and inescapable reality in any organization. Although many people fear and even avoid conflict, it is, if handled appropriately, an extremely valuable and productive PR tool. Whereas conflict is inevitable, positive and productive growth from conflict is not. In order for conflict to have a positive effect, it must be directed, guided, and supported. Fullan, Bertani, and Quinn (2005) suggest "Successful districts are collaborative, but they are not always congenial and consensual. Working in a high-trust yet demanding culture, participants view disagreement as a normal part of change and are able to value and work through differences."

To gain the most positive results, school leaders must recognize those elements of conflict that contribute to unproductive organizational and individual behavior. Second, they must understand the types of conflict that occur so that they can structure communications appropriately.

Conflict Contaminants

Conflict contaminants are occurrences or happenings that have a detrimental effect on the school climate. Several authors (e.g., Harvey & Drolet, 1994; Roberts, 1982) refer to these contaminants as pollutants that clog and choke an organizational climate. Although they are not inherent in the conflict itself, they provide the conditions in which negative conflict grows and thrives. Following are some of the contaminants that commonly affect schools:

1. *Negativism.*   People get into more harmful types of conflict in environments where negativity abounds. Negative environments also have a higher incidence of conflict (Harvey & Drolet, 1994). This is true because feelings of doom and gloom are nurtured.
2. *Unrealistic expectations.*   When unrealistic expectations are placed on employees and students, negative and unproductive conflict likely. For example, unproductive conflict occurs when teachers or students are asked to achieve projects or goals within unrealistic time lines or guidelines.
3. *Poor communication skills.*   Without effective communication skills, individuals and schools leave themselves vulnerable to rumors, misinformation, and missed information. These products also contaminate the communication process.
4. *Personal stressors.*   Personal stressors may include health problems, financial difficulties, poor organizational abilities, and poor interrelationship skills. People having difficulties in these areas are more likely than others to engage in unproductive types of conflict (Harvey & Drolet, 1994).
5. *Lack of support and trust.*   Individuals in schools need to feel supported and trusted. These feelings enhance creativity, communication, and personal and organizational growth and development. When these qualities are missing, the probability of negative conflict increases. People who operate in an environment that supports the way things have always been done, rather than acting on the knowledge they know to be better, will fear repercussions for their candor and repeat past mistakes and re-create past problems (Pfeffer & Sutton, 2000).
6. *Preference protection.*   Preference protection is exemplified by the "my way or the highway" syndrome. Individuals need to spend more time thinking about where they are going and less time arguing about how they are going to get there. Individuals or organizations with tunnel vision feel that their preferred way is the only way. This disposition not only creates negative conflict, but also inhibits organizational creativity and growth.
7. *Savior syndrome.*   Some individuals try to fix everyone's problems. They constantly engage in harmful conflict. "When you try to solve someone else's problems, you do two perilous things. First, you rob the other person of the opportunity to grow. . . . Second, you increase the chances that you will become an actor in the conflict yourself" (Harvey & Drolet, 1994, pp. 75–76). A strong principal encourages others to own up to their problems; they act as a consultant, not a savior.
8. *Jumping to conclusions.*   Some individuals jump to conclusions before getting all the information necessary to make an effective decision. In such a situation, conflict is almost certain because not all the facts have been considered. Jumping to conclusions often escalates the original problem and creates additional problems.

Conflict Types

Harvey and Drolet (1994) identified five types of conflict. Their categorization is useful because it breaks conflict into definable and understandable categories. If school leaders cannot define conflict, they cannot manage it.

Value Conflict.   Value conflict involves individual values, beliefs, or convictions, making this type of conflict the most difficult to resolve. Values are more than simple preferences. As Harvey and Drolet (1994) explain, value conflicts "often involve convictions held on faith, independent of evidence or logic" (p. 80). These convictions are likely to be deep-seated beliefs that have been individually tested over time. The process of developing a shared vision to guide teaching and learning in learning communities uncovers hidden values, based on newly developing cultural understandings.

Tangible Conflict.   Tangible conflict can also be referred to as resource conflict because it occurs over measurable resources. Measurable resources may include time, money, supplies, parking spaces, classroom space and location, personnel, benefits, and technology. Tangible conflicts in schools have steadily escalated because resources have declined and special-interest groups have become more influential. Tangible conflict, however, is one of the easier types of conflict to resolve if resources are available or can be creatively gained. If ignored, tangible conflicts can spawn secondary conflicts. For example, two teachers having a conflict over sharing classroom space (a tangible conflict) can grow to dislike each other.

Interpersonal Conflict.   Interpersonal conflict results when an individual has strong feelings of dislike about another individual. Most interpersonal conflicts occur as a result of another type of conflict. Although interpersonal conflicts are common in schools, they are resolved very infrequently. Next to value conflicts, interpersonal conflicts are the most difficult type of conflict to resolve.

Territorial Conflicts.   Territorial conflicts occur as the result of territorial invasions or as the result of someone expecting another to expand his or her present territory (or responsibility). Consider the elementary teacher who, for the first time in his 15-year career, is asked to share his classroom with another teacher. He feels the room is his private property. Conflict is generated by a territorial invasion. Or consider a biology teacher who has been told by her principal that her teaching load will increase to include a health class. Resistance produces conflict based on territorial expansion. Whereas tangible conflict is based solely on material resources, territorial conflict is not necessarily measurable resources.

Perceptual Conflicts.   Conflicts frequently contain a small core of truly incompatible goals, surrounded by a thick layer of misperceptions of the adversary's motives and goals. People in conflict frequently form distorted images of one another. These distorted images cause people to jump to conclusions about the motives and goals of others. Conflicting parties often have mirror-image perceptions of one another—each attributes the same virtues to themselves and vices to their adversaries (Meyer, 1987). For example, when both sides believe that they are doing beneficial things for students, they see their adversaries doing detrimental things. Perceptual conflict may occur between teachers and parents. Parents may have a perception of a teacher that is created from the comments and opinions of their child. Most perceptual conflicts occur because individuals fail to get the facts. Perceptual conflicts are easier to resolve if they do not grow into another type of conflict.

Schools functioning as professional learning communities seek to reduce all types of unproductive conflict by collaboratively developing a shared vision for student learning, working together toward that vision, and accepting collective responsibility for all students. Consequently, fewer value, tangible, interpersonal, territorial, and perceptual conflicts occur in professional learning communities than in conventional schools.

Conflict-Resolution Strategies

Handled ineffectively or ignored, conflict can lead to dysfunctional behavior. Managed effectively, conflict can be beneficial, enhancing individual and group growth and development. The following fourteen diverse conflict-resolution strategies are presented as alternatives for high-achieving schools and their leaders to resolve conflict (Ball, 1989; Filley, 1975; Harvey & Drolet, 1994; Huse, 1975; Meyer, 1987).

1. *Expanding or developing resources.*   Scarcity of materials, time, territory, personnel, information, or influence may produce conflict (Ball, 1989). This problem may be resolved by expanding existing resources or by developing new resources. For example, the conflict between two teachers fighting over limited instructional materials may be alleviated by buying more materials.

2. *Compromising.*   A compromise is a settlement in which each individual gives up part of what he or she wants in order to resolve the issue. Compromise is most effective when parties believe they are making reasonably equal concessions.

3. *Using group dynamics intervention.*   Group dynamics interventions include actions such as multicultural awareness, cooperative learning approaches, team building, personality inventories, trust building, and questioning strategies. They help individuals and organizations better understand each other. For example, placing conflicting groups together allows the parties to get better acquainted. Misperceptions may be clarified, goal compatibility may be identified, and conflicts may be resolved.

4. *Using outside intervention.*   Sometimes tensions and suspicions between conflicting groups are so high that direct communication is impossible. In such cases, outside intervention may be needed. Outside intervention consists of a third party entering a conflict situation to assist resolution. It can occur formally (involving a negotiator, arbitrator, or intervenor) or informally (offering friendly advice).

5. *Conducting interdependence analysis.*   According to Harvey and Drolet (1994), "When individuals and organizations understand that their interests are dependent and that they need each other for future success, a basis exists for resolving conflict" (p. 88). This is the "I need you and you need me so let's work out something we can both live with" resolution strategy.

6. *Altering organizational structure.*   This is a conflict-resolution strategy whereby structural changes are made in the organization. In a school setting, the structural alteration may include changing a teacher's job responsibilities, changing the physical space of a school or a classroom, creating a new organizational chart, terminating or reassigning a teacher, or changing a student's class schedule. There is a potential downside to this approach. The symptoms of the conflict may be relieved without rectifying the underlying problem.

7. *Seeking additional information.*   Too often, conflict occurs because of the lack of information or the use of misinformation. Seeking additional information is an important resolution strategy because it allows us to gain a deeper understanding of the conflict and helps us clarify misunderstandings.

8. *Maintaining constant communication.*   A constant communication channel helps to prevent unproductive conflict. For example, many teachers attempt to communicate with parents through classroom newsletters, conferences, and telephone calls. These teachers know that the more aware parents are of what is going on in the classroom, the less trouble they have with conflict based on misperception.

9. *Issuing a direct order.*   A direct order is one of the most common types of strategies used today. However, because it requires little or no participation by the conflicting parties, most parties lack the commitment to resolve the conflict or prevent future conflict. Harvey and Drolet (1994) suggest using a direct order when a resolution is needed immediately and when authority is acceptable to the parties involved.

10. *Clarifying roles.*   Many times, conflict will occur because people are unclear about their own roles or the roles of others in their organization. An effective role clarification process includes having each individual define his or her own role responsibilities and expectations and the role responsibilities and expectations for others in their organization. When completed, the results are compared. Points of conflict (different perceptions or expectations about roles and responsibilities) often emerge. This permits roles to be redefined or clarified to prevent further conflict.

11. *Appealing to a higher value.*   This strategy appeals to values, beliefs, or goals that are deemed more important than the immediate conflict. Teachers often say, "We are all in this for the sake of the students." This is a value or belief statement that overarches most conflict in schools. A teacher may agree to do something he or she would rather not "for the good of the students." Organizations and their leaders have been known to create or expose a common threat as a strategy for building group cohesiveness and cooperation. Social, economic, and educational barriers are often dropped as people help each other cope with a common enemy. The struggle creates a cohesive and cooperative spirit, effusing people with the value of uniting behind a common enemy.

12. *Using avoidance.*   Avoidance is probably the most overused resolution strategy. Although helpful in dealing with some conflict, it can actually exacerbate a problem. Most problems do not resolve themselves.

13. *Taking a democratic vote.*   A democratic vote is a "majority wins" strategy for resolving conflict. A verbal vote can be taken to determine how many individuals are for or against an issue. The group with the most votes wins. The negative side of using this strategy is that it creates winners and losers. Whenever possible, win-win resolutions to conflict are preferable.

14. *Initiating conciliatory gestures.*   Sometimes conflict is so intense that communication comes to an impasse. At such times, a conciliatory gesture—a soft answer, a warm smile, or a concession—by one party may elicit reciprocal conciliatory acts by the other party (Meyer, 1987; Osgood, 1962, 1980). Conciliation begins when one side

announces its desire to reduce tension and describes the conciliatory act prior to performing it. After the act is completed, the adversary is asked to reciprocate in an equal manner. This then elicits public pressure on the adversary to participate in the conciliatory process. The intent of conciliation is to edge both conflicting parties toward greater cooperation and less tension, and eventually toward conflict resolution. Repeated conciliatory acts breed greater trust and cooperation.

Matching Conflict Types with Appropriate Resolution Strategies

One of the most difficult aspects of managing conflict is matching the conflict type with the most appropriate resolution strategy. Table 6–3 demonstrates the relationship between the conflict types and resolution strategies discussed here. Keep in mind that all conflict-resolution strategies are situational, modifiable, and combinable. Therefore, educators must carefully reflect on their choices before selecting a conflict-resolution strategy. Reflection is important because it permits the simulation of possible outcomes based on the understanding of the context in which the conflict occurred.

Understanding the causal situations surrounding conflict guides school leaders in selecting conflict-resolution strategies that coincide with the context of the problem. Although Table 6–3 will facilitate matching appropriate conflict-resolution strategies to conflict types, the following questions should also be considered:

TABLE 6–3

Matching Resolution Strategies with Conflicts

Conflict-Resolution Strategy	Value Conflict	Tangible Conflict	Interpersonal Conflict	Territorial Conflict	Perceptual Conflict
Expanding or developing resources		++		++	
Compromising	+	+		+	
Using group dynamics intervention		+	++	+	+
Using outside intervention			+	++	+
Conducting interdependence analysis	++		+	+	+
Altering organizational structure		++	+	+	
Seeking additional information	+		+		++
Maintaining constant communication			+		++
Issuing a direct order	+	+	++	+	
Clarifying roles			+	++	+
Appealing to a higher value	++	+	+	+	
Using avoidance	+		+		
Taking a democratic vote	++	+			
Initiating conciliatory gestures	+	+	++	+	

+ *Strategy match for the conflict type.*

++ *Preferred strategy match for the conflict type.*

Source: Harvey & Drolet, 1994. Copyright 1994 by Technomic Publishing Company, Inc. Adapted with permission.

1. What is the source of the conflict? What additional conflicts are likely to arise as a result of this conflict?
2. Do the conflicting groups or individuals have the necessary communication or problem-solving skills to work through their differences?
3. Do potential losses outweigh possible gains?
4. Who stands to gain—one party or all parties?
5. How much time is available for resolving the conflict?
6. Is the issue major or minor?
7. Is additional research or information needed?
8. Are tempers too hot for a productive resolution?
9. Will a temporary solution suffice for the present?
10. What communication failures are at the base of the conflict?

Establishing meaningful lines of communication between the surrounding community and any given educational institution is dependent on the successful development of conflict-resolution systems. Conflict in the home translates into conflict in the classroom. Only by working in unison and acknowledging the constant barrage of social differences can community and school leaders hope to reach the diverse population in our educational systems.

Only by training educators in the vast new technological advantages of the twenty-first century can we hope to make education more feasible for the next generation of students. Conflict is born of differences; mutual respect is the product of understanding these differences and making the appropriate changes in technique and style. Change theorists refer to problems as our friends, and without conflict, schools are less likely to become learning communities. Recent studies in the causes of conflict and social behavior management have produced some invaluable conflict-management resources.

The Thomas-Kilmann Conflict Mode Instrument (TKI) has been a leader among conflict-resolution assessment tods (Thomas & Kilmann, 2002). This instrument is a catalyst in learning how our conflict-handling styles affect personal and group dynamics. Many of the multicultural barriers in society and in our schools can be better understood and eliminated once we realize that "conflict-handling behaviors are neither good nor bad. Rather, conflict resolution is simply a matter of expanding skill sets and choosing the most effective group of behaviors for a particular situation." The TKI inventory provides invaluable data about conflict-handling style and the five distinct modes of dealing with ethnic, gender, and multicultural difficulties:

- ◆ Competing. High assertiveness and low cooperativeness. The goal is to "win."
- ◆ Avoiding. Low assertiveness and low cooperativeness. The goal is to "delay."
- ◆ Compromising. Moderate assertiveness and moderate cooperativeness. The goal is to "find a middle ground."
- ◆ Collaborating. High assertiveness and high cooperativeness. The goal is to "find a win-win situation."
- ◆ Accommodating: Low assertiveness and high cooperativeness. The goal is to "yield."

School and community leaders alike acknowledge the merits of the TKI model. Many require that their employees attend TKI workshops that specialize in effectively developing better communication and conflict-management skills. Learning to understand and accept one's own cultural biases and misgivings enables a person to begin facing the challenges of an ever-changing multicultural society.

SUMMARY

This chapter has provided a two-pronged approach to understanding the role of communication in PR. The first prong seeks to establish an understanding of professional learning community conditions associated with high-achieving schools and the role of skillful communication in advancing these conditions. The second prong utilizes communication theory to provide a foundation for successful school communication, consisting of three core communication competencies:

Competency 1: Listening effectively

Competency 2: Defining and decoding nonverbal communication

Competency 3: Understanding and managing conflict.

QUESTIONS AND SUGGESTED ACTIVITIES

CASE STUDY

1. It is now time to begin work on Greenhill's improvement plan. Describe your thoughts and concerns as you begin working on the plan. What concepts can you apply from this chapter to help you? Where should you begin?
2. Create a detailed school improvement plan, one that will incorporate the benefits of professional learning communities and respect the input of the school staff, parents, community, students, and the state agency.
3. What kinds of conflict contaminants were evident in the case study? What types of conflict did the contaminants lead to?
4. After answering question 3, list and describe several resolution strategies for dealing with the conflict in this case study.

CHAPTER

5. Reflect on the following statement: The meaningful participation of the school community in defining the direction of the school also results in an enhanced culture of collective responsibility for all of the students. Rewrite this statement in your own words. Then provide an example of this statement in action within your school setting.
6. As a listener, what first impressions do you make? Ask for feedback from a colleague and a few close friends to help you with your self-analysis.
7. On the basis of the results of your self-analysis, describe areas for improving your listening skills. Use key concepts of the strategic listening process to help you identify your listening strengths and weaknesses.

8. Walk the halls of your school, paying particular attention to various classroom arrangements. What nonverbal characteristics create a climate conducive to learning, and what nonverbal characteristics detract from a favorable climate?
9. Evaluate your success at implementing the framework of visual communication skills covered in this chapter. Select two or three areas in which improvement is needed and develop an action plan.
10. Consider two recent conflict situations in which you were involved. Describe the context for each situation, the contributing factors, and the strategies you used (or wish you had used) for conflict resolution.

SUGGESTED READINGS

Doyle, D., & Pimental, S. (1997). *Raising the standard: An eight-step action guide for schools and communities*. Thousand Oaks, CA: Corwin Press.

Furman, G. (Ed.). (2002). *School as community: From promise to practice*. New York: State University of New York Press.

Health, R. (Ed.). (2001). *Handbook of public relations*. Thousand Oaks, CA: Sage.

O'Hair, D., Friedrich, G., & Dixon, L. (2005). *Strategic communication in business and the professions* (5th ed.). Boston: Houghton Mifflin.

O'Hair, D., Stewart, R., & Rubenstein, H. (2006). *A speaker's guidebook* (3rd ed.). New York: St. Press.

O'Hair, M. J., McLaughlin, H. J., & Reitzug, U. C. (2000). *Foundation of democratic education*. Belmont, CA: Wadsworth.

Spaulding, A. (2002). Committees and conflict: Developing a conflict resolution framework. *Journal of School Public Relations, 23*(3), 19–26.

Spaulding, A., & Correa, C. (2005). Crisis management and media relations: Preparing for media involvement in a school crisis. *Essays in education*. Retrieved December 31, 2005, from http://www.usca.edu/essays.

Veugelers, W., & O'Hair, M. J. (Eds.). (2005). *Network learning for educational change*. London: Open University Press.

Warner, C. (1997). *Everybody's house: The schoolhouse*. Thousand Oaks, CA: Corwin Press.

Wilson, G. (1996). *Groups in context: Leadership and participation in small groups*. New York: McGraw-Hill.

REFERENCES

Argyle, M. (1988). *Bodily communication* (2nd ed.). London: Methuen.

Atkinson, L. A. (2005, November). *Atkinson schools as learning organizations: Relationships between professional learning communities and technology-enriched learning environments*. Paper presented at a meeting of the University Council for Educational Administration, Nashville, TN.

Averso, R. (2003, November). *Leading to learn: The role of shared school vision*. Paper presented at a meeting of the University Council for Educational Administration, Portland, OR.

Ball, S. (1989). Micro-politics versus management: Towards a sociology of school organization. In S. Walker & L. Barton (Eds.), *Politics and the processes of schooling* (pp. 218–241). Philadelphia: Open University Press.

Bernhardt, V. (2002). *The school portfolio toolkit: A planning, implementation, and evaluation guide for continuous school improvement.* Larchmont, NY: Eye on Education.

Brewer, C. A., & Suchan, T. A. (2001). *Mapping Census 2000: The geography of U.S. diversity.* Washington, DC: U.S. Government Printing Office.

Burgoon, J. K., Buller, D. B., & Woodall, W. G. (1989). *Nonverbal communication: The unspoken dialogue.* New York: Harper & Row.

Carroll, T. G. (2001). Do today's evaluations meet the needs of tomorrow's networked learning communities. In W. F. Heinecke & L. Blasi (Eds.), *Methods of evaluating educational technology.* Greenwich, CT: Information Age.

Darling-Hammond, L., & McLaughlin, M. W. (1995). Policies that support professional development in an era of reform. *Phi Delta Kappan, 76*(8), 587–604.

Darling-Hammond, L., & Snyder, J. (1992). Reframing accountability: Creating learner-centered schools. In A. Lieberman (Ed.), *The changing contexts of teaching* (pp. 11–36). Chicago: University of Chicago Press.

Dolan, K. (1996). *Communication: A practical guide to school and community relations.* New York: Wadsworth.

Eaker, R., DuFour, R., & DuFour, R. (2002). *Getting started: Reculturing schools to become professional learning communities.* Bloomington, IN: National Educational Service.

Eibl-Eibesfeldt, I. (1972). Similarities and differences between cultures in expressive movement. In R. A. Hinde (Ed.), *Nonverbal communication* (pp. 297–314). Cambridge, England: Cambridge University Press.

Ekman, P., Friesen, W. V., & Ellsworth, P. (1972). *Emotion in the human face: Guidelines for research and an integration of the findings.* New York: Pergamon.

Filley, A. (1975). *Interpersonal conflict resolution.* Glenview, IL: Scott Foresman.

Fullan, M. G. (1991). *The new meaning of educational change.* New York: Teachers College Press.

Fullan, M. G. (2003). *Change forces with a vengeance.* New York: Routledge Falmer.

Fullan, M. G., Bertani, A., & Quinn, J. (2005). *Leading in tough times: New lessons for district-wide reform.* Center for Development and Learning. Retrieved December 31, 2005, from http://www.cdl. org/-resourcelibrary/articles/leading_in_tough_times.php?type=subject&id=36.

Glickman, C. D. (1993). *Renewing America's schools: A guide to school-based action.* San Francisco: Jossey-Bass.

Golen, S. (1990). A factor analysis of barriers to effective listening. *Journal of Business Communication, 27,* 25–36.

Hall, E. T. (1973). *The hidden dimension.* Garden City, NY: Anchor.

Harper, R. G., Wiens, A. N., & Matarazzo, J. D. (1978). *Nonverbal communication: The state of the art.* New York: Wiley.

Harvey, T., & Drolet, B. (1994). *Building teams, building people: Expanding the fifth resource.* Lancaster, PA: Technomic.

Henderson, A. T., & Mapp, K. L. (2002). *A new wave of evidence: The impact of school, family and community connections on student achievement.* Austin, TX: Southwest Educational Development Laboratory.

Hewes, D. E., & Graham, M. L. (1989). Second-guessing theory: Review and extension. In J. A. Anderson (Ed.), *Communication yearbook 12* (pp. 213–248). Newbury Park, CA: Sage.

Hord, S. M. (1997). *Professional learning communities: Communities of continuous inquiry and improvement.* Austin, TX: Southwest Educational Development Laboratory.

Huffman, J. B., & Hipp, K. K. (2003). *Reculturing schools as professional learning communities.* Lanham, MD: Scarecrow Press.

Huse, E. (1975). *Organizational development and change.* New York: West.

Lambert, L. (1998). *Building leadership capacity in schools*. Alexandria, VA: Association for Supervision and Curriculum Development.

Lambert, L. (2003). *Leadership capacity for lasting school improvement*. Alexandria, VA: Association for Supervision and Curriculum Development.

McLeod, S. (2004, December 7). *Data-driven teachers*. Minneapolis: University of Minnesota, School Technology Leadership Initiative (STLI).

McNulty, R., & O'Hair, M. J. (1998). *Crucial elements of communication to address when initiating change*. Paper presented at the annual meeting of the Association for Supervision and Curriculum Development, San Antonio, TX.

Meyer, D. G. (1987). *Social psychology*. New York: McGraw-Hill.

Miles, M. B. (1993). Forty years of change in schools: Some personal reflections. *Educational Administration Quarterly, 29*(2), 213–248.

Newmann, F. M., & Wehlage, G. G. (1995). *Successful school restructuring: A report to the public and educators*. Madison: University of Wisconsin.

O'Hair, D., Friedrich, G., & Dixon, L. (2005). *Strategic communication in business and the professions* (5th ed.). Boston: Houghton Mifflin.

O'Hair, M. J. (1998a). *The strategic listening process*. Unpublished manuscript, University of Oklahoma.

O'Hair, M. J. (1998b). *The framework of visual communication skills*. Unpublished manuscript, University of Oklahoma.

O'Hair, M. J., McLaughlin, H. J., & Reitzug, U. C. (2000). *The foundation of democratic education*. Fort Worth, TX: Harcourt Brace.

O'Hair, M. J., & Reitzug, U. C. (1997). Restructuring schools for democracy: Principals' perspectives. *Journal of School Leadership, 7*(3), 266–286.

O'Hair, M. J., Reitzug, U. C., Cate, J., Averso, R., Atkinson, L., Gentry, D. R., et al. (2005). Creating professional learning communities in Oklahoma: School university-community partnerships to enhance student achievement. In W. Veugelers & M. J. O'Hair (Eds.), *Network learning for educational change* (pp. 72–97). London: Open University.

O'Hair, M. J., & Ropo, E. (1994). Unspoken messages: Understanding diversity in education requires emphasis on nonverbal communication. *Teacher Education Quarterly, 21*(3), 91–112.

O'Hair, M. J., & Spaulding, A. M. (1996). Institutionalizing public relations through interpersonal communication: Listening, nonverbal, and conflict resolution skills. In T. Kowalski (Ed.), *Public relations for educational organizations: Practice in an information age*. New York: Prentice Hall.

Osgood, C. E. (1962). *An alternative to war or surrender*. Urbana: University of Illinois Press.

Osgood, C. E. (1980, June). *GRIT: A strategy for survival in mankind's nuclear age?* Paper presented at the Pugwash conference on New Directions in Disarmament, Racine, WI.

Pfeffer, J., & Sutton, R. (2000). *The knowing-doing gap*. Boston: Harvard Business School Press.

Putnam, R. D. (2000). *Bowling alone: The collapse and revival of American community*. New York: Simon & Schuster.

Roberts, M. (1982). *Managing conflict from the inside out*. San Diego, CA: Learning Concepts.

Sanchez, W. (1995). Working with diverse learners and school staff in a multicultural society. *ERIC Digest*, ERIC Clearinghouse on Counseling and Student Services. Retrieved April 30, 2002, from http://www.ed.gov/databases/ERIC Digests.com.

Thomas, K. W., & Kilmann, R. H. (2002). *Thomas-Kilmann conflict mode instrument (TKI)*. Retrieved April 30, 2002, from http://www.careerlifeskills.com.

Thurston, P., Clift, R., & Schacht, M. (1993). Preparing leaders for change-oriented schools. *Phi Delta Kappan, 75*, 259–265.

Tichy, N. M., & Devanna, M. A. (1986). *The transformational leader*. New York: Wiley.

Williams, L. (2005, November). *A phenomenological study of technology's impact on collaboration: Perceptions of secondary school administrators.* Paper presented at a meeting of the University Council for Educational Administration, Nashville, TN.

Wilmore, E. L. (2002). *Principal leadership: Applying the new Educational Leadership Constituent Council (ELCC) standards.* Thousand Oaks, CA: Corwin Press.

Yukl, G. (2002). *Leadership in organizations* (5th ed.). Upper Saddle River, NJ: Prentice Hall.

Zunin, L., & Zunin, N. (1972). *Contact—The first four minutes.* New York: Ballantine Books.

CHAPTER 7

Programming in Public Schools

Theodore J. Kowalski

CASE STUDY: HIGH HOPES GONE SOUR

A little more than three years ago, when Nancy Turner arrived in Lawrence, she was hailed as the superintendent who was going to radically improve the local public schools. Many taxpayers, however, have concluded that the expectation has not yet been fulfilled. Although patrons readily agree that the school system has not deteriorated under her leadership, most are quick to point out that she has failed to produce meaningful improvements. Dr. Turner fully realizes that the survival clock is ticking because her contract is up for renewal in another year.

A small, working-class midwestern city, Lawrence has faced many of the problems plaguing urban areas, including intense criticism of its public schools. The city's political elites, individuals who possess tremendous power, have frequently made the schools their scapegoat by suggesting that most of the city's problems are rooted in a mediocre education system. As examples, an economic downturn and job losses were attributed to a perception that the schools had not properly prepared graduates for the workforce. And when juvenile crime increased, poor school discipline was blamed. Such negative perceptions existed even before Dr. Turner was employed; however, the school board members had described her to the community as a dynamic change agent who would reverse the district's sliding productivity.

The belief that the schools were at the center of the community's problem was the main reason why Dr. Turner's predecessor, Dr. Murray West, had been dismissed. Dr. West's relationship with the board deteriorated after his detractors, including many district employees, portrayed him as an out-of-touch academic who was too detached from the day-to-day operations.

Dr. Turner pursued the job in Lawrence knowing the last two superintendents had had a combined tenure of only four years. An experienced administrator, she thought she knew all the risks that were associated with this position. Her apprehensions were reduced by the fact that the mayor and the entire school board supported her selection, political support that was instrumental in her receiving an initial five-year employment contract.

Superintendent Turner had barely placed the family pictures on her desk when she realized that she had underestimated the complexity of Lawrence and the intensity of dissatisfaction in the school district. Unlike in her previous superintendent assignments, she found herself inundated with paperwork that confined her to the office. For instance, every purchase over $500—and there were many—required her personal review and signature. She also had discovered other discomforting facts:

◆ She was the only "outsider" on the administrative team; all the others were former teachers in the school system who had been promoted to administrative positions.

◆ There were 37 standing committees functioning in the district, and no consequential decision was made without going through one of them. More noteworthy, committee recommendations were far more likely to be political than rational.

♦ She could find no record of an administrative staff member being fired, disciplined, or even reprimanded during the last 10 years. When principals or central office personnel got into trouble or did not complete their work satisfactorily, they were usually transferred to another administrative assignment.

♦ The school board members had involved themselves in routine administrative decisions for at least the last four years.

♦ The district's two employee unions (the teachers union and the staff union) were very powerful. They had lucrative contracts and exerted considerable influence in school board elections.

♦ There was no policy governing communication except for a phone chain that was deployed in the event that schools had to be closed unexpectedly. In the absence of policy, administrators often ignored telephone calls and letters from patrons.

♦ The school board and administration rarely expressed interest in listening to the sentiments of stakeholders. For example, no efforts had been made to identify public opinion.

After two months in Lawrence, Dr. Turner had shared her concerns about the school district with several other superintendents. They advised her to become more active in the community and to initiate meetings with teachers and various stakeholders. They believed that the district's closed political climate (i.e., indifference toward stakeholder opinions) made her vulnerable to becoming yet another scapegoat.

Dr. Turner first decided to delegate most of her routine managerial responsibilities to an assistant superintendent, Bill Evans, a longtime employee with 38 years of experience in the district. This allowed her to spend more time out of the office. She joined local organizations to broaden her contact with the public, and she made herself available to speak before community groups. She had two motives. She wanted to share information, and she wanted to obtain information. She quickly discovered that many individuals, including employees, were reluctant to communicate with her. And even when she was able to engage them, employees usually complained that they were underappreciated, or they spoke despairingly about other employees. Some parents hinted that they were dissatisfied with some principals and teachers, but typically they would not elaborate.

After one year, Dr. Turner's goal of devoting more time to communicating with internal and external stakeholders experienced a setback. Mr. Evans, the assistant superintendent who had assumed many of the routine management responsibilities, decided to retire. The board president immediately exerted pressure on Dr. Turner to promote a principal, Gene Glenn, to the vacated position. Initially, she resisted, indicating that she wanted to conduct an open search and hopefully find someone who would inject new ideas into the organization. But surmising that she probably would not win a confrontation with the board, she tried to make the best out of the situation. She offered to promote Mr. Glenn in exchange for the board's support of two recommendations: the creation of a new administrative position (director of public information services) and a reorganization of the administrative staff. A majority of the board accepted the compromise.

Betty Simmons, a lifelong Lawrence resident and high school journalism teacher, was selected to be the director of public information services. The board praised Dr. Turner for selecting a district employee, a decision that also was reported favorably by the local media. The reorganization of staff, by contrast, became highly controversial. Dr. Turner recommended consolidating four positions into two, and she wanted to conduct open searches for the two positions. If her plan was approved, the four administrators affected could apply for the new positions, elect to retire (all were eligible), or be reassigned to teaching positions (all had tenure as teachers). The four administrators mounted a vigorous campaign against the recommendation, and because of their political influence, they persuaded the board members to table the superintendent's recommendation on their reassignment indefinitely. The board president advised Dr. Turner that the board had not agreed to remove current administrators as part of a reorganization plan. The media, siding with the four administrators, described the superintendent's recommendation as a "senseless game of musical chairs that only intensified employee dissatisfaction and public confidence."

The failed realignment plan made Dr. Turner more vulnerable politically. After less than two years, detractors were openly criticizing her. In addition, her decision to delegate important responsibilities to Mr. Glenn proved to be counterproductive. He was disloyal and covertly criticized her performance to board members. Even worse, he became a hero and role model for other disgruntled administrators, and he secretly worked to scuttle the superintendent's efforts to improve the district's climate. For example, even though the board had approved adding the position of director of public information services, they rejected Dr. Turner's recommendation to appropriate $35,000 for planning and operations in this area.

The situation faced by Dr. Turner illustrates how a closed organizational climate attenuates effective communication and prevents positive school-community relations. Despite widespread dissatisfaction with the public schools, administrators and school board members continued to insulate themselves from realities of the community's changing environment. And instead of pursuing authentic reforms, they opted to create the illusion that the next superintendent would be the district's savior—a political ploy that unfortunately has been used in many low-performing school districts (Kowalski, 1995). By deceiving the public and perhaps themselves, the school board and administrative staff have put a revolving door on the superintendent's office; more importantly, they have prevented the school system from improving.

This chapter explores public relations (PR) programming in public schools. The content is premised on the belief that effective PR plans are needed at both the district and the individual school levels. Ideally, the former plan is developed first and then the latter plan is created to augment it. This integrative approach balances centralization and decentralization, ensuring that a reasonable degree of uniformity and control is provided, while allowing schools to adapt to the real needs of their stakeholders.

SETTING THE TONE AT THE DISTRICT LEVEL

As described in Chapter 1, PR is all about communication. Recognizing this fact, Bohen (1998) emphasized the importance of organizational leadership in creating a climate in which communication is an asset:

> A superintendent sets the tone, the style, and the philosophy of a school system's organizational approach to communication. Superintendents need to have public-relations expertise at their fingertips, and, without apology, they must commit resources to managing community relations or public affairs. (p. 219)

Promoting and modeling open two-way communication, however, is not an easy assignment for most superintendents. Many of them have been socialized to believe that open communication and community involvement spawn conflict and that the media are the enemy (Batory, 1999). Therefore, they prefer to insulate themselves from disgruntled employees, disappointed parents, and aggressive reporters (Borja, 2004). Moreover, many of them have never studied communication in the context of school administration, and therefore, they rely on trial and error or intuition to build relationships (Kowalski, 2005).

Unfortunately, some administrators' negative dispositions toward communicating openly stem from personal experiences. In a recent book (Johnston et al., 2002), an administrator described his apprehensions about being open with others:

> During a particularly tumultuous time of contentious labor negotiations and dealing with a new board member whose agenda was my "head on a platter," it dawned on me how tense I was each morning when I walked down the driveway to pick up the daily newspaper. My stomach and my shoulders would knot up, and I would hold my breath as I slipped the rubber band off the paper and scanned the headlines while returning to the house. I always hoped the headlines said nothing controversial or negative about me or anyone else in my school district. I realized I also hoped that no one else in public education was being beaten up either. (p. 21)

Despite such apprehensions, highly effective administrators know that schools probably will not improve appreciably unless they and others collaborate to build an acceptable vision for the future and a plan to reach it. Based on this belief, eight superintendents (Johnston et al., 2002) reflected on their experiences concerning visioning and planning and then developed a list of lessons they had learned while pursuing these tasks:

- ◆ Rely on multiple forms of input to draw conclusions about a community.
- ◆ Study the history and culture of a school district before trying to change it.
- ◆ Participate in community organizations and inspire others to do community service.
- ◆ Develop a network of key supporters in the community who can be resources in both positive and negative situations.
- ◆ Seek participation from community groups, even from those with differing perspectives.
- ◆ Develop and use a media relations plan.
- ◆ Give the district a human face in the community by being part of the community. (p. 30)

Given the organizational structure of public schools, PR planning and programming should begin at the district level. Collaborative visioning and planning should be modeled, reinforced, and nurtured by superintendents who are both effective communicators (Kowalski, 2005) and democratic leaders (Petersen & Kowalski, 2005).

Current Context

Thirty years ago a school PR program that included a good newsletter, six positive stories in the local newspaper, a strong PTA, and consistent bond levy promotions was considered effective. But communities have changed, and so have standards for good practice. In the past, families obtained information from sources close to home—resources such as the local church, neighbors, and the local newspaper. Today, information is readily available from a much wider array of sources. In an information-rich environment, stakeholders have access not only to more data, but also to different types of data. When their interpretations of these data are negative, they feel more confident in criticizing public institutions, administrators, and teachers.

Contrary to popular thought, however, criticism of public education did not originate with the advent of the current reform movement. Nearly a decade before the well-known report *A Nation at Risk* was published in 1983, Unruh and Willier (1974) observed that intense criticism had placed public education officials on the defensive. They also explained that the condemnations had come from many sources and in unexpected ways. Arguing that the assault on public schools was basically unwarranted, they pointed out that "what's right with the schools is far greater than what's wrong" (p. 150). Then, as today, two facts were evident: The public's attention focused on problems and deficiencies, many of which were beyond the control of educators; and public school officials did little to counteract invalid criticisms.

Both technology and the drive for school reform have created unprecedented opportunities for local school district officials to provide more balanced coverage of schools. As an example, technology facilitates improved communication, allowing superintendents and other administrators to engage in two-way communication with multiple publics. They can exchange information through channels such as Web pages, e-mail, and cable television broadcasts, and their communication can serve both professional and political purposes. Most notably, they can exchange information in ways that help school personnel respond to changing needs and wants and help stakeholders better understand and appreciate what school personnel are doing to help students and the community (Kowalski, 2006). School reform pressures also provide opportunities to educate the public. As examples, reporters remain interested in education stories, and continued attention from state legislatures sustains open and candid discussions about schools. Technology and school reform, however, enable rather than guarantee success. Superintendents are more likely to capitalize on these opportunities when they accept the broad PR definition provided earlier in Chapter 1.

PLANNING AT THE DISTRICT LEVEL

The process of program planning is discussed in detail in Chapter 9. The purpose here is to identify aspects of planning that are important at the district level. The discussion is divided into four subtopics: organizational considerations, preplanning responsibilities, plan components, and postplanning responsibilities.

Organizational Considerations

Organizational format and planning level are two key variables defining a school district's PR programs. Organizational format pertains to control and responsibility; planning level pertains to the extent to which the program has been purposefully designed. The three basic organizational options are summarized in Figure 7–1.

Centralization is the most commonly used option. In a centralized PR approach, the superintendent or another district-level administrator (e.g., PR director) designs, controls, manages, and otherwise operates the program. The two perceived advantages of this strategy are control and technical efficiency. Control is exercised by having policy and rules that are intended to produce uniformity and compliance. Technical efficiency is thought to result from having one PR expert in charge of the program. Advocates argue that costs can be reduced in the following ways:

◆ Fewer employees need to be prepared to engage in PR.
◆ Fewer employees require supervision to perform PR functions.
◆ Principals, other administrators, and teachers are not burdened with PR responsibilities.
◆ The program is highly controlled through policies and rules, and therefore, the probability of errors or other problems that could prove to be costly (politically, as well as economically) is reduced.

Centralization of authority, however, errs on the side of too much control (Fullan, 2001). As examples, communication may suffer because employees do not see PR as a personal

FIGURE 7–1
Organizational Options for
Public Relations

CENTRALIZATION

Top-down approach: PR functions are planned
and managed by the superintendent or a
designee. Principals have little direct role.

DECENTRALIZATION

Bottom-up approach: PR functions are planned
and managed independently at each school. The
superintendent may coordinate but does not
directly manage PR.

HYBRID

Both top-down and bottom-up approach: A PR
plan is developed at the district level first and
school plans become extensions of it. All
administrators have direct PR responsibilities.

responsibility (Kowalski, 2006), and school personnel may not be able to adjust their communication to meet the specific needs of the clientele being served (Pawlas, 1995).

With *decentralization*, PR authority is delegated to school principals based on the following premises: Community relations are best executed on a school-by-school basis, and principals and other school-based personnel have a greater understanding of their clientele than do district-level administrators. Accordingly, decentralized PR programs are thought to have the greatest advantages in districts where culture, social conditions, and economic conditions vary markedly across the publics being served. Decentralization of authority, however, errs on the side of chaos (Fullan, 2001) because the superintendent relinquishes control over much of the program, raising the possibility of inconsistent communication and PR errors. As examples, building goodwill for the passage of a bond referendum and redrawing district attendance boundaries are decisions that affect all district residents. Having individual principals communicate independently with the public on these matters is likely to produce conflicting information and competing perspectives. In addition, the quantity and quality of communication provided to the public are apt to vary substantially simply because the principals are not equally prepared for or committed to the task (Kowalski, 2006).

With a *hybrid* approach, control and responsibility are shared between district and school administrators. The intention is to meld centralization and decentralization so that PR planning occurs at both the district and the school levels. More precisely, school plans are developed as extensions of the district plan, and the nature of specific functions determines the division of PR responsibilities. This integrative approach symbolically reinforces a belief that all administrators and district employees have a responsibility to engage in PR. In addition, human resources are more likely to be maximized because many employees participate in formal PR activities. Dividing PR responsibilities, however, can generate conflict; for example, a PR director and a principal may disagree over the control of a school's newsletter. In general, however, the integrated approach is considered the best choice, especially for school districts that serve diverse publics.

Preplanning Responsibilities

In order to build an effective plan, the superintendent and support staff must complete several essential tasks (see Figure 7–2). The first pertinent task is to *define the community*. Discussing collaboration between schools and communities, Kirst and Kelley (1995) emphasized the importance of administrators defining their relevant publics. According to them, the information produced by the defining process enables school officials to accurately understand demographic conditions, including "racial composition, cultural and language diversity, poverty levels, and indicators of risk factors for children" (p. 37).

Defining research also extends to determining needs and wants. A need is essentially a gap between what should be and what is. Since public schools exist to serve their communities, accurately determining real community needs is an essential administrative activity. Given the political nature of public institutions, superintendents may also want to identify patron wants.

Much of the information required for defining research can be extracted from existing databases maintained by the school district or other agencies (e.g., state statistical

Preplanning
- Defining the community
- Defining the school district
- Benchmarking
- Validating the PR mission

Plan components
- PR mission statement
- Collaborative PR vision
- PR goals
- Communication calendar
- Relevant laws and policies
- Messages and themes
- Publications
- Web page specifications
- Information services
- Media outlets
- Program evaluation

Postplanning
- Providing human and material resources
- Developing an evaluation process
- Providing orientation and information

FIGURE 7–2
Building a School District PR Program

reports). Some data, however, must be collected through surveys or other assessment procedures. Chapters 9 and 12 provide specific information about planning and data collection/analysis.

Administrators also must *define the school district*. This process is nearly identical to the one used to define the community. Here, however, emphasis is placed on identifying school district strengths and weaknesses and on interpreting these attributes in relation to needs and desired program initiatives. As with community data, much of the information needed to define the organization may already exist in documents such as accreditation reports, annual reports filed with the state department of education, student records, staff surveys, student surveys, program evaluation reports, and follow-up studies of high school graduates.

Benchmarking is a third essential task that entails comparing your school district to highly effective school districts. The goal is to improve operations by identifying and then adopting standards that are found in productive school systems. Since these standards are not static, benchmarks need to be revised periodically—preferably every year. Benchmarks have been used extensively in business planning, and they must be relevant, achievable, and measurable if they are to have a positive effect.

Validating the PR mission is the fourth task. A PR mission provides a brief, but concise statement of an organization's purpose in communicating, both internally and externally. Whereas a district's overall mission is established primarily by state government, a PR mission statement is not. Therefore, the responsibility rests with the school board and su-perintendent (Kowalski, 2006). First and foremost, these mission statements should detail the purposes of the PR function.

Plan Components

Planned programs are considered ideal practice because operating with a written plan pro-vides a distinct advantage for administrators and other employees. As examples, an effec-tive plan provides direction in the form of goals and accountability in the form of assessment and evaluation procedures. Topor (1992) suggested that a PR plan should re-semble a mosaic, communicating a dynamic and powerful message to viewers. Most no-tably, the plan should focus on the big picture, ensure a balance between individual elements, and include smaller pieces, each with its own value.

Without a plan, superintendents and principals can only guess if PR initiatives are mov-ing in the right direction. Unfortunately, having a written PR plan has not been the norm in public education; many district programs have simply evolved from past practice and tradition. This condition is considered problematic because it contributes to indifference toward PR and results in the process being managed through trial and error.

A district PR plan is influenced by variables such as enrollment, social composition, tra-dition, and philosophy. Since these factors are not constant across a district, no single plan is universally effective. Even so, the following components are recommended:

- ◆ *PR mission statement.* This component details what the PR function is intended to do.
- ◆ *Collaborative PR vision.* This component details what the PR function should look like in meeting its mission at some designated point in the future.
- ◆ *PR goals.* This component specifies particular objectives related to achieving the col-laborative vision.
- ◆ *Communications calendar.* This component details tasks and deadlines for the period covered by the planning document.
- ◆ *Summary of relevant laws and policies.* This component provides essential information about communicating with employees, students, and the general public. Examples include policies for allowing the public to use school buildings, policies concerning media relations, and rights and privacy provisions.
- ◆ *Messages and themes.* These components help garner support for the organization, and they help people understand the directions in which the organization is moving. Good themes are concise, rhythmic, memorable, and easy to understand (e.g., a "Quest for Quality" or "Public Education: A Sound Investment in America"; Bagin, Ferguson, & Marx, 1985, p. 112). More so than the mission statement, messages and themes are cultural. That is, they express symbolically the values and beliefs of the organization; they are an overt expression of organizational culture and philosophy (Deal & Kennedy, 1982).
- ◆ *Publications.* This component identifies district publications and provides informa-tion regarding their purpose, content, and distribution.
- ◆ *Web page specifications.* This component provides an address for the district's Web page and outlines the information that is provided through this medium. In addition,

the relationship between the district's Web page and individual school Web pages is addressed.

◆ *Information services*. This component provides a list of information services in the district. Examples include procedures such as how to contact the superintendent, how to get a matter on the school board agenda, and how to obtain general information about the school district. It also identifies organizational components that generate or distribute information.

◆ *Media outlets*. This component identifies all pertinent media outlets and provides contact information.

◆ *Program evaluation*. This component specifies how and when the PR program is assessed and evaluated.

Postplanning Responsibilities

After a district PR plan has been developed, three other important responsibilities must be met. First, no plan can be pursued effectively without adequate resources. Therefore, the superintendent must ensure that the district is *providing human and material resources* to support implementation. Often, school officials make the mistake of believing that a PR plan is fiscally neutral; that is, that the plan can be implemented with little or no cost. If designed and managed appropriately, however, a PR plan could produce a favorable cost-benefit ratio for the school district. For example, effective use of communication and information may facilitate the quality of administrative decisions—an outcome that could reduce expenditures associated with correcting mistakes or collecting the same data repeatedly.

Although a good plan includes specifications for assessment and evaluation, the superintendent also must ensure that the district is *developing an evaluation process*. She or he does this by setting expectations and assigning responsibility.

Even the best of plans falter when they remain hidden from employees, and especially from employees who are expected to implement them. For this reason, the superintendent must *ensure* that school district personnel understand the purpose of the plan and that they are aware of the plan's content. In most school systems, this process is carried out at the school level, where the principal or a PR director is *providing orientation and information*.

STAFFING A DISTRICT PR PROGRAM

The issue of whether to employ a PR director is often determined by district enrollment. Smaller school systems, those with less than 1,500 students, rarely employ an administrator for this specific role. In other districts, however, the trend has been to employ such a person, at least on a part-time basis. Studies of PR directors (e.g., Zoch, Patterson, & Olson, 1997) indicated that their overall responsibilities typically fall into two roles: manager and technician. In the former, these administrators concentrate on how to do things well; in the latter, they focus on providing technical assistance to others so that they can fulfill their responsibilities.

In the recent past, it was relatively common for a superintendent to relegate PR responsibilities to an English teacher or an administrator who appeared to have a knack for communicating. Both the present context of public education and the refinement of the PR profession (more specifically, the infusion of sociological, psychological, and economic theory) suggest that perpetuating such past practices is not advisable. Ideally, candidates for this position should have academic preparation and experience in both administration and public relations (or at least communication or journalism).

The district's PR director should be an integral part of the administrative team. Preferably, this individual should have easy and open access to the superintendent; having the director report directly to the superintendent is the best way to achieve this objective. This usually is possible in all but the very largest school systems.

When creating a PR division, superintendents should carefully consider the name they give to this entity. Quoting Edward Bernays, Davis (1986) wrote, "Words are as fragile as lace or a soap bubble. The words and their meanings get kicked around . . . so today the words 'public relations' are so muddy in meaning that to some they do mean press agentry or flackery" (p. 14). Consequently, many superintendents and school board members prefer using a title such as "Division of Communication Services," "Community Relations Division," or "Division of School-Community Relations." However, the selected title should reflect the scope of responsibilities assigned to the division.

After determining who will be responsible for the PR function and after naming the division, the superintendent should answer other key questions:

◆ Where should the division's office be located?
◆ How many employees will be assigned to the division and what roles will they have?
◆ What material resources are necessary to support the division?
◆ How will the division interface with individual school principals?

SCHOOL-LEVEL PROGRAMS

Few people argue that good human relations are not important to organizational effectiveness, nor would they wittingly shun any practice that helped to achieve such goodwill. Good human relationships engender respect, cooperation, and collaboration and are essential to organizational success. But good human relationships do not happen naturally; they must be planned and implemented with careful deliberation. This kind of planning in any organizational context requires an effective PR program that incorporates the best in human relations and communication practices (West, 1985).

Need for School-Level Programs

The case for developing school-level PR programs as extensions of a district program is framed by two issues. First, misperceptions are more likely to be eradicated at the school level than at the district level because parents and other citizens have more contact with educators in schools. Even today, many people view PR as being synonymous with verbs like *cover up, obfuscate, misrepresent,* and *lie* (Martinson, 1995). In addition, the benefits derived from a PR program often go unnoticed until a crisis occurs or attempts to acquire needed resources fail. A strong school-level PR program can be instrumental in eradicating these conditions.

Second, needs, including those pertaining to PR, are not constant across schools, even in the same school district. Therefore, having individual school PR programs as extensions of a district program is considered effective practice. School-based PR programs require support and nurturing from district-level officials. For example, the school board should provide appropriate policy and encouragement, the superintendent should provide overall direction and fiscal resources, and the PR director should provide counsel and direct assistance. In addition, central office personnel should contribute to effective PR by promoting values and beliefs foundational to open, two-way communication. Even the best-conceived plan is likely to fail if it must be used in an organizational culture that restricts the principles of modern PR.

Building a School-Level Program

Pertinent school board policy and a district-level PR plan provide a foundation for a school-level PR plan because they establish purpose and parameters. Consequently, information contained in them needs to be shared and discussed by teachers and other staff members before initiating the planning process. Most importantly, employees need to understand the purpose of PR and recognize why this function is being pursued at both the district and the school levels. Many teachers and principals, for example, view PR narrowly as a responsibility for the school board and superintendent.

Though there is no single recipe for school PR planning, there are several tasks that are considered essential to every approach.

- ◆ *Creating a school PR committee.* This committee coordinates PR activities and advises the principal. It should be large enough to ensure that all stakeholder groups are represented, but not so large that communication and decision making suffer. Typically, such a committee would include representatives of the following groups: teachers, professional staff members (e.g., representatives of media specialists, guidance counselors), parents, support staff (e.g., food services, secretarial services), and possibly district administration (e.g., the district PR director or another person who serves on the district PR committee; West, 1985). In high schools, a representative of the students also may be included. A diverse committee brings different attitudes, opinions, and solutions to the table, and the diversity of inputs often strengthens the quality of decisions.
- ◆ *Identifying relevant publics.* One reason why school-level plans are important pertains to demographics. Each school has its own set of publics, and although they may be very similar among schools in a given district, they are never identical.
- ◆ *Identifying the media outlets used by relevant publics.* This information informs school personnel about available channels that can be used to communicate with stakeholders (Gronstedt, 1997).
- ◆ *Conducting external research.* A school plan should be predicated on real needs in the community being served (Gronstedt, 1997). Therefore, those needs should be identified and validated. In addition, relationships between school personnel and community members should be evaluated (Grossman, 1998).
- ◆ *Conducting internal research.* Given the broad definition of PR presented in this book, an assessment of needs and relationships within the school also is important. This includes communication between school and district personnel (Grossman, 1998).

- ◆ *Validating the school's PR mission.* A school's PR mission is shaped by school board policy, the district PR plan, and the specific needs of the school. The statement should be written in the present tense and reflect accurately what the school's PR program is supposed to do.
- ◆ *Developing a PR vision.* As discussed in relation to a district PR plan, the school vision presents an image of what the school PR program should look like in meeting the school's PR mission at some designated point in the future. Written in the future tense, the ideal vision is collaborative and attainable.
- ◆ *Developing goals.* Goals provide benchmarks for measuring progress toward the vision. If the time frame for reaching the PR vision is 10 years, goals provide periodic (e.g., annual) objectives that determine if satisfactory progress is being made (Gronstedt, 1997).
- ◆ *Developing messages and themes.* Messages and themes, explained previously in relation to district-level PR programs, are equally relevant to school programs (Armistead, 2002).
- ◆ *Adopting strategies and tactics.* Strategies are overall procedures for goal attainment. Tactics are the actions that must occur to carry out these procedures.
- ◆ *Interfacing the school and district PR plans.* As noted, a school plan should be an extension of a district plan. Therefore, the principal needs to ensure that these plans are complementary and that there are no contradictions in them.
- ◆ *Evaluating the plan.* As discussed in relation to district-level PR programming, the utility of plans is attenuated without an evaluation component.

SCHOOL-LEVEL RESPONSIBILITIES

Based on the conviction that PR is every school employee's responsibility, administrators should be aware of the role each employee group is expected to perform. In large measure, the principal's own role depends on whether he or she is the person responsible for coordinating PR.

Principal's Role

The principal focuses on improving relations with and among building-level personnel and between school personnel and external stakeholders. His or her role parallels the superintendent's role in several important ways. First, both administrators are instrumental in recommending PR policy: the superintendent directly to the school board, principals indirectly through the superintendent. Both administrators deal with the media: the superintendent fairly often, and principals periodically. As a consequence, both are obliged to develop good relationships with journalists (West, 1985).

A study of Texas high school principals and PR directors (Schueckler & West, 1991) found that principals expressed a need to improve their PR performance in the following five ways:

1. Operating their office more effectively;
2. Using common sense, good judgment, discretion, and a sense of proportion when dealing with others;

3. Becoming better listeners;
4. Being tactful and diplomatic in their relationships; and
5. Adopting an open-door policy for students, teachers, parents, and others.

The PR directors added three additional areas in which principals could improve their PR performance:

1. Striving to have the best PR program possible,
2. Recognizing the accomplishments of others, and
3. Keeping the superintendent informed of potential PR problems.

Writing about the PR role of elementary school principals, West (1993) noted:

[T]hey communicate with a variety of groups daily, most typically students, teachers, support staff and parents, but also central office personnel, their peers, and sometimes their superintendents, depending on the size of the system. They also communicate with business/industry representatives engaged in adopt-a-school programs. In these relationships they may at one moment assume an instructional leadership posture and at another an entrepreneurial stance. As entrepreneurs they strive to communicate their school's excellence to the neighborhoods that support them. (p. 10)

Faculty's Role

As the largest category of employees in a school system, teachers have an immense impact on PR. One of their most effective PR postures is treating students as clients. This means that they must know their subject matter and be able to deliver it in a manner that is educational and interesting. It also means that teachers must have high expectations for students and that they should recognize and reward appropriate behaviors. In carrying out this PR role, teachers model behavior they want their students to emulate. Perhaps the most important factor in creating satisfying relationships between home and school is a properly qualified and proficient teacher of high moral standing who works hard and cares about children (Swink, 1989).

In summary, a teacher is expected to maintain ongoing communication with parents, be a good listener, and maintain a professional and caring demeanor. Above all, the teacher should never minimize the parent or the child (Ediger, 2001).

Staff's Role

Other school employees, professional and nonprofessional, also have a PR responsibility. Guidance counselors and nurses, for example, should develop close relationships with students and parents so that they can advise them on pertinent matters. Librarians open up a world of books and visual learning materials to children, and they must be sensitive to community standards. Working just outside the principal's office, secretaries and clerks generally are the initial point of contact for visitors, and their attitudes toward and treatment of these people shape opinions toward the school (Ediger, 2001). Even custodians and food services employees influence relationships, both through their job performance and through their communicative behavior.

OTHER WAYS TO IMPROVE PUBLIC RELATIONS

The school PR plan provides direction for a variety of functions that determine whether school personnel establish positive relationships with their target publics. The most cogent of these functions are described here.

Multicultural Public Relations

The value of a multicultural approach to PR is well documented in the literature (e.g., Grunig & White, 1992; Kern-Foxworth & Miller, 1992). Social-interpretive communication theory, discussed by Banks (1995), indicates that effective multicultural PR is determined by the degree to which communication

- ◆ Reinforces participants' self-concepts,
- ◆ Affirms participants' cultural identities,
- ◆ Enhances the parties' relationship,
- ◆ Accomplishes the parties' strategic goals,
- ◆ Embraces the constitutive nature of communication,
- ◆ Recognizes the contextual nature of meanings,
- ◆ Accepts the diversity of interpretations, and
- ◆ Remains open to reinterpretation.

The more that is known about a school's external publics, the better the chance for implementing multicultural communication. A sociological inventory is one tool for social composition. Such an inventory could cover population characteristics, customs and traditions, political structure, social tensions, economic conditions, community groups, communication channels, and previous community efforts (Gallagher, Bagin, & Kindred, 1997).

Unfortunately, many schools do not attempt to communicate with all relevant publics. For example, various studies (e.g., Gibson, 1983, 1987; Rodriguez, 1992) have found that school personnel in diverse communities often ignore the culture and communication patterns of certain racial and ethnic groups. Multicultural communication has become a critical factor in building community relations, and this topic is discussed later in Chapter 10.

Planning Public Meetings

All open meetings sponsored by the district or a school affect organizational image and, therefore, should have a PR purpose. Basically, these meetings constitute opportunities to balance criticism, concerns, and problems with positive information that showcases successful programs, model students, and outstanding employees.

Procedures and personal behavior are important elements of public meetings. At the district level, the superintendent and, at the school level, the principal set the tone for normative communicative behavior. If he or she engages in open, honest, and appropriate communication, other employees are usually prompted to model this behavior (Kowalski, 2005).

Encouraging Citizen Participation

Over the past three or four decades, there has been a growing recognition that schools do not function well when they are isolated from their communities (Kowalski, 2003). Accordingly, involving as many district residents as possible should be one of the PR programming goals. Citizen participation has become more necessary, but more difficult due to the fact that many taxpayers no longer have children or even grandchildren attending local public schools. As a result, public opinion related to schools is often based on secondhand information sources.

There is a myriad of approaches that can be used to involve citizens. Arguably, parent-teacher conferences and parent-teacher associations (e.g., PTA or PTO) have been and should continue to be effective strategies (Ubben, Hughes, & Norris, 2004); however, they are restrictive in that they involve only the stakeholder group that already has the greatest level of contact with schools. The following are options that could be deployed to broaden citizen participation:

- *Open houses*. Open houses can attract nonparents as well as parents (Nicholson & Myhan, 2002). The keys are to invite the entire community and to give nonparents a reason to attend. For example, if the school media center is available to senior citizens, an open house is an excellent opportunity for displaying the resources that are available.
- *District and school Web pages*. A high percentage of residents in the typical school system rely on the Internet and the portion of it known as the World Wide Web for information. A user-friendly, information-rich Web page can be a tremendous asset with respect to communicating with the entire community. To be effective, however, district and school Web pages need to be updated regularly so that the information provided is timely (Ubben et al., 2004).
- *Advisory committees*. District and school advisory committees are an effective way to involve key individuals within various publics (McKenna & Willms, 1998). School councils, such as those associated with site-based management, are a prime example.
- *Opinion polling*. Periodic opinion polling serves two important purposes: It provides data essential to organizational development, and it conveys a message to stakeholders that you care about their opinions (Copeland, 2002; Glass, 1997).
- *School partnership programs*. School partnerships have multiplied considerably since 1980. Though most involve businesses or other governmental agencies, some engage nonparent district residents (Kowalski, 2006). As an example, a school district developed a senior citizen tutor program in which volunteers spent three hours per week tutoring students.
- *Community pride rooms*. Recognizing that a majority of taxpayers had no direct contact with public schools, some forward-thinking administrators have developed community pride rooms in schools. The rooms contain both historical artifacts and information resources (e.g., newspapers, magazines, Internet access) that are attractive to residents (Kowalski, 2002).

In seeking to broaden citizen participation, administrators may find it useful to network with colleagues to determine what is being done in other schools and to share information about effective strategies (Pawlas, 1995).

Maximizing the Use of Technology

Effective district and school leaders see technology not only as a tool for transforming teaching and learning (e.g., Bailey, 1996), but also as a vital resource for building relationships (Whitehead, Jensen, & Boschee, 2003). Most organization executives discover that cost and value are related when it comes to technology. That is, the more value technology produces, the less likely it is to be perceived as costly (Rhodes, 1997).

The list of opportunities to deploy technology in PR programs is virtually endless; two of them, Web pages and networking, are discussed separately. The following are other examples of ideas that have been implemented in districts and schools:

◆ *Electronic newsletters* not only provide information to relevant publics, but also can serve as an effective marketing tool with respect to determining the public's needs and wants (Walker & Donohue, 2004). Such newsletters may be published by the district, a school, or an individual. For example, some school board members provide information to constituents via an e-newsletter (Klagge, 1999).

◆ An *interactive computer station* for visitors is a good idea for district administrative offices and larger schools (Fry, 2001). Visitors can access information and directions quickly.

◆ *Annual technology fairs* often attract many community residents, some of whom would not otherwise visit schools (Fry, 2001).

◆ *Technology learning opportunities and development assistance* for community members are less recognized activities. For example, some schools provide computer literacy programs for adults or other technology-based adult education courses. In some communities, school personnel have helped local businesses develop Web pages, listservs, and related Internet products (Whitehead, 2000).

District or School Web Pages

In recent years, district and school Web sites have become one of the most widely used technological products; however, this medium presents potential problems as well as benefits. Consequently, administrators should be sure comprehensive policies and rules governing Web pages are in place (Levine, 2001) that at a minimum address the following issues:

1. *Roles and responsibilities*. Policy should address the following roles and their responsibilities: (a) a Webmaster to oversee the technical aspects of the site, (b) an editor to monitor the content that is published, and (c) an instructional development specialist to train district staff.

2. *Education value*. The Web site is intended to support the PR function, which in turn supports the school's teaching and learning objectives. Therefore, content must be regularly reviewed for value to ensure that information is accurate, fair, and relevant to the viewing publics.

3. *Student privacy*. The Federal Education Rights and Privacy Act, the Children's Online Privacy and Protection Act, and the Federal Bureau of Investigation (FBI) provide safeguards that administrators should follow. In the fall of 2000, for example, the FBI urged schools not to put student photos on Web sites. A district

policy should be adopted regarding student confidentiality before a Web site is allowed to post information, and, at a minimum, photo release forms should be revised to include use in electronic formats.

4. *Copyright laws.* Most school districts already have policies regarding adherence to fair-use provisions of copyright laws (a topic discussed previously in Chapter 4), but these should be revisited periodically to ensure awareness that Internet publishing is considered a "public performance" and that stricter guidelines pertain to material transmitted via this medium. The three critical copyright issues for Web pages are permissions (policy on granting and getting permission to use material from a Web site), fair use, and public domain (Is the material available without permission?; Butler, 2004).

5. *Use policy.* Web pages can have passive or dynamic servers. The latter permits material to be posted and discarded, typically by all or selected employees. When dynamic servers are used, policy should outline the purposes of the Web site, standards for acceptable material, and conditions under which material can be altered or removed (Reilly, 2003).

6. *Technical standards.* Cogent standards include issues such as the size of files permitted to be placed on the Web page and the server used for the Web page (e.g., Will the school district's server be used for individual school Web pages?). Although many districts use the schoolname.K12.state.us designation, others purchase a .com or .org domain name. Levine (2001) recommends that school officials take action to protect Web page content from individuals who seek to parody it or use it to present antieducational messages.

7. *Commercial sites and services.* A school's Web policy should forbid the use of third-party sites that have not been approved by school personnel. For example, an unscrupulous business enterprise may create sites or fund-raising programs that have no official ties to the district or school.

In addition to developing pertinent policies and rules, administrators have other responsibilities in relation to Web pages. Padgett (2005) recommends the following actions by principals:

◆ Establish and communicate the purpose of the Web page.
◆ Publicize the page to make all publics aware that it exists.
◆ Make the page visually attractive and information-rich.
◆ Visit the page at least once a week to ensure that it is being properly maintained and updated.

Administrators also should see that a school's Web page conveys symbolic messages reinforcing institutional mission, vision, and culture. For example, school officials who profess that students, the community, and academic achievement are important send mixed messages when they include only pictures of themselves, buildings, and athletic events on the Web page.

An ideal Web site is visually appealing to its audience. The primary goal for the administrator is to ensure the site assumes the personality of the school. A homepage that is thoroughly effective will serve to welcome visitors to the school's total environment.

Homepage basics should include the school phone number, its location, and driving directions from major highways. Staff names and contact information are also well-advised additions. If possible, it is worthwhile to display links to district and student services so that user-friendliness is attained. The key consideration, and one that the principal must attend to, is that information included on the Web site must be valuable to its users. This requires an inquiry process of some sort, which will render the needed facts. Finally, a Web page should be a key source of information. For example, many of them contain online school "report cards" and important information for parents, staff, and students. With effective translations, a Web site can help a school reach out to minority parents and citizens who no longer have children in school.

Networking

Network-based communication describes a variety of systems that enable educators to communicate with other people through computers and networks (Romiszowski & Mason, 1996). Broadly categorized, communication occurring over networks is either synchronous or asynchronous. Though both are text-based, synchronous communication takes place in real time, just as if two people were talking on the telephone. Examples of synchronous formats include virtual hallways, network videoconferencing, and chat rooms. Common asynchronous network communication mediums (those having time lapses) are e-mail, newsgroups, listservs, threaded forums, and electronic bulletin boards (Hawkes, 2001).

Two-way communication, horizontal and vertical, is vital in any organization. If formal information channels are not kept open, rumors and misinformation flourish through informal channels, and ultimately, employee morale suffers. Although there are some disadvantages of network communication (e.g., loss of verbal communication), the process allows educators to connect to other educators, parents, or other persons in an efficient manner. Networks exist among school districts (e.g., connecting all the school districts in a state or region), within a school district (e.g., connecting all the schools and offices in a district), among peer administrators across districts (e.g., superintendent or principal networks in a state or region), and among workstations in a school. The refinement of wireless networking has made school-level connections more feasible, especially in older facilities. For example, laser, infrared, and radio frequency options allow networking where wiring would be unduly expensive or unsafe (Ahmed, 2004).

Networking also is a means for connecting classrooms to the public. If done properly, students, teachers, and administrators will have access to supportive communities when they venture electronically outside of their physical learning environment. Conversely, networking gives district residents, business executives, and other agency officials opportunities to become more involved in public education (Conte, 1998).

Although there are many formal ways to communicate about PR activities, one of the best ways is to exchange information through a network connecting persons who serve on the district's school PR advisory committees. In larger school systems, the network should be coordinated by the PR director. Such a network also can encourage informal exchanges among principals and PR committee members.

PUBLIC RELATIONS IN SITE-BASED SCHOOLS

Site- or school-based management (SBM) plans are now required in several states. For example, school systems in Kentucky and Texas must develop and implement SBM plans annually as a way of decentralizing governance. Proponents of SBM believe that people affected by educational decisions ought to be involved in making those decisions because involvement leads to greater commitment to the eventual success of the decision (McNergney & Herbert, 1998); thus, SBM committees often are given the power to make important decisions in designated areas of operation.

Schwahn and Spady (1998) have analyzed and recommended the best future-focused change strategies for education. They echo the recommendation of Peters and Waterman (1982), who urged that visionary business leaders "get close to their customers." The philosophy of a client focus encourages leaders to ask their colleagues and themselves repeatedly if they meet or exceed their customers' needs, present, emerging, and future (Schwahn & Spady, 1998). Exceptional principals work hard to find opportunities to form and discuss school goals and purposes, as well as mission, with staff, parents, students, community members, and others in the school system (Ashby & Krug, 1998). In those districts where SBM, total quality management, and strategic planning are reinforced by broadening dramatically the circle of participation, PR skills become even more important.

Traditionally, superintendents and principals have depended heavily on legal and organizational authority. Under SBM, they facilitate and support decisions made democratically. Observers often err in concluding that decentralization minimizes the importance of administration; in fact, concepts such as SBM reshape practice. As an example, district superintendents continue to make important leadership decisions that ultimately determine whether decentralization will function as intended (Thompson & Wood, 1998). Moreover, superintendents usually determine whether the district will have a full-time PR administrator, communications team, and effective communications policy (Gallagher et al., 1997; Ledell, 1996; Norton, Webb, Dlugosh, & Sybouts, 1996). In this vein, they have considerable influence on how PR functions are carried out under decentralized governance.

SUMMARY

The tone for effective PR in districts and schools is set by the superintendent. He or she almost always has more influence than any other individual on planning, staffing, and budgeting. Equally important, the superintendent's communicative behavior has symbolic importance, especially with respect to determining whether open, candid, and two-way communication is the norm (Kowalski, 2005).

Principals also have a great deal of responsibility for shaping and managing PR activities. Most notably, they are expected to develop a school-based planning committee, a school-based PR plan, and appropriate support technology. In addition, they need to utilize these resources in ways that improve PR specifically and instructional effectiveness generally. In this vein, their ability to build and maintain a school Web page, communication networks, and community involvement greatly influences the overall effectiveness of their own practice.

QUESTIONS AND SUGGESTED ACTIVITIES

CASE STUDY

1. For years, the school district has been blamed for many of the city's problems. To what extent is the district's closed climate (i.e., its reluctance to interact with external forces) a contributing factor to the district's being made a scapegoat?
2. In what ways did the superintendent underestimate the complexity of the community?
3. What negative communication patterns existed in the school district? How did these negative patterns affect the superintendent?
4. Why were many parents reluctant to have open dialogue with the superintendent?
5. The superintendent tried to increase PR activities in two ways: by creating a new position in public information services and by personally spending more time outside of her office. Were these prudent decisions? Why or why not?
6. What actions might the superintendent take to build more open communication with the school board members?

CHAPTER

7. What is the ideal relationship between a district PR plan and a school PR plan?
8. Why is it important to have a building-level PR program?
9. Who is responsible for engaging in good PR in districts and schools?
10. What is benchmarking? Why is this concept relevant to PR?
11. In what ways are public meetings a PR function?
12. Why is the superintendent's communicative behavior symbolically important with respect to PR?
13. What are the attributes of a good district PR plan?
14. What is defining research? What role does it play in PR planning?

SUGGESTED READINGS

Armistead, L. (2000). Public relations: Harness your school's power. *High School Magazine*, 7(6), 24–27.

Arnett, J. S. (1999). From public enragement to engagement. *School Administrator*, 56(8), 24–27.

Bete, T. (1998). Eight great community relations ideas. *School Planning & Management*, 37(5), 49–57.

Bruckner, M. (1998). Make friends before we need them: Operating a key communicator program. *Journal of Educational Relations*, 19(1), 6–12.

Bushman, J., & Boris, V. (1998). Listening to the public. *American School Board Journal*, 185(12), 27–29.

Carroll, S. R., & Carroll, D. (2000). *EdMarketing: How smart schools get and keep community support.* Bloomington, IN: National Educational Service.

Copeland, S. (2002). Use of public opinion surveys. *Journal of School Public Relations*, 23(4), 67–83.

Deasy, J. E. (2000). Moving from oversight to insight: One community's journey with its superintendent. *Phi Delta Kappan*, 82(1), 13–15.

Enderle, J. (2000). Three school districts honored for their community relations efforts. *School Planning & Management*, 39(5), 26, 28–31.

Gronstedt, A. (1997). The role of research in public relations strategy and planning. In C. L. Claywood (Ed.), *The handbook of strategic public relations and integrated communications* (pp. 47–59). New York: McGraw-Hill.

Grossman, J. W. (1998). *Public relations plans.* Rockville, MD: National School Public Relations Association.

Holliday, A. E. (1996). 99 ways to increase/improve school-community relations. *Journal of Educational Relations, 17*(3), 2–6.

Kaplan, G. R. (1992). *Images of education: The mass media's version of America's schools.* Arlington, VA: National School Public Relations Association.

McLaren, P. (1998). *Life in schools.* New York: Longman.

McNergney, R. F., & Herbert, J. M. (1998). *Foundations of education.* Boston: Allyn & Bacon.

Plucker, J. A., & Slavkin, M. L. (2000). No school is an island. *Principal Leadership, 1*(1), 48–53.

Schwahn, C. J., & Spady, W. G. (1998). *Total leaders.* Arlington, VA: American Association of School Administrators.

Soholt, S. (1998). Public engagement: Lessons from the front. *Educational Leadership, 56*(2), 22–23.

Uline, C. L. (1998). Town meeting and community engagement. *Journal of School Leadership, 8*(6), 533–557.

Watson, A. (1998). The newspaper's responsibility. *Phi Delta Kappan, 79*(10), 728–734.

REFERENCES

Ahmed, S. F. (2004). Unplugged facilities. *American School & University, 77*(3), 369–371.

Armistead, L. (2002). Ten steps for planning public relations. *Education Digest, 67*(6), 57–61.

Ashby, D. E., & Krug, S. E. (1998). *Thinking through the principalship.* Larchmont, NY: Eye on Education.

Bagin, D., Ferguson, D., & Marx, G. (1985). *Public relations for administrators.* Arlington, VA: American Association of School Administrators.

Bailey, G. D. (1996). Technology leadership: Ten essential buttons for understanding technology integration in the 21st century. *Educational Considerations, 23*(2), 2–6.

Banks, S. P. (1995). *Multicultural public relations: A social-interpretive approach.* Thousand Oaks, CA: Sage.

Batory, J. P. (1999). The sad state of education coverage. *School Administrator, 56*(8), 34–38.

Bohen, D. B. (1998). Communication: Illusions and realities. In R. R. Spillane & P. Regnier (Eds.), *The superintendent of the future: Strategy and action for achieving academic excellence* (pp. 219–236). Gaithersburg, MD: Aspen Publishers.

Borja, R. R. (2004, October 24). Educators, journalists spar over media access. *Education Week, 21*(8), 1, 24–25.

Butler, R. P. (2004). Web page construction and copyright law: How much do I need to know? *Knowledge Quest, 32*(4), 41–42.

Conte, C. (1998). Technology in schools: Hip or hype? *Education Digest, 63,* 28–33.

Copeland, S. (2002). Use of public opinion surveys. *Journal of School Public Relations, 23*(4), 67–83.

Davis, B. R. (1986). *School public relations: The complete book.* Arlington, VA: National School Public Relations Association.

Deal, T. E., & Kennedy, A. A. (1982). *Corporate cultures: The rites and rituals of corporate life.* Reading, MA: Addison-Wesley.

Ediger, M. (2001). Effective public school relations. *Education, 121*(4), 743–750.

Fry, P. L. (2001). Getting the word out. *Technology & Learning, 21*(10), 54–56.

Fullan, M. (2001). *Leading in a culture of change.* San Francisco: Jossey-Bass.

Gallagher, D. R., Bagin, D., & Kindred, L. W. (1997). *The school and community relations* (6th ed.). Boston: Allyn & Bacon.

Gibson, M. A. (1983). *Home-school-community linkages: A study of educational opportunity for Punjabi youth* (Final report). Stockton, CA: South Asian American Education Association.

Gibson, M. A. (1987). The school performance of immigrant minorities: A comparative view. *Anthropology & Education Quarterly, 18*(4), 262–275.

Glass, T. E. (1997). Using school district public opinion surveys to gauge and obtain public support. *Community Journal, 7*(1), 101–116.

Gronstedt, A. (1997). The role of research in public relations strategy and planning. In C. L. Caywood (Ed.), *The handbook of strategic public relations and integrated communications* (pp. 47–59). New York: McGraw-Hill.

Grossman, J. W. (1998). *Public relations plans*. Rockville, MD: National School Public Relations Association.

Grunig, J. E., & White, J. (1992). The effect of world views on public relations theory and practice. In J. E. Grunig (Ed.), *Excellence in public relations and communication management* (pp. 31–65). Hillsdale, NJ: Erlbaum.

Hawkes, M. (2001). Variables of interest in exploring the reflective outcomes of network-based communication. *Journal of Research on Computing in Education, 33*(3), 299–315.

Johnston, G., Gross, G., Townsend, R., Lynch, P., Novotney, P., Roberts, B., et al. (2002). *A view inside public education: Eight at the top*. Lanham, MD: Scarecrow Press.

Kern-Foxworth, M., & Miller, D. A. (1992, May). *Embracing multicultural diversity: A preliminary examination of public relations education*. Paper presented at the annual conference of the International Communication Association, Miami, FL.

Kirst, M. W., & Kelley, C. (1995). Collaboration to improve education and children's services: Politics and policy making. In L. Rigsby, M. Reynolds, & M. Wang (Eds.), *School-community connections: Exploring issues for research and practice* (pp. 21–44). San Francisco: Jossey-Bass.

Klagge, J. C. (1999). Democracy on the Net. *American School Board Journal, 186*(1), A24–A25.

Kowalski, T. J. (1995). *Keepers of the flame: Contemporary urban superintendents*. Thousand Oaks, CA: Corwin.

Kowalski, T. J. (2002). *Planning and managing school facilities* (2nd ed.). Westport, CT: Bergin & Garvey.

Kowalski, T. J. (2003). *Contemporary school administration: An introduction* (2nd ed.). Boston: Allyn & Bacon.

Kowalski, T. J. (2005). Evolution of the school superintendent as communicator. *Communication Education, 54*(2), 101–117.

Kowalski, T. J. (2006). *The school superintendent: Theory, practice, and cases* (2nd ed.). Thousand Oaks, CA: Sage.

Ledell, M. A. (1996). Common ground: A way of life. *School Administrator, 53*(10), 8–11.

Levine, E. (2001). A Web policy primer. *American School Board Journal, 188*(7), 20–23.

Martinson, D. (1995). School public relations: Do it right or don't do it at all! *Contemporary Education, 66*(2), 82–85.

McKenna, M., & Willms, J. D. (1998). Co-operation between families and schools: What works in Canada. *Research Papers in Education: Policy & Practice, 13*(1), 19–41.

McNergney, R. F., & Herbert, J. M. (1998). *Foundations of education*. Boston: Allyn & Bacon.

Nicholson, J. I., & Myhan, J. G. (2002). Twenty practical parental involvement tips. *Journal of Early Education & Family Review, 10*(2), 13–17.

Norton, M. S., Webb, L. D., Dlugosh, L. L., & Sybouts, W. (1996). *The school superintendency*. Boston: Allyn & Bacon.

Padgett, R. (2005). A portal to great PR. *Communicator: The Monthly Newsletter of the National Association of Elementary School Principals, 29*(3), 5–6.

Pawlas, G. E. (1995). *The administrator's guide to school-community relations*. Princeton Junction, NJ: Eye on Education.

Peters, T., & Waterman, R. (1982). *In search of excellence*. New York: Harper & Row.

Petersen, G. J., & Kowalski, T. J. (2005, November). *School reform strategies and normative expectations for democratic leadership in the superintendency*. Paper presented at the annual meeting of the University Council for Educational Administration, Nashville, TN.

Reilly, R. (2003). Your school wants a Web page: Plan carefully. *Multimedia Schools, 10*(2), 60, 62, 64.

Rhodes, L. A. (1997). Building leadership technology. *School Administrator, 54*(4), 12–16.

Rodriguez, C. E. (1992). *Student voices: High school students' perspectives on the Latino dropout problem* (Report of the Fordham University, College at Lincoln Center Student Research Project). New York: Latino Commission on Educational Reform.

Romiszowski, A. J., & Mason, R. (1996). Network-based communication. In D. Jonasson (Ed.), *Handbook of research for educational communications and technology* (pp. 438–456). New York: Simon & Schuster Macmillan.

Schueckler, L. P., & West, P. T. (1991). Principals and PR directors mostly agree on the ideal PR role for senior high school principals, but substantially disagree on their PR performance. *Journal of Educational Public Relations, 13*(4), 24–26.

Schwahn, C. J., & Spady, W. G. (1998). *Total leaders.* Arlington, VA: American Association of School Administrators.

Swink, E. (1989). What factors in a school create satisfying home–school–community relations? *Journal of Educational Public Relations, 12*(1), 19–20.

Thompson, D. C., & Wood, R. C. (1998). *Money and schools.* Larchmont, NY: Eye on Education.

Topor, R. (1992). *No more navel gazing!* Mountain View, CA: Topor & Associates.

Ubben, G. C., Hughes, L. W., & Norris, C. J. (2004). *The principal: Creative leadership for effective schools* (5th ed.). Boston: Allyn & Bacon.

Unruh, A., & Willier, R. A. (1974). *Public relations for schools.* Belmont, CA: Lear Siegler/Fearon.

Walker, T., & Donohue, C. (2004). Decoding technology: Creating e-newsletters. *Child Care Information Exchange, 157,* 61–62.

West, P. T. (1985). *Educational public relations.* South Beverly Hills, CA: Sage.

West, P. T. (1993). The elementary school principal's role in school–community relations. *Georgia's Elementary Principal, 1*(2), 9–10.

Whitehead, B. M. (2000). How does technology measure up? *Principal, 80*(2), 45–46.

Whitehead, B. M., Jensen, D. F., & Boschee, F. (2003). *Planning for technology: A guide for school administrators, technology coordinators, and curriculum leaders.* Thousand Oaks, CA: Corwin.

Zoch, L. M., Patterson, B., & Olson, D. L. (1997). The status of the school public relations practitioner: A statewide exploration. *Public Relations Review, 23*(4), 361–375.

CHAPTER

Programming in Private and Nontraditional Public Schools

Theodore J. Kowalski

CASE STUDY: SELLING THE SCHOOL

Located in an established area of a northeastern city, Metropolitan Hebrew High School (MHHS) has a tradition that dates back to 1951. Many of the alumni are prominent citizens in the community and regular contributors to the school. Until recently, the school's principal has not had to worry about enrollments because a new generation of alumni children always filled the available spaces and the enrollment remained stable at about 300 students. In the past three years, however, the incoming freshman class has declined about 5% each year. Urged by the school's board of directors, the headmaster has conducted a study to determine why the school is losing enrollment. His findings attributed the enrollment decline to three factors.

1. There has been a gradual exodus of Jewish families from the immediate community to more-affluent suburbs that have excellent public schools. The population of Jewish families with school-age children has declined 22% in just 10 years.
2. The public school district in which MHHS is located recently opened a new mathematics-science magnet school. Housed just blocks from MHHS, the magnet school is equipped with modern computers and science laboratories.
3. A group of retired public school teachers has opened a charter high school in the community. Although it is housed in an old elementary school and enrolls just 83 students, nearly half of those students did or probably would have attended MHHS.

The headmaster's report included the following information:

◆ MHHS defines itself as both a religious and an academic institution. In the past, parents have paid more attention to religious values, but presently, they appear to be placing more emphasis on academics.
◆ Restricted resources have limited both improvements to the facility (now more than 50 years old) and the acquisition of technology.
◆ In just seven years, 30% of the faculty have resigned or retired.
◆ The school publishes a newsletter that is mailed to both parents and other donors twice each year. The publication's primary purpose is to solicit donations.
◆ Annual contributions since 2000 have averaged about $59,000 per year—about $210 per pupil. Last year, however, approximately 85% of financial gifts to the school came from just 11 donors.
◆ The school's last capital campaign occurred 29 years ago and raised $1.5 million. About half of the funds was used to start a foundation account; the other half was used to pay for facility improvements. Currently, the school's endowment is $3.6 million.
◆ Tuition is currently $7,600 per year, and it is estimated to increase by an average of 3% per year for the foreseeable future.

♦ In addition to tuition revenues and annual donations, the school receives support from two local synagogues; each contributes $25,000 per year. These funds are used primarily for tuition scholarships.

♦ The school has neither a public relations (PR) plan nor a recruitment plan. Parent volunteers assist the headmaster with sending recruitment letters to potential students.

♦ The school does not employ teacher aides, and the school has only one secretary, who is assigned to the headmaster. Twenty-one volunteers work one day per month in the school—assisting teachers, working in the cafeteria, or helping with clerical tasks. Just a few years ago there were over 40 volunteers.

After reading the headmaster's report, the board of directors has decided to embark on a five-year program to reverse enrollment trends. The members have instructed the headmaster to outline a plan of action, advising him that a failure to reverse enrollment trends could mean the demise of the school. They also have expressed fears that charging additional tuition could exacerbate rather than solve the declining enrollment problem.

The overall problem faced by the headmaster at the school in this case study is not especially unusual, especially for private school principals in urban areas. Revenues, enrollments, and infrastructure are intertwined; as enrollments declined, so did revenues and so did the possibilities for improving facilities and providing modern equipment. Improved public schools, charter schools, and other private schools present greater competition, and there is only a limited capacity to compete with these schools. In the midst of enrollment declines and considerable faculty turnover, the headmaster is faced with the reality that either he reverses the school's downward spiral or the school will close.

Over the past two decades, interest in private schools and alternative forms of public education has grown considerably. The reasons are varied, but many of them are rooted in convictions that parental choice[1] is an effective reform initiative. Consider just three arguments supporting this belief:

1. Students from low-income families, trapped in areas served by the most ineffective and troubled public schools, could benefit from having options that are otherwise unavailable to them (Hill, 1996; Viteritti, 1996).

2. Reformers embracing market mechanisms[2] (Friedman & Friedman, 1981) believe that ineffective public schools will either improve or close if forced to compete for students. Moreover, competition is seen as a relatively inexpensive reform strategy.

3. Reformers guided primarily by the value of liberty believe that parents across all income levels should have the freedom to select schools for their children. In their

---

[1]Parental choice is a liberty provision allowing parents to select a preferred school. Choice can exist (a) within a public school district (e.g., a student can attend any school in the district in which he or she resides), within a state among public school districts (e.g., a student can attend any public school within the state in which he or she resides), and (c) public/private choice (e.g., providing support either through vouchers or tuition tax credits to allow a student to attend any public or private school in the state in which he or she resides).

[2]Defined as the concepts central to the marketplace economy, where competition among providers is believed to produce organizational change and development.

eyes, school choice results in greater parental support for education, and therefore, it benefits students (Vasallo, 2000).

Ideas promoting more alternatives to traditional public schooling have not gone unchallenged. Consider some of the more prevalent criticisms:

◆ Teachers unions and political leaders sympathetic to them have been especially vocal in denouncing programs such as vouchers, tuition tax credits, and charter schools. They see these ideas as merely diversions that further reduce public education's scarce resources and that potentially diminish the political influence of unions (Brouillette & Williams, 1999).

◆ Less-educated parents with more modest means are less likely to exercise choice. Therefore, choice systems could lead to less equity and more racial, ethnic, and socioeconomic stratification (Goldhaber, 1999; Good & Braden, 2000).

◆ Market-driven reform strategies have spawned ideological concerns related to the concept of school as community (Bryk, Lee, & Holland, 1993) and to the potential for greater racial segregation (Smith & Meier, 1995) and social segregation (Walford, 1996).

◆ Rather than serving the needs of inner-city students from low-income families, choice caters to families in the middle and upper classes (Witte, 1995).

◆ Private schools can and do reject students. The propensity to attend them increases with both income and ability, and in private schools, tuition declines with student ability—a factor making private schools attractive to higher-achieving students. Hence, choice programs, and especially those funded through vouchers, can entice these students to leave traditional public schools (Epple & Romano, 1998).

◆ Choice programs raise fundamental legal questions; if legislation promoting this concept is enacted without corresponding revisions to school finance laws and policies, local control over public education will be eroded (Hilton, 1994).

◆ A relatively recent study from Harvard University's Civil Rights Project claims that in the case of charter schools, choice has resulted in racial isolation (Colgan, 2003).

Despite such disapproval, efforts to create more options to traditional elementary and secondary public schools keep gaining momentum.

This chapter examines PR application in institutions that must compete for students. Private schools and then nontraditional public schools are discussed. This subject matter is relevant for aspiring administrators because some of them will eventually practice in private or nontraditional public schools. For the remaining students, the topic is cogent because they will be practicing in traditional public schools that will directly and indirectly compete with these institutions for students.

PRIVATE SCHOOLS

The popularity of private schools is attested to by the fact that the rate of enrollment increases in these institutions is getting larger; between 1970 and 1986, private school enrollment in the United States increased by 2%, but rose by 6% between 1986 and 1996

(Smith, 1997). During the period from 1997 to 2007, total private school enrollment is expected to increase by 3%, rising from 5.9 to 6.1 million (Smith, 1997). According to the Council for American Private Education (CAPE; 2005), 11.5% of all elementary and secondary school students in the United States attended private institutions during the 2003–2004 school year.

Nature of Private Schools

Although state governments have virtually ensured the continued existence of public schools, private schools have had to rely on attractive programs, values, and aspects of climate and culture to recruit and retain students. Success has usually depended on the delivery of a challenging, personalized academic curriculum in a socially defined atmosphere. Therefore, compared to public schools, private schools have had to exist in a more competitive environment—a condition that elevated the importance of PR for their administrators.

Generalizations about private schools are precarious because these institutions have different missions and serve different clientele. Generally, five criteria are used to describe differences among these schools (also see Figure 8–1):

Affiliation Based on Religion
- Religiously affiliated or sponsored
- Religiously nonaffiliated (independent or nonsectarian)

Cost
- Expensive (high-cost schools)
- Moderate (moderate-cost schools)
- Inexpensive (low-cost schools)

Admission Based on Religion
- Religion not considered
- Religion considered, but not a required factor
- Religion an essential factor

Admission Based on Academics
- Highly selective
- Selective
- Nonselective

Student Residence
- Residential only (boarding schools)
- Combined residential and nonresidental
- Nonresidential only

FIGURE 8–1
Types of Private Schools

1. *Religious affiliation.* This criterion identifies whether a school is affiliated with or subsidized by an organized religion, religious order, parish, church, synagogue, or other religious institution. Schools having such an affiliation are generally referred to as parochial schools[3]; those that do not are classified as independent or nonsectarian schools.

2. *Cost.* The cost of sending a student to a private elementary or secondary school varies markedly in this country. Generally, secondary schools cost more than elementary schools, and geographic location, mission, and economic realities play some part in determining tuition and fee rates. High-cost schools, usually found in urban and suburban locations, have distinctive student populations generally characterized by students from high-income families. They rely heavily on tuition revenues and private gifts. By comparison, moderate-cost and low-cost schools typically are parochial schools that rely on a mix of tuition revenues, private gifts, and subsidies provided by the sponsoring congregation, parish, or religious order.

3. *Religious admission standards.* Not all parochial schools use religion-based admission criteria. Most Catholic and Lutheran schools, for example, accept students of different faiths, although some may give preference to students based on religion (e.g., in parish-supported Catholic elementary schools). Some schools, however, admit only students who adhere to specified religious tenets, values, and beliefs. These schools typically require parents (and possibly students) to sign statements stipulating their acceptance of the specified religious principles and committing them to abide by those principles. The intent of these statements is to socialize students to think and behave according to the dictates of the sponsoring religion's doctrine (Peshkin, 1986). Conservative Christian schools sponsored by various Protestant denominations constitute the vast majority of schools restricting admission based on religious beliefs or church membership. Other schools restricting admission based on religion include Muslim academies and some Hebrew day schools.

4. *Academic admission standards.* Private schools often have different admission standards based on student ability and past achievement. Some are highly selective, some are moderately selective, and some have open admission policies.

5. *Student residence.* A small percentage of private schools are boarding schools; these are institutions requiring students to live on campus in dormitories or other facilities. Other schools admit both boarding and day students (i.e., students who commute). The vast majority of private schools do not offer boarding as an option.

Religious affiliation is arguably the criterion most widely used to distinguish among private schools. For example, the National Center for Education Statistics (1997) categorizes schools on the basis of religious affiliation and then uses subdivisions in these two categories to report data. The subcategories are shown in Figure 8–2 and defined as follows:

◆ *Catholic—Parochial Schools.* These are primarily elementary schools sponsored by and affiliated with parishes. (The term *parochial school* actually refers to a parish-based

---

[3]Parochial schools also are defined more narrowly to include only parish-sponsored schools.

Religious Schools
- Catholic
  * Parish owned or controlled (narrowly defined as parochial)
  * Diocesan owned or controlled
  * Religious order owned/controlled
- Conservative Christian
- Other religious affiliated (other than Catholic or conservative Christian, e.g., Lutheran)
- Other religious unaffiliated (e.g., nondenominational Christian schools)

Nonsectarian Schools
- Regular (no special focus)
- Special emphasis (e.g., Montessori schools)
- Special education (includes schools for gifted and talented students)

FIGURE 8–2
Subcategories for Religious and Nonsectarian Schools

school, but over time, the term has been used to connote any religiously affiliated or sponsored school.)

◆ *Catholic—Diocesan Schools.* These schools are sponsored by and affiliated with a diocese (e.g., a diocese high school).

◆ *Catholic—Private Order Schools.* These schools, predominately high schools, are owned and operated by religious orders (e.g., Jesuit, Marianist, and Christian Brothers schools).

◆ *Other Religious—Conservative Christian Schools.* This category includes only conservative Christian schools, whereas a general reference to "fundamentalist schools" usually has a broader connotation.

◆ *Other Religious—Affiliated Schools.* This category includes religious-based schools other than Catholic and conservative Christian schools. Examples include Lutheran, Episcopal, Seventh-Day Adventist, Hebrew, and Muslim schools.

◆ *Other Religious—Unaffiliated Schools.* These schools have a religious mission and philosophy, but are not affiliated with any particular religion, church, or denomination. They are often referred to as interdenominational religious schools.

◆ *Nonsectarian Regular Schools.* This category includes private schools without a religious affiliation and without a special focus.

◆ *Nonsectarian Special Emphasis Schools.* This category includes private schools without religious affiliation, but having a special mission or philosophical focus (e.g., Montessori schools).

◆ *Nonsectarian Special Education Schools.* This category includes private schools without religious affiliation and serving only special needs students ranging from students with disabilities to gifted and talented students.

Historically, religiously affiliated schools have accounted for the vast majority of private elementary and secondary schools in the United States, with a high percentage being Catholic schools. In 1965, Catholic schools educated 88% of the students attending this country's private schools; from that year to 1983, however, the number of Catholic schools declined by 30%. In 1983, only 46% of the students enrolled in private schools were attending Catholic schools (Cooper, 1984). Responding to enrollment concerns and rising costs, Catholic schools across America launched a marketing campaign in the early 1990s called "Discover Catholic Schools, 1992" (Rist, 1991). This effort helped to reverse the declining enrollment trend. In 1993–1994, there were 26,093 private elementary and secondary schools, and the Catholic Church operated about one-third of them (32%) and enrolled slightly more than half (51%) of the nation's students attending private schools (McLaughlin & Broughman, 1997). In the fall of 1999, there were 27,223 private elementary and secondary schools in the United States. Among the three primary types of private schools—Catholic, other religious, and nonsectarian—other religious schools were the most numerous, followed by Catholic schools and then nonsectarian schools, representing 49, 30, and 22% of all private schools, respectively (Broughman & Colaciello, 1999). In 2000, Catholic schools of various types enrolled 48.6% of all private elementary and secondary school students (CAPE, 2005).

Over the past few decades, the trend has been toward more private schools, and therefore, the aggregate enrollment in these schools has been increasing. The largest increase in the number of schools in the last quarter of the twentieth century was experienced among those identified as "conservative Christian" and Baptist (CAPE, 2005). However, the numbers of Jewish schools, Montessori schools, and special education schools also have increased since 1960 (Broughman & Colaciello, 1998; McLaughlin & Broughman, 1997). Interest in parochial schools has been greatest in urban areas, largely because many minority families have lost confidence in their local public schools. Even when religion is not a factor, some families have selected parochial schools because they think that the public schools lack discipline and academic focus. Some studies (e.g., Convey, 1992) have even found academics to be the prime motivator for parents enrolling their children in religiously affiliated schools.

In the past 25 years, the popularity of entrepreneurial schools also has grown. These institutions are intended to produce a profit for their owners or stockholders. For-profit private schools, however, should not be confused with either public schools operated under contract by private businesses or charter schools. Unlike these two types of schools, for-profit schools may not be required to abide by all policies and regulations governing public schools, and they do not receive direct public funding. For-profit schools are most prevalent in urban areas, where they attract primarily affluent parents. Lieberman (1986), a leading spokesperson for entrepreneurial schools, argues that these institutions create levels of competition with public schools not achieved by other types of private schools. As an example, he describes competition between Catholic and public schools as typically "genteel" (p. 216) because Catholic school officials fear that criticizing public schools might alienate church members who send their children to public schools. Lieberman believes that entrepreneurial school officials have fewer inhibitions about being critical, and therefore, their marketing and recruitment strategies often aggressively emphasize public education's perceived deficiencies.

Financial Realities

Private schools receive no tax dollars directly from state or local government. Therefore, they rely primarily on the following funding sources:

- ◆ Tuition and fees,
- ◆ Capital campaigns and other forms of annual fund-raising,
- ◆ Major private gifts and endowments, and
- ◆ In the case of religiously affiliated schools, fiscal support from parishes, congregations, or religious orders.

Compared with public school funding, private school revenue streams are less assured and more irregular. Private school administrators, however, typically have more flexibility in making resource allocation decisions, initiating fund-raising activities, and investing funds.[4] Seeking greater flexibility in using public fiscal resources, many public schools have established their own educational foundations in recent years. These separate legal entities allow foundation boards to expend money collected from private donors (Merz & Frankel, 1997).

Virtually all private schools are experiencing increasing expenditures, the most significant of which involve personnel costs. Catholic schools, for example, used to be staffed primarily by men and women in religious orders, employees who received little compensation. As the number of religious vocations declined, personnel budgets had to be increased significantly so that lay teachers and administrators could be hired. Even so, public school teachers almost always earn more and receive more benefits than private school teachers (Choy, 1997). A study in the mid-1990s, for example, found that public elementary schools generally spent twice as much per pupil as did religiously affiliated elementary schools—and much of the difference was attributable to personnel costs (Larson, 1995). Many parish-sponsored schools, funded heavily by weekly collections, suffered considerably as personnel costs escalated. Unable to divert more parish revenues, pastors faced the difficult choice of raising tuition or closing the school. For many of these parish schools, higher tuition produced a seemingly hopeless cycle of budget–enrollment decline problems.

In addition to personnel, operating costs in private schools have been affected by the following conditions:

- ◆ *Capital improvements*. Many private schools have had to enlarge, renovate, or replace their facilities.
- ◆ *Risk management*. Many private schools have had to expand liability coverage and pay higher insurance premiums.
- ◆ *Technology*. In order to remain competitive, private schools have had to divert resources to the deployment of technology in classrooms and in administrative offices.
- ◆ *Rising energy prices*. In many parts of the country, the cost of heating and cooling school buildings has gotten progressively higher.

---

[4]States' laws govern the types of investments that may be made by public agencies, including school districts.

Public schools typically address such fiscal challenges by securing added funding either through state support or through local tax revenues. Private school officials, however, have to rely on a mix of tuition increases, budget cuts, and fund-raising activities to meet escalating costs.

Private schools typically have endowments that include revenues raised through periodic capital campaigns, annual alumni contribution drives, grants, and gifts from philanthropic organizations and foundations. The need to raise funds independent of tuition places even more pressure on private school administrators to engage in effective PR.

Attraction of Private Schools

A number of writers (e.g., Greeley & McManus, 1987; Rothstein, Carnoy, & Benveniste, 1999) have pointed out that private schools, and especially religious schools, emphasize organizational climate as an asset. "Climate" refers to the general characteristics of a school, including its physical attributes, social structure, organizational design, and culture (the values and beliefs held in common by those who constitute the school community) (Kowalski, 2003). A school's climate has been compared to an individual's personality (Sargeant, 1967). Religious schools, in particular, often claim to provide a "family atmosphere" congruent with the philosophical convictions of the families represented by their students. Even lay administrators and teachers are expected to be role models in these cultures, symbolically expressing through their dress and their behavior the school's moral values and beliefs (Kelly & Bredeson, 1991). In addition, researchers (e.g., Choy, 1997; Kowalski & Swaringin, 1982; McLaughlin, O'Donnell, & Ries, 1995) have found that the sense of community and the levels of job satisfaction and morale have usually been higher in private schools than in public schools.

Public perceptions of private schools are shaped primarily by comparison. When private schools are compared to urban public schools, for instance, most people believe that private schools are more effective academically, safer, and more orderly. Even when compared to all public schools, many people view private schools as setting higher student expectations, tolerating less misbehavior, and requiring more academic tasks. Not surprisingly, some researchers (e.g., Convey, 1992; Crawford & Freeman, 1996) have found that instruction and discipline often outweigh religious considerations when parents decide to send their children to religious schools. Yet attitudes about instruction and discipline are not easily separated from religious convictions. Parochial schools are formed to promote a central (frequently spiritually oriented) mission or set of values that gets translated into learning and behavior expectations (Kowalski, 2003). Some Christian schools, for example, have infused discipline with religious values, a decision that reinforces positive parental attitudes (Simmons, 2004).

In the final analysis, however, there are multiple reasons why parents choose private schools (Newman, 1995). Dissatisfaction with public schools, commonly focused on inadequate discipline and low academic standards, is certainly one of them. Closer scrutiny, however, reveals that dissatisfaction is usually rooted in a broader and more abstract issue. Many parents believe that public schools lack a sense of moral purpose; that is, they see public schools as places where their values are ignored or, even worse, openly ridiculed. Philosophical and political differences over the purposes of public education have

TABLE 8–1

Public and Private Schools: Key Considerations

Factor	Comparison
Structure	Laws and regulations largely shape public schools; distinctive missions and philosophies largely shape private schools.
Funding	Public schools rely on tax revenues; private schools rely on a combination of tuition, gifts, subsidies, and grants.
Expenditure decisions	Public school administrators are restricted by laws and state policies governing the expenditure of tax revenues and by local school board approval; private school administrators are typically restricted by board or pastor approval.
Students	Mandatory attendance laws and little competition ensure clientele for public schools; private schools must compete for students. Public schools must serve all eligible students; private schools can be and often are selective in admitting students.
Market status	Public schools are considered quasi-monopolies; private schools function in a competitive market in which the future is not assured.
Mission	Public schools typically have broad missions reflecting a range of purposes and expectations; private schools typically have a narrow mission based on religious and/or academic criteria.
Programming	Public schools offer a wide range of programs intended to serve student needs and interests; private schools' programs are often more basic and focused on serving the needs of a more homogeneous population.
Parental involvement and volunteers	In many public schools, parent and volunteer involvement is viewed as a luxury; in many private schools, this involvement is viewed as a necessity.
PR structure	In public schools, PR responsibilities exist at both the district and the school levels: in private schools, school administrators rarely have support from a larger organizational structure.
PR foci	Public schools tend to concentrate on information exchanges between the schools and the community; private schools focus largely on marketing, recruitment, and fund-raising.

presented a challenge to educational leaders from the very beginning of this nation's public schools.

Table 8–1 provides a list of general comparisons between public and private schools. These factors help frame the context of practice in private schools.

NONTRADITIONAL PUBLIC SCHOOLS

Increasingly, competition to traditional public schools also comes from other public schools, as the concept of parental choice gains political support. National surveys conducted over the past decade show that the majority of the public supports some form of school choice, but also believes that such programs should generate minimal contro-versy (Hausman & Brown, 2002). Therefore, choice among public schools usually is supported more than choice among public and private schools. Fowler (2002) notes that at the superficial level, school choice deals with how students should be assigned to schools and which schools should receive public funding. Beneath the surface, however, the debate is premised on the wisdom of moving public education from the public-sector economy to the marketplace. Proponents (e.g., Chubb & Moe, 1990) argue that by forcing schools to recruit students in order to survive, educators will become more responsive to real needs and wants and be compelled to be innovative. Opponents counter that public schools of choice draw needed resources from regular programs (Fusarelli, 2002) and provide an opportunity for racial and economic segre-gation (Eaton, 1996).

Four types of nontraditional public schools are discussed here because their PR needs and programming often are closer to those of private schools than they are to those of other public schools. One type, career-technical high schools (or vocational schools), has existed in this country since the early part of the last century. The other three types, charter schools and certain types of magnet and alternative schools, have become popular much more recently.

Charter Schools

Charter schools became a major reform initiative in the 1990s. Although it is difficult to precisely define these institutions because of varying state statutes (Good & Braden, 2000), they basically are hybrids. That is, they are funded much like public schools, but op-erate much like private schools. A primary intent of charter schools is to balance freedom (by virtue of being excused from traditional state policies and rules governing public schools) and accountability (by virtue of having to produce evidence of sufficient student performance). Proponents argue that charter schools give parents a choice and by provid-ing competition, they pressure traditional public schools to improve (Vergari, 1999). Re-gardless of how charter schools may be described, they are intended to meet the needs of students who are underserved in traditional public schools; thus, "they represent at least an implicit criticism of the status quo" (Perreault, 2004, p. 27). With respect to PR, char-ter schools resemble private schools in two important ways:

> First, they are self-governing institutions with wide-ranging control over their own curriculum, instruction, staffing, budget, internal organization, and much more. The second similarity is that nearly all of them are schools of choice. Nobody is assigned against his or her will to attend (or teach in) a charter school. (Manno, Finn, & Vanourek, 2000, p. 737)

In 2005, 40 states and the District of Columbia had charter school laws, and more than 3,600 charter schools enrolling approximately 800,000 pupils were operating across the United States (Center for Education Reform, 2005). State charter school laws differ markedly, as evidenced by variations in the following five areas:

1. *Authority to grant a charter.* Typically, charters must be granted by a state agency (e.g., department of education or state board of education); however, some states allow local school boards to grant charters.

2. *Alliances (partnerships)*. Charter school legislation in all but 4 of the 41 jurisdictions—that is, all but Arkansas, Kansas, Iowa, and Mississippi—includes provisions related to alliances or partnerships. Three states—Florida, New Mexico, and Rhode Island—have language in their statutes encouraging partnerships (Education Commission of the States, 2004).

3. *Eligible recipients*. Whereas some states grant charters only to licensed teachers, other states have broader eligibility criteria, allowing businesses, parents, and community groups to receive a charter.

4. *Time limits*. Because accountability is a focal point of charter schools, charters are typically granted for only a few years. Some states—for example, Michigan—essentially do not place a time limit on a charter.

5. *Status of the school*. Some states grant charters to both public and private schools, and some, but not all, states allow charter schools to operate as entrepreneurial schools.

As a matter of public policy, charter school laws have faced and continue to face opposition. The following are the more common criticisms of these institutions:

- Charter schools often reduce state fiscal allocations to regular public schools.
- The fundamental promise of charter schools—that they will improve public education through competition—is an unproven hypothesis.
- Race and economics, and not curricula or policies, influence many families enrolling children in charter schools. Therefore, these schools contribute to segregation.
- Many charter schools lack sound management and financial plans.
- Charter schools often operate in unsafe environments that are not conducive to effective teaching.
- Many charter schools practice selective admissions; for example, students with special needs are often not admitted.
- Not all states have a well-conceived evaluation plan, resulting in more emphasis being placed on process than on progress.

Given this disparagement, positive relationships between charter schools and their surrounding school districts are atypical (Perreault, 2004).

Imaging and marketing are extremely important responsibilities for charter school administrators because they must recruit a sufficient number of students in order to survive. Because they often recruit students vigorously and because they compete most directly with traditional public schools, their marketing and promotional efforts often force public school administrators to engage in student recruitment. In Dayton, Ohio, for example, the city public schools spent over $500,000 on advertising in the 28-month period between July 2003 and November 2005. Responding to media inquiries, the board president explained that district officials were forced to compete for students after having lost approximately 22% of the district's enrollment to 33 charter schools, all of which have opened since 1998 (Elliott, 2005).

Despite their overall growth, a considerable number of charter schools have failed after only a few years of operation. Common reasons for their demise have included mismanagement, financial difficulties, unsuitable facilities, and failure to meet the academic goals stipulated in their charter (Paglin, 2001). However, the number of new schools has been greater than the number of failed schools, and therefore, charter schools remain a major competitor to traditional public elementary and secondary schools—and they are expected to become even more competitive in the future.

Magnet Schools

Magnet schools emerged in the late 1960s, largely in response to forced desegregation in public schools (Rossell, 2005). Their primary purpose was to attract students from their home schools so that benefits would accrue to both the community (e.g., via desegregated schools) and the individual (e.g., via a more personally relevant curriculum)(Waldrip, 2005). As an example, advocates believe that white students from suburban areas will attend inner-city schools with predominately minority enrollments if the curriculum is sufficiently attractive. Magnet schools, however, are public schools focusing on particular academic subjects, and they operate as part of public school districts.

There are two types of magnet schools: whole-school magnets and programs-within-a-school magnets. A *dedicated magnet school* has no set attendance boundaries, and students must apply and be accepted to them. It is estimated that this category accounts for approximately one-third of all magnet schools (Hausman & Brown, 2002). Since this is the only type of magnet school that must recruit a sufficient number of students in order to survive, it is the only type relevant to our discussion of PR in this chapter.

Career-Technical High Schools

Career-technical high schools emerged in the United States nearly 100 years ago with the passage of the Smith-Hughes Act in 1917. Their mission was to prepare students with job-specific skills (Zehr, 1999). Today, the titles of these schools vary across states; for example, they still may be referred to as vocational schools, area vocational schools, career centers, or trade schools—but career-technical schools became the preferred title among educators who work in these institutions during the 1990s (Reese & Thompson, 2002). Private vocational schools are referred to as proprietary vocational schools, and because they are not public schools, PR programming issues for them are covered by material in the previous section on private schools.

Often, career-technical schools serve a particular region of the state, drawing students from multiple local school districts. Such schools are commonly known as joint or collaborative schools. In large school districts, typically over 7,000 students, there may be a sufficient number of students to operate a career-technical school solely within the school district. Both district-specific and joint-venture schools, however, face the same challenge of maintaining a sufficient enrollment.

Threats to vocational education became more frequent and intense during the 1980s as America moved toward becoming an information-based society. Preparing students for manufacturing jobs, in particular, became a questionable human capital investment, and the term *vocational* assumed a somewhat negative connotation (Reese & Thompson, 2002). In response to the need for skills required in high-technology workplaces, many vocational school administrators broadened the curriculum and shifted the focus of instruction toward subjects such as electronics and computer-assisted drafting. And as noted, they elected to rename these institutions as career-technical schools.

Alternative Schools

Only a handful of public alternative schools existed 50 years ago. Prior to the 1960s, distinctive options to traditional public elementary and secondary education were found primarily in private schools (Deal & Nolan, 1978; Smith, Gregory, & Pugh, 1981). As national and state policy makers shifted their attention from equality issues to excellence issues during the 1970s, interest in alternative schools waned. While some alternative schools survived, many local district officials lost interest in establishing new ones. Interest in these schools shifted again in the late 1980s, largely because many leading reformers believed that equity and excellence could be pursued concurrently (Kowalski, 2003). Since then, there has been a proliferation of alternative schools; by 2000, over half the states had enacted some type of provision requiring alternative public schools. The primary intent of such legislation is to improve education opportunities for students excluded or about to be excluded from regular programs (Barr & Parrett, 2001) and to respond to national reform initiatives such as the No Child Left Behind Act.

In fact, there are three types of alternative schools; Raywid (1994) described them as follows:

- ♦ *Type I schools* are institutions of choice that any student may attend until high school graduation. These schools are innovative and have nontraditional organizational and administrative structures.
- ♦ *Type II schools* are placement institutions enrolling disruptive students for a temporary period. These schools provide an alternative to expulsion, and they focus on behavior modification in order to reduce or eliminate problems that caused discipline concerns in traditional schools.
- ♦ *Type III schools* are referral institutions enrolling students with academic, social, or emotional difficulties. These schools focus on rehabilitating students so that they can succeed in a traditional school.

Both Type II and Type III schools attempt to change the student, behaviorally in the former and behaviorally and/or academically in the latter. Type I schools, however, focus on changing the school environment. The dissimilar missions reflect differences in how sponsoring district officials frame problems associated with students not succeeding in traditional schools. Whereas Type II and Type III schools are predicated on the belief that the student is the problem, Type I schools are predicated on the belief that traditional school environments are the problem (Kowalski & Reynolds, 2003). Leading alternative-school scholars (e.g., Conrath, 2001; Gregory, 2001; Raywid, 1995) contend that most students who encounter difficulty in traditional schools do so because their learning styles and intellectual talents do not conform to traditional school norms. Placing these students in Type I rather than in Type II schools has proven to be more effective (Wehlage, Rutter, Smith, Lesko, & Fernandez, 1989).

Therefore, Type I alternative schools are institutions of choice, and like other nontraditional public schools discussed here, they must recruit and maintain a sufficient number of students to ensure their existence. In this vein, they and the other nontraditional public schools require some aspects of PR programming (e.g., student recruitment) that have not been integral for traditional public schools.

PUBLIC RELATIONS IN PRIVATE AND NONTRADITIONAL PUBLIC SCHOOLS

Positioning is a technique used in the commercial sales world to associate a product with consumer needs. Being able to maintain adequate enrollment levels in private and nontraditional public schools depends largely on the ability of school officials to position their institutions appropriately so that they are attractive to consumers. In the case of private schools, administrators are expected to ascertain and evaluate market conditions (marketing) and convince parents that tuition is a beneficial investment (selling). In the case of nontraditional public schools, administrators must engage in the same activities; however, their efforts typically extend beyond parents to include entire communities. They are expected to demonstrate that their schools are beneficial to students and, more generally, to the community and public education.

Having to compete for students requires most private school administrators to sell their programs to multiple publics spanning age groups and interest levels. Brochures, newsletters, buttons, wearing apparel, bumper stickers, and even athletic teams have been used to build and advertise an all-inclusive image. Public school administrators, by comparison, have not commonly developed effective sales strategies, and this fact became painfully apparent as they tried to counter a confidence crisis that intensified during the 1980s as a result of stinging criticisms contained in reform reports (Hanson, 1992).

For contemporary private schools, advertising foci typically have included educational (and religious) philosophy, tuition, discipline, financial aid, athletic programs, social standing of the student population, and average ability and achievement scores. Nontraditional public schools have been more likely to emphasize curriculum, human and material resources, educational philosophy, and student achievement. Administrators have a responsibility to maintain high ethical standards when promoting their institutions. As examples, making false promises, denigrating other schools, and using high-pressure tactics to recruit students are considered unethical acts. More pragmatically, unscrupulous advertising and recruiting tactics have proven to be ineffective most of the time, and they have the potential to destroy a school's reputation (Barbieri, 1991).

Defining the School

To be successful, both private and nontraditional public schools need to establish a market niche. To do this, administrators must develop defining statements—testimonials that realistically and accurately give a school a special identity. The purpose is to highlight differences between a particular school and other schools in the vicinity. Defining statements should be based on actual experiences as characterized by current and former students or by other verifiable evidence. Some private high schools, for example, use testimony from alumni appearing in paid media ads as a defining device. Typically, these ads feature a graduate who attributes her or his career success to study skills, moral values, and self-discipline acquired in high school. Schools also define themselves symbolically—through logos or mottos—or through well-developed brochures (Abella, 1989).

Effective schools that have defined themselves positively overshadow schools that have not. Identity should communicate a deep commitment to an educational and possibly a religious philosophy. In defining a school, administrators should be guided by three objectives (Cheney, 1991):

1. *Coherence.* The image is presented clearly and comprehensively.
2. *Symbolism.* The image represents values and attitudes.
3. *Positioning.* The image differentiates the school from other institutions.

The importance of being able to connect to potential consumers has prompted private and nontraditional public school officials to rely less on their own judgment and more on data-collection techniques such as focus groups. A focus group, for example, infuses the opinions and sentiments of actual and potential stakeholders into the defining process. Parents who are part of a focus group may be asked to talk about what they like best about the school, or they may be urged to identify problems and other elements of the school that are alienating to them and to students. Ideally, all stakeholders should have an opportunity to participate in image building because their broad participation enhances the likelihood of creating an accurate image. In addition, their involvement fosters ownership, and as a result, they are more likely to play an active role in promoting the image that is created. When parents join school staff and alumni in promoting an image based on proven educational benefits, they often are able to override prevailing concerns and doubts.

Since societal conditions surrounding schools are not static, administrators need to periodically revise image statements. Religiously affiliated schools provide a good example in this regard. At one time, they relied entirely on religious values to sell their institutions to parents. By engaging in effective marketing, they discovered that academic excellence (Leahy, 1989) and firm discipline (Meade, 1991) had become equally attractive issues. In light of this knowledge, some inner-city parochial school administrators have stressed that moral values and discipline philosophy are preconditions for productive teaching and learning; thus, they connect all three issues and present them as distinguishing characteristics for their institutions (Meade, 1991).

Interrelating Marketing, Public Relations, and Student Recruitment

Largely because neither private schools nor nontraditional public schools are guaranteed a steady flow of students, marketing and PR must be treated as interrelated functions. Collectively, the two functions require these tasks:

◆ Monitoring the environment to detect changing needs and wants,
◆ Interpreting known needs and wants,
◆ Defining the school, and
◆ Communicating information about relevant programs and building goodwill.

Student recruitment (i.e., selling the product) is an extension of marketing and PR. Except in large-enrollment private schools and nontraditional public schools that function within the framework of a large local district, one administrator or staff member usually has responsibility for all three functions.

Selling or student recruitment typically receives the most attention from administrators because they know that continued operation depends on having a sufficient number of the right types of students. There are both quantitative and qualitative dimensions to this assignment. Quantitatively, these schools must enroll a sufficient number of students; qualitatively, they must enroll students who fit the school's image and mission. Consider several examples of why attracting the right type of students is important:

♦ A high-tuition private school targets its recruitment activities to upper-income families in order to enhance its image as an elitist institution.
♦ A charter school targets its recruitment efforts to parents who are willing to do volunteer work as a means of strengthening parental involvement in education.
♦ A Lutheran high school targets its recruitment activities to families belonging to 10 local parishes that were instrumental in creating the school.

The quantitative dimension of recruitment usually addresses an economic goal—getting enough students (and tuition income) to ensure viability. The qualitative dimension usually addresses philosophical and programmatic goals—getting enough of the right type of student to validate image or to fulfill commitments.

The qualitative dimension of student recruitment can be an especially sticky wicket for charter school administrators because legal parameters and political community expectations often constrict them. For instance, charter schools often are expected to enroll a sufficient number of preferred students while maintaining a racial and economic balance similar to that found in other public schools (usually in the same district). Or they may be expected to provide a broad curriculum to serve the needs of all types of students, including special education programs. Nontraditional public school administrators also face important admissions questions that rarely create conflict for private school administrators. For instance, under what circumstances may a charter school deny admission to an applicant? A study of the 36 state charter school laws in effect at the time revealed that all but 2 contained some provision ensuring that underrepresented groups have equal access to these institutions (Ausbrooks, 2001). So although charter schools can and do deny some students admission, administrators in these institutions typically have less latitude than private school principals in this regard.

Parental commitment is arguably important in every school, but it is particularly critical in schools of choice. When parents select a school, they usually feel a special sense of responsibility; and in the case of private schools, tuition payments almost always deepen this feeling. Consequently, parents who become disillusioned, disappointed, or mistreated often act swiftly to transfer their children to another school. Recognizing this proclivity, administrators in schools of choice should continuously reinforce the convictions that initially influenced parents—action that requires them to first know these reasons and then to validate them.

Organizing the Public Relations Function

In traditional public schools, marketing and PR activities are often divided between district and school initiatives. In schools of choice, these responsibilities often belong entirely or primarily to the principal or assistant principal. The greatest challenges related to providing a coherent PR program are commonly faced by principals in small parochial schools. These administrators rarely have administrative support staff, yet they are expected to build and maintain community relations, recruit students, and perform the managerial and leadership duties assumed by all other principals.

Some private school principals have relegated marketing and PR responsibilities to teachers or parent volunteers. Though this option may appear prudent, it usually has proven to be ineffective for at least three reasons:

1. The individuals selected were not prepared adequately for these assignments.
2. The individuals selected failed to devote a sufficient amount of time to these assignments.
3. Marketing, PR, and recruiting got fragmented because each task was being executed by a different employee or volunteer.

Recognizing these problems, administrators may combine marketing and PR with recruiting and fund-raising. This decision makes it more likely that either a half-time or a full-time specialist could be employed. For example, private schools often compensate fund-raisers on a commission basis; that is, they receive a percentage of the funds they raise. Table 8–2 contains information about different organizational options for addressing these responsibilities.

TABLE 8–2

Organizational Options for Administering Public Relations and Marketing

Option	Advantages or Disadvantages
Not assigning responsibilities to an employee	Assigning responsibilities to volunteers almost always leads to serious problems. Neither coordination nor continuity is likely. However, minimal resources need to be allocated.
Assigning responsibilities to the principal	Principals already have myriad leadership and management duties; overloading them with additional assignments may detract from their primary responsibilities in areas such as curriculum development and instructional leadership. However, minimal resources are allocated.
Distributing the duties among two or more existing employees or volunteers	PR and marketing are likely to get fragmented; these two duties may be low priorities for the individuals who are assigned.
Employing a PR or marketing specialist	This option requires considerable resources, but it is likely to provide the most comprehensive and effective leadership. Combining PR and marketing with fund-raising and student recruitment responsibilities may reduce personnel costs.
Employing a PR or marketing consultant	Resources required vary depending on the quantity and quality of service provided. Administrators lose some control over these functions.

Building a Public Relations Calendar

A PR-marketing-recruitment calendar is one tool that helps principals deal with conditions caused by less-than-adequate resources. The calendar is a guide for daily, weekly, and monthly activities. A sample calendar is illustrated in Table 8–3. All events and responsibilities pertaining to PR, marketing, and recruitment should be placed on the calendar and updated daily or at least weekly.

Internal and external audiences should be considered when preparing the calendar. Within the school, all officials, including members of the governing board, should receive periodic updates of the calendar to ensure that they are aware of scheduled activities, programs, and communication efforts. Pertinent parts of the calendar should also be shared with teachers, support staff, and relevant external audiences. Thus, parts of the calendar should be shared with parents, local government officials, fund-raising groups, the media, and even other school administrators.

The calendar also is used to ensure that communication exchanges are occurring between appropriate parties and that potential scheduling conflicts are avoided. For instance, the calendar can be used to monitor schedules for college recruiters and alumni relations activities in a given school year. The PR calendar also provides a composite of activities, and therefore, it indirectly helps the principal or others working with PR to allocate resources effectively.

Communicating with External Targeted Audiences

Communication can be viewed as an inside-out or outside-in process. In the former, school officials disseminate messages through outlets such as newsletters, recruitment brochures, press releases, public service announcements, outdoor advertising, open houses, community service projects, and lectures. In the latter, community input is gathered and analyzed using opinion surveys, telephone interviews, and focus groups (Carroll & Carroll, 2001). We usually recognize that politics prompts public school administrators to maintain contact with all stakeholders and not just parents (Kowalski, 2003). However, we are less likely to recognize that private school administrators need to do the same thing. Although

TABLE 8–3
Sample Public Relations-Marketing-Recruitment Calendar

Program/Event	Date	Start/End Time	Target Audience	Objective
Alumni reception	9/22	6:00–9:00 P.M.	Alumni in local area	Communicate goals for annual fund drive
TV program	9/23	4:00–4:30 P.M.	Potential students	Promote the school
Parent advisory meeting	9/23	7:00–9:00 P.M.	Parents	Get information about problems, positive experiences, etc.
Deadline for newsletter copy	9/24	5:00 P.M.	Potential contributors	Get materials on time

private schools are not dependent on tax revenues (and hence not dependent on political referenda), their image and acceptability are affected by public opinion. Moreover, they are subject to public policy decisions; for example, a state legislature or state board of education could enact laws or policies affecting their operations.

Individuals and groups with whom school officials should exchange information are known as *targeted audiences*. In order to maintain contact with them, administrators must be able to (a) identify them, (b) initiate and maintain contact with them, and (c) put forth the effort to exchange vital information with them. Moreover, administrators need to be cognizant that both their motives for communicating with targeted audiences and their personal behavior while doing so are evaluated constantly. For example, a principal who communicates with relevant publics only when the school or he wants something from them may be viewed as a manipulative administrator. Likewise, a poorly prepared newsletter filled with grammatical errors or misspelled words may harm a school's image, rather than building goodwill.

Communicating with targeted audiences serves several purposes. The process may sustain interest in the school, provide information about accomplishments or activities, or call attention to planned actions, such as fund drives, athletic events, or school social events. Generally, each communication should focus on two overarching goals: reinforcing the school's effectiveness and reminding the public of the school's special role in the local community.

Two-way communication with the public also produces information that can be used by principals to make a variety of decisions (Tarter & Hoy, 1996). Often referred to as environmental scanning (Hanson, 2003), monitoring the community helps administrators engage in organizational development. Changing economic, social, and political conditions, for example, can affect the welfare of schools of choice in a relatively brief time. As an example, a downturn in a local economy may cause some parents to withdraw their children from private schools because they no longer can afford the tuition. In the case of nontraditional public schools, new programs or realigned attendance boundaries for the traditional public schools may negatively affect charter or career center enrollments.

Student and Parental Involvement

In business, selling a product is easier when a potential buyer knows the characteristics of a satisfied consumer. The same principle is true for schools of choice. Students and parents who praise the school and talk about its successes often prove to be effective recruiters. Stated differently, satisfied students and parents can be goodwill ambassadors who independently relate positive attitudes to friends, neighbors, and relatives. These individuals also can contribute to PR in other ways, such as providing testimonials that appear in ads and publications (Warner, 1994).

A school advisory committee is another way to broaden participation in a PR program. Students and parents serving on the committee usually have valuable insights about the following topics:

◆ How the school's PR efforts are received in the community;
◆ The school's strengths and weaknesses;

♦ Ways that parents can become more involved in the school's operations;
♦ How marketing, recruiting, and fund-raising could be improved; and
♦ Family-oriented social events that build goodwill.

Involving parents and students on the PR committee also conveys a powerful symbolic message: The school engages families. Parental involvement partially explains why parent–teacher associations have been a potent force in developing school image. Most parents react positively to messages telling them that they are welcome in the school and that their direct involvement is welcomed and appreciated.

Many parochial schools depend on parent volunteers (including grandparents) to offset resource deficiencies. Some schools have even developed volunteer "gift option" booklets—a communication device that details volunteer opportunities. Further, the booklets provide specifications for time and talent so that parents can select an activity that fits their schedule and interests or abilities.

Parental involvement is truly a win-win situation because the benefits extend beyond PR to the students themselves. Research indicates that parental involvement and home-learning activities positively influence student grades, attendance, and behavior (Simon, 2001). Hence, the high rate of parental involvement in schools of choice may partially explain the relatively high rate of student success reported by many of these schools.

Future Issues

Because their future is not ensured, private and nontraditional public schools remain highly dependent on effective strategic planning and PR. Having to compete for students affects virtually every aspect of their operations, and this reality has been magnified in the present school reform environment. Initiatives such as school choice, charter schools, vouchers, and tuition tax credits remain popular topics. The widespread adoption of charter school laws, for example, already has spawned consequential questions about the future of both private and public schools. For instance, the success and possibly future existence of both types of schools are likely to depend on their ability to define themselves effectively.

Increasingly, private and nontraditional public school principals are realizing that they must devote more time and fiscal resources to PR. This will require several improvements over past practices. Principals will need to possess a PR knowledge base, acquire the skills necessary to deploy that knowledge, and embrace values and beliefs that are congruous with the modern definitions of PR discussed previously in Chapter 1.

SUMMARY

From a process perspective, PR principles are applicable to private schools and public schools because all of these institutions are more effective when they maintain a symbiotic relationship with their external publics. In private and nontraditional public schools, however, the immediate need to recruit students elevates the importance of certain aspects of PR; for example, marketing, imaging, and selling are absolutely essential.

Though private school administrators always have had to recruit students, conditions in the marketplace have changed. In the past, for instance, parochial schools attracted students primarily on the basis of religious values; today, academics and discipline are at least equally important considerations. Such changes reflect the vibrant nature of market conditions and illustrate why integral PR functions such as marketing, imaging, selling, and two-way communication play a major role in determining whether a school is responsive to its targeted audiences.

Current economic and political policy trends suggest that market-driven reform ideas will be increasingly adopted by state legislatures. Most states, for example, already have charter school laws. Growing numbers of private and nontraditional public schools coupled with their increasingly vigorous recruitment efforts already have forced many school districts, especially in urban areas, to engage in student recruitment. The adoption of voucher or tuition tax credit legislation would intensify the level of competition. Therefore, traditional school administrators now have a vested interest in understanding how private and nontraditional public schools conduct their PR programs.

QUESTIONS AND SUGGESTED ACTIVITIES

CASE STUDY

1. Assume you are the headmaster of the Metropolitan Hebrew High School. What steps would you take to meet the school board's directive?
2. Is it possible that the absence of a PR plan has contributed to enrollment declines at the school? Why or why not?
3. Evaluate the school's newsletter. How could you make it more effective?
4. In light of increased competition and an out-migration of Jewish families from the local community, what information should the headmaster obtain to define the school?
5. Are the problems facing the Metropolitan Hebrew High School typical for urban parochial schools? If so, in what ways? If not, why not?
6. What actions could increase parental involvement in this school's activities?

CHAPTER

7. In what ways are charter schools, career centers, and certain types of magnet and alternative schools similar to private schools?
8. How do the similarities between private and nontraditional public schools affect PR planning and programming?
9. Why should schools of choice define themselves?
10. Compare marketing, imaging, and selling. In what ways are these three functions different?
11. Assigning marketing, recruiting, and other PR functions to staff with other full-time assignments or to volunteers often produces fragmentation. What is fragmentation? Why is it likely to occur?
12. In small private schools, connecting fund-raising and PR may be a prudent decision. Why?
13. Why should administrators in traditional public schools understand how private schools are organized and operated?

SUGGESTED READINGS

Barr, R. D., & Parrett, W. H. (2001). *Hope fulfilled for at-risk and violent youth* (2nd ed.). Boston: Allyn & Bacon.

Bushweller, K. (1997). Working miracles: Catholic schools' success formula. *American School Board Journal, 184*(1), 14–19.

Coleman, J. S., & Hoffer, T. (1987). *Public and private high schools: The impact of communities.* New York: Basic Books.

Convey, J. J. (1992). *Catholic schools make a difference: Twenty-five years of research.* Washington, DC: National Catholic Educational Association.

Cooper, B. S., & Gargan, A. (1996). Private, religious schooling in the United States: Emerging trends and issues. *Journal of Research on Christian Education, 5*(2), 157–178.

Dana, J. A. (2004). Public engagement: A 21st century necessity for school success. *Journal of School Public Relations, 25*(1), 8–21.

DeBlois, R. (1997). Public vs. private: Time for an honest discussion that could benefit all schools. *NASSP Bulletin, 81*(589), 90–98.

Gestwicki, C. (1992). *Home, school, and community relations: A guide to working with parents* (2nd ed.). Albany, NY: Delmar.

Henry, M. E. (1993). *School cultures: Universes of meaning in private schools.* Norwood, NJ: Ablex.

Hess, F. M. (2001). Whaddya mean you want to close my school? The politics of regulatory accountability in charter schooling. *Education & Urban Society, 33*(2), 141–156.

Hogan, S. D., & Knight, H. (1988). *Successful planning for private schools: The administrator's guide.* Arlington, VA: Thornsbury Bailey & Brown.

Holcomb, J. H. (1993). *Educational marketing: A business approach to school–community relations.* Lanham, MD: University Press of America.

Holland, P. B. (1997a). Catholic school lessons for the public schools. *School Administrator, 54*(7), 24–26.

Holland, P. B. (1997b). The folly of public/parochial comparisons. *School Administrator, 54*(7), 28–31.

Houle, J. C. (2002). Engaging the public in public schools through school choice. *Journal of School Public Relations, 23*(2), 148–158.

James, C., & Phillips, P. (1995). The practice of educational marketing in schools. *Educational Management & Administration, 23*(2), 75–88.

Perreault, G. (2004). Life on the bleeding edge: Philosophy, practice, and public relations in charter schools. *Journal of School Public Relations, 25*(1), 22–31.

Reid, K. S., & Johnson, R. C. (2001, December 5). Public debates, private choices. *Education Week, 21*(14), 32–38.

Schenk, J. A., & Schaid, J. A. (2002). Strategic planning imperatives for educators: Creating advantage in an emerging competition-based market. *Journal of School Public Relations, 23*(2), 131–147.

REFERENCES

Abella, M. (1989). The exciting world of public relations. *Momentum, 20*(1), 38–39.

Ausbrooks, C. Y. (2001, April). *How equal is access to charter schools?* Paper presented at the annual meeting of the American Educational Research Association, Seattle, WA.

Barbieri, R. (1991). Morality in marketing. In R. Cowan (Ed.), *The next marketing handbook for independent schools* (pp. 14–17). Boston: National Association of Independent Schools.

Barr, R. D., & Parrett, W. (2001). *Hope fulfilled for at-risk and violent youth: K–12 programs that work* (2nd ed.). Boston: Allyn & Bacon.

Broughman, S. P., & Colaciello, L. A. (1998). *Private school universe study, 1995–96.* U.S. Department of Education, National Center for Education Statistics. Washington, DC: U.S. Government Printing Office.

Broughman, S. P., & Colaciello, L. A. (1999). *Private school universe survey: 1997–98.* U.S. Department of Education, National Center for Education Statistics. Washington, DC: U.S. Government Printing Office.

Brouillette, M. J., & Williams, J. R. (1999). *The impact of school choice on school employee labor unions: Unionization rates among private, charter, and traditional government schools suggest reason for union opposition to school choice.* Midland, MI: Mackinac Center for Public Policy.

Bryk, A. S., Lee, V. E., & Holland, P. B. (1993). *Catholic schools and the common good.* Cambridge: Harvard University Press.

Carroll, S. R., & Carroll, D. (2001). Outside-inside marketing. *School Administrator, 58*(7), 32–34.

Center for Education Reform. (2005). *Charter schools.* Retrieved November 10, 2005, from http://www.edreform.com/index.cfm?fuseAction=stateStats&pSectionID=15&cSectionID=44.

Cheney, C. (1991). In other words. In R. Cowan (Ed.), *The next marketing handbook for independent schools* (pp. 36–44). Boston: National Association of Independent Schools.

Choy, S. P. (1997). *Public and private schools: How do they differ? Findings from "The Condition of Education, 1997."* Washington, DC: U.S. Government Printing Office.

Chubb, J., & Moe, T. (1990). *Politics, markets and America's schools.* Washington, DC: Brookings Institution.

Colgan, C. (2003). Study: Charters are "places of racial isolation." *American School Board Journal, 190*(9), 16.

Conrath, J. (2001). Changing the odds for young people: Next steps for alternative education. *Phi Delta Kappan, 82*(8), 585–587.

Convey, J. J. (1992). *Catholic schools make a difference: Twenty-five years of research.* Washington, DC: National Catholic Educational Association.

Cooper, B. (1984). The changing demography of private schools. *Education & Urban Society, 16*(4), 429–442.

Council for American Private Education. (2005). *Facts and studies.* Retrieved on November 13, 2005, from http://www.capenet.org/facts.html.

Crawford, J., & Freeman, S. (1996). Why parents choose private schooling: Implications for public school programs and information campaigns. *ERS Spectrum, 14*(3), 9–16.

Deal, T. E., & Nolan, R. R. (1978). An overview of alternative schools. In T. Deal & R. Nolan (Eds.), *Alternative schools: Ideologies, realities, guidelines* (pp. 1–17). Chicago: Nelson-Hall.

Eaton, S. (1996). Slipping toward segregation: Local control and eroding desegregation. In G. Orfield & S. Eaton (Eds.), *Dismantling desegregation: The quiet reversal of* Brown v. Board of Education (pp. 265–285). New York: New Press.

Education Commission of the States. (2004). *Charter school laws and partnerships: Expanding opportunities and resources.* Retrieved November 10, 2005, from http:// www.ecs.org/clearinghouse/ 51/12/5112.doc.

Elliott, S. (2005, November 21). Schools defend ad splurge. *Dayton Daily News,* A1, A7.

Epple, D., & Romano, R. E. (1998). Competition between private and public schools, vouchers, and peer-group effects. *American Economic Review, 88*(1), 33–62.

Fowler, F. C. (2002). School choice. *Clearing House, 76*(1), 4–5.

Friedman, M., & Friedman, R. (1981). *Free to choose.* New York: Avon Books.

Fusarelli, L. D. (2002). Charter schools: Implications for teachers and administrators. *Clearing House, 76*(1), 20–24.

Goldhaber, D. D. (1999). School choice: An examination of the empirical evidence on achievement, parental decision making, and equity. *Educational Researcher, 28*(9), 16–25.

Good, T. L., & Braden, J. S. (2000). Charter schools: Another reform failure or a worthwhile investment? *Phi Delta Kappan, 81*(10), 745–750.

Greeley, A. M., & McManus, W. (1987). *Catholic contributions: Sociology and policy.* Chicago: Thomas More Press.

Gregory, T. (2001). Fear of success? Ten ways alternative schools pull their punches. *Phi Delta Kappan, 82*(8), 577–581.

Hanson, E. M. (1992). Educational marketing and the public schools: Policies, practices, and problems. *Educational Policy, 6*(1), 19–34.

Hanson, E. M. (2003). *Educational administration and organizational behavior* (5th ed.). Boston: Allyn & Bacon.

Hausman, C., & Brown, P. M. (2002). Curricular and instructional differentiation in magnet schools: Market driven or institutionally entrenched? *Journal of Curriculum & Supervision, 17*(3), 256–276.

Hill, P. T. (1996). The educational consequences of choice. *Phi Delta Kappan, 77*(10), 671–675.

Hilton, J. J. (1994). Local autonomy, educational equity, and school choice: Constitutional criticism of school reform. *New England Journal of Public Policy, 10*(1), 293–305.

Kelly, B. E., & Bredeson, P. V. (1991). Measures of meaning in a public and in a parochial school: Principals as symbol managers. *Journal of Educational Administration, 29*(3), 6–22.

Kowalski, T. J. (2003). *Contemporary school administration: An introduction* (2nd ed.). Boston: Allyn & Bacon.

Kowalski, T. J., & Reynolds, S. (2003). Knowledge, dispositions, and career orientations of alternative school principals. *Connections: Journal of Principal Preparation & Development, 5*, 22–31.

Kowalski, T. J., & Swaringin, C. (1982, Spring). Measured differences in public and non-public elementary school teacher morale. *Private School Quarterly*, 25–32.

Larson, M. (1995). *Public and religious elementary school costs and programs.* Unpublished Ed.D. dissertation, Arizona State University.

Leahy, M. A. (1989). A new determination. *Momentum, 20*(3), 48–51.

Lieberman, M. (1986). *Beyond public education.* New York: Praeger.

Manno, B. V., Finn, C. E., & Vanourek, G. (2000). Beyond the schoolhouse door: How charter schools are transforming U.S. public education. *Phi Delta Kappan, 81*(10), 736–744.

McLaughlin, D. H., & Broughman, S. (1997). *Private schools in the United States: A statistical profile, 1993–94.* U.S. Department of Education, National Center for Education Statistics. Washington, DC: U.S. Government Printing Office.

McLaughlin, D. H., O'Donnell, C., & Ries, L. (1995). *Schools and staffing in the United States: A statistical profile, 1993–94.* U.S. Department of Education, National Center for Education Statistics. Washington, DC: U.S. Government Printing Office.

Meade, J. (1991). Keeping the faith. *Teacher Magazine, 3*(1), 34–36, 41–45.

Merz, C., & Frankel, S. S. (1997). School foundations: Local control or equity circumvented? *School Administrator, 54*(1), 28–31.

National Center for Education Statistics. (1997). *Private schools in the United States: A statistical profile, 1993–94.* Retrieved on November 14, 2005, from http://nces.ed.gov/pubs/ps.

Newman, J. W. (1995). Comparing private schools and public schools in the 20th century: History, demography, and the debate over choice. *Educational Foundations, 9*(3), 5–18.

Paglin, C. (2001). Why charter schools stumble—and sometimes fall. *Northwest Education, 6*(3), 20–25.

Perreault, G. (2004). Life on the bleeding edge: Philosophy, practice, and public relations in charter schools. *Journal of School Public Relations, 25*(1), 22–31.

Peshkin, A. (1986). God's choice: The total world of a fundamentalist Christian school. *Educational Leadership, 43*(4), 36–41.

Raywid, M. (1994). Alternative schools: The state of the art. *Educational Leadership, 52*(1), 26–31.

Raywid, M. A. (1995). Alternative and marginal students. In M. C. Wang & M. C. Reynolds (Eds.), Making a difference for students at risk (pp. 119–155). Thousand Oaks, CA: Carwin Press.

Reese, S., & Thompson, J. (2002). Celebrating 75 years of success. *Techniques, 77*(2), 19–45.

Rist, M. C. (1991). Parochial schools set out to win their share of the market. *Executive Educator, 13*(9), 24.

Rossell, C. H. (2005). Whatever happened to . . . magnet schools? *Education Next, 5*(2), 44–49.

Rothstein, R., Carnoy, M., & Benveniste, L. (1999). *Can public schools learn from private schools? Case studies in the public and private nonprofit sectors.* Washington, DC: Economic Policy Institute.

Sargeant, J. C. (1967). *Organizational climate in high schools.* Danville, IL: Interstate Publishers.

Simmons, B. S. (2004). Discipline as a source of public relations in a Christian school. *Journal of School Public Relations, 25*(1), 60–69.

Simon, B. S. (2001). Family involvement in high school: Predictors and effects. *NASSP Bulletin, 85*(2), 8–19.

Smith, G., Gregory, T., & Pugh, R. (1981). Meeting student needs: Evidence for the superiority of alternative schools. *Phi Delta Kappan, 62*(8), 561–564.

Smith, K. B., & Meier, K. J. (1995). School choice: Panacea or Pandora's box? *Phi Delta Kappan, 77*(4), 312–316.

Smith, T. M. (1997). *The pocket condition of education, 1997.* Washington, DC: U.S. Government Printing Office.

Tarter, C. J., & Hoy, W. K. (1996). Toward a contingency theory of decision making. *Journal of Educational Administration, 36*(3&4), 212–228.

Vasallo, P. (2000). *More than grades: How choice boosts parental involvement and benefits children* (Policy Analysis No. 383). Washington, DC: Cato Institute.

Vergari, S. (1999). Charter schools: A primer on the issues. *Education & Urban Society, 31*(4), 389–405.

Viteritti, J. P. (1996). Stacking the deck for the poor: The new politics of school choice. *Brookings Review, 14*(3), 10–13.

Waldrip, D. (2005). *A brief history of magnet schools.* Retrieved on November 11, 2005, from http://www.magnet.edu/about.htm.

Walford, G. (1996). Diversity and choice in school education: An alternative view. *Oxford Review of Education, 22*(2), 143–154.

Warner, C. (1994). *Promoting your school: Going beyond PR.* Thousand Oaks, CA: Corwin Press.

Wehlage, G., Rutter, R., Smith, G., Lesko, N., & Fernandez, R. (1989). *Reducing the risk: Schools as communities of support.* Philadelphia: Falmer.

Witte, J. F. (1995). Three critical factors in the school choice debate. *Social Science Quarterly, 76*(3), 502–505.

Zehr, M. A. (1999, May 19). Debating the direction of vocational education. *Education Week, 18*(36), 27.

PART III
Administrative Applications

CHAPTER 9

Building Effective Public Relations Plans

Robert H. Beach

A COLD NIGHT . . . GETTING COLDER

Ira Hoskins, standing by his window in a cold sweat, had just returned from a very hot board meeting. It was cold outside. A light rain was falling and the mist was beginning to rise. For the first time in his superintendency, he had been threatened with a revocation of his contract. Marshal had expressed his belief that the failure of the county to raise the half-cent sales tax for the school district was Ira's fault. Marshal had said it was "a direct result of the superintendent's lackadaisical approach to getting people behind the district's efforts." But Ira felt that he had kept on top of this.

The intercom buzzed and Alice said that Bill Watson was on the phone. Ira picked up the phone, "Hi, Bill, quite a board meeting."

Bill responded, "Ya, well, Ira, I just wanted to let you know that I'm 110% with you on this."

"Thanks, Bill," Ira responded. "Any suggestions?"

"Well, things can't go on the way they are now. It's just a matter of time before the board will act and, well, when that begins to happen, even I will have to side with the majority—but I know you'll get things cleaned up. And remember, we can go back to the commission in six months, so you have a good shot at this. Got to go, Ira."

"Thanks, Bill," and Ira punched off.

Ira felt he had made many contacts within the community, even to the point of being out of the house four nights a week. Things were okay at the *Dispatch*. Mabel Blane, at the paper, called Ira whenever questions on school issues were being covered. True, they had printed Pete Johnston's comment that the real problem in the district was the "pigheaded nature of the county commission and a lack of gray matter on the part of the older elements in the community," which, when coming from the principal of the district's newest school, was not as helpful as it might have been. With the families having kids in school down to 20% and about 35% of the community's citizens being older than 65, this comment had created quite a flurry. Still, the *Tribune* and the two TV stations rarely covered stories about the district. Ira had formed a public relations (PR) task force just after this incident, and they had been charged with providing his office with suggestions for improving community relations. They had come up with two or three good ideas.

Well, with Henry and Mary supporting Marshal and with Bill moving to the middle of the road, things looked as bleak as the weather outside. Thinking of his new principal who had become well known in PR circles, Ira checks his rotary file and dials your number.

Good PR does not just occur. As the case study illustrates, it has to be created. Issues relating to PR are, as Richardson (2002) indicated, among the major stressors in a superintendent's job. High public expectations, concerns regarding student achievement, and negative press coverage all contribute to the dilemma that Ira Hoskins finds himself in. Education has changed, and the forces impacting education have, over the past three decades, increased both in number and in scale. Differing cultural expectations for schools, a concern over violence, and the demand for school safety are examples of problems that now necessitate responses by school leaders—responses that were hardly national in scope 30 years ago. Then, a superintendent often attended to the PR needs of a small district by going to the Lions Club lunch, talking with people at the barber shop, and networking with community leaders. Although these classic methods are still valid, such an ad hoc approach would now be considered inadequate, especially if it constituted the total PR program.

Issues of national diversity, safety, and controversy surrounding other social problems have reached even the small district. Consequently, effective school PR should go beyond intuitive actions and focus on a coherently guided system for managing inter- and intradistrict information flows.

As education's problems have expanded and become more complex, the PR efforts made by school administrators have had to expand. These broader efforts have required a more sophisticated and comprehensive perspective on school PR, such as the one presented in this book. Within this perspective, planning assumes a central role in determining goals and prescribing strategies to achieve them. Ultimately, this affects the very future of the district.

Historically, emphasis on educational planning was rudimentary, highly authoritative, and inflexible. But with social change, this rigid approach has proven to be less than successful. Over time, multiple planning theories have evolved, and some have been quite successful. The dominant planning tool in use today is known generically as *strategic planning*, but it has multiple forms.

Strategic planning emerged in the 1980s, but has roots in the rationalism movement that developed much earlier. Cook (1995) was a major figure in adapting this tool to educational use. He saw strategic planning as "the means by which an organization continually re-creates itself toward extraordinary purpose" (p. 41). Others disagree. As Black and Gregersen (2002) pointed out, "the eight mistakes, twelve steps, and so on offered by others about change are often correct in direction but overly complicated in reality" (pp. 8–9). Bryson (2004) noted that when implementing strategic planning, the causes of failure "are legion" (p. 242). Beach and Lindahl (2004a) noted that "alternative approaches to change exist" (p. 212).

Unlike these early, overly structured attempts to control the planning process, modern versions of planning now emphasize adherence to process with flexibility and with stakeholder involvement.

A sound approach to district planning will assist in positioning the school to meet new issues prior to their becoming problematic. An effective PR program can assist with that positioning and is an important part of the overall district plan. An effective planning-based PR program will better prepare schools for a future that the district's PR effort has helped shape.

PLANNING IN EDUCATION

Planning has long been considered a management function and, therefore, an area of interest for educational administrators. As a discipline, educational planning can trace its roots to the work of Simon (1955), who created a theory of planning known as *rationalism*. This

216 PART THREE ■ Administrative Applications

theory views the organization as a highly rational entity that seeks a series of logically derived linear steps to a "best" solution. Today, rationalism is referred to as "traditional planning" and is the underlying structure for both long-range and strategic planning. Simon's theory, however, had several problems related to (a) a natural confusion between ends and means, (b) the organization's inability to produce truly rational outputs, (c) the inability to define a "best" solution, and (d) normal human limitations. As a result, a competing perspective, known as *incrementalism*, was proposed by Lindblom (1959). Incrementalism accepts the organization as it is and, within this context, proposes pursuing opportune increments to a loosely defined objective. But it, too, is flawed: Over time, the fuzziness related to processes and objectives subjects the organization to political activism and a loss of focus.

Yet another approach to planning grew out of the organizational development movement and related disciplines. It became known as *goal-free* or *developmental planning* and received attention in education as a result of the work of Clark (1981). Here the organization recognizes that an early focus on goals can lead to conflict; goals are therefore given attention only later in the planning process. The initial focus of developmental planning is on creating shared values and vision. The involvement of stakeholders has become an axiom of this planning approach. However, this theory also tends to suffer from ambiguity in process and goals.

Concerns for plan implementation and the readiness of the organization to undergo a proposed change process may be more important to success than a purist application of specific theories. In most change settings, one can simultaneously find applications for rationalism, incrementalism, and developmental planning (Beach, 1993).

Existing methods for dealing with growth in district size (enrollment), for satisfying elevated demands for accountability, and for incorporating business methodologies were adapted by administrators to guide education planning. Although rational models were initially used, with long-range and strategic planning models being the most common, educators sought ways to operationalize more systematic processes in shaping a positive future. The primary difference between these two approaches is that long-range rational models are more internally focused and based on an extrapolation of trends from past organizational data. Strategic planning has an internal focus (trend analysis), but it also explores external issues (environmental scanning) with an analysis of their potential organizational impact (Howell, 2000). With time, strategic planning was subjected to extensive criticism because of a perceived lack of adequate attention to the human aspect of planning. Such criticism has contributed to the infusion of developmental theory concepts, which have resulted in "softer" forms of strategic planning. Now it is generally accepted that all planning theory can be relevant, regardless of which perspective one uses as a basic model: "Mix and match" to suit each unique problem has become standard. Bryson (1999) noted that there must be a "willingness to be flexible regarding what constitutes a strategic plan" (p. xv).

The development of a PR program involves several elements that are in the domains of educational planning and organizational change. Planning is future oriented—seeking to achieve a better future than any anticipated. Change involves the institutionalization of planning products—the PR management system or program. A traditional planning process rests on acquired district data and begins with the goals of the system that have been articulated in relation to the overall organization's vision and mission. At some point, a problem set presents itself; this is simply the recognition, by individuals in the organization, that one or more issues need resolution. Such awareness can occur in many ways, including tirades by irate citizens and recognition derived from internal data analysis. This recognition may be made through the planning process in anticipation of a problem actually arising; this represents "best practice." Additional information is then developed relating to the problem set, the organization, outside forces, and similar factors. A search for potential solutions is initiated in conjunction with an examination of available resources and possible constraints or barriers. A solution or solution strategy is eventually selected and implemented. Finally, an evaluation is conducted to determine the effectiveness of the process and preferred solution.

Two major problems have plagued educational planning at all levels. First, although every group—teachers, administrators, and boards of education—agrees that effective planning is vital, each group thinks that the responsibility for planning rests elsewhere. The administration should work with different groups and different units within the district as a means of avoiding this mind-set. Throughout the district, each unit should be expected to develop an individual plan. However, if not coordinated and linked to the mission of the district, this can become both confusing and counterproductive as different, perhaps contrary, perspectives are communicated across the community. Everyone in the school community has to work together to develop a common vision and plan. Networks of concerned citizens, internal and external to schools, should combine their efforts and resources to set future goals and paths to attain those goals.

The second planning problem involves a reliance on top-down planning approaches. It has become clear that the "We'll tell you what you need to know" approach is no longer acceptable. Modern PR programs, especially in public schools, encourage total school and community involvement.

The potential value of PR planning is addressed by Kaufman, Herman, and Watters (2002). They distinguished between *inside-out* and *outside-in* planning. *Inside-out* planning makes the organization the primary client, "as if one were looking from within the organization outside into the operational world where learners complete, graduate, or get certified; and where citizens live, play and work" (p. 31). *Outside-in* planning views society as the primary agent and beneficiary, "as if one were looking into the organization from outside, from the vantage point of society, back into the realm of organizational results and efforts" (p. 32). Kaufman et al. indicated that the difference between the two perspectives is how one views the world. In the inside-out mode, the client (and beneficiary) is the organization; its survival and well-being will likely be paramount. The outside-in mode sees the basic client (and beneficiary) as society, and anything the school can or should contribute is identified and considered in that light. A comparison of "what is" may be made against "what should be" in order to determine what to keep and what to change.

Whatever the mode or comparison, educational leaders must seek to develop and legitimize a school system's PR program and should strongly consider a planning system that incorporates the following characteristics:

◆ *Simplicity*. Most school systems do not have the resources to establish a full-time planning position. This being the case, an effective system will involve planners who hold other full-time professional positions. Time constraints will require a planning system that is simple, straightforward, and easily managed.

◆ *Visibility*. An effective plan should establish both the purpose and the underlying principles that ground a PR program. Visibility should be a prime consideration in communicating key elements of the program and in shaping public expectations related to the PR function.

◆ *Accountability*. Outcomes of the plan should be tangible and measurable. Planning raises expectations that outcomes will be achieved. Planners must be sensitive to the need to evaluate and visibly demonstrate planning outcomes.

◆ *Brevity*. An effective plan should communicate with a wide variety of constituents. It should be succinct and to the point, with language and structure appropriate to a wide audience.

◆ *Implementability*. The best plan is of questionable value if it is not implemented. Concerns relating to implementation issues should be pervasive throughout the entire planning process.

Gallagher, Bagin, and Kindred (1997) provided a planning checklist that suggests a way to determine where to go and how to get there in school PR planning:

1. A legally adopted policy on school-community relations is indicated.
2. The larger goals and specific objectives of the program must be consistent with the philosophy of the school system and the laws of the state.
3. To the extent possible, the larger goals and specific objectives must be stated in measurable terms.
4. The strategies for attaining the objectives must involve members of various special publics when such involvement is feasible.
5. A distinction must be made in the plan between short- and long-term objectives.
6. The objectives of the school-community relations program must reflect an assessment of need or the gap discovered between what is and what should be.
7. The program must be planned and tailored to the nature of the school and the community with which it is identified.
8. The communication channels selected for disseminating various kinds of information must be appropriate for the audiences involved.
9. The program must involve a continuing audit of the results it produces.
10. Each individual having responsibility in the program must know exactly what he or she is trying to accomplish.
11. The plan must include guides for resolving issues of emotional and intellectual concern to members of the community.
12. To the extent possible, provision must be made in the plan for long-range in-service education of the staff.
13. Program strategies and activities must be adapted to available human resources, funds, and facilities. (pp. 47–48)

A workable planning format requires a projection of future trends and the development of a long-term vision for the PR program. Plans must be realistic and make sense to a wide variety of school constituents. These considerations suggest involving both members of the school family and members of the community in the planning process. These are the stakeholders.

Typically, a planning team should range between 7 and 12 people, at least half of whom represent the community. Teams should be broad enough to be representative, but not so large as to make consensus difficult. The typical planning team often includes central office administrators, building administrators, teachers, and noncertified staff. Community representatives may include both parents and nonparents. Representatives may also reflect constituencies that have a strong vested interest in education: business, government, human services, the ministry, and industry. The planning team is led by the school system administrator responsible for planning and typically includes the superintendent of schools if he or she is not the individual holding primary responsibility for the planning effort. The superintendent's presence lends credibility and reinforces the high priority of the PR planning function.

Although it is unlikely that all planning team members will be experienced planners, it is desirable to select participants who have strong people skills and a commitment to working together. Staff development efforts can create an awareness of the major processes and issues in planning. In their research, Brown, Perry, and McIntire (1995) found that while "teachers and principals . . . desire significantly more participation by students, parents and community members," educators must realize that in planning, "team building is a prerequisite . . ." (p. 3). Individuals should be selected who can work toward consensus, which requires an ability to put aside individual biases and agendas and to base decisions on objective data. It has been observed that "people trained in the technical aspects of the job, in how groups function, and in what members and leaders can do to help groups function more effectively make good group members" (Wheelan, 1999, p. 14).

EFFECTIVENESS IN PLANNING

Planning is predicated on a very broad background of research and theory. Beach and Lindahl (2004b) have noted that the knowledge base in planning is sufficiently extensive so as to be virtually inaccessible to the typical practitioner. However, effectiveness can be achieved by working toward specific guidelines and by using known methodologies. The planning methodology presented here is an effective process for developing a PR program. It is a blend of various planning theories and experiences. It must be noted that this is only one approach among many and it is an elaborate tool for which consultant assistance might be needed. This approach is presented because a considerable body of research, literature, and professional materials exists that can be used in supporting PR planning efforts.

Effective planning processes attempt to predict the external environment that the organization will have to deal with in accomplishing goals. Too often organizations focus inwardly and, thus, fail to see outside their boundaries—a process that is essential to predicting the future. Effective planning recognizes that significant change is likely to be initiated from outside the organization, through societal change and policy mandates. Stakeholders from outside the educational community must be involved. Educators cannot assume what the public wants or needs to know about schools. They must ask the public what it needs or desires.

The process of looking at the environment with a concern for the future arises in planning from the work of Etzioni (1967), where he defined and described a concept known as *mixed scanning.* This is a process where the planner addresses the major elements in the environment that could have an impact on the district and then focuses on only those that are of particular concern. The remaining elements are addressed incrementally.

Planning is a process of developing an understanding of the needs of the organization in order to foretell and make ready for the future. Effectiveness in PR planning involves using the same process for clarifying the present, forecasting the future, deciding what actions should occur (the plan), and then implementing those actions.

Effectiveness in planning is associated with effective leadership. The leader must be committed to future-oriented thinking and planning. Fenwick English made the point that most practitioners get bogged down in activity and see planning as the doing as opposed to the thinking (Kaufman, 1992). Thinking "strategically" requires a mind-set different from that typical of many traditional planners: It requires flexibility as a key ingredient. The same shift in mind-set is needed in the development and implementation of a PR program. Public relations involves much more than "informing the public." Effective PR programs now reach out to parents, the community, businesses, and other constituencies for total involvement in planning, decision making, and evaluation. Crowson (1998) has pointed out that considerable community support for schools can be an indirect product of participation strategies.

Over time, planning links the purpose and beliefs of the organization to its goals; it requires a clear, collective understanding of internal and external environments as they presently exist, and it enables planners to objectively position the organization as future trends are projected; it projects a future based on the assumption that the internal and external environments continually change; it requires reaching out beyond the boundaries of the organization to identify the perceptions of external constituents; and finally, it involves an ongoing process of reshaping the direction of the organization so that it can effectively respond to change.

Kaufman (1992) cited six critical success factors for thinking and planning strategically: (a) being willing to move out of today's comfort zone to use new and broader limits for thinking, planning, doing, and evaluating; (b) distinguishing between ends and means by focusing on what, not how; (c) utilizing all three levels of results (mega, macro, and micro); (d) using an ideal vision as the underlying reason for planning without being limited by current restraints or naysayers; (e) developing objectives that will include measures that tell you what you have accomplished; and (f) defining "need" as a gap in results, not as insufficient resources, means, or methods.

THE PLANNING PROCESS

In adopting any planning process, an administrator should recognize that most school systems have limited planning resources, including time. Figure 9–1 illustrates a process that is straightforward, yet features the essential steps found in any effective planning process. The eight steps illustrated include district profile database development, profile analysis and assessment, plan articulation, capacity analysis, the action plan, the finalized action plan, implementation of the plan, and an annual evaluation review.

When undertaking these steps, it is important to take the opportunity to involve various stakeholders in the actual work processes. The developmental theorists believe that

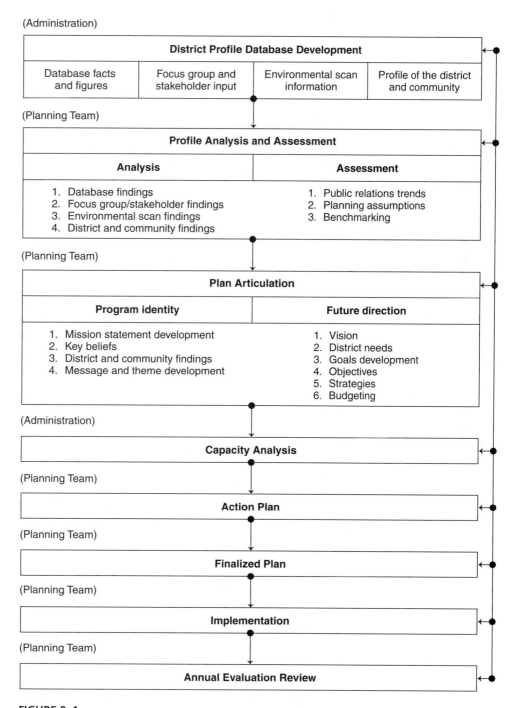

FIGURE 9–1

A Public Relations Planning Process

this has a powerful social benefit. Not only can this involvement help with simple labor concerns, but also it becomes an opportunity for faculty and other groups to become familiar with the details of the organization. Most faculty do not have a complete and comprehensive understanding of the school at all levels. As individuals learn about the organization, there tends to develop a simultaneous growth in their personal understanding relative to how they fit within the school, an understanding that transcends a focus on just the teaching function and creates a perception of the individual's place in the full school environment. This involvement in planning processes helps reduce resistance to the change being planned. Most faculty do not want to decide things; rather, they wish to have some input into those things that impact their lives.

Step 1: District Profile and Database Development

Bernhardt (1998) stated, "Data provide power . . . to make good decisions" (p. xiii). As you will note, the process recommended here is data based. As a first and ongoing step, the school system's administration assembles hard data relative to the organization and its external environment, especially the local community. Database sources cited by Gallagher et al. (1997) and Kaufman et al. (2002) suggest that strong emphasis should be placed on assessing both the internal characteristics of the school system and the external demographics. Much of the external community information required can be extracted from the existing databases maintained by the school district or other agencies. For example, principals may have already completed surveys of students and parents, and the local chamber of commerce may have studies that include educationally related components. The following are information sources one school district employed to expand its database:

1. A demographic review of the community conducted by school officials that included income, age, race, gender, location, occupation, hobbies, interests, lifestyle, and connections to organizations;
2. Results from an opinion poll conducted with parents;
3. Data collected in conjunction with broad referenda that reveal voter preferences with respect to tax increases;
4. Public reactions to critical decisions made by the school board in the past three years;
5. Demographic data extracted from state and county statistical reports (e.g., population projections); and
6. Opinions expressed by focus groups consisting of community leaders.

In addition, organizing community and school focus groups to query stakeholders as a means of better understanding their values, attitudes, and expectations regarding the district's direction is recommended. Focus groups may be organized by identifying constituent groups that interact with the schools and then scanning their respective memberships to identify each group's perception of the PR function and its perceptions and concerns that the PR unit should prepare to address.

Obtaining unbiased responses can be a problem; in this case, one solution may be to elicit anonymous responses. This option becomes more plausible with the assistance of technology. Using present-day technology can significantly improve analysis and assessment efforts. A local school computer laboratory can be used, when networked, to provide an anonymous response system for a small group, or a Web-based Standard Query Language (SQL) capture form can be created that will also capture anonymous responses from external groups. These are powerful tools for generating information held by stakeholders. Proprietary software such as BlackBoard™, WebCT™, and FrontPage® can be used to serve the same purpose with larger groups, especially when anonymity is not a serious concern.

Database analysis serves two important purposes in the planning process: It provides planners with a common understanding of the organization, and it suggests trends that must be planned for or planned around. In the typical district, most analysis can be done using desktop technology. Database software, such as Microsoft® Access and FileMaker Pro™, which can be found in almost all districts, can provide powerful support for analysis. Someone in the district will be able to use these tools. However, the district probably has more powerful database tools in place, and the use of these should be explored.

Specifically, data structure issues should be discussed. These are concerns relative to how different data elements, such as name, grade, and age, relate to each other. Some of the data elements necessary for PR planning may have to be created. Other desktop tools, designed for analysis, are commonly used: Microsoft® Excel is an outstanding example. More-powerful mainframe software, such as SPSS® (the former Statistical Package for the Social Sciences), will handle most districts' analysis needs (desktop versions are available). Although a standard analysis tool, SPSS® requires a greater level of knowledge to use, and it is somewhat expensive. Analysis tools for free-form questions also exist. QSR Internationals© N6 (a non-numerical, unstructured data indexing, searching, and theorizing system) can assist in looking at responses to open-ended questions that may be generated from focus groups.

Standard word processing and presentation software, such as Microsoft's® Word, PowerPoint, and Publisher, can assist with the preparation and distribution of information. The development of most PR materials can be undertaken with these tools prior to production by professional service providers. These tools provide fundamental assistance to the district in understanding—that is, to defining—itself and in disseminating such information to the community.

The process for defining the organization, the district, is nearly identical to that discussed previously for the community. Much of the information required may already exist. The following are examples of resources used by a school district:

1. Accreditation reports;
2. Annual reports for the state department of education (e.g., free lunch data);
3. Student records, such as grade reports and standardized test scores, (these data should be disaggregated);
4. Staff surveys of opinions, perceptions, and attitudes;
5. Student surveys relating to curricular and extracurricular needs and interests;
6. Surveys of higher education officials (e.g., admission standards);
7. Follow-up studies of graduates;
8. Program evaluation outcomes (e.g., state and regional accreditation reports);
9. Staffing reports identifying ratios and needs;
10. School facility feasibility studies;
11. Student discipline records; and
12. Reports from energy and safety audits.

Because administrators may find it difficult to be objective in drawing inferences from these data, a validation process, such as using consultants or an external review panel, is often employed. Figure 9–2 presents output from an analysis of hard data.

An important element in the development of planning data is the external scanning of the environment. This activity is undertaken as a means of determining what factors exist or are developing outside the organization that create either an opportunity or a challenge to the district. This process is based on an awareness of societal and community trends, such as the knowledge that within two years, the new car factory will bring 250 more children into our district of 500 students. Along the same lines would be the recognition that the district is decreasing in size each year with a proportional loss in economies of scale. The planning committee can reflect on things that are developing and that may impact the district's environment in informal sessions using techniques such as brainstorming and nominal group processes. Following are some guiding frameworks that may make this process easier: (a) The district's competitors—charter schools, private schools, etc; competitors include everything that reduces resources or quality; (b) forthcoming state demands, changes in standards and curriculum, and mandates for school operations; (c) community shifts in demographics and attitudes; and (d) new and developing technologies.

"What if" questions can also be formalized by conducting scenario-building sessions, where participants develop projections as to how specific trends could impact the district. The same trend may generate multiple scenarios.

Constituent group: Chamber of commerce
Question: What is the primary purpose of a school public relations program?

Response priority
1. Convince the public of the value of school
2. Keep the public informed about school events
3. Promote school levies or bond issues
4. Communicate about school life
5. Promote extracurricular athletics
6. Involve parents in school activities
7. Communicate school policy

Values and attitudes (summary)
Local businesspeople value public relations for a wide variety of reasons. Convincing the public of school, a number one priority, reflects business's desire to support the value of excellence. Attitudes are positive, with substantial support present for a public relations program.

Organizational expectations (summary)
The business community will expect a diverse, multifaceted approach to public relations to effectively market the schools to the community.

FIGURE 9–2
Output Format for an Analysis of Focus Group Responses

Finally, the data set should include a profile of the community. This is just a statement reflecting demographics, resident attitudes and beliefs, economic status, and other factors felt to be important. A similar profile should be developed for the district. This should be an unvarnished look at the positive and negative aspects of the local schools.

Three problems will present themselves at this point. The first relates to what data will be useful, the second to how best to collect these data in an ongoing fashion, and the third to how to elicit unbiased responses to questions from participants. These concerns will be answered over time. If expertise is not available among district staff, then perhaps a local university or business partner can assist in this effort as part of its service activity. An approach to minimizing concerns in these three areas should be worked through in advance because some expertise is required.

You have reached the end of Step 1.

STOP

Planning is not a linear process. At this point in the process, an understanding of Step 7 becomes paramount. Next, read the information on implementation, which is found in Step 7, in this chapter.

Step 2: Profile Analysis and Assessment

An analysis, the second step in the planning process, represents the first activity of the planning team. The context for the analysis is the profiles of the community and the district. Using the database, the focus group and stakeholder responses, and the environmental scans, planning team members develop findings for responses of (a) each category of data, (b) responses in each focus group, and (c) the collective stakeholders. Data obtained by scanning both internal and external sources is analyzed to identify trends that will impact planning. Emphasis must be placed on reaching consensus through answering questions similar to the following:

1. *Finding*. What do the data show has occurred over time? Specific pieces of data are examined over a five-year period to identify trends.
2. *Projected future*. What do these data imply in the three- to five-year future? What future trends may be predicted?
3. *Comments/qualifications*. What scenarios/events may intervene to impact the data? What does the projected future assume and depend on? (Ricks, Carr, & Buroker, 1991, p. 66)

Figure 9–3 illustrates a possible format for the results of an analysis related to focus groups.

Focus group and stakeholder input from activity within the community is a second data type that can be utilized. Data are gathered by asking open-ended questions of constituent groups and then extracting information on values, attitudes, and expectations reflective of the group response.

After completion of the above analyses, planners examine PR trends and the mandates imposed by federal regulations, the state department of education, or the local board. More specifically, planners assess trends related to the database, project actions to be taken, estimate impacts on the organization, consider the probability of occurrence, and project

Database Demographics

Finding (Summary)
A review of demographic data over a 5-year period reveals a dramatic decline in the percentage of families in the community with children in school. From a past high of 31%, the current data imply that only 22% of the district's families now have children.

Projected Future
This trend is projected to continue in the future as the population ages. It does not appear likely that younger families will immigrate into the district as a result of new business and industry expansion.

Comments and Qualifications
Fewer families will have a direct stake in the educational process. This will lessen support for schools.

FIGURE 9–3
Output Format from an Analysis of Hard Data

trend duration. The potential impact on planning decisions is also defined. Figure 9–4 illustrates a format for organizing the results of a typical trend analysis.

Once trends and mandates are analyzed, it is essential to monitor future directions and to reassess trend data over time. An analysis of important trends and mandates is followed by the development of a balance sheet designed to assess organizational strengths and weaknesses. The balance sheet provides planners with the opportunity to classify certain key factors:

1. *Assets:* advantages enjoyed over time and likely to continue in the future;
2. *Liabilities:* temporary negative conditions that may be overcome in the short term;
3. *Barriers:* disadvantages experienced over time and likely to continue in the future;
4. *Favorable probabilities:* future advantages the organization may exploit to strengthen its position (Ricks et al., 1991, pp. 88–90); and
5. *Threats:* predictable future conditions that may jeopardize the organization's capacity to meet its purposes.

Figure 9–5 illustrates the organization of these factors into a typical balance sheet.

The assessment step also involves the development of planning assumptions. A *planning assumption* is a simple statement predicting a future condition that will need to be planned for or planned around. It is not a goal or an action statement that addresses how a problem will be met. A planning assumption is an assumed condition, usually identified by examining data over time and projecting how related external and internal variables may impact future data. Examples of planning assumptions are given below:

Data. Five-year data trends show that the number of families in the community without children is increasing.

Assumption. There may be some erosion in future support for schools.

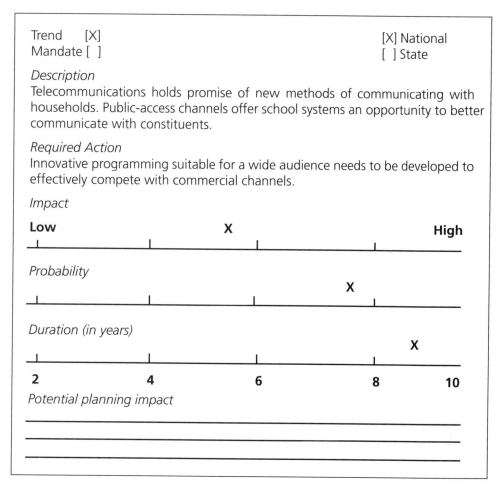

Trend   [X]   [X] National
Mandate [ ]   [ ] State

Description
Telecommunications holds promise of new methods of communicating with households. Public-access channels offer school systems an opportunity to better communicate with constituents.

Required Action
Innovative programming suitable for a wide audience needs to be developed to effectively compete with commercial channels.

Impact

Low   X   **High**

Probability

                                                    X

Duration (in years)

                                                           X

2   4   6   8   10
Potential planning impact

FIGURE 9–4
Format for an Analysis of Trends and Mandates

Data. Demographic data and projections indicate a stable population base with insignificant population in-migration.

Assumption. There may be little change or a slight decline in the number of children entering school in the future.

Data. Economic data project the slow growth of new industry in the community.

Assumption. There may be some improvement in the tax base supporting the schools.

Data. National and state data indicate a dropping birth rate.

Assumption. Competition for state educational dollars may be reduced.

Present

1. *Assets*

Financial support has been and
will be present to support a
public relations program.

2. *Liabilities*

A lack of public relations expertise
exists in the school system.

3. *Barriers*

Historically, some segments of the school
public have been resistant to supporting
a public relations plan.

Future

4. *Favorable probabilities*

Technological advances in communications
will open new awareness to better
communication with the public.

5. *Threats*

Educational restructuring may demand
resources that might otherwise
support public relations efforts.

FIGURE 9–5
A Typical Balance Sheet

A final step in profile analysis and assessment is benchmarking. The purpose of benchmarking is to identify conditions most associated with goal attainment so that these conditions can be replicated and even improved. Fortune 500 corporations such as AT&T, DuPont, Ford, Motorola, and Xerox have used benchmarking as a standard management tool.

Most administrators in other districts are willing to share their knowledge and skills, including the detailed plans and strategies they have developed for school improvement. Such information can be accessed more quickly and economically than in the past. Consider the following ways that this information can be transmitted:

1. Telephone surveys;
2. Site visits;
3. Attendance at national conferences where this information is discussed;
4. Web page data;
5. Plans, reports, or other documents that can be faxed, e-mailed, or sent by regular mail; and
6. Videotapes.

Step 3: Plan Articulation

Completion of the analysis phase leads planners to the development of the actual plan. The plan consists of two components: establishing the program's identity and determining the district's future direction.

The public relations program of the Ashtown Community School is intended to involve, educate, and inform parents and community of the school system's purposes, program, and activities. Through the program, the public will develop greater understanding and insight into the schools, which will lead to greater appreciation of the school's contribution to the community. The program is structured to offer greater opportunity for expanded school communication to ensure community input in school activity.

FIGURE 9–6
Sample Mission Statement

Establishing the Program's Identity.   Development of a program identity serves to establish both the purpose of and the key beliefs about the district and its PR function. This process is essential in defining the program in that it serves to shape the expectations of the school's public and to set parameters that will guide in developing the program's direction. Establishing an effective program requires a sustained effort on the part of the organization to communicate both the program's purpose and its key guiding principles to all involved. The development of a program mission statement and a belief system provides the primary communication message in this process.

The development of a clear, concise *mission statement* is essential for PR planning. A mission statement should be structured in a fashion that will maximize its impact on both the members and the external constituents of the organization. The following guidelines should be observed in developing an organizational mission statement:

1. Keep the statement as brief as possible. An effective mission statement should not exceed one or two paragraphs and should provide guidance for a sense of organizational purpose and direction, a definition of operational scope, resource allocation parameters, and a foundation for strategic goals and objectives.
2. Use language that is understandable to the constituencies being addressed. The mission statement should be readily understood by members of the organization and by the people external to it.
3. Make sure the mission statement contains all required elements. Check the statement to see that it captures all dimensions of the organization.
4. Design and construct the statement for widespread dissemination. The statement should appear throughout the organization and should be predominantly displayed through organizational publications and posted in public areas.

A sample mission statement is found in Figure 9–6.

The development and articulation of a *belief system* represent a second step in clarifying the identity of the PR program. The primary purpose of a belief system is to establish the relationship between the program and its employees, clients, and external constituents. A belief system meets this purpose by establishing values and philosophies that provide the parameters for the program's operation. It serves to define the culture of the program, while setting expectations for conduct. It also provides basic premises around which policies, rules, and regulations are developed.

Beliefs serve as constants as the program responds to internal and external challenges. The strength of the program is established through actualization of the district's and the program's belief system. In developing a belief system, the program should be described as it is, as well as the way it aspires to be. The belief system cannot be imposed on the organization externally, but rather should be articulated from the traditions that are held within the organization itself.

The belief system should give rise to the behavioral expectations of all involved with the program. Equally important is the behavior of employers toward individuals, which should maintain an underlying consistency and be in accord with the belief system.

Typically, programs are encouraged to build their belief systems on a maximum of 10 major tenets. Keep it simple and clear. Shared belief systems are a basic element in school culture and will take time to emerge. A typical tenet is illustrated in Figure 9–7.

Once the mission and goals (drawn from an understanding of future direction) are written, administrators are in a position to craft the organization's messages and themes. These elements of the PR plan serve two critical purposes: (a) They help garner support for the organization, and (b) they help people understand the directions in which the organization is moving. Good themes are usually concise, rhythmic, memorable, and easy to understand. Themes used by schools include such ringing phrases as "Quest for Quality," "Getting Better for Kids," "Public Education: A Sound Investment in America," and "Champions of Learning" (Bagin, Ferguson, & Marx, 1985, p. 112). More so than the mission statement, messages and themes are cultural. That is, they express symbolically the values and beliefs of the organization; they are an overt expression of organizational culture and philosophy. Themes can be very powerful. To be effective, though, they should be predicated on reality. Consider, for example, administrators who decide on the theme "Established Excellence" when in fact test scores in the district have been declining for 15 years. False claims are likely to be challenged, and if they are proven to be false, the school district suffers. Themes and messages should be positive, honest, and truly reflective of the district's vision, mission, and goals.

Determining the District's Future Direction.   The first task in determining future direction is the development of vision statements that predict the future environmental con-

> Effective public relations requires two-way communication between the school and community.

FIGURE 9–7
One Tenet of a Belief System

> Population trends in the nation and in our service area will continue to show an increase in the percentage of families without school-age children. Families of this type have less vested interest in participating.

FIGURE 9–8
A Strategic Vision Statement

ditions to which the program must respond in meeting its purposes. A vision statement should be framed to address both desired educational outcomes and the conditions that must be met if the program is to retain its capacity to meet its purposes. An example of a vision statement is provided in Figure 9–8.

Most plans feature four to seven vision statements. Because vision statements drive the plan's development, it is necessary to limit them to what is deemed most significant to the program and to ensure that they are integrated.

At this point in the process, an assessment of district needs should be made. Attempting to plan for a future that does not incorporate an understanding of existing and projected needs would be futile. A need is the gap between what exists and what is desired in the future. In the broadest terms, it is what the district requires to be in the desired future.

Once visions and needs are clarified, formed, and adopted, they are directly linked to the purposes of the program through the development of goals. Goals constitute broad general desires based on projections of variables that will impact the program's future. Each goal should clearly indicate a priority direction for the organization that reflects the vision statements. A sample goal is given in Figure 9–9.

The establishment of future direction is a goal-setting process; this involves drafting visions, establishing needs and goals, devising strategies, and setting measurable objectives. The process relies on information found in the database and in the conclusions drawn through analysis. Information from both of these sources must be continually referenced throughout the goal-setting process.

The identity established for the program is equally important to the process. All outcomes of the goal-setting process must be congruent with previously developed elements that define the organization's identity. This brings forward an interesting problem associated with all planning processes. You probably have experienced this. The planning process is discussed and illustrated, as it must be, in a linear form. In actuality, the process, while appearing to move forward in linear fashion, is in fact recursive—folding back on itself, with overlapping interacting elements and with events often happening in parallel.

Historically, a superintendent could establish the goals for a district's PR program simply by decree. Largely due to changes in the way we perceive organizations, this is now a sure way to doom any planning effort in just about any large (especially public) organization. Examples of this are easy to find. Assume an administrator does in fact set a goal for a PR program such as *increase public receptivity to higher fiscal support for the school district*. This, of course, is read as *higher taxes*. Teachers are members of the community, that is, the public. If the teachers do not agree with raising taxes, improved salary and working conditions aside, then the goal comes into conflict with the beliefs of some of the very people

---

The school system shall place increased emphasis on keeping those without school-age children well informed about the schools, their programs, and their importance to the community.

FIGURE 9–9
Sample Strategic Goal

who will be involved with its successful attainment. When asked by other members of the community if new funding really is needed, some teachers will present an individual perspective, perhaps masked by other issues—"not if they would stop spending on those computers"—which is at variance with district efforts. An important and needed goal can become a source of contention within the school itself and within the community. This is a basic consideration in developmental planning models.

Goals are better established by a process of articulation where the teachers and other members of the organization, as well as community stakeholders, have input into their formulation. It is difficult to move an educational institution to a place where it does not wish to go. If a goal is important for an organization, yet does not arise naturally from within the stakeholder group, then it may be that time must be devoted by the administration to pre-planning. This is a time to stop and reflect on whether or not the change is positive and actually needed. It is a time to reflect on whether or not the organization has the capacity to change. Perhaps time is needed to improve stakeholder understanding of the organization and to build capacity for change. Questions such as these need to be answered: Why are new monies required? How will this improve instruction? How will the children benefit? This process of understanding can be enhanced by creating task forces that focus on a problem. When stakeholders work on investigating a problem, even an unrelated problem, and find solutions, it builds a stronger understanding of the institution.

An additional problem can be associated with goal formation: A beautiful solution is stated, but no goal. Take, for example, this goal: *Establish better relationships with the press*. This looks like a natural, even required goal, but it is not. It is only one means (a solution) to some other goal, perhaps the fiscal support goal above. Better press relationships are necessary to achieve some larger end. This is end-means confusion and a pit into which even experienced planners fall. The goal is the end; the solution strategy is the means of achieving the end. When solutions are substituted for goals, the process of finding better alternatives is truncated and unexplored, with many potentially better solutions overlooked. Consider a teacher who has the goal of obtaining a new text for a reading class. The text is, of course, a means to better student reading performance. Other methods of reading improvement, such as a pull-out program, may not be examined when the textbook "goal" is accepted.

In any serious PR program, there usually will be more than one goal. In addition, because goals tend to be of a general nature, a greater degree of specificity must be supplied. This is done by establishing objectives in support of each goal, as noted, thus creating a cascade or hierarchy from goals to objectives. Objectives are usually stated in performance terms. Figure 9–10 shows an illustration of two objectives related to a goal.

The goal and objectives illustrated in Figure 9–10 should have been developed through a process of problem articulation, data generation and analysis, and a search for alternative solutions. This last element, developing alternative solution strategies, requires specific attention.

Each goal should be linked by one or more strategies that in turn shape the objectives that define component activities related to the goal. In forming strategies, the organization concentrates on identifying alternative actions that hold promise for maximizing the organization's likelihood of reaching its goals. Strategy formulation may be accomplished by addressing the sequence of questions shown in Figure 9–11.

Problems can arise in many ways. They may "come out of the woodwork," be the result of a review of instructional test scores or other data analyses, or arise from reflections on what must be accomplished in meeting the institution's PR goals. In the last case, there will be a series of linked problems, each requiring a solution. The linking of individual problems and their solutions ultimately becomes the program itself. Solving these problems requires developing a set of possible solutions and choosing an acceptable and workable solution for each problem.

Strategies are the alternatives the organization selects to best enable it to meet its objectives. These objectives are most often programmatic aspects of the total organizational effort, constituting the substance of what it will take to make the projected future a reality (Ricks et al., 1991).

Problem: The print media publishes articles related only to district problems.

Goal A: Increase the number of publicized columns that present district achievements and successes.

> *Objective 1:*
> Within 3 months have established a file on each major local print media provider and subfiles within each to include the name, address, phone numbers, topical areas of interest, etc., for each educational correspondent and reporter.
>
> *Objective 2:*
> Within 6 months ensure that 90% of the local print media's educational correspondents and reporters have met personally the district's public relations officer.

FIGURE 9–10
A Goal-Objective Hierarchy

What is our organization doing now?
The school district currently sends a newsletter to citizens of the school system featuring school programs.

What are the deficits of our current activity?
Many residents do not read the newsletter because they do not perceive school news to be important to them.

What needs to occur to overcome deficits?
The readership base of the newsletter needs to be significantly expanded.

Strategy
The district newsletter shall be expanded to include other information of vital community interest as a means of expanding the readership base.

FIGURE 9–11
The Strategy Development Process

By the beginning of next year, the school system shall effectively communicate information about district programs to 60% of all families without children in the district.

FIGURE 9–12
A Simple Objective

Objectives should be measurable and feature a clearly defined time frame (see Figure 9–12). Typical time frames for objectives are from three months to five years.

Projecting time lines and establishing ways to measure the achievement of objectives involve a "best guess" consideration of how effective the developed strategy will be in driving the desirable programmatic outcome. In setting objectives, you have to project the impact of the strategy in shaping both standards for measuring success and projected time lines.

No PR office can function without an adequate budget. When budgets are slim and teachers' salaries are frozen, the PR staff is often an easy target, criticized as "fluff" and described as something the district can live without. The budget of any division of a school district has both direct and symbolic importance; that is, the amount of money dictates the program scope and conveys a message to employees and the community about the importance placed on this function.

At this point in the planning process, the costs of plan implementation can be reasonably estimated. Funding for the PR office must include an estimate of the resources required for the development and implementation of the PR plan if that plan is to be implemented. Hall and Hord (2001) commented:

> We have seen change efforts where even required equipment and materials were not forthcoming. We are not talking about delayed delivery but the complete lack of planning and budgeting for equipment and materials. All too frequently, we are amazed to observe that other types of basic resources, such as training, are not provided. (p. 157)

Major failures in planning can be attributed to a lack of support for teacher time, well-developed materials, and ongoing staff development. If an organization cannot fund its plans, it should not attempt major change. The failure of a plan leads to demoralization, and a lack of adequate resources will lead to failure.

Step 4: Capacity Analysis

The foregoing clearly indicates that prior to the final adoption of the plan, consideration must be given to whether or not the organization has adequate resources to carry it out. To this end, the organization is charged with the responsibility of conducting a capacity analysis to determine the plan's viability.

Capacity analysis is a preliminary examination of the ability of the organization to support plan objectives. "Capacity" comprises multiple elements. *Fiscal requirements* are defined as the amount of money needed, over time, to accomplish each objective. *Human requirements* are an estimate of the personnel (or personnel time) required to conduct plan activities. Each variable should be projected for each objective (Ricks et al., 1991). Figure 9–13 represents a typical capacity analysis.

It is becoming common to find plans being created that have not involved a close inspection of the district's facilities. This is an especially important undertaking. As an example, a

Goal
The school system shall place increased emphasis on keeping those without school-age children informed about schools, their programs, and their importance to the community.

Objective
By next year the school system shall effectively communicate information about district programs to 60% of all families without children in school.

Anticipated activity - newsletters

1. Evaluate newsletter content
2. Assess public views and needs
3. Reformat newsletters
4. Bid graphics/printing
5. Assemble mailing list
6. Distribute

Anticipated outcome

Fiscal requirements	Amount	Current %	New Funding
Supplies	$ 3,000.00	50%	$ 1,500.00
Equipment/printing	$ 7,000.00	65%	$ 4,550.00
Personnel	$ 60,000.00	100%	$ 60,000.00
Information acquisition	$ 2,000.00	100%	$ 2,000.00
Printing	$ 15,000.00	75%	$ 11,250.00
Mailing	$ 6,000.00	80%	$ 4,800.00
Total cost	$ 93,000.00		$ 84,100.00

Human resources	% Time
Director Jane Doe	Director 50%
Other participants (describe)	Secretary 100%
	Newsletter Editor 25%

FIGURE 9–13
Capacity Analysis

common surprise can occur with the improvement of the district's technology resources. The PR office announces the arrival of the district's new computers for the new lab, only to see a delay in implementation for several months while the lack of adequate power and cooling in the designated space is addressed. Problems such as this are an embarrassment that can be avoided by assessing the physical capacity of the system relative to the plan.

Therefore, close attention to capacity analysis is critical if credibility is to be preserved. Planning raises expectations in the community and in the schools. Credibility is damaged if the organization does not have the capacity to move its PR plan forward. Consequently, failing to conduct a capacity analysis properly can result in serious problems after planning.

Step 5: The Action Plan

Each adopted objective in the plan should be finalized and forwarded to the administrator responsible for PR for action planning. *Action planning* consists of identification, in chronological order, of the activities that must be undertaken to achieve each strategy of each objective. This consists of evaluating each strategy and listing what steps must be taken in a who, what, when framework. Prior to initiating an action plan, the administrator in charge should carefully examine the vision statement, goal, and strategies related to each objective. The action plan should be consistent with both the vision statement and the specific goal being addressed and should directly reflect the strategies around which the related objective(s) is based. A classic example of an action plan is illustrated in Figure 9–14. An assumption underlying the example is that the plan is extensive, with several components or parts. The development of the action plan involves considerable thought and reflection by the planning team as to how best to accomplish the project.

Step 6: The Finalized Action Plan

A central purpose of planning is to create one or more documents that support communication to all district employees, stakeholders, and community members. Codifying the plan's elements produces a document that can be distributed. This document should reflect results from the steps that have gone into the planning process, including, at least, the community and district profiles, significant findings from the profile analyses and assessment (especially vision, mission, and goals), and the various other outputs from the plan. This is done in textual format, by section. A section should be created that relates goals, objectives, and strategies. Finally, the action plan should be presented in relation to those goals, objectives, and strategies. This is the plan—tentatively. It is tentative in that the planning committee and core stakeholders should be provided with an opportunity to review the plan and to make adjustments as appropriate. At this point, if not earlier, a project manager (the individual who will be responsible for implementing the plan) should be named.

Project: **Public Relations Improvement**   Page 12 of 28

Section: **Media Relations (MR)**

Activity	Definition	Agent	Start Date	End Date	Cost	Special Notes
MR 15	Establish joint protocols	Smith, H.	6/7/07	8/7/07	$150	None
MR 16	Develop protocol brochure	Jones, L.	6/15/07	8/21/07	$500	3 Color
MR 17	Distribute brochure	Kim, K.	8/22/07	8/23/07	$50	None

FIGURE 9–14
A Classic Action Plan

The tentative designation also recognizes that the plan will require a review by the superintendent and board. There may also be a requirement for a legal review. Again, expect some plan modifications. Associated with the plan may be some need for the creation of board-approved policy supporting the process of implementation.

Prior to implementation, materials will have to be created that reflect the plan, its purpose, district goals, and the departmental and individual expectations for implementation. The plan must be flexible, so there really is no "Final Plan."

Step 7: Implementation

In a technical sense, the information presented in this and the next section is not compatible with the title of this chapter. However, these sections are essential parts of any planning process. Concerns related to implementation are critical and must be addressed if any plan is to be made manifest. Experience dictates that *the back end must drive the front end*. Everything associated with a plan's development must reflect the understanding that no matter how fine the elements of a plan are, if they cannot be implemented, the plan probably will fail.

Overlooking important variables can contribute to this failure. Typical factors that must be addressed prior to implementing the plan includes clear goals and expectations; organizational tranquility to faculty demographics—age, gender, education; ability of stakeholders to observe the innovation; plan flexibility; preparedness for change; available materials and resources; faculty time and energy; user commitment; ongoing aid and training; administrative support; peer consultation; understanding; communication capacity; staff skills; definition of proposed activities; resources—staff development; learning time; physical constraints; project size; post-project funding arrangements; positive/negative experiences with change; and teacher competence.

Of course, many planners plan with no serious intent to implement. Many reasons for this exist. Planning can be a political process designed as a defense when a board member asks, Do we have a plan? This is understandable, but it is bad practice.

Therefore, understanding how each element of the plan will be implemented is critical. As an example, if a strategy is developed for adding 10 television announcements informing the community of pending open board meetings, while, at the same time, no funds exist for advertising, what are the chances the plan will be implemented? While this is an obvious example, more subtle considerations exist. In any serious planning effort, there will be individual winners and losers. In a small office where plans are unrelated to a greater organization or where there will be no large losses, this may be a trivial concern. In a larger setting, where department chairpersons are changed, where offices without windows are reassigned, or where any other status-changing impact will be felt, resistance to change is created. Alienate enough people, and you will find yourself in a position like the bright-eyed leader who is charging forward, but with no followers. He is just a guy out jogging! Concerns for issues such as this are the reason for emphasizing stakeholder involvement at all levels of the planning process. How any planned action will impact stakeholders drives consideration as to the effectiveness of the action. Implementation concerns drive planning. The back of the process drives the front!

When implementation begins, the process shifts from planning to change. As Hall and Hord (2001) noted, "An organization does not change until the individuals within it change" (p. 7). They viewed implementation as a process where the planner, now a change agent, addresses the concerns of stakeholders. Concerns can be categorized by stages. This categorization is done first by probing, essentially on a one-on-one basis, to determine how each individual is viewing proposed or ongoing plan implementation. This probing yields information on concerns and use (implementation). At the same time, the system is probed to determine how implementation is spreading out among stakeholders. Levels of use are determined and early adopters of the change can assist others who have yet advanced to this level. Finally, an assessment is made as to the implementation's fidelity (faithfulness) to the plan. All of the probing, feedback, and fidelity assessments are ongoing, with the overall purposes of reducing concerns, increasing plan adoption—change, and maintaining a reasonable level of fidelity, while allowing for flexibility.

You have reached the end of Step 7.

STOP

If this is the first time you have read this section, return to Step 2 above and continue the planning process. If not, continue on to Step 8.

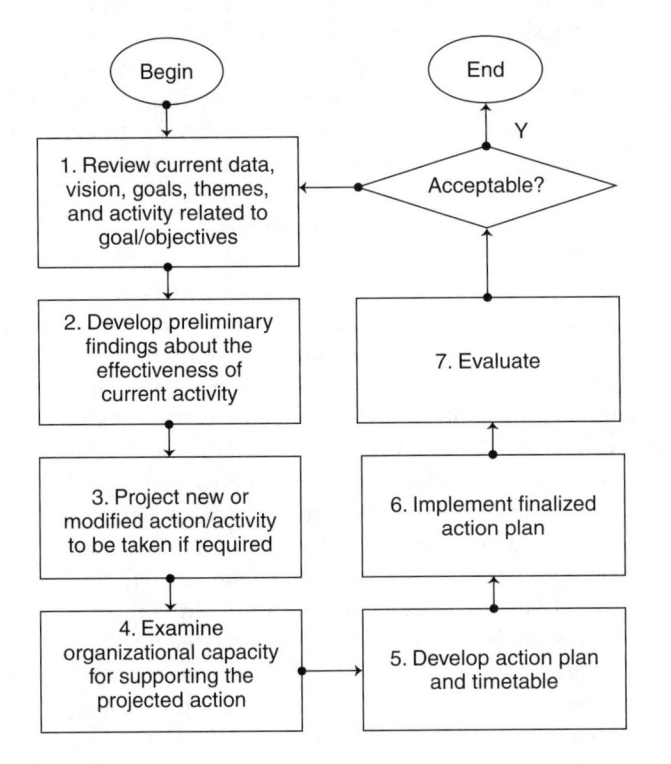

FIGURE 9–15

Steps in an Action Plan Review

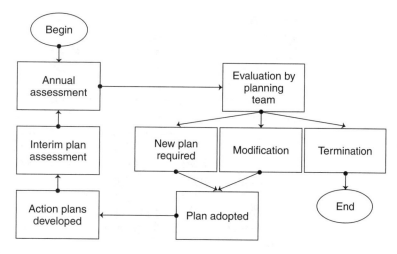

FIGURE 9–16
Annual Planning Cycle

Step 8: Annual Evaluation Review

To maximize the effectiveness of a PR plan, the planning process should be ongoing. Unlike those of more traditional long-range plans, the components of a modern plan are considered dynamic. As the future unfolds, the plan must be revisited, readjusted, and updated. Changes in both the internal and the external environments over time require flexibility. An annual planning cycle (see Figure 9–16) is necessary to ensure that the plan becomes a part of the culture of the PR program.

In establishing an annual evaluation review of the plan, it is considered most desirable to reconvene the original planning team each year to review progress on the plan and to reconsider its viability in the face of changing conditions. Figure 9–16 presents a simple flowchart illustrating a planning cycle that features flexibility in promoting termination, modification, or regeneration of objectives on an annual basis. Through this configuration, the plan becomes dynamic over time as changes in the environment result in restructuring activities each year.

PITFALLS WHEN PLANNING

Even though the planning system presented in this chapter is intended to provide planners with a simple, straightforward tool, users should be aware of pitfalls that may be encountered in its implementation. Even the best-planned efforts may become bogged down unless careful attention is given to avoid the following problems:

1. *Overreliance on data.* Databases utilized in planning should be designed to lead to the identification of general conditions that must be planned for or planned

around. Adding extensive, detailed information to databases may not contribute to making accurate generalizations and may, in effect, bog down planners in trivia.

2. *Compromised analysis.* Planners often differ in their perceptions of what major priorities ought to be. All too often competing views may be adopted in the same plan because of the planners' inability to reach consensus. When this happens, plans soon proliferate and often exceed the capacity of the organization to complete.

3. *Strained resources.* Planners are urged to consider the importance of tailoring the scope of plans to available resources. Resources include faculty and staff time. Exceeding available resources will lead to unmet objectives and goals and, as a consequence, unmet public expectations.

4. *Failure to consider mandates.* Educational reform often leads to mandates for change outside the control of local planners. Failure to consider such mandates and incorporate them appropriately in plans may lead to overextension and competition for resources.

5. *Unexpected consequences.* Things happen that were not foreseen. Calabrese et al. (2003) provided an interesting example of a citizen updating his trucks and making fuel cheaper (fewer deliveries) for other citizens, which resulted in several layoffs, which subsequently saw the removal of five students, which, in this small community, amounted to a loss of 1% in state aid to the school! Cheaper fuel versus higher school taxes!

6. *Assumptions about the future.* The future is not fixed. It can change in an instant, and assumptions made from trend analysis and environmental scanning can become invalid within months or within even shorter time periods. Change may outpace projections and may be sufficiently complex that it is not predictable with any precision. Be flexible and alert (Napier, Sanaghan, Sidle, & Saraghan, 1997, p. 14).

7. *Assumptions about citizens.* Because citizens desire involvement in school affairs does not mean that they will be willing to participate and independently seek relations with the school (Snowden & Gorton, 2002, p. 239).

Careful consideration of the pitfalls outlined above will help ensure a timely planning process that will generate a high-utility product.

SUMMARY

Public relations is an often overlooked, but very important component of any successful organization. School systems have not given it enough attention because of the lack of resources, knowledge, or skill levels—or because of the failure to realize the impact that a good PR program can have on the employees, clients, and external constituents. Boards of education and superintendents, because of the attention being given to education by the media, much of which is negative, have begun to focus on better ways of communicating with the public.

The development of a PR program requires careful planning that not only takes into account current activities in the organization, but also focuses on the future. It is important to understand the community both internally and externally, as it now exists, but it is just as important to project the future environment that will have to be dealt with in order for the organization to meet its purpose. The image of the organization can be significantly enhanced through an effective and efficient PR program.

Even at a time when educators are expected to do more with less, a PR strategy will be invaluable to a school district. It is not a matter of whether one is needed, but rather a matter of getting started and moving forward in explaining to the constituents, employees, and clients where the system is, where it wants to go, and how it expects to get there. A positive image takes time, resources, and effort to establish, but the dividends are endless.

QUESTIONS AND SUGGESTED ACTIVITIES

CASE STUDY

1. What seems to be the central problem for this district?
2. How would you proceed to change the PR planning process in the district?
3. What PR goals and objectives would you develop for the district?
4. In response to Ira's call, what will you tell him about the problem?

CHAPTER

5. Why is it important to scan the environment when planning?
6. Why is it important to avoid end-means confusion?
7. Assume that you are a superintendent of a district with 3,500 students. Who would you involve in the PR planning process?
8. Discuss potential barriers that may prevent school administrators from properly planning a PR program. What actions can be taken to overcome these barriers?
9. What problems might occur if an organizational capacity analysis is not completed?
10. What problems can arise when major stakeholders are not involved in the development of a PR plan?

SUGGESTED READINGS

Bradford, R. W., & Duncan, J. P. (2000). *Simplified strategic planning: A no-nonsense guide for busy people who want results fast.* Worcester, MA: Chandler House Press.

Conner, P., Lake, L., & Stackman, R. (2003). *Managing organizational change.* Westport, CT: Praeger.

Fearn-Banks, K. (1995). *Crises communications: A casebook approach.* Mahwah, NJ: Erlbaum.

Harris, A. (2002). *School improvement: What's in it for schools?* New York: Routledge Falmer.

Stone, N. (1995). *The management and practice of public relations.* London: Macmillan.

Tucker, K., Derelian, D., & Rouner, D. (1997). *Public relations writing: An issue-driven behavioral approach.* Englewood Cliffs, NJ: Prentice Hall.

REFERENCES

Bagin, D., Ferguson, D., & Marx, G. (1985). *Public relations for administrators*. Arlington, VA: American Association of School Administrators.

Beach, R. (1993). Emerging perspectives on planning and change processes. *Journal of School Leadership, 3*(6), 646–665.

Beach, R. H., & Lindahl, R. A. (2004a). A critical review of strategic planning: Panacea for public education? *Journal of School Leadership, 14*(2), 211–234.

Beach, R. H., & Lindahl, R. A. (2004b). Identifying the knowledge base for organizational improvement. *Planning & Changing, 35*(1&2), 2–32.

Bernhardt, V. (1998). *Data analysis for comprehensive schoolwide improvement*. Larchmont, NY: Eye on Education.

Black, J. S., & Gregersen, H. B. (2002). *Leading strategic change: Breaking the brain barrier*. New York: Prentice Hall.

Brown, D., Perry, C., & McIntire, W. (1995). Parents, students, community members: Teachers and administrators desire their increased participation in making educational decisions. *Journal of Educational Relations, 16*(4), 2–8.

Bryson, J. M. (1999). *Strategic management in public voluntary service: A reader*. New York: Pergamon.

Bryson, J. M. (2004). *Strategic planning for public and non-profit organizations* (3rd ed.). San Francisco: Jossey-Bass.

Calabrese, R., Patterson, J., Koenigs, A., Johnson, R., Neill, S., Rasmussen, C., et al. (2003). Fighting for survival: A rural midwestern community and its schools. *Planning & Changing, 34*(1&2), 19–31.

Clark, D. (1981). In consideration of goal-free planning: The failure of traditional planning systems in education. *Educational Administrative Quarterly, 17*(3), 42–60.

Cook, W. (1995). *Strategic planning for America's schools*. Arlington, VA: American Association of School Administrators.

Crowson, R. (1998). *School-community relations, under reform*. Berkeley, CA: McCutchan.

Etzioni, A. (1967). Mixed scanning: A third approach to decision-making. *Public Administration Review, 27*(5), 385–392.

Gallagher, D., Bagin, D., & Kindred, L. (1997). *The school and community relations*. Boston: Allyn & Bacon.

Hall, G., & Hord, S. (2001). *Implementing change: Patterns, principles, and potholes*. Boston, MA: Allyn & Bacon.

Howell, E. (2000). *Strategic planning for a new century: Process over product* (Report No. EDO-JC-00-08). Los Angeles: ERIC Clearinghouse for Community Colleges. (ERIC Document Reproduction Service No. ED447842)

Kaufman, R. L. (1992). *Mapping educational success: Strategic thinking and planning for school administrators*. Newbury Park, CA: Corwin Press.

Kaufman, R., Herman, J., & Watters, K. (2002). *Educational planning: Rethinking, restructuring, revitalizing*. Lanham, MD: The Scarecrow Press.

Lindblom, C. E. (1959). The science of muddling through. *Public Administration Review, 19*, 79–88.

Napier, R., Sanaghan, P., Sidle, C., & Saraghan, P. (1997). *High impact tools and activities for strategic planning: Creative techniques for facilitating your organization's planning process*. New York: McGraw-Hill Trade.

Richardson, L. (2002). The challenge of boundary spanning in school district leadership. *Planning & Changing, 33*(3&4), 202–203.

Ricks, J., Carr, P., & Buroker, C. (1991). *Strategic planning for schools: A manual designed for school district organizational planning.* Dayton, OH: Wright State University.

Simon, H. A. (1955). A behavioral model of rational choice. *Quarterly Journal of Economics, 69,* 99–118.

Snowden, P., & Gorton, R. (2002). *School leadership and administration* (6th ed.). New York: McGraw-Hill.

Wheelan, S. (1999). *Creating effective teams: A guide for members and leaders.* Thousand Oaks, CA: Sage.

CHAPTER 10

Community Relations

Theodore J. Kowalski

CASE STUDY: A MENTOR'S QUESTIONABLE ADVICE

In the Rock Ridge School District, administrators fondly refer to Edgar Palmer as the "sage." During his 28-year tenure as principal of Adams Elementary School, 17 other administrators moved in and out of principal positions in the district's other 7 schools. When asked to explain how he has been able to remain in his challenging position for such a long time, Edgar quickly responds, "It's a combination of hard work, positive relationships with teachers, concern for students, and good old common sense."

Last year, after Dr. Karen Lewis was employed as principal of North Middle School, the Rock Ridge superintendent appointed Edgar to be her mentor. In an effort to reduce turnover, the superintendent had initiated a mentoring program for all newly employed principals and assistant principals. Though Karen had been a teacher for 12 years and an assistant principal for 4 years, she had been neither a principal nor a Rock Ridge employee previously. Mentors were required to meet with their protégés at least once a month for one year, and at the end of that period, they had to file a summary report with the superintendent. At Edgar's urging, he met with Karen twice a month.

Edgar needed little encouragement when it came to offering advice, especially to other principals. Despite the fact that he had never been a middle school principal, he made a myriad of suggestions to Karen. Knowing that she had recently completed a doctoral degree in school administration, he also reminded her repeatedly that his knowledge did not come from reading textbooks or from listening to professors. "My wisdom," he told her, "has come from dealing with real problems, real students, real teachers, and of course, real parents."

Karen liked Edgar personally, but she did not agree with some of his suggestions. However, she never revealed her disagreements during their discussions. Typically, she listened politely and occasionally asked questions. During a meeting in mid-October, however, she became quite troubled after he suggested that community involvement in general and parental involvement specifically were a bad idea. He commented, "I've lived in Rock Ridge a long time and I've outlasted four superintendents and a whole lot of principals. Regardless of what you may think, most residents really don't want to be highly involved in schools. They feel pretty good about the way we run things. Sure, there are a few malcontents, but they have an axe to grind or just have a need to rebel against authority."

"Do you think most parents are pleased with our schools?" she inquired.

"Absolutely. But you have to be careful when it comes to parents because some of them are the worst troublemakers. Good parents respect teachers and administrators, and they don't challenge our decisions. They trust us to do the right things for their children. The complainers think they know more than we do. They think that having gone to school qualifies them as education experts. Well, they're wrong—but, of course, it's best not to tell them that. So I just try to stay away from them. Unfortunately, that's not always possible. Sometimes you have to meet with them—usually to give them bad news."

After listening to Edgar, Karen tried to decide if she was astonished or depressed by his comments. His views contradicted her convictions, but she decided not to challenge him. Instead, she conferred with two other persons: Elaine Bratski, one of her former professors, and Susan Miles, an experienced elementary principal in Rock Ridge. Professor Bratski told Karen that Edgar's opinions were misguided, and she advised Karen to challenge his views. Mrs. Miles gave her different advice.

"Even if Edgar is wrong on this issue, challenging him is not a good idea. He has political clout, especially with the teachers' union and the school board. For example, one of the board members is his nephew, and another board member is his best friend. If I were you, I'd smile and keep quiet. This first year will pass quickly."

Anticipating her next meeting with Edgar, Karen tried to decide if Dr. Bratski or Mrs. Miles was correct on this issue. She was certain about one thing, however: The "sage" would have more advice for her at their next meeting.

The case study demonstrates that administrators often disagree concerning community and parental engagement in public education. This disagreement can confuse novice principals and result in internal conflict. For example, Dr. Lewis may wonder why her former professor and her mentor have such different perspectives, and she may feel that she has to choose between her professional convictions and political expediency. Her ability to deal effectively with this uncertainty and conflict, however, depends on her personal knowledge. That is, she is better prepared to handle this challenge if she is aware of the knowledge base on community and parental involvement.

As pointed out in Chapter 1, members of the school administration profession often refer to public relations (PR) as "community relations," primarily because they believe that PR is a politically unacceptable term. In truth, PR "strives to help organizations develop and preserve the variety of relationships that ensure long-term success" (Austin & Pinkleton, 2001, p. 5); therefore, it is a broader process than the one described in early definitions (i.e., definitions that focus entirely on persuasion, press agentry, and advertising). As defined in this book, community relationships are integral and essential to school PR, and they are arguably the primary objective of this administrative process.

In promoting ideal relations between schools and their publics, Holliday (1988) identified four core purposes or processes:

1. Promoting a school climate that is conducive to teaching and learning,
2. Encouraging a maximum level of parental involvement,
3. Building the public's knowledge of education as a means of garnering support, and
4. Involving citizens in collaborative projects, partnerships, and similar initiatives to maximize human and material resources.

This perspective is nested in two premises: that information leads to support and participation and that support and participation enhance productivity (i.e., student learning). Unfortunately, trend lines for educational challenges and community participation have been moving in different directions; as the challenges have multiplied, participation has waned.

The content of this chapter addresses relationships between schools and their communities and the pivotal roles administrators play in building them. First, the nexus between relationships and communication is examined. Second, methods for improving community relations are discussed. Then, focused attention is given to constructing positive relationships with parents—arguably the most important of a school's multiple publics.

RELATIONSHIPS AND COMMUNICATION

The reluctance among some school administrators to develop relationships with others stems from misguided beliefs about organizational efficiency. Most notably, these administrators believe that interactions with employees and persons outside the organization produce conflict and the conflict then diminishes organizational efficiency (Hanson, 2003). For example, there is a school board in a small rural district that meets only once a month on a Saturday morning at 8:00 A.M. The board conducts its meetings in the superintendent's conference room, and there is no seating provided for visitors. The underlying rationale for this arrangement is to discourage local residents from attending board meetings—an action rooted in the belief that interaction with patrons spawns conflict.

In truth, conflict is inevitable in all organizations, and its effect on schools is determined largely by the manner in which it is managed (Hoy & Miskel, 2005). Recognizing this fact, forward-thinking administrators are disposed to capitalize on the positive by-products of conflict, especially in relation to pursuing organizational improvements. This more positive perspective of relationships was summarized by Uline, Tschannen-Moran, and Perez (2003):

> Conflict is a natural part of collective human experience. In our efforts to cooperate with one another, we have differences of opinion about how best to accomplish our common goals. We seek to protect our individual interests within these efforts and forestall outside influences, fearing discord in the face of these conflicting forces. Conflict is often unsettling. It can leave participants shaken and ill at ease, so it is often avoided and suppressed. Yet conflict, when well managed, breathes life and energy into relationships and can cause individuals to be much more innovative and productive. (p. 782)

Typically, administrators committed to involving stakeholders are guided by a mix of philosophical, professional, and political convictions. Philosophically, they believe that citizens have a right to be informed about public schools (Gotts & Purnell, 1985), and therefore, they accept democratic administration as a normative standard (Miretzky, 2004; Petersen & Kowalski, 2005). Professionally, they rely on empirical evidence showing that stakeholder participation enhances authentic reform (Crowson & Boyd, 2001; Fullan, 2001). And politically, they realize that change is less probable in a community in which stakeholders are alienated and unwilling to financially support improvement efforts (Duke, 2004; Hoyle, Björk, Collier, & Glass, 2005).

Unfortunately, administrators do not always understand how relationships influence school improvement efforts and how PR influences positive relationships. The quality of relationships is determined by four variables described by Huang (1997):

- ◆ *Control mutuality:* mutual agreements about power sharing;
- ◆ *Trust:* the extent to which persons in a relationship trust each other;
- ◆ *Satisfaction:* feelings that the relationship is successful and mutually beneficial; and

◆ *Commitment:* feelings that the relationship is sufficiently important to warrant effort and resources.

Administrators may attempt to manipulate or otherwise control relationships unilaterally. For example, a principal may prey upon weak teachers by demanding their loyalty in return for "administrative protection." Such behavior also has been observed in relationships between superintendents and school board members (Kowalski, 2006). This form of relationship management, however, usually produces misunderstandings and dissatisfaction (Grunig & Huang, 2000). One of the attributes of a comprehensive PR program is that the process provides a framework for mutuality relative to control, trust, satisfaction, and commitment.

Positive relationships are capable of producing three types of capital deemed essential for school reform:

1. *Political capital* in the form of increased financial support (Valenzuela & Dornbush, 1994),
2. *Social capital* in the form of positive dispositions and interrelationships among citizens (Smylie & Hart, 1999), and
3. *Human capital* in the form of increased citizen knowledge and skills (Bourdieu, 1986; Coleman, 1990).

The association between these products and school reform is illustrated in Figure 10–1. Simply recognizing the potential value of relationships, however, is insufficient; administrators also must know how to cultivate them. The most frequent process errors are intermittent and inconsistent communication. As an example, the only time that some superintendents communicate with or seek input from stakeholders is when there are ulterior motives—such as persuading stakeholders to vote for a tax increase. Astute taxpayers usually recognize when someone is trying to manipulate them, and therefore, self-serving, intermittent communication can produce more ill will than goodwill (Kowalski, 2005).

Positive associations among people are more probable when the interactants engage in *relational communication,* an interpersonal and symmetrical paradigm focusing on participant perceptions of exchanges (Littlejohn, 1992). Interpersonal communication involves two-way exchanges in which persons influence one another's behavior over and above their organizational role, rank, and status (Cappella, 1987). Symmetrical communication

FIGURE 10–1
Relationships, Capital, and School Reform

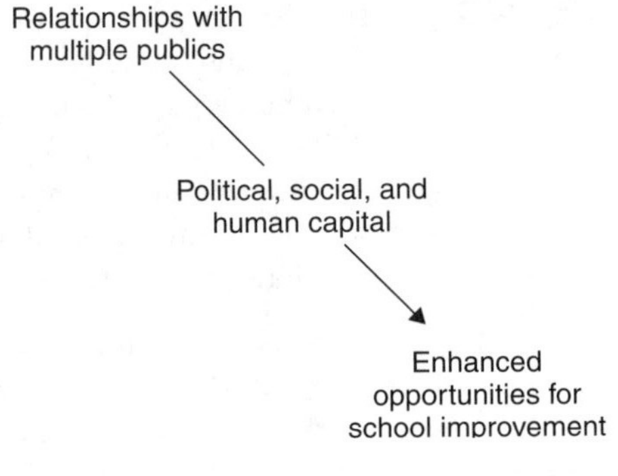

Relationships with
multiple publics

Political, social, and
human capital

Enhanced
opportunities for
school improvement

is intended to benefit all interactants (Grunig, 1989), and therefore, the interactants behave similarly in order to minimize their formal authority and actual power differences (Burgoon & Hale, 1984). The purpose of relational communication is to maintain positive relationships between school employees and stakeholder publics (Bruning & Ledingham, 2000).

When executed properly, relational communication produces mutual understandings, mutual influence, negotiation, openness, credibility, and trust. These characteristics are integral to positive organizational development (i.e., pursuing change on the basis of known community needs), and organizational equilibrium (i.e., providing services that meet community needs) is more probable (Toth, 2000) for at least two reasons: First, administrators who communicate interpersonally and symmetrically are better able to identify and address unmet needs (Conrad, 1994). Second, communities satisfied with their public schools are more likely to treat these institutions as assets rather than liabilities (Bruning & Ledingham, 2000).

IMPROVING COMMUNITY RELATIONS

Even in its formative years, public education was expected to maintain a symbiotic relationship with local communities. This belief reflected a philosophical disposition centered primarily in the value of liberty (Kowalski, 2003). During the last two decades of the twentieth century, however, a mix of political and professional convictions was responsible for a renewed interest in school-community relations. The transformed attention emanated primarily from the following conclusions:

- ◆ The percentage of citizens who have no direct contact with schools has grown incrementally over the past three or four decades. As a result, there is a wide gap between public education and the public (Richardson, 1997).
- ◆ Public schools here deteriorated and their ineffectiveness is jeopardizing the country's economic welfare (National Commission on Excellence in Education, 1983).
- ◆ Educators are either incapable of or unwilling to reform schools (Sarason, 1996).
- ◆ School improvement will not occur unless a broad base of stakeholders participates in and supports proposed changes (Bauman, 1996).

The political context of school reform during the mid-1990s was reflected in three convictions offered by Banach and Frye (1996):

1. The public will abandon reforms that did not appear to be effective and then demand alternatives to traditional public schools (e.g., school choice or charter schools).
2. Politicians will legalize alternative change initiatives intended to create competition for traditional public schools; they will do so not because they are convinced that the ideas are effective, but rather because they want to appease a disgruntled constituency.
3. Educators will not respond well to these alternative initiatives because the governance structure, the political environment, and the existing policies and procedures in local school systems are not conducive to change.

These and related opinions provided momentum for democratic approaches to school reform—that is, strategies that are dependent on community involvement.

Building and maintaining community relations are arguably broad topics. Williams and Chavkin (1989) found that most successful programs shared the following characteristics:

- ◆ Guidance by written policy,
- ◆ Support from administrators,
- ◆ Training for both staff and parents,
- ◆ Use of partnership approaches,
- ◆ Two-way communication,
- ◆ Networking, and
- ◆ Ongoing evaluation and modifications.

In this portion of the chapter, the processes of identifying and analyzing publics and communicating with them are explored. Focused attention is then given to communication and community diversity.

Identifying and Analyzing Publics

Public schools serve multiple publics, and defining them accurately is a prelude to improving community relations. The reason is that administrators should know the individuals with whom they need (or want) to cultivate relationships. A public can be viewed as any group that has a stake in the district or school in question (Richardson, 1997). Generally, publics are divided into four categories:

- ◆ Internal publics (i.e., groups within the organization, such as teachers, students),
- ◆ External publics (i.e., groups outside the organization, such as taxpayers),
- ◆ Media publics (e.g., print and broadcast reporters and editors), and
- ◆ Regulatory publics (e.g., governmental agencies that have authority to affect schools).

To qualify as a public in our context here, the population in question should be distinguishable, bound by one or more homogeneous characteristics, relevant to the welfare of public education, politically influential (or potentially influential), and accessible.

After publics are identified, they should be analyzed. The following are areas that are commonly assessed and evaluated:

- ◆ *Demographic analysis*—each public's characteristics, such as gender, age, income, or political disposition;
- ◆ *Cultural analysis*—each public's customs, rituals, values, and dispositions toward education;
- ◆ *Interest analysis*—each public's concerns, such as tax issues or quality of education issues;
- ◆ *Communication analysis*—each public's dominant language, communication channels, and normative communicative behavior;
- ◆ *Social-political analysis*—each public's social standing and political influence; and

◆ *Leadership analysis*—each public's leadership structure, including the key individuals who shape opinion and influence action.

Communicating with the Community

Rising communication expectations for school administrators are attributable to several conditions; foremost are (a) America's development as an information-based society, (b) the rapid development of technology, and (c) a disjunction between many taxpayers and the public schools (Kowalski, 2006). Despite the fact that these conditions have been widely publicized, it is doubtful that the rate of communication improvements in schools has kept pace with the rate of technology improvements in society (Keil, 2005). For example, administrators and teachers often do not take full advantage of the Internet as a communication tool (Moore, 2005).

Ideally, communication is addressed as part of a PR plan that is an extension of or integrated with an institutional strategic plan. The PR plan should address alternatives for communicating with identified publics, list resources available to support communication, and provide guidance to employees about their roles and responsibilities as communicators. According to Kernan-Schloss and Plattner (1998), communication responsibilities should be framed by three questions:

1. What is needed from each public to enhance a symbiotic relationship and support school improvement efforts?
2. What do educators expect from members of each public?
3. What do members of each public expect from educators?

School administrators are required to communicate with others in and out of the school. The frequency of contact among school employees often makes internal communication less problematic for them. Recognizing that principals are usually more apprehensive about external communication, Thomas (1996) offered them the following suggestions:

◆ Use clear and simple language.
◆ Frame the essential questions that will guide dialogue, especially if the topic is school reform.
◆ Establish an open process for conducting dialogue.
◆ Manage disagreements by promoting civility, rather than by refusing to deal with conflict.
◆ Promote ownership of ideas (process and product) by using collective pronouns such as "our" and "we" and by avoiding divisive pronouns such as "their" and "they."
◆ Capitalize on existing communication resources.

Moore (2005) adds that administrators should reengineer established communication options and capitalize on new options. The slowness with which many administrators adapted to electronic mail reminds us that this advice is not always heeded.

The communication challenge for administrators is difficult both because many administrators have not been prepared academically to be communicators (Kowalski, 2005; Osterman, 1994) and because they are expected to have positive relationships with diverse publics. As an example, communicating with middle school students and their parents about the school's Internet policy may require two separate approaches. In many schools, just communicating with parents may require multiple approaches because of language, social, literacy, and interest differences. Arguably, communicating with parents of high school students is often more difficult than communicating with elementary school parents because the latter are typically more involved in their children's education (Keil, 2005).

In order to be effective communicators, principals and other administrators must first learn to be good listeners (Richardson, 1997). They also must be able to use multiple outlets and engage in both direct communication (e.g., conversing with parents about a student problem) and indirect communication (e.g., providing general information) in order to reach diverse publics. Though the quantity and quality of communication outlets available to administrators vary across districts and schools, the following are the most frequently used:

- ◆ Print media (e.g., newspapers),
- ◆ Broadcast media (e.g., radio and television),
- ◆ Internet (e.g., school Web pages, electronic mail),
- ◆ School- or district-sponsored publications or broadcasts (e.g., school newsletters, handbooks, policy manuals, high school radio broadcasts),
- ◆ Public forums,
- ◆ Open houses,
- ◆ Extracurricular events (e.g., plays, interscholastic athletics),
- ◆ Academic programs (e.g., award ceremonies, graduation),
- ◆ Parent groups,
- ◆ Partnership programs, and
- ◆ Conferences (e.g., parent-teacher conferences).

When pursuing community relations, administrators should always remember two facts: Disseminating information is not synonymous with communicating (Ubben, Hughes, & Norris, 2004), and communicating in the identical way with all publics usually is not effective (Watts & Tutwiler, 2003). Errors related to the first fact can be reduced by ensuring that community members have multiple channels for providing information and asking questions; advisory committees, focus groups, opinion polls, and school Web pages are examples. Errors related to the second fact can be reduced by pursuing principles of multicultural education and by recognizing differences among constituent publics.

Deploying a Multicultural Perspective

The population of most school districts has become more diverse over the last half century, and communities continue to become more heterogeneous in terms of race, ethnicity, religion, wealth, and age (National Center for Educational Statistics, 2004). This demographic profile is considerably different from the one that existed 100 years ago—a time when many of the standards for effective practice in school administration were established (Kowalski, 2006). Communicative behavior is derived from a set of values, attitudes, and beliefs shared within the particular cultural context in a process called socialization (Mavrelis, 1997). Administrators who do not understand diversity are at a distinct disadvantage with respect to developing community relationships because they are unprepared to communicate in alternative ways. For example, principals may incorrectly conclude that poverty is an issue affecting only racial or cultural minorities (Fuller, 2003).

The topic of multicultural communication was introduced in Chapter 7. This process is intended to ensure that school officials understand cultural and ethnic differences that influence communicative behaviors and to ensure that they apply this knowledge in their personal communicative behavior. Language differences among diverse publics are easy to recognize; however, other pertinent aspects of multicultural communication are more difficult to diagnose. The following examples of cultural characteristics among three prevalent publics are provided by Watts and Tutwiler (2003):

- ◆ Attitudes and behaviors among members of the African-American community are often influenced by concerns related to racism and past incidents of biased treatment. Therefore, "a sense of kinship often extends beyond blood relations to other members of the community" (p. 52).
- ◆ Attitudes and behaviors among members of the Asian-American community are often influenced by distinct boundaries between family and school. Consequently, members of this community are not prone to challenge school authority to set curriculum and achievement standards.
- ◆ Attitudes and behaviors among members of the Latino community are often influenced by a conviction that the family is an essential resource for coping with problems. Therefore, members of this community are prone to respond negatively to any action that appears to challenge the family's role, especially in relation to values.

Minority group residents often feel they are at a disadvantage when their values conflict with the majority's values about education issues, such as grading, testing, and discipline (Garcia & Ortiz, 2004). Often educators do not understand that both their own communicative behavior and the communicative behavior of minority citizens are culture bound. This is why the principles of multicultural communication should be an integral part of the district's PR plan. In addition, administrators should provide staff development on this topic, facilitate efforts to engage in multicultural communication, and model the principles they want others to follow.

POSITIVE RELATIONSHIPS WITH PARENTS

Ask a group of aspiring principals to define the role of parents and you will probably receive at least three different answers. Some will say that they are customers; this is not unexpected, since even the executive director of the American Association of School Administrators has referred to parents in this manner (Houston, 2000). Some will say that they are owners; this response is predicated on the reality that public schools belong to the community and, therefore, all community members are technically owners. Some will say that parents are clients; this is not surprising, since researchers (e.g., Hoy, Smith, & Sweetland, 2003) often refer to them in this manner. Though distinctions among these answers may appear to be only semantic, the three characterizations differ markedly from a philosophical perspective.

The word *customer* connotes accommodation (Jones, 1997), as in the adage "The customer is always right." The word *owner* connotes organizational dominance, as in the adage "The boss is always right." But the word *client* has a very different meaning. A relationship between a professional and a client is based on a degree of dependency in which the professional helps the client. Therefore, persons who view educators as professionals believe that calling parents and students customers is "as chilling as the sound of a fingernail scratching on a blackboard" (Bayer, 1996, p. 82).

One of the distinguishing characteristics of public school administration is that practitioners must apply their knowledge in highly political contexts (Wirt & Kirst, 2001). In fact, parents are at various times customers, owners, and clients; consequently, building positive relationships with them is a complex assignment intended to develop mutual understanding and benefits (Martinson, 1999). Even so, many educators who see themselves as professionals remain uncomfortable with treating parents and other stakeholders as customers (Chambers, 1998). In order to better understand school and community relations, both the need for parental relationships and the techniques for building and maintaining them are discussed here.

Need for Parental Relationships

Educators often recognize that far too many students are detached from schools, probably because they witness indifference in their classrooms on a daily basis. According to Constantino (2003), levels of student engagement are determined by an intricate mix of desires, attitudes, motivation, and behavior. Each of these variables is influenced by conditions pertinent to a student's (a) individual characteristics (e.g., personality, health), (b) peers, (c) family, and (d) school. Unfortunately, educators are less likely to discern that many parents also are disengaged from schools (Steinberg, 1996).

Why is parental engagement important? This question should be answered in three ways:

1. *Philosophically*, parent relationships are justified by the values that guide a democratic society—values such as citizen participation and shared decision making (Petersen & Kowalski, 2005).

2. *Politically*, administrators are more likely to improve schools if they have parental support (Bauman, 1996), and they are more likely to gain support if they have positive relationships with parents (Petersen & Kowalski, 2005; Kowalski, 2006).

3. *Professionally*—that is, from an educational perspective—the answer is more complex. Parents who are involved with teachers and administrators are likely to focus on the intellectual growth of their children and to reaffirm the importance of education; conversely, they avoid negative judgments, such as simply comparing their children to other students (Constantino, 2003).

Though each perspective is important, the educational dimension has taken center stage in recent years. After conducting a macroanalysis of 85 studies, Henderson and Berla (1994) concluded that parent involvement has produced a myriad of educational benefits, as demonstrated by the following examples:

◆ Students whose parents were involved with schools usually had higher grades, higher test scores, greater self-esteem, higher levels of motivation, and better attendance records.

◆ Parents who were involved had higher levels of sensitivity to the social, emotional, and educational development of their children; they had a more accurate understanding of teacher roles and were more committed to supporting teachers and the school.

◆ Educators who are in schools having high levels of parent involvement had higher morale, more respect from parents, and a better understanding of parental problems and cultural differences.

◆ Schools that had high levels of parent involvement had greater community support, better reputations, and higher-quality programs than did schools that had low levels of parent involvement.

Overall, there is considerable evidence supporting the conclusion that parent involvement is critical to both the academic and the emotional growth of children (e.g., Lim, 2003; White, 1998). Even so, many parents in general and most parents of secondary students specifically have little contact with their children's schools (Dodd, 1998). Typically, teachers say that collaborating with parents would be more of a priority if administrators endorsed such efforts and provided them time to pursue collaboration (Miretzky, 2004). On the other hand, parents often say that they would be more collaborative if their participation was encouraged and valued by teachers (Chavkin & Williams, 1987).

Rhetoric aside, parents do not establish positive relationships with teachers naturally. In promoting and facilitating the development of these associations, principals and teachers are expected to be the initiators. They are more likely to accept this role if they understand the social conditions that make educator-parent relationships increasingly essential to student learning. Consider, for example, the following pertinent conditions that are found in most schools:

◆ *Diversity*. The demographic profile of most school systems has changed markedly in the last half century. Today, the population of the typical public school district is heterogeneous with respect to race, religion, political values, social standing, education levels, and income (as discussed previously in Chapter 2). By interacting with parents, educators gain a clearer understanding of how demographic variables affect students (Watts & Tutwiler, 2003).

◆ *Parent role*. The treatment of parents has changed over time. In the formative years of public schools, parents often were deeply involved, especially in smaller rural schools. During the period from 1950 to 1970, however, the treatment of parents gradually changed from participant to guest. Moreover, mothers were far more likely than fathers to visit schools, largely because planned activities such as plays, music programs, and parent-teacher conferences were usually scheduled during normal school hours when fathers were working. As the economy changed and many mothers began working (Sherman, 1994), neither parent in two-income families was available during school hours (Fuller & Marxen, 2003). Though many schools now schedule evening events, planned activities alone do not ensure engagement.

◆ *Family structure*. Increasingly, the structure of families has become less uniform. Many students are now being raised by one parent, by grandparents, or by a legal guardian (Watts & Tutwiler, 2003). If all or most families had two parents with one of them available during the school day, generic approaches to dealing with parents would be more successful. Since this is not the case in virtually all schools, an individualized approach based on an understanding of family conditions is essential.

- ◆ *Family hygiene*. Assisting students living in dysfunctional families has become an increasingly difficult challenge (Dodd, 2000). Unless educators are able to intervene, the negative effects of these conditions will attenuate learning outcomes. For example, students reared in dysfunctional families are often characterized by (a) distrust, (b) low self-esteem, (c) an inability to have fun, and (d) shame (Fuller & Marxen, 2003).
- ◆ *Parent availability*. Educators often see themselves as being blameless when it comes to parental disengagement. For example, they conclude that parents do not get involved with schools because they have other priorities (e.g., work, social activities). However, several studies (e.g., Dauber & Epstein, 1991) have concluded that lack of time does not fully explain disengagement. The ways schools are organized and the attitudes of principals and teachers are other cogent factors (Dauber & Epstein, 1993).

Principals quickly learn that their interactions with parents are likely to be unpleasant if these interactions occur only when they are responding to or providing negative news. Administrators who cultivate positive relationships with parents find it much easier to deal with unpleasant situations. This is because principals are better able to be proactive (focus on what will or can be done to correct the situation), positive (make a commitment to solve the problem), and candid (share all pertinent information) with parents who trust them (North, 2005).

Lastly, diversity has increased the need for parental relationships. In the recent past, researchers (e.g., Baker & Stevenson, 1986; Lareau, 2000; Lareau & Shumar, 1996) have raised a number of questions concerning the effect of wealth and social status on a child's education. For example, do parents of privileged children participate more in schooling and provide more educational resources than do parents of children living in poverty? Studying parental involvement in a suburban school district where there were social class and racial differences, McGrath and Kuriloff (2005) found that parental participation can produce negative outcomes if not properly managed by principals. Involvement in their study was dominated by a relatively few upper-middle-class white mothers, and they "often acted, perhaps unintentionally, in ways that tended to exclude other mothers, especially African American mothers." The researchers urged principals to exert the leadership necessary to prevent parental involvement from becoming another factor contributing to educational inequities.

Building and Maintaining Parental Relationships

In order to improve parental engagement, administrators and teachers must first define this process accurately (Coleman & Churchill, 1997). Typically, educators agree on two points: The need for parental involvement is real, and parental involvement in schools should be based on a multidimensional perspective (Grolnick, Benjet, Kurowski, & Apostoleris, 1997). But without an effective, meaningful framework to guide them, educators see parental engagement as nothing more than "a series of disconnected activities with little relevance to family or classroom environments" (Coleman & Churchill, 1997, p. 144).

Engagement became a popular word during the reform-minded political environment of the 1980s and 1990s. Often, however, the concept was misinterpreted (Wadsworth, 1997).

Engagement, especially in the context of PR, is not manipulation; rather, it is the building of a reciprocal relationship that is uncharacteristic of political transactions and entrepreneurial exploitations (Thompson, 1998). And though collaboration is a form of co-learning (Herman, 1998), parental engagement is more than parents spending a few hours a week helping their children do homework.

The most widely referenced definition of school-family collaboration was developed by Epstein and associates (1997). It includes six functions:

1. Home-to-school communication,
2. School-to-home communication,
3. Parents as volunteers,
4. Parent involvement in school governance and decisions,
5. A positive home learning environment, and
6. Greater collaboration and connection with the community.

Discussing participation in the context of a learning community, Kowalski, Petersen, and Fusarelli (in press) identified six characteristics pertinent to parental engagement:

1. Support for change,
2. Continuous learning,
3. Collaboration,
4. Open, two-way communication,
5. Inquiry, and
6. Mutual respect.

Collectively, such typologies provide a framework that allows principals and teachers to develop a comprehensive definition of parent relationships.

The next step is conducting an engagement audit using your accepted definition. This is done so that you can determine gaps between the quantity and quality of existing relationships and those of desired relationships. Ideally, data regarding relationships are collected and analyzed continuously using feedback loops—that is, asking questions, receiving answers, making decisions or changes, and providing feedback as educators and parents have interactions (Soholt, 1998). Regardless of how parental involvement is diagnosed, the following components are usually effective:

◆ Inventory the number of interactions that occur, and group them by activities (e.g., music programs, parent-teacher conferences, athletic events, discipline problems).

◆ Collect and analyze teacher and parent opinions regarding (a) the productivity of these interactions, (b) the effectiveness of communication during these interactions, and (c) mutual treatment during these interactions.

◆ Collect and analyze data to determine why some families have not had any interactions with school personnel.

◆ Determine what types of information parents (a) find most useful, (b) find least useful, and (c) want, but do not receive.

◆ Determine which teacher-initiated or administrator-initiated activities require or encourage parental involvement.

◆ Seek suggestions about ways to improve interactions.

Perhaps most notably, an engagement audit is an effective way to determine if common barriers to parent relationships exist. Many of the common barriers are issues that are best addressed by teachers and parents directly; examples include ambivalence toward parental involvement (Eccles & Harold, 1993) and differing perceptions of meaningful relationships (Krasnow, 1990). Principals, however, can be quite influential with respect to other variables, such as a lack of administrative support for teacher and parent interaction and a lack of time for parent conferences (Miretzky, 2004).

Procedurally, the pursuit of parental engagement also may include the following steps identified by White (1998):

- *Creating an action team.* The action team coordinates the process and ensures that it is ongoing.
- *Developing an involvement plan.* The plan is typically developed by the action team and provides goals and strategies for improving parental involvement.
- *Developing an appropriate parent involvement policy and regulations.* Once the involvement plan is approved, the principal needs to ensure that the policy and regulations facilitate its implementation.
- *Securing support for parent involvement.* Even the best plan will fail if those attempting to implement it do not have sufficient human and material resources.
- *Providing staff development for educators.* Because parental involvement is defined as a multifaceted process, the principal needs to ensure that all professional staff understand it and are prepared to implement it.
- *Evaluating and revising the involvement plan periodically.* Evaluation should be a formative process in which periodic adjustments are deemed beneficial.

Figure 10–2 illustrates all elements of an engagement plan.

An engagement plan is most likely to be developed and implemented in schools that have environments conducive to relationships. The following are common characteristics of these schools:

- *Positive institutional climates.* The social relationships both among staff and between staff and parents are friendly, open, compassionate, and respectful (Lim, 2003).
- *Cultures that promote democratic leadership and participation.* Parent involvement is viewed as essential to democratic decision making (Petersen & Kowalski, 2005).
- *Open, two-way communication.* Multiple channels are used to ensure that communication among school personnel and between school personnel and parents occurs continuously (Kowalski, 2006).
- *Enabling programs.* School-sponsored programs are adopted to encourage and support parental involvement (Lim, 2003).
- *Respect for diversity.* School personnel recognize and understand diversity and individualize parent relationships to maximize collaboration (Lim, 2003).

Some districts and schools have developed "parent partnerships." True partnerships are agreements in which two parties concur with respect to goals and process, usually within a legal or moral framework—for example, a partnership between a school and a local business. Collaborative relationships involving schools and parents are more accurately

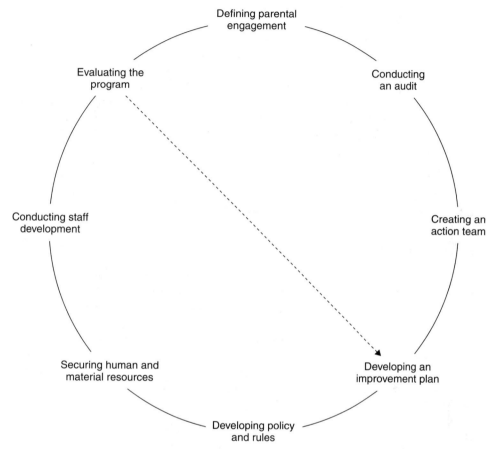

FIGURE 10–2
Elements of a School-Parent Engagement Plan

defined as "an on-going, developmental process of mutual or reciprocating empowerment" (Shepard, Trimberger, McClintock, & Lecklider, 1999, p. 34). That is, teachers and parents empower each other, enabling both parties to have a more positive influence on student learning. The goal of an effective PR program is to provide administrators and teachers with the resources necessary to cultivate these collaborative relationships.

SUMMARY

This chapter examined community relations as an integral component of school PR. Rather than having one homogeneous public, schools actually have multiple publics distinguishable by demographic variables. Identifying and analyzing them are essential to erecting an effective two-way communication process, and such a process is essential to school-community relations.

Focused attention was given to parents because they are arguably the most influential public with respect to student learning. The need for school-family relationships has increased incrementally, both because society has become more diverse and because changes in family structure have made parental involvement more elusive. To build and maintain school-family relations, administrators must play a proactive role in which they define ideal parental involvement, assess current levels of involvement, and erect an involvement plan. Equally important, administrators must encourage and facilitate the implementation of that plan.

QUESTIONS AND SUGGESTED ACTIVITIES

CASE STUDY

1. Discuss the compatibility of professionalism and politics in relation to school administration.
2. After having read this chapter, do you agree or disagree with Principal Palmer's opinions of community and parental engagement?
3. Evaluate the advice that Mrs. Miles gave to Dr. Lewis. Do you agree with her advice? Why or why not?
4. Assume that Dr. Lewis decides to challenge Mr. Palmer's views on engagement. How should she do this?
5. Do you believe that Dr. Lewis should request a meeting with the superintendent to discuss Mr. Palmer's views? Why or why not?

CHAPTER

6. Are the terms *community relations* and *public relations* synonymous? Why or why not?
7. How can principals identify and analyze relevant publics?
8. In what ways has diversity created challenges for community relations?
9. In what ways has diversity created challenges for parental involvement in schools?
10. Is it ever possible for parental involvement to have negative effects? If so, in what ways?
11. Why is communication critical to relationships?
12. Discuss ways principals can influence the development of community relations.

SUGGESTED READINGS

Brent, B. O. (2000). Do classroom volunteers benefit schools? *Principal, 80*(1), 36–43.

DeCastro-Ambrosetti, D., & Cho, G. (2005). Do parents value education? Teachers' perceptions of minority parents. *Multicultural Education, 13*(2), 44–46.

Epstein, J. L., & Jansorn, N. R. (2004). School, family, and community partnerships link the plan. *The Education Digest, 69*(6), 19–23.

Griffith, J. (Ed.) (2005). Parent involvement: Emerging models and applications. *The Elementary School Journal, 106*(2), 81–187. (See entire issue).

Halsey, P. (2005). Parent involvement in junior high schools: A failure to communicate. *American Secondary Education, 34*(1), 57–69.

Hindman, J. L. Brown, W. M., & Rogers, C. S. (2005). Beyond the school: Getting community members involved. *Principal Leadership (Middle School Edition), 5*(8), 36–39

Holliday, A. E. (1997). 106 ways to better school-community relations. *The Education Digest, 62*(5), 15–19

Houston, P. D. (2003). Time to re-public the republic. *School Administrator, 60*(8), 10–12.

Johnson, J., & Friedman, W. (2006). Dear public: Can we talk? *School Administrator, 63*(2), 26–30.

Neely, E. (2005). Communication with parents: It works both ways. *Leadership, 34*(5), 24–27.

Padgett, R. (2006). Better public relations on Websites. *The Education Digest, 71*(5), 54–55.

Sanders, M. G. (2003). Community involvement in schools: From concept to practice. *Education and Urban Society, 35*(2), 161–180.

Sanders, M. G., & Lewis, K. C. (2005). Building bridges toward excellence: Community involvement in high schools. *The High School Journal, 88*(3), 1–9.

Walser, N. (2005). Parents as partners in school reform. *Harvard Education Letter, 21*(5), 4–6.

REFERENCES

Austin, E. W., & Pinkleton, B. E. (2001). *Strategic public relations management: Planning and managing effective communication programs.* Mahwah, NJ: Lawrence Erlbaum Associates.

Baker, D. P., & Stevenson, D. L. (1986). Mothers' strategies for children's school achievement: Managing the transition to high school. *Sociology of Education, 59*(3), 156–166.

Banach, W. J., & Frye, E. T. (1996). Bound for glory. *Thrust for Educational Leadership, 26*(6), 18–22.

Bauman, P. C. (1996). *Governing education: Public sector reform or privatization.* Boston: Allyn & Bacon.

Bayer, A. A. (1996). What is wrong with customer? *College Teaching, 44*, 82.

Bourdieu, P. (1986). The forms of capital. In J. Richardson (Ed.), *Handbook of theory and research for sociology education* (pp. 141–258). New York: Greenwood.

Bruning, S. D., & Ledingham, J. A. (2000). Organization and key relationships: Testing the influence of relationship dimensions in a business to business context. In J. Leningham & S. Bruning (Eds.), *Public relations as relationship management: A relational approach to the study and practice of public relations* (pp. 159–174). Mahway, NJ: Lawrence Erlbaum Associates.

Burgoon, J. K., & Hale, J. L. (1984). The fundamental topoi of relational communications. *Communication Monographs, 51*, 193–214.

Cappella, J. N. (1987). Interpersonal communication: Definitions and fundamental questions. In C. R. Berger & S. H. Chaffee (Eds.), *Handbook of communication science* (pp. 184–238). Newbury Park, CA: Sage.

Chambers, L. (1998). How customer-friendly is your school? *Educational Leadership, 56*(2), 33–35.

Chavkin, N. F., & Williams, D. L. (1987). Enhancing parent involvement: Guidelines for access to an important resource for school administrators. *Education & Urban Society, 19*, 164–184.

Coleman, J. (1990). *Foundations of social theory.* Cambridge: Harvard University Press.

Coleman, M., & Churchill, S. (1997). Challenges to family involvement. *Childhood Education, 73*(3), 144–148.

Conrad, C. (1994). *Strategic organizational communication: Toward the twenty-first century* (3rd ed.). Fort Worth, TX: Harcourt Brace College Publishers.

Constantino, S. M. (2003). *Engaging all families: Creating a positive school culture by putting research into practice.* Lanham, MD: Scarecrow Education.

Crowson, R. L., & Boyd, W. L. (2001). The new role of community development in educational reform. *Peabody Journal of Education, 76*(2), 9–29.

Dauber, S., & Epstein, J. L. (1991). School programs and teacher practices of parent involvement in inner-city elementary and middle schools. *Elementary School Journal, 91*(3), 289–305.

Dauber, S., & Epstein, J. L. (1993). Parent attitudes and practices of involvement in inner-city elementary and middle schools. In N. F. Chavkin (Ed.), *Families and schools in a pluralistic society* (pp. 53–71). Albany: State University of New York Press.

Dodd, A. W. (1998). Parents: Problems or partners? *High School Magazine, 5,* 14–17.

Dodd, A. W. (2000). Making schools safe for all students: Why schools need to teach more than the 3 R's. *NASSP Bulletin, 84*(614), 25–31.

Duke, D. (2004). *The challenge of educational change.* Boston: Allyn & Bacon.

Eccles, J. S., & Harold, R. D. (1993). Parent-school involvement during the early adolescent years. *Teachers College Record, 94*(3), 568–587.

Epstein, J. L., Coates, L., Salinas, K. C., Sanders, M. G., & Simon, M. G. (1997). *School, family, and community partnerships.* Thousand Oaks, CA: Corwin Press.

Fullan, M. (2001). *Leading in a culture of change.* San Francisco: Jossey-Bass.

Fuller, M. L. (2003). Poverty: The enemy of children and families. In G. Olsen & M. L. Fuller (Eds.), *Home-school relations: Working successfully with parents and students* (2nd ed., pp. 273–289). Boston: Allyn & Bacon.

Fuller, M. L., & Marxen, C. (2003). Families and their functions: Past and present. In G. Olsen & M. L. Fuller (Eds.), *Home-school relations: Working successfully with parents and students* (2nd ed., pp. 12–43). Boston: Allyn & Bacon.

Garcia, S. B., & Ortiz, A. A. (2004). *Preventing disproportionate representation: Culturally and linguistically responsive pre-referral interventions.* Denver, CO: National Center for Culturally Responsive Educational Systems.

Gotts, E. E., & Purnell, R. F. (1985). *Improving home school communication* (Fastback #230). Bloomington, IN: Phi Delta Kappa Educational Foundation.

Grolnik, W., Benjet, C., Kurowski, C., & Apostoleris, N. (1997). Predictors of parent involvement in children's schooling. *Journal of Educational Psychology, 89,* 538–548.

Grunig, J. E. (1989). Symmetrical presuppositions as a framework for public relations theory. In C. H. Botan (Ed.), *Public relations theory* (pp. 17–44). Hillsdale, NJ: Lawrence Erlbaum Associates.

Grunig, J. E., & Huang, Y. H. (2000). Antecendents of relationships and outcomes. In J. Ledingham & S. Bruning (Eds.), *Public relations as relationship management* (pp. 23–54). Mahwah, NJ: Lawrence Erlbaum Associates.

Hanson, E. M. (2003). *Educational administration and organizational behavior* (5th ed.). Boston: Allyn & Bacon.

Henderson, A. T., & Berla, N. (1994). *A new generation of evidence: The family is critical to student achievement.* Washington, DC: National Committee for Citizens in Education.

Herman, H. T. (1998). Parent involvement: Must we choose sides? *High School Magazine, 5,* 26–31.

Holliday, A. E. (1988). In search of an answer: What is school public relations? *Journal of Educational Public Relations, 11*(2), 12.

Houston, P. (2000). Treating parents as our customers. *School Administrator, 57*(5), 54.

Hoy, W. K., & Miskel, C. G. (2005). *Educational administration: Theory, research, and practice* (8th ed.). New York: McGraw-Hill.

Hoy, W. K., Smith, P. A., & Sweetland, S. R. (2003). The development of the organizational climate index for high schools: Its measure and relationship to faculty trust. *High School Journal, 86*(2), 38–49.

Hoyle, J. R., Björk, L. G., Collier, V., & Glass, T. (2005). *The superintendent as CEO: Standards-based performance.* Thousand Oaks, CA: Corwin Press.

Huang, Y. H. (1997). *Public relations strategies, relational outcomes, and conflict management strategies.* Unpublished doctoral dissertation, University of Maryland, College Park.

Jones, R. (1997). Kids as education customers. *Education Digest, 62*(1), 10–14.

Keil, V. (2005). Communicating for results. *Principal Leadership, 5*(8), 28–31.

Kernan-Schloss, A., & Plattner, A. (1998). Talking to the public about public schools. *Educational Leadership, 56*(2), 18–22.

Kowalski, T. J. (2003). *Contemporary school administration: An introduction* (2nd ed.). Boston: Allyn & Bacon.

Kowalski, T. J. (2005). Evolution of the school superintendent as communicator. *Communication Education, 54*(2), 101–117.

Kowalski, T. J. (2006). *The school superintendent: Theory, practice, and cases* (2nd ed.). Thousand Oaks, CA: Sage.

Kowalski, T. J., Petersen, G. J. & Fusarelli, L. (in press). *Communication in school administration: Leading change in an information age.* Lanham, MD: Rowman & Littlefield.

Krasnow, J. (1990). *Improving family-school relationships: Teacher research from the schools.* Boston: Institute for Responsive Education.

Lareau, A. (2000). *Home advantage: Social class and parental intervention in elementary education.* Lanham, MD: Rowman and Littlefield.

Lareau, A., & Shumar, W. (1996). The problem of individualism in family-school policies. *Sociology of Educaion.* (Special Issue on sociology and educational policy: Bringing scholarship and practice together), 24–39.

Lim, S. (2003). Parent involvement in education. In G. Olsen & M. L. Fuller (Eds.), *Home-school relations: Working successfully with parents and students* (2nd ed., pp. 134–158). Boston: Allyn & Bacon.

Littlejohn, S. W. (1992). *Theories of human communication* (4th ed.). Belmont, CA: Wadsworth.

Martinson, D. L. (1999). School public relations: The public isn't always right. *NASSP Bulletin, 83*(609), 103–109.

Mavrelis, J. (1997). Understanding differences in cultural communication styles. *High School Magazine, 5*(6), 30–32.

McGrath, D. J., & Kuriloff, P. J. (2005). *They're going to tear the doors off this place: Upper-middle class parent school involvement and the educational opportunities of other people's children.* Retrieved November 28, 2005, from http://plsc.uark.edu/ritter/edfd5353-mcgrath.html.

Miretzky, D. (2004). The communication requirements of democratic schools: Parent-teacher perspectives on their relationships. *Teachers College Record, 106*(4), 814–851.

Moore, E. H. (2005). Six steps to better school communications. *American School Board Journal, 192*(9), 20.

National Center for Educational Statistics. (2004). *Digest of education statistics, 2004.* Retrieved November 28, 2005, from http://nces.ed.gov/programs/digest/d04/tables/dt04_019.asp.

National Commission on Excellence in Education. (1983). *A nation at risk: The imperative for educational reform.* Washington, DC: U.S. Government Printing Office.

North, T. A. (2005). When bad news bursts the bubble. *Principal Leadership, 5*(8), 22–25.

Osterman, K. F. (1994). Communication skills: A key to collaboration and change. *Journal of School Leadership, 4*(4), 382–398.

Petersen, G. J., & Kowalski, T. J. (2005). *School reform strategies and normative expectations for democratic leadership in the superintendency.* Paper presented at the annual conference of the University Council for Educational Administration, Nashville, TN.

Richardson, J. (1997). Engaging the public to improve student learning. *Journal of Staff Development, 18*(3), 24–28.

Sarason, S. B. (1996). *Revisiting the culture of the school and the problem of change.* New York: Teachers College Press.

Shepard, R. G., Trimberger, A. K., McClintock, P. J., & Lecklider, D. (1999). Empowering family-school partnerships: An integrated hierarchical model. *Contemporary Education, 70*(3), 33–37.

Sherman, A. (1994). *Wasting America's future: The Children's Defense Fund report on the cost of child poverty.* Boston: Beacon Press.

Smylie, M., & Hart, A. (1999). School leadership for teacher learning and change: Human and social capital development. In J. Murphy & K. S. Louis (Eds.), *Handbook of research on educational administration* (2nd ed., pp. 421–441). San Francisco: Jossey-Bass.

Soholt, S. (1998). Public engagement: Lessons from the front. *Educational Leadership, 56*(2), 22–23.

Steinberg, L. (1996). *Beyond the classroom: Why school reform has failed and what parents need to do.* New York: Simon & Schuster.

Thomas, G. (1996). Keys to effective public management in school reform. *Thrust for Educational Leadership, 25*(1), 16–17.

Thompson, S. (1998). Moving from publicity to engagement. *Educational Leadership, 55*(8), 54–57.

Toth, E. L. (2000). From personal influence to interpersonal influence: A model for relationship management. In J. A. Ledingham & S. D. Bruning (Eds.), *Public relations as relationship management* (pp. 205–220). Mahwah, NJ: Lawrence Erlbaum Associates.

Ubben, G., Hughes, L., & Norris, C. (2004). *The principal: Creative leadership for effective schools* (5th ed.). Boston: Allyn & Bacon.

Uline, C. L., Tschannen-Moran, M., & Perez, L. (2003). Constructive conflict: How controversy can contribute to school improvement. *Teachers College Record, 105*(5), 782–816.

Valenzuela, A., & Dornbush, S. (1994). Familism and social capital in the academic achievement of Mexican origin and Anglo adolescents. *Social Science Quarterly, 75,* 18–36.

Wadsworth, D. (1997). Building a strategy for successful public engagement. *Phi Delta Kappan, 78*(10), 749–752.

Watts, I. E., & Tutwiler, S. W. (2003). Diversity among families. In G. Olsen & M. L. Fuller (Eds.), *Home-school relations: Working successfully with parents and students* (2nd ed., pp. 44–70). Boston: Allyn & Bacon.

White, L. J. (1998). National PTA standards for family/parent involvement programs. *High School Magazine, 5,* 8–12.

Williams, D. I., Jr., & Chavkin, N. F. (1989). Essential elements of strong parent involvement programs. *Educational Leadership, 47*(2), 19–20.

Wirt, F., & Kirst, M. (2001). *Political dynamics of American education* (2nd ed.). Berkeley, CA: Wadsworth.

CHAPTER 11

Media Relationships

Theodore J. Kowalski

CASE STUDY: MISMANAGING A SENSITIVE SITUATION

School administrators face many unforeseen situations, but those that produce the most anxiety involve an inappropriate relationship between teacher and student. Not long ago a high school football coach was placed on paid leave after one of his players reported that the coach had asked the student to have sex with his wife. The story made its way to school officials, who then acted to remove the coach from the school environment pending a legal investigation.

Knowing that rumors would circulate as soon as reporters started asking questions about the coach's suspension, the school's principal called a faculty meeting. Without releasing details, he emphasized to the faculty and staff that they should not discuss personnel matters because this topic was deemed to be confidential. In essence, the principal urged school employees not to discuss the situation, and especially not to discuss it with reporters. Following the faculty meeting, the principal met with the school's counselors and told them to monitor student behavior closely in the event that there were additional students who had similar encounters with the coach.

Despite efforts to keep the matter private, the story was leaked to a local newspaper prior to the conclusion of a police investigation. On the very day law enforcement officials arrested the coach and his wife, a story confirming the investigation and the alleged sexual misconduct appeared in the local paper as front-page copy.

Faced with a media crisis, the school board designated one of its members to be the official spokesperson to reporters. This board member was to handle all media inquiries, including those made directly to school district employees. But the appointment of a media spokesperson did not deter television crews and newspaper reporters from descending on the high school. Interviews were sought with students and teachers. Though the principal had attempted to control conversations between school employees and the media, he did not take parallel action to control students. Both the principal and other school officials were stunned as they watched the local television news that evening. Students who had no real knowledge of the incident were embellishing tales to reporters.

The next morning the local newspaper carried several articles, each including anonymous quotes from students and school employees. In fact, information in one of the articles was clearly wrong, but school officials decided not to call the matter to the reporter's attention. The newspaper that printed the story was a small local publication, and they figured that making a correction was not worth the effort. But shortly after the story appeared, the Associated Press picked it up and ran it across the country. The error was now compounded, and school officials faced a dual problem: dealing with the coach's inappropriate behavior and dealing with misinformation about the incident.

As the story gained national attention, community members demanded that the school board and administration gain control of the situation. Responding to increasing levels of political pressure, the superintendent convinced the school board to employ a private investigator for $10,000; his charge was to determine whether any employees had prior knowledge of the sexual misconduct involving the coach and his wife. The employment of the investigator, however, only intensified criticism. The school district was in poor financial

CHAPTER 11 ■ Media Relationships **267**

condition, and taxpayers were angered that money had been spent for this purpose. Several taxpayers wrote letters that appeared in the newspaper stating that school board members and administrators should have conducted the investigation. Even worse in the eyes of critics, the private investigator concluded his work in less than three weeks and reported that he did not find any evidence that employees had prior knowledge of the misconduct.

Eventually, the coach and his wife pleaded guilty. After they did so, parents of two teenagers who were found to be victims of their crimes sued the school district, alleging that school officials had failed to adequately protect their children from the coach. When asked about the lawsuits, school administrators and the board member spokesperson refused to comment.

The media and the public accused school officials of having breached their duty in three areas. First, they were blamed for not having provided proper and sufficient supervision of employees. Second, they were blamed for managing the problem carelessly, especially in relation to employing the private investigator. Third, they were blamed for jeopardizing the district's financial welfare by creating the potential for further financial losses via the lawsuits.

Reasonable people recognize that school administrators cannot anticipate every problem they encounter. However, they expect superintendents and principals to manage problems effectively once they materialize. The preceding case reminds us that there are serious repercussions for school administrators who have neither a positive relationship with the media nor a plan to manage media coverage. Naming a school board member to be the media spokesperson, failing to anticipate the willingness of students and employees to make anonymous comments to reporters, and consistently refusing to respond to media queries exemplify errors that justifiably created a public perception that key school officials were incompetent. Once their ability to manage the situation involving the coach was challenged, virtually every subsequent decision was criticized.

When administrators or their employing institutions receive unfavorable press coverage, the finger of blame has often been pointed at reporters. In large measure, the proclivity of superintendents and principals to blame journalists stems from a pervasive attitude that the media's only interest in public education is to sensationalize this institution's weaknesses. For example, a report by Public Agenda, a nonpartisan public-opinion research firm, confirmed that school administrators have been very displeased with the quality of press coverage given to public education (Batory, 1999). In truth, both administrators and journalists usually share the blame for poor relationships. On the one hand, many administrators do not understand journalism; they act aloof when dealing with reporters, and they attempt to avoid or manipulate reporters (Borja, 2004). On the other hand, many reporters attempt to cover public education without understanding the governance structure of this institution; they accuse administrators of overstating positive information while concealing negative information (Spicer, 1997) and they view administrators as clumsy bureaucrats or domesticated public servants and not as true professionals.

Discussing effective media relations, a veteran college president (Raisman, 2000) noted that the first rule for administrators is to realize that the media are neutral when it comes to covering education. That is, most reporters are not predisposed to glamorize or destroy schools. Over the past few decades, this wisdom has been repeated in books and journal articles about school public relations (PR) in an effort to counteract a long-standing belief that contact between administrators and journalists usually produces contempt on both sides. In this information-based society, maintaining a positive relationship with reporters is essential. As the opening case study teaches, poor or nonexistent relationships intensify tensions that surround unpleasant situations when administrators must respond to criticism or a crisis situation (Polansky & Montague, 2001). In an information-based society, three realities frame a normative disposition toward the media:

1. The public demands accurate, complete, and timely information about governmental agencies.
2. In the current school reform environment, administrators need to introduce and explain improvement initiatives to the public.
3. Nearly two decades of concentrated criticism make it imperative that administrators be able to build public confidence and support.

This chapter addresses the need for and development of a positive media relations program. Decisions related to this topic are discussed at the organizational and personal levels. The chapter content is framed by two objectives: to identify ways that administrators can enhance the image and effectiveness of districts and schools and to identify ways that administrators can better prepare themselves to manage potentially threatening situations when the media are demanding data and comments.

ORGANIZATIONAL DECISIONS

The media are broadly divided into print and electronic outlets. The former include newspapers, newsletters, journals, and magazines; the latter include television, radio, and Web-based outlets. Superintendents, principals, and other administrators do not build relationships with the media; they build them with persons who are media employees (e.g., reporters, editors, photographers). Therefore, the term *media relations* refers to the patterns of communication that occur between organization members and media personnel (Ridgway, 1996). Working without a media relations plan is like tightrope walking; administrators have to make spontaneous decisions about what to communicate and how to communicate. This casual attitude usually produces inconsistent, unpredictable, and largely negative relationships with reporters (Gonring, 1997).

Media Relations Plan

District and school administrators are expected to lead and manage, and with respect to PR, developing a media relations plan is one of the most important leadership responsibilities. According to Gonring (1997), an organization's media relations plan should be shaped by fundamental questions related to four key variables:

1. *Organizational purpose (Why does the organization exist?)* Purpose raises questions about the organization's value to society. In the case of schools, the overarching purpose is to provide an essential service.

2. *Ownership (Who owns the organization?)* In the case of schools, ownership is either public or private. This consideration is especially pertinent to determining the extent to which the organization is expected to interact with the publics being served.

3. *Media interest in the organization (To what extent do the media seek to report on the organization?)* In the case of schools, interest is typically high. This variable prompts administrators to think about circumstances that cause media interest to fluctuate.

4. *Organizational expectations (What does the organization hope to accomplish by interacting with the media?)* In the case of schools, building a positive image, producing political support, and securing economic resources are almost always cogent objectives.

The formation of a media relations plan is enhanced when the following attributes are present:

♦ *Direction.* The district or school has a policy that provides parameters for the plan's goals and strategies. As an example, the policy should detail expectations regarding the exchange of information between the organization and its multiple publics.

♦ *Clarity.* The plan is written in language readily understood by those affected.

♦ *Unity.* The plan is an extension of a more comprehensive PR plan in order to ensure that interactions with media personnel are connected to more global communication and information management objectives.

♦ *Sponsorship.* The plan is supported and approved by the superintendent and school board.

The relationships of the four key variables and these attributes are illustrated in Figure 11–1.

Since contextual variables differ across districts and schools, implementing, without modification, a media relations plan developed by administrators in another organization, even when that plan has been successful, is ill advised. Why? The success of almost any type of plan depends not only on substantive content, but also on the circumstances under which it is implemented (Fullan, 1999). Therefore, there is no assurance that the same initiative will produce a consistent product across organizations. Internal variables—such as organizational philosophy and goals—and external variables—such as local media and community conditions—almost always influence outcomes (Kowalski, 2004). Therefore, media plans should be tailored to meet a specific institution's needs and goals and should take into account available human and material resources that affect implementation.

In general, effective media relations plans are characterized by the following procedures, which are also shown in Figure 11–2:

♦ *Needs assessment.* This process identifies gaps between ideal and real practices related to dealing with the media. For example, school officials want more positive than negative media coverage, so they collect, sort (positive versus negative), and quantify articles to determine if there is a discrepancy between the media coverage desired and the media coverage received.

♦ *Problem identification and analysis.* This process is used to make judgments about identified needs. Assume that 65% of the media stories about a school were negative over

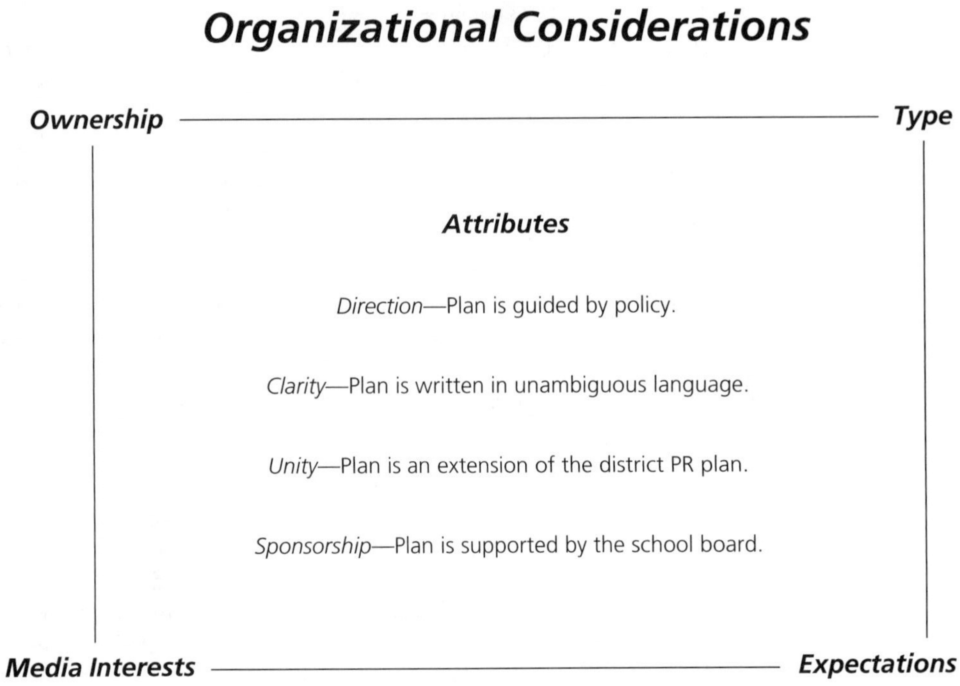

Organizational Considerations

Ownership ——————————————————————————————— Type

Attributes

Direction—Plan is guided by policy.

Clarity—Plan is written in unambiguous language.

Unity—Plan is an extension of the district PR plan.

Sponsorship—Plan is supported by the school board.

Media Interests ——————————————————————————— Expectations

FIGURE 11–1
Media Relations Plan: Considerations and Attributes

the past year; obviously, the school district has not achieved its goal of generating more positive than negative articles. At this stage, administrators seek to determine whether problems (e.g., lack of voter support for a tax referendum) resulted from not having achieved the ideal and to estimate the effects of those problems.

♦ *Goal setting.* This process entails replacing, reaffirming, or modifying existing objectives in order to increase the probability that identified needs could be met in the next year. In the district where two-thirds of the media stories over the past year were negative, for instance, administrators may decide to add the goal of producing at least one positive story monthly over the course of the next year.

♦ *Strategy development.* This process focuses on prescribing actions and behaviors for goal attainment. For instance, what actions are recommended to ensure that one positive story will be produced each month? Key questions surrounding the plan's development are listed in Table 11–1.

Media relations plans for education institutions should be designed to address three populations: district (or school) personnel, print and electronic media personnel, and stakeholders served by the district (or school) and media (Kosmicki & Bona, 1996). Administrators have most readily recognized that the plan should benefit school employees by communicating needs, problem statements, goals, and strategies. They also have been inclined to recognize that the needs and interests of the community at large should be infused into the planning process. Unfortunately, they have been less inclined to deal with

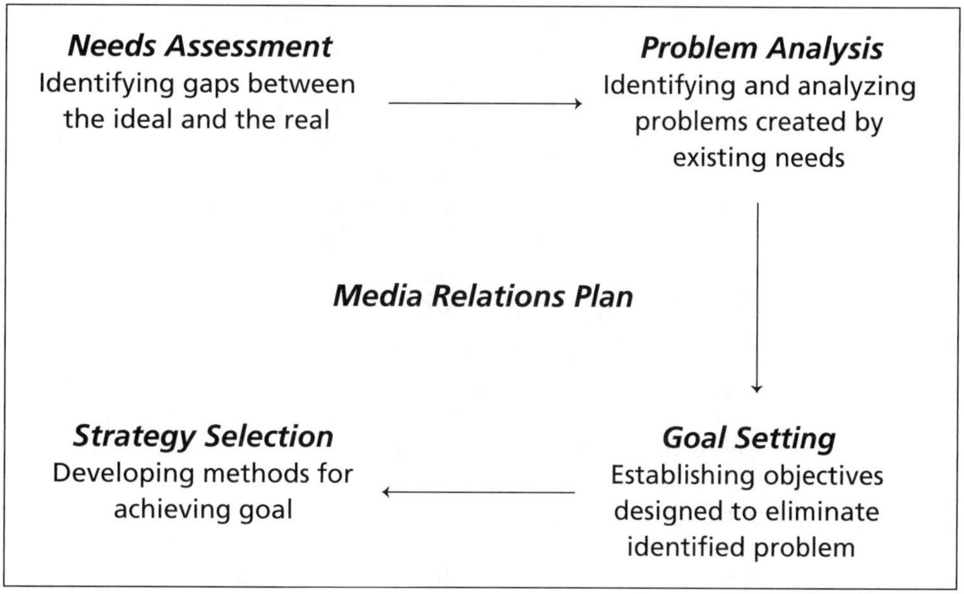

Needs Assessment
Identifying gaps between
the ideal and the real

Problem Analysis
Identifying and analyzing
problems created by
existing needs

Media Relations Plan

Strategy Selection
Developing methods for
achieving goal

Goal Setting
Establishing objectives
designed to eliminate
identified problem

FIGURE 11–2
Basic Elements of a Media Relations Plan

TABLE 11–1
Key Questions for Developing a Media Relations Plan

Question	Relevance
What has been the history of media relations?	Discovering the past so that ideal and real performance can be compared
What media have a primary interest in the schools?	Identifying the media that have the most contact with and the greatest impact on schools
Which journalists are assigned to cover schools?	Identifying reporters who have the most contact with and the greatest impact on schools
What messages need to be delivered?	Setting goals based on identified needs
What are the interests and goals of the targeted media?	Selecting strategies that maximize opportunities for desired coverage
What do targeted media deem newsworthy?	Informing staff of the areas that are likely to receive coverage
Who will assume management of the plan?	Identifying one individual who assumes overall responsibility for implementation and who serves as a resource person to other administrators
Who will receive or use the media relations plan?	Ensuring that the plan is written appropriately for those who use and are affected by it
How often will the plan be revised?	Ensuring that the plan is evaluated and that goals and strategies are revised periodically

the media's needs and interests. Given the fact that reporters and editors have the power to shape and control information, and thus to influence public opinion (Gonring, 1997), not addressing the media's needs and interests is a serious planning error. Generally, the media relations plan should be viewed as a tool for connecting the three populations. As an example, updated local, regional, and state media lists should be developed as an appendix to the plan. This information can be used both to initiate and to respond to media contacts. The value of an effective plan is most apparent when school officials face crisis situations (Cook, 2001), such as the one depicted in the opening case study.

Determining Responsibility

The size of educational institutions (in terms of enrollment and employees) has been a major factor in determining responsibility for media relations. In very large school systems (over 20,000 students), we are likely to find a PR director and a coordinator of media relations who reports to him or her. In midsize districts (between 5,000 and 20,000 students), we are likely to find a full-time PR director who assumes the responsibility for media relations. In the remaining districts, however, assignment of this responsibility varies markedly—from having a full-time coordinator to totally ignoring the responsibility. These differences are especially noteworthy with respect to public schools because most school systems in this country are relatively small; among the approximately 14,000 school systems, only 10% enroll more than 5,000 students (Kowalski, 2006). In most small-enrollment districts and especially those with fewer than 1,500 pupils, superintendents often do not have either a PR director or a media coordinator. Consequently, the responsibility for media relations must be either assumed personally or relegated to another administrator who has primary responsibilities in other areas.

Primary responsibilities associated with media relations beyond planning follow:

- ◆ Preparing employees to interact with journalists,
- ◆ Providing consultation to employees when they interact with journalists,
- ◆ Adjudicating conflict between employees and journalists,
- ◆ Developing and managing press releases and press conferences,
- ◆ Preparing and disseminating positive news,
- ◆ Advising the superintendent (or designee) on relevant policy and regulations affecting the media, and
- ◆ Serving as a contact person for media inquiries.

The last duty almost always falls on superintendents and principals when it is not assigned. That is, reporters will automatically call the administrator in charge of the district or school when they need information. When administrators are unprepared to respond to these requests, their reputation and the institution's reputation can suffer. Therefore, it is advisable to designate a media contact person, even in the smallest districts. In making such an assignment, the following criteria are helpful:

- ◆ *Knowledge of the district's policies and plans concerning communication.* The spokesperson should be familiar with all policies and plans that affect communication so that interactions with the media are carried out properly.
- ◆ *Information management skills.* The spokesperson must be well informed with respect to information sources and the methods required for retrieving information.

♦ *Communication skills.* The spokesperson's knowledge and information-gathering skills are of limited value if he or she is unable to communicate effectively.

♦ *Trust of district officials.* The spokesperson should have the confidence of the superintendent, administrative staff, and school board.

♦ *Personal relationship with the media.* The spokesperson should have credibility and a good relationship with reporters.

♦ *Ability to perform under pressure.* A spokesperson plays a critical role in crisis management, and the person needs to maintain a proper demeanor at all times.

On occasion (as in the case study presented in this chapter), a media contact person is appointed after a crisis occurs. This certainly is not advisable (Kowalski, 2002) for several reasons. As examples, the designee would not be listed in the crisis plan, and would not be prepared to assume the assignment. However, if this course of action is pursued, the superintendent should appoint only one media spokesperson, and the designee should have the necessary knowledge and skills for the assignment, including specific insights into the crisis in question (Armistead, 1996).

Assigning a school board member to be the media spokesperson, either permanently or in the midst of a crisis, usually is not a good idea. Most board members do not possess the requisite knowledge, they have no independent authority, and they do not report to the superintendent. If a board member serving in this role neglects his responsibilities or errs in pursuing them, political realities prevent the superintendent from intervening.

WORKING WITH PRINT MEDIA REPORTERS

Like all professionals, school administrators accumulate craft knowledge—that is, wisdom gained through practice. One pearl commonly passed from generation to generation is the caveat—a paraphrase of Mark Twain—that educational leaders ought not to fight with persons who buy their ink by the barrel (Akers, 1983). While serving as executive director of the American Association of School Administrators, Paul Salmon developed a list of old-fashioned, commonsense guidelines for successful practice. Among them were the following two pieces of advice: Recognize the importance of empowerment and effective communication, and develop a positive relationship with the media (Shannon, 1994). Many seasoned administrators, nevertheless, point out that these guiding principles are easier to set than they are to follow. Good media relationships, even in the context of a well-developed media relations plan, require nurturing. The parties involved must be able to overcome any misperceptions and prejudices they may have about each other.

Developing Positive Relationships

Sooner or later administrators discover that they cannot prevent media contacts; however, they should learn that they can affect the conditions under which they occur. If a superintendent does not know the local reporter covering education, for example, she or he should initiate contact so that the two can meet in a relatively stress-free situation. Otherwise, contact will be initiated by the reporter, often as a request to interview the superintendent about a rumor, scandal, or problem. Meeting a reporter for the first time under such conditions can be highly stressful because the two parties do not know if they should trust each other. Moreover, interviews by reporters are not casual conversations (DeLapp, 1991). If the meeting does not go well, the relationship between the administrator and the reporter may already be headed in a negative direction. When inviting a reporter to a get-acquainted meeting, the administrator should be clear about purpose; media personnel are generally wary if they think an administrator is trying to be manipulative (Bridges & Nelson, 2000). Once the administrator and the reporter are acquainted, they can move forward to build credibility and trust and pave the way to an open-door policy that gives the reporter access to the administrator (Sielke, 2000).

A positive relationship between administrators and reporters also depends on the parties understanding and respecting each other's roles (Raisman, 2000). As an example, principals who want to be treated as professionals should learn to treat journalists as professionals. Unfortunately in the past, many administrators typecast reporters as troublemakers who were interested in covering only negative stories (McQuaid, 1989). Early in their relationship, the administrator and the reporter should exchange thoughts about role expectations.

Accommodating Deadlines

Reporters routinely have deadlines—times established for them to complete research, writing, and editing. Completed stories typically must be submitted hours before publication or airing because the copy may require the approval of several editors as well as technical development (e.g., determining where and how the article will be placed in the newspaper). Time parameters necessitate expeditious information exchanges; thus, reporters are often aggravated when school officials fail to return telephone calls or return them only after deadlines have passed.

Some administrators wrongly assume that ignoring a reporter's inquiries ensures a story's demise. When inquiries are not answered within the requested time frame, reporters are likely to write the story sans the school district's perspective. Therefore, responding within requested time parameters provides some protection against one-sided reporting—and is a courtesy that strengthens personal relationships between administrators and reporters (Frohlichstein, 1993).

At times, responding within the requested time frame is not possible. For example, suppose a reporter requests that she receive a summary of student test scores from the superintendent of a small district within 24 hours. Having no support staff in district administration, he is unable to meet her request. Under such circumstances, the superintendent should give the reporter an honest explanation and an estimate of the time needed to fulfill the request. If the reporter behaves ethically, she should explain why test data for this district are not included in her article, and she should make arrangements to do a follow-up article after she receives them.

Relationships with New Reporters

Richard Colvin, a former education reporter for the *Los Angeles Times* and now director of the Hechinger Institute at Columbia University's Teachers College, commented, "Administrators need to know that the relationship between schools and the media already exists. It is an administrator's responsibility to make it a positive relationship" (as quoted in White, 1998, p. 8). In most school districts, administrators have to overcome two problems in trying to follow this advice. First, reporters covering education, especially for low-circulation outlets, almost always have other assignments. Consequently, they may not spend much time interacting with school administrators, either because they are more interested in their other assignments or because their other assignments are considered more important (Posner, 1994). Second, education assignments are low-level appointments at many newspapers and broadcast outlets, often given to the least experienced reporters. Those who do well covering schools generally get promoted out of the assignment (McQuaid, 1989).

Most media personnel know little about the inner workings of schools and even less about the history, culture, or current problems of a specific district or school when they are initially assigned to this beat. Consequently, helping them to learn about education in general and about local schools specifically is one way to build trust. In terms of building relationships with administrators, media personnel are much like new teachers: Both are more apt to trust administrators who are sincere in helping them become more proficient.

Assisting media personnel in covering school board meetings—a difficult assignment for those who know little about the structure and politics of public education—is one way to build trust. Typically, a reporter's article must be prepared right after the meeting ends. Faced with a tight deadline, there is little or no opportunity to conduct postmeeting interviews, to check name spellings and titles, or to confirm statements. Anticipating these conditions, administrators could aid the media personnel in the following ways:

- Send reporters an agenda several days in advance of the meeting.
- Highlight and explain action items.
- List the names and titles of individuals scheduled to participate in agenda items.
- Offer to meet with reporters prior to the board meeting to answer questions they may have about the agenda.
- Offer to meet with reporters after the board meeting to answer questions and provide information (e.g., identifying persons who are in pictures taken by reporters).

In addition to providing assistance in covering board meetings, administrators can build trust by helping media personnel in the following ways:

- *Identify and explain pressing education issues of the day.* Often reporters are unaware of emerging issues, and even when they are aware, their understanding of them is often shallow.
- *Provide research and related information.* Reporters appreciate receiving background material that potentially strengthens their articles or reports.
- *Direct reporters to outside sources.* Reporters usually appreciate receiving tips about individuals outside the school district who could provide additional or different perspectives.
- *Share documents when permissible and appropriate.* Often administrators have access to documents that can clarify or validate an issue; reporters appreciate having material that adds accuracy to their coverage (Rhoades & Rhoades, 1991).

Dealing with Negative News

What is negative news? It is any report or article that focuses on a problem, conflict, or scandal that places a district or school in a less-than-favorable light. Negative news frustrates administrators because the positive image that results from long-term efforts may be damaged by just one incident. Negative media stories can focus on the district or on school (e.g., the unsafe conditions in a school building) or on people in the district or school (e.g., violent acts by students or employee misconduct). When faced with these stories, administrators often become defensive. As an example, they may claim an unscrupulous reporter is trying to advance his own career by victimizing them or the schools. Even if true, expressing such feelings does not make the negative story disappear or neutralize the story's effects.

Reporters, including those having a positive relationship with administrators, are trained not to look the other way when problems surface. Journalists typically see themselves as public watchdogs—individuals with the responsibility to reveal and report on problems in public institutions. Therefore, choosing to ignore negative news is a big mistake (Shaw, 1987). Reporters and other stakeholders are likely to view silence either as an admission of guilt or as evidence of incompetence. The following guidelines facilitate the formulation and issuance of a managed response.

- ◆ *Never try to suppress a story by lying or refusing to comment.* Just one lie can destroy your credibility, and saying "no comment" suggests that you have something to hide.
- ◆ *If a problem really exists, share your perspective on the issue as quickly as possible.* Make yourself accessible to the media and provide your side of the story.
- ◆ *Have the top-ranking administrator speak to the media.* Hearing from the superintendent or principal conveys the message that the district or school is not taking the matter lightly.
- ◆ *Have an action plan to deal with the problem.* Negative reactions are often attenuated when school officials demonstrate that they are prepared to deal with the situation. You should indicate the steps you will take to deal with the problem.
- ◆ *Communicate the action plan in language that can be understood by the reporter and readers.* Unless the public understands your description of the district's response, they are not apt to focus on your affirmative actions.

As with all organizational conflict, negative news can lead to positive change if it is managed properly. For example, consider an elementary school principal faced with the problem of crowded classrooms. After several parents wrote letters to the newspaper editor complaining about the situation, the education reporter was directed to do a series of articles on this issue. Instead of being defensive, the principal admitted the problem existed and acknowledged that the parental concerns had merit. She also accommodated the reporter's information requests by including the district's long-range facility plan calling for an addition at the school within two or three years. Last, she carefully explained that state law required taxpayers to approve the planned addition via a tax referendum. Skillfully, the principal capitalized on the conflict initiated by the parental complaints. She acknowledged that the problem was real; she focused on the fact that the district officials already had a plan to resolve the problem; and she pointed out that taxpayers, including the complaining parents, would play a pivotal role in determining if the district's solution would be implemented.

Speaking Off the Record

Speaking off the record means different things to different people; more importantly, the rules regarding such communication vary among reporters. Therefore, the general rule is to "never say anything to a reporter you are not willing to see in print or hear on the evening news" (Howard & Mathews, 2006, p. 113). Yet experienced reporters often have been able to get administrators to speak to them "off the record," usually by promising the administrators anonymity or confidentiality—that is, the administrators are assured either that they will not be identified as the source of the information or that the story will be pursued through other sources. Even when such promises are honored, and often they are not, the story can get traced back to the administrator who provided the information.

Some administrators have deluded themselves into believing that speaking to reporters off the record enhances their image with the media. This is a precarious conviction because having secret conversations with reporters can have the opposite effect. For example, some reporters may treat the administrator as an informant; others may view the administrator as a manipulative individual who selectively discloses information intended to harm others. Such perceptions evoke suspicions that the administrator is not always truthful (Howard & Mathews, 2006).

Refusing to Comment

When confronted with difficult questions or accusations, administrators have often responded by saying "no comment" or "I can neither confirm nor deny your accusation." Although these responses appear to be rational and safe, they actually convey negative messages. Million (2000) contends that administrators who answer "no comment" are perceived as trying to avoid additional scrutiny or as trying to conceal something. The public is prone to draw the same conclusion. Consequently, experienced reporters rarely retreat after receiving a "no comment" response; instead, they usually are motivated to dig deeper.

Rather than not commenting, you may find the following responses to be more effective choices:

◆ *"I don't have the details to answer your question at this time. Can I get back to you later?"* This response is effective when the administrator needs to collect and analyze data. An example would be answering questions about an accident in a science lab before school district officials have concluded an investigation of the matter.
◆ *"Can I have _____ contact you regarding this issue?"* This response is effective when the question pertains to a matter that could be better addressed by another school official (e.g., the school's attorney or the business manager).
◆ *"I am not at liberty to provide this information because _____."* This response is effective when the administrator knows that the requested information is protected by law (e.g., the contents are from an employee's personnel file).
◆ *"I am not sure the information you want can be revealed. I'll check and get back to you promptly."* This response is effective when the administrator is uncertain whether the requested information can be made available (e.g., the details of an out-of-court legal settlement).

◆ *"I need to confirm the information before I respond. I'll contact you as soon as I am able to do that."* This response is effective when the administrator is unaware of the situation raised by the reporter (e.g., the arrest of an employee).

In some instances, administrators cannot respond to reporter questions because the information being sought is legally protected. Consider a case where parents accuse administrators of engaging in unfair discipline practices. The administrators feel helpless to respond to the media inquiries because federal laws prohibit them from releasing discipline information contained in a student's record (Surratt, Majestic, & Shelton, 1998). But rather than saying "no comment" to reporter questions, the administrators could either explain why they cannot discuss information in the student's file or request that the parents sign a release allowing them to do so. A refusal to sign such a release often conveys a message that the parents are the ones who do not want all the facts presented to the media (Surratt et al., 1998).

Avoiding Lies

One of the cardinal PR principles for administrators is "Never lie to the media." A school official often finds it tempting to mislead reporters, especially when the circumstances are personal or when the official believes that reporters are adversaries. An administrator who lies or obscures facts, however, rarely prevents a good reporter from finding the real story (Posner, 1994).

Although answering certain questions is painful, giving untruthful answers can be deadly. Experience has proved that lies come back to haunt those who tell them. If caught lying, administrators can lose credibility, public trust, and positive relationships with the media that took years to build—a tremendous price to pay for having gained the convenience of keeping reporters temporarily at bay (Howard & Mathews, 2006).

Staying on Track

When reporters contact administrators, they usually have a specific topic in mind, and they want input in a timely manner so that they can meet their deadline. Understandably, they get frustrated with school officials who do not cooperate with them—that is, officials who (a) avoid answering their questions, (b) answer their questions with questions, or (c) try to change the subject by meandering to other topics. If there is another story the administrator believes merits media attention, he or she should make the suggestion at the end of the interview (Ordovensky & Marx, 1993). During the interview, the administrator should answer questions directly and avoid being evasive; he or she should try to facilitate, not hinder, communication with the reporter (Parker, 1991).

Getting the School's Story to the Media

As noted earlier, administrators often complain that the media present relatively few positive stories about schools. What educators wish to see or hear in the media, however, may be of little interest to reporters—not because the story is positive, but because it is not news. If administrators want to get their stories printed or broadcasted, they have to know what is newsworthy. Answering the following questions can help you determine if a story merits media attention:

♦ Would I want to hear this story?
♦ Who is the audience for this story?
♦ Why should taxpayers care about the story?
♦ Can the story be connected to larger issues currently in the news?
♦ Are there interesting photo opportunities that accompany the story? (This is an especially cogent question for television outlets.)

Frequently, stories that administrators want to see in print do not lend themselves to being newspaper articles. A folk dancing group at a high school and a Thanksgiving skit at an elementary school exemplify activities that reporters may not see as newsworthy, but they could make their way into print because they are suitable for stand-alone photos—that is, photos that are used without accompanying stories. Media coverage for schools is enhanced when administrators understand how news stories and features are used, but it is also enhanced when administrators understand the *importance of timing*. Features that are not suitable for news stories can attract media attention if they are brought forward at an opportune moment. If stories can be linked to current events, they often have a better chance of being published. For example, a story about an outdoor science laboratory might be used in conjunction with the state legislature's deliberation of an environmental protection bill.

Besides understanding the nature of news and the value of timing, administrators need to understand the local media markets. Consider, for example, the tremendous differences faced by superintendents in urban and rural districts. A small-town newspaper is usually more willing to cover "puff" pieces—stories that have no news value and little human interest, but are published to maintain good relations between the newspaper and the school district. Hence, reporters for these papers might write a short article (with a photo) about a principal having lunch with the straight-A students, whereas reporters at large-circulation newspapers covering urban districts are likely to reject the idea. In addition, reporters are often the friends and neighbors of school officials in smaller communities. These contacts can serve to draw the reporter's attention to a desired story (Parker, 1991).

Preparing News Releases

Writing a news release is a relatively simple process and a good way to eliminate misunderstandings. Since an administrator is initiating contact with journalists, timing is an important consideration; that is, getting reporters to pay attention to the release depends on whether the content is newsworthy or related to current issues in the news.

Reporters should be informed if you are presenting them with an "immediate" or an "embargoed" release; this declaration should appear at the top of the first page. An immediate release is intended to be released to the public as soon as possible; an embargoed news release is provided to the media for use at a later time (e.g., on a date specified by the issuer). The release should be printed and include the full name and telephone number of the contact person the reporter should call for additional information. According to Ordovensky and Marx (1993), the release should be written in journalistic style and address the following five W's:

- Who is issuing the release?
- What is the release about?
- When will the event in question take place?
- Where will the event in question take place?
- Why will the event in question take place?

The effectiveness of a press release is enhanced when the most important information is placed at the beginning, starting with a headline that grabs the reader's attention (Albrecht, 1997). Larger newspapers and broadcast media outlets often receive multiple news releases from public agencies, so reporters often sort through them on the basis of the headline and the first few paragraphs.

News releases may contain facts and opinions. Facts should be stated concisely, and if opinions are included, quotes from individuals expressing the opinions should be provided. Since news releases should not be very long (typically two or three pages), only the most important or effective quotes should be used. The release should be written just as you would like to see it appear in the newspaper the next day. Table 11–2 contains a summary of basic guidelines that can be used to structure press releases.

Planning and Conducting News Conferences

News conferences present a greater challenge than do news releases. This may explain why school administrators do not do the former as often as the latter. Ordovensky and Marx (1993) identified three possible reasons why school officials would schedule such a conference:

1. They need to communicate with multiple media outlets simultaneously.
2. Reporters indicate that they need to ask them questions about breaking news.
3. The district's or school's most knowledgeable source needs to be available to the media, but this person has only a limited amount of time to devote to reporters.

Since the goal is to communicate with multiple media outlets simultaneously, giving reporters as much notice as possible is helpful. An advisory, containing basic information about the purpose of the news conference and pertinent logistics (date, time, location, and parking), should be sent to reporters at least several days in advance when possible.

A news conference is more likely to be successful when it is planned properly. Here are suggestions you should follow:

- Select a time of day and a location that are convenient for reporters.
- Select a site that (a) can accommodate media equipment, (b) is convenient for reporters, and (c) is appropriate for the topic.
- Several hours before the conference is scheduled to begin, contact reporters and politely ask them if they will be attending. The call reminds them of the conference and symbolically conveys the fact that you consider their attendance to be important.

TABLE 11–2

Guidelines for Preparing a News Release

Guideline	Benefit
Identify the issuing organization immediately.	Reporters or editors know the source before reading the document; identification can provide credibility.
Identify the contact person.	Questions, comments, and decisions are directed to the appropriate person.
Provide a headline.	The reader is able to discern the nature of the release immediately; in large media markets, this can be critical.
Develop a strong first paragraph.	The first paragraph captures the reader's attention. It should provide a concise, engaging summary of the news release.
Brevity is a virtue.	Reporters and editors are more likely to read the entire document if it is not unduly lengthy.
Avoid using educational jargon.	The material in the release is more likely to be used by journalists if they do not need to make clarifying inquiries.
Double-space the document.	The reader has room to do editing and to insert comments or notes.
Provide vital time-related information.	State the date of the release and the intended date for publication or broadcast; doing so increases the likelihood that the release will be used as intended.
Insert either "more" or "###" at the end of each page.	The former notation informs the reader that additional information follows the end of a page; the latter informs the reader that the release is finished.
Predetermine distribution.	This action makes it more likely that the release will reach all intended audiences.
Include a brief overview of the district or school.	This action ensures that all readers will have an accurate description of the district or school issuing the release.
Provide supplementary material for complicated information.	Providing explanations in the news release will lengthen this document; some reporters may refuse to deal with it simply because it is too lengthy. If explanations of complicated content (e.g., test scores, budgets) need to be provided, use appendices or attachments.

◆ Be prepared to distribute pertinent materials at the start of the conference. These include one or more relevant news releases and information packets containing supportive data.

◆ Anticipate reporter questions and be prepared to answer them.

◆ Inform attendees how they can get additional information.

◆ Avoid confrontational encounters with reporters and have a contingency plan if communication exchanges become emotional.

- ◆ Determine a procedure for conducting the conference in an orderly manner.
- ◆ Have a planned ending for the conference. The preferred method is to announce that only one more question can be asked.
- ◆ Inform school personnel that they should not leave the conference abruptly when it ends. Reporters may wish to interview them. Accordingly, only personnel who may be interviewed should attend the conference.
- ◆ News conferences should be scheduled sparingly because reporters are likely to ignore them if they believe such conferences are held for frivolous reasons. Always determine if the topic is newsworthy before scheduling a conference.

Correcting the Record

As in all human endeavors, mistakes are made in media stories about schools, and these errors are made on both sides of the fence—by reporters and by school officials. When they occur, administrators are foolish to ignore them. Even slight errors, such as misstating a person's official title, could have negative repercussions. Regardless of who is at fault, the administrator should point out the problem directly to the reporter. Lodging a complaint with an editor may create the perception that the primary intent is to discredit the reporter. If errors recur because the reporter is careless or unfair, then discussing the matter with the appropriate editor may be warranted.

The reasons why school officials elect not to correct the record vary. Several years ago, for example, a newspaper reporter mistakenly wrote that a school district agreed to pay $250,000 to a junior high school girl who had sued her teacher for sexual harassment. After the story broke, school officials took disciplinary action against the teacher. Countless stories about the lawsuit and the disciplinary action followed. Though reporters covering the story changed, they consistently relied on previous media reports for their historical background. Therefore, the report that the school district had paid the settlement was restated countless times over the next five years. The superintendent could have corrected the record by explaining that the damages were actually paid using the district's insurance pool and not the district's operating budget—but he did not. Initially, he remained silent in an effort to protect the reporter—a person he considered a friend. Later he concluded that correcting the record would not matter.

In some instances, administrators conclude that corrections only make matters worse. For example, they may argue that repeating damaging or negative information about student test scores is not in the district's best interests. Regardless of the situation, however, you should point out an error to the reporter. After you do that, the two of you can discuss whether making a correction is in the best interests of all parties.

WORKING WITH ELECTRONIC MEDIA REPORTERS

Today, electronic media span radio, television, and the World Wide Web. These outlets require additional preparation from school administrators. When interviews are conducted by broadcast media reporters, for example, school officials have to be concerned about not only what they say, but also how they speak and, in the case of television, how they look when they speak. Administrators often find that electronic media reporters are more direct and confrontational than their print media peers (Walker, 1990).

Television

The tenor of a live or taped interview is crucial because both the administrator and the reporter communicate with audiences nonverbally, as well as with words. Consequently, personal appearance, gestures, and facial expressions can be more powerful than words. Given the special challenges presented by television, administrators should be prepared for this experience. In this vein, the following recommendations should be helpful:

- *Before you agree to do an interview, find out if it will be live or taped.* Taped interviews allow you to pause before answering or to stop and start over if you decide to rephrase your answer.
- *Anticipate the interview questions that will be asked.* Preparing answers to anticipated questions gives you an advantage. Having a colleague do a simulated interview with you can also be helpful.
- *Focus on nonverbal behavior.* Concentrate on the reporter's nonverbal behavior and your own nonverbal behavior. For example, an interviewer who is reading material while you are answering may be sending the message that he or she is not interested in your responses; smiling before you answer helps to build rapport with the interviewer and the audience.
- *Avoid one-word and excessively long answers.* Either option presents a problem. The former provides too little information; the latter creates the impression that you are attempting to dominate the interview (e.g., to avoid other questions).
- *Focus on a message that you want to present.* Identify two or three key points you want to emphasize prior to the interview, and then inject them periodically into your responses.
- *Dress appropriately.* Dress can be distractive; that is, your appearance can cause viewers to pay more attention to how you look than to what you have to say. Both overdressing and underdressing are problems that may prompt the interviewer and the audience to question your credibility.
- *Give the interviewer suggested questions.* Some reporters may not cooperate and may ask their own questions, but most often they will use your questions. The suggested questions are another technique for getting your message across to the audience (Ordovensky & Marx, 1993).
- *Maintain eye contact with the interviewer and try to ignore the cameras.* The audience is observing a conversation; if you ignore the interviewer, your behavior may be interpreted negatively. One exception to this recommendation is satellite interviews in which the reporter and the interviewee are not physically in the same studio.
- *Be careful what you say during a commercial break.* The interviewer may repeat your comments to the audience after the commercial break has ended.
- *Avoid being manipulated or intimidated.* An interviewer and the audience can usually sense when you are defensive or anxious (Howard & Mathews, 2006).

◆ *Use related questions to make points.* If you are trying to stress the importance of passing a bond referendum for a new school, you may ask: "What programs will have to be curtailed if the referendum fails?"

◆ *Avoid being derailed.* You should not allow the reporter to dominate the content. To remain focused on your message, you need to inject transitions at the end of your answers. For example, you might say, "Rather than spending all of our time talking about financial problems, can we now focus on academic programs?"

◆ *Avoid being defensive.* Try to remain confident, especially if the reporter attempts to confuse you by asking inappropriate questions or questions unrelated to the interview topic.

◆ *Avoid nervous habits.* Tapping your finger on the table or shuffling your papers presents an image that you are uneasy.

◆ *Do not tolerate constant interruptions.* If the reporter keeps interrupting you, politely request that you be given adequate time to answer questions.

◆ *Use visuals to enhance critical points.* Television is a medium that favors the use of pictures, graphs, and charts (Parker, 1991).

In larger media markets, television reporters are assigned to cover school districts. Occasionally, they will attend board meetings, usually looking for short pieces that can be integrated into the nightly news broadcast. These spots provide opportunities for administrators to deliver a message, but the time is limited—often less than one minute. Thus, words for these short pieces must be chosen carefully (Parker, 1991).

Radio

Reporters working for radio stations often contact administrators without advance notice seeking a few sound bites that can be used to enhance a story. Most often these interviews are conducted via telephone. If the reporter intends to make an audiotape of your conversation, she or he should inform you to that effect and then seek your permission.

Radio offers an excellent opportunity for direct audience involvement via call-in shows (Austin & Pinkleton, 2001). Consequently, station personnel may invite administrators to participate in scheduled programs where the purpose is to conduct an in-depth interview coupled with audience participation. If you are contacted to do such a program, you should accept only if you have extensive knowledge of the topic(s) to be discussed. If not, recommend another person to the reporter.

Though many of the suggestions for appearing on television are relevant to radio, there are several notable differences between these two mediums:

◆ You usually are able to rely on notes and prepared statements when responding to radio interview questions.

◆ Your nonverbal behavior and personal appearance are usually nonfactors; the exception is a radio interview conducted before a live audience.

◆ You usually have greater opportunity to discuss essential points in detail on radio because the time frames generally are longer than they are on television.

◆ Presenting statistical data on the radio is more difficult because you cannot use charts or other visual aids to influence the audience.

Web-Based Outlets

Increasingly, information about districts and schools is being made available via the Internet. The increasing availability of streaming media content via broadband is driving traditional sources of audio content, such as radio stations, to use the Internet to develop original online content (Cox, 2000). Newspapers also are making their content available online, typically within 24 hours after publication. In the case of established media outlets, the Internet provides a medium for reaching more people, and it provides opportunities for users to retrieve past articles or broadcasts quickly and easily. However, the content is still produced by journalists who are employed by these businesses.

Other forms of online journalism present a unique challenge to school administrators. Examples of these outlets include online journals, community Web pages, education association Web pages (e.g., those of the state department of education, school boards association, teacher organizations), political action group Web pages, and Web logs (or "blogs"). A *blog* is a Web page that provides a personal journal for an individual or group of individuals (Lasica, 2001) and is typically updated daily; blogs are more about politics than about technology (Wikipedia, 2005). Online journalism outlets often are interactive (i.e., they provide opportunities for the public to respond) and hypertextual (i.e., they offer hyperlinks to related stories, archives, and selected resources) (Deuze, 2005).

Relationships with persons who generate stories about schools through Internet-only outlets are difficult to develop for at least three reasons. First, administrators often will never meet these individuals; in some instances, their identities are purposely concealed. Second, many of these individuals are not professional journalists; therefore, they develop their own reporting standards. Third, many of them are driven by political motives; therefore, their reporting decisions may be based on emotions and self-interests, rather than rationality. Even so, administrators should identify and then monitor Internet sources that provide news, opinions, and other types of information relevant to the employing district or school.

SUMMARY

In an information age, school officials are expected to provide information frequently, accurately, and honestly. Their ability to do so usually depends on their relationships with journalists. Effective relationships require both parties to understand each other's roles and to develop a mutual appreciation for these roles and responsibilities. Table 11–3 includes a summary of media relations suggestions discussed in this chapter.

Being criticized by the media, directly or indirectly, is painful for administrators. When this occurs, you may be tempted to hide, express indifference, or make excuses. None of these reactions, however, is advantageous. Even worse, you may opt to publicly counterattack; this myopic rejoinder virtually ensures that future interactions with journalists be acrimonious. Effective administrators recognize that conflict, including disputes with journalists, is inevitable, and rather than ignoring the problem or surrendering to it, they capitalize on the situation. They do this by viewing conflict both as a learning opportunity

TABLE 11–3
Summary of Media Relations Suggestions

Issue	Suggestions
Organizing the program	Develop a media relations plan that is connected to the district's PR plan; determine who will be responsible for administering public information functions; determine who will serve as spokespersons.
Gaining an understanding of journalists	Learn about the role and responsibilities of journalists and use that knowledge to form opinions about the media.
Building and maintaining positive relationships	Media relations are about personal relationships—between you and reporters. Take the initiative to meet them and always try to be cooperative.
Answering media inquiries	Make yourself accessible, honor deadlines, and never lie. When you cannot answer, provide an explanation instead of saying "no comment."
Speaking to a reporter off the record	Do not do it under any circumstances.
Dealing with negative news	If the news is true, admit it, and then focus attention on your plan to resolve the problem.
Issuing news releases	Make sure the content is newsworthy, follow the format presented in this chapter, and accommodate reporter questions.
Holding news conferences	Make sure the topic merits a conference; schedule the conference to accommodate reporters; plan carefully so that you maintain control.
Conveying your message	Pursue positive stories by capitalizing on media interests.
Correcting errors	Always bring errors to the attention of the reporter, and then determine if issuing a formal correction is in the best interest of all parties.
Working with electronic media	Understand how messages are shaped via radio, television, and Web-based outlets.

(at the personal and the organizational levels) and as an opportunity for organizational growth (Kowalski, 2006). As an example, a forward-thinking superintendent responded to negative media stories about crowded classrooms by first educating her administrative staff about possible solutions and then convincing the school board to support a school construction referendum.

Though it may appear that some reporters are interested in covering only negative school stories, the media actually report both positive and negative stories. In most school systems, the quantity of positive and negative stories is basically equal over time (Shaw, 1987). Unfortunately, positive stories often capture less attention than negative stories, and this partially explains why many administrators believe the media are predisposed to be critical. As an administrator, you should seek to develop relationships with reporters because in an information-based society, journalists have the power to shape public opinion.

QUESTIONS AND SUGGESTED ACTIVITIES

CASE STUDY

1. Was it a good idea for the school board to name one of its members as the official media spokesperson to deal with this scandal? Why or why not?
2. Evaluate the principal's decision to urge the faculty to remain silent.
3. What actions could the principal have taken to control media access to students?
4. Should the superintendent have been more visible in making media statements with regard to this case? Why or why not?
5. By refusing to comment about the scandal, did school officials encourage or discourage journalists from pursuing related stories?
6. What actions could the superintendent or principal have taken to communicate with stakeholders about the scandal immediately after it became public?
7. Why were many residents in the school district angry about the employment of a private detective?

CHAPTER

8. What is a media relations plan?
9. What information should be contained in a media relations plan?
10. Content in the chapter stresses the point that media relations are really about personal relationships. What does this mean?
11. When and how should administrators react to errors in media articles or stories?
12. Why should school administrators have a basic understanding of journalism?
13. As an administrator, you should be aware of differences among newspaper, radio, and television interviews. What are these differences?
14. In attempting to build positive relationships with journalists, administrators may communicate "off the record." Is this effective practice? Why or why not?
15. When confronted with negative news, some administrators have opted to be unavailable to reporters. Is this effective practice? Why or why not?
16. Experts advise administrators not to respond to reporter questioning by saying, "No comment." What is the basis of their advice?

SUGGESTED READINGS

Burgess, D. (2000). Managing public scrutiny. *American School & University, 72*(5), 38–40.

Cook, G. (2001). The media and the message. *American School Board Journal, 188*(6), 16–22.

Cook, G. (2003). The perception challenge. *American School Board Journal, 190*(12), 53–54, 57.

Engeln, J. (2000). A complete turnabout. *High School Magazine, 7*(6), 28–31.

Fox, J. A., & Levin, J. (1993). *How to work with the media.* Newbury Park, CA: Sage.

Frohlichstein, T. (1993). Dealing successfully with media inquiries. *NASSP Bulletin, 77*(555), 82–88.

Hennessey, A. (1992). Getting the word out: Working with your local school reporter. *Phi Delta Kappan, 74*(1), 82–84.

Kowalski, T. J. (2002). Working with the media during a crisis situation: Perspectives for school administrators. *Journal of School Public Relations, 23*(3), 178–196.

Lawrence, J. R. (2004). Good news to share with gusto. *School Administrator, 61*(1), 36.

Levin, B. (2004). Media-government relations in education. *Journal of Education Policy, 19*(3), 271–283.

Million, J. (2000). No comment, NO WAY! *Education Digest, 65*(9), 59–60.

Ordovensky, P., & Marx, G. (1993). *Working with the news media.* Arlington, VA: American Association of School Administrators.

Owen, A. R., & Karrh, J. A. (1996). Video news releases: Effects on viewer recall and attitudes. *Public Relations Review, 22*(4), 369–378.

Paciancia, D. (1995). Getting out the good news. *American School Board Journal, 182*(6), 39–40.

Pohl, R. J. (1994). Beyond confrontation. *American School Board Journal, 181*(2), 54.

Polansky, H. B., & Montague, R. (2001). Handling an emergency: A defining moment. *School Business Affairs, 67*(7), 13–15.

Sielke, J. (2000). So, you want positive press? An in-depth look at what the media really want when they come knocking. *School Business Affairs, 66*(10), 26–29.

Sperbeck, J. M. (1997). Some media relations success stories. *Journal of Applied Communications, 81*(3), 24–39.

Townsend, R. (1993). Coping with controversy. *School Administrator, 50*(9), 24–27.

REFERENCES

Akers, J. T. (1983, April). *Don't fight the man who buys his ink by the barrel.* Paper presented at the Annual Meeting of the National School Boards Association, San Francisco. (ERIC Document Reproduction Service No. ED246553)

Albrecht, D. G. (1997). *Promoting your business with free (or almost free) publicity.* Englewood Cliffs, NJ: Prentice Hall.

Armistead, L. (1996). What to do before the violence happens: Designing the crisis communication plan. *NASSP Bulletin, 80*(579), 31–37.

Austin, E. W., & Pinkleton, B. E. (2001). *Strategic public relations management: Planning and managing effective communication programs.* Mahwah, NJ: Erlbaum.

Batory, J. P. (1999). The sad state of education coverage. *School Administrator, 56*(8), 34–38.

Borja, R. R. (2004, October 24). Educators, journalists spar over media access. *Education Week, 21*(8), 1, 24–25.

Bridges, J. A., & Nelson, R. A. (2000). Issues management: A relational approach. In J. A. Ledingham & S. D. Bruning (Eds.), *Public relations as relationship management: A relational approach to the study and practice of public relations* (pp. 95–116). Mahwah, NJ: Erlbaum.

Cook, G. (2001). The media and the message. *American School Board Journal, 188*(6), 16–22.

Cox, B. (2000). *Rise of broadband forcing local media outlets online.* Retrieved November 8, 2005, from http://www.internetnews.com/bus-news/article.php/392341.

DeLapp, T. (1991). Interviews are not conversations. *Thrust for Educational Leadership, 20*(3), 46–47.

Deuze, M. (2005). *Online journalism: Modeling the first generation of news media on the World Wide Web.* Retrieved November 8, 2005, from http://www.firstmonday.org/issues/issue6_10/deuze.

Frohlichstein, T. (1993). Dealing successfully with media inquiries. *NASSP Bulletin, 77*(555), 82–88.

Fullan, M. (1999). *Change forces: The sequel.* Philadelphia: Falmer Press.

Gonring, M. P. (1997). Global and local media relations. In C. L. Caywood (Ed.), *The handbook of strategic public relations and integrated communication* (pp. 63–76). New York: McGraw-Hill.

Howard, C. M., & Mathews, W. K. (2006). *On deadline: Managing media relations* (4th ed.). Long Grove, IL: Waveland Press.

Kosmicki, R. J., & Bona, F. E. (1996). Media relations: How to relate to the press. In R. L. Dilenschneider (Ed.), *Dartnell's public relations handbook* (pp. 59–75). Chicago: Dartnell Corp.

Kowalski, T. J. (2002). Working with the media during a crisis situation: Perspectives for school administrators. *Journal of School Public Relations, 23*(3), 178–196.

Kowalski, T. J. (2004). *Case studies on educational administration* (4th ed.). Boston: Allyn & Bacon.

Kowalski, T. J. (2006). *The school superintendent: Theory, practice, and cases* (2nd ed.). Thousand Oaks, CA: Sage.

Lasica, J. (2001, May 24). Blogging as a form of journalism. *Online Journalism Review.* Retrieved November 9, 2005, from http://ojr.usc.edu/content/story.cfm?request5585.

McQuaid, E. P. (1989). The rising tide of mediocre education coverage. *Education Digest, 54*(8), 7–10.

Million, J. (2000). No comment, NO WAY! *Education Digest, 65*(9), 59–60.

Ordovensky, P., & Marx, G. (1993). *Working with the news media.* Arlington, VA: American Association of School Administrators.

Parker, J. (1991). *Accessing the media.* Guide developed for the Kent (WA) Public Schools. (ERIC Document Reproduction Service No. ED339337)

Polansky, H. B., & Montague, R. (2001). Handling an emergency: A defining moment. *School Business Affairs, 67*(7), 13–15.

Posner, M. A. (1994). Read all about it. *Case Currents, 20*(1), 8–13.

Raisman, N. A. (2000). Building relationships with the media: A brief working guide for community college leaders. *New Directions for Community Colleges, 28*(2), 21–27.

Rhoades, L., & Rhoades, G. (1991). Helping the media add depth to education news. *Clearing House, 64*(5), 350–351.

Ridgway, J. (1996). *Practical media relations* (2nd ed.). Brookfield, VT: Gower.

Shannon, T. A. (1994). Salmon's laws. *Executive Educator, 16*(4), 52–54.

Shaw, R. C. (1987). Do's and don'ts for dealing with the press. *NASSP Bulletin, 71*(503), 99–102.

Sielke, J. (2000). So, you want positive press? An in-depth look at what the media really want when they come knocking. *School Business Affairs, 66*(10), 26–29.

Spicer, C. (1997). *Organizational public relations: A political perspective.* Mahwah, NJ: Erlbaum.

Surratt, J., Majestic, A., & Shelton, S. (1998). Both sides of the story: Media relations. *American School Board Journal, 185*(2), 47, 52.

Walker, K. B. (1990). Confrontational media training for administrators: Performance and practice. *Public Personnel Management, 19*(4), 419–427.

White, J. (1998). Media misconceptions. *Thrust for Educational Leadership, 27*(6), 8–10.

Wikipedia. (2005). *Wikipedia the free encyclopedia.* Retrieved November 9, 2005, from http://en.wikipedia.org/wiki/Blog.

CHAPTER

Collecting and Analyzing Decision-Oriented Data

A. William Place
Maryanne McNamara
James F. McNamara

CASE STUDY: GOOD INTENTIONS AREN'T ALWAYS ENOUGH

Having to spend extra time hunting for a parking space at the John F. Kennedy Elementary School was not in Jane West's plan for this April evening. As director of communications for the Lancaster School District, Dr. West was ending a two-week marathon of scheduled meetings in each of the district's seven elementary schools. The purpose of these meetings was to share information with parents about a proposed new year-round calendar to be piloted in the district beginning in September.

Persons attending each elementary school campus meeting had been asked to fill out and return a questionnaire related to their interest in having their children participate in the new year-round school pilot program. Questionnaire responses from previous elementary school meetings indicated that, in general, parents were supportive of the program. However, West was cautious about this finding because she realized that (a) attendance at the previous meetings had been low, (b) those in attendance had come from what are considered to be more affluent sections of the district, and (c) many of those attending had not returned their questionnaires.

After searching several minutes for a parking spot, West was convinced that low attendance would not be an issue at tonight's meeting. As she entered the cafeteria, she saw that all seats were taken and that a few parents were standing. She was surprised to see the large numbers of preschool children accompanying their parents.

The audience was largely Hispanic, and West was pleased that she'd had the good sense to arrange to have an interpreter at the meeting, since many of the residents in this area of the school district were new immigrants.

When West turned on the overhead projector and began her presentation, she heard shouts coming from several areas of the room. "No! We don't want to hear about something that you've already decided for us." "We can't afford to have our children out of school at odd times of the year. How will we find babysitters?" "We've heard rumors that you're going to force all of the children in *this* neighborhood to go to school this summer." "Why is it that no one has asked *us* what we think about a year-round school program?"

West, though startled, recovered quickly: "Your children brought information home last month, and the local newspaper published two articles on this pilot program just last week. We're now asking you to fill out this questionnaire so that we'll *know* how you feel." But her enthusiasm to share more information about the program was quickly eroded as she realized that the angry questions and comments were not going to stop.

At the close of the meeting, a frustrated West had her assistants pass out the questionnaires. "Before you go home could you please fill these out?" she asked. "We'll pay close attention to your responses."

Several parents had already left the building before the questionnaires were distributed. A few people crumpled the sheets when they saw that the forms were written in English. Most people, however, simply left the questionnaires on their empty seats. As the last of her audience filed out, West leaned over and dejectedly picked up a few of the questionnaires that had floated to the floor.

Early the next morning Jane West sat in her office thinking about the series of meetings she had conducted on the year-round school pilot program. Last night's meeting at the John F. Kennedy Elementary School had made it clear that something more needed to be done to get clarity on whether or not families with children in district schools were interested in exploring year-round schools. What should she do to get accurate information on how the pilot program could best work for them? Would "working best for them" be different for different types of families?

THE IMPORTANCE OF DATA IN THE TWENTY-FIRST CENTURY

Public relations (PR), as defined in Chapter 1, includes providing vital and useful information to the public and employees and playing an integral role in planning and decision-making functions. This chapter is most concerned with the concepts of two-way communication and the use of data for the purposes of planning and decision making. *Decision making* is defined as a process of generating an outcome based on a variety of cognitive, social, and contextual influences (Jones & Beck, 1996). Administrators can make better decisions when they collect and analyze data directly related to these three areas (McNamara, 1993, 1994a).

The latest trends in leadership promote data-driven decision making. For example, Austin and Pinkleton (2001) state: "Research helps practitioners get accurate information quickly at a relatively low cost to aid them in sophisticated planning and problem solving" (p. 3). There is also an emphasis on research-based practices on the federal level in the No Child Left Behind legislation. Gathering and analyzing information is more than a trend; it is an essential component of modern leadership that is critical to the planning, visioning, and decision making of educational administration. This process of dealing with data, like other elements of PR, entails effective two-way communication.

Gathering and analyzing data about the thoughts, feelings, and characteristics of a community is even more important today because of increased diversity in society. While the case study at the beginning of this chapter provided an obvious example where research prior to meeting with a segment of the district would have been helpful, there are many times when knowledge of subtle differences could be very helpful to administrators. In the past, the dominant culture has sometimes emphasized one-way communication. Today, in our multicultural society, one-way communication, even if it is well intentioned with a good message, is not sufficient for good leadership. Successful practice must include collecting and analyzing data from the various community groups and perspectives. One of the issues addressed in the case study at the beginning of this chapter is the need to understand why different cultures affect schools in dramatic ways.

Collecting Data

As administrators collect data, they should start with the basics. For example, to measure anything, even a child's height, the assessor should have a clear understanding of purpose (why the measurement is being done) and process (how the measurement will be done). In the case of children's height, the researcher may need to order furniture or tell custodial staff how high to place coat racks or simply be interested in the distance from the bottom of the children's feet to the top of their head. One accurate way to collect these data is to have each child take off his or her shoes and stand up straight with their back to a tall enough measuring stick. Even with this rather simple task, the researcher must make important decisions that may influence how data will be used—for example, deciding whether to report data in inches or meters.

For educational leaders, decision-making data are often complex and difficult to access. For instance, determining community perceptions of a particular program can be a very intricate assignment. First, the administrator must understand interactions between the program being studied and other programs. That is, how does this program affect other programs, and how do other programs affect this program? Second, the administrator must answer basic questions: What population or sample of a population will be studied? What measure of perception will facilitate making a decision? Third, the administrator must determine whether qualitative data, quantitative data, or both are needed. Whereas quantitative data deal with numbers, qualitative data typically entail thick and rich descriptions, often of situations that are difficult or impossible to study quantitatively.

Qualitative approaches may be preferable when the population or sample is quite small and when the variable being measured is complex (i.e., when the task involves interrelated variables that cannot be neatly separated). If, however, the population or sample is large and data can be isolated and clearly defined, then quantitative methods are likely to be more useful. Qualitative approaches are preferable when achieving depth of understanding is important; quantitative approaches are preferable when ascertaining general perceptions is the goal. Selection of methodology ought not to be based on the evaluator's preference, but rather should be determined by the type of information needed.

In modern organizations, there is a large inventory of tools that can be used to formalize the collection and analysis of relevant information. It is helpful to think of these tools as systematic procedures used to complete tasks associated with one or more of the major phases in a decision model (McNamara & Chisolm, 1988). When used as intended, these tools improve the capacity to make more effective managerial and policy decisions.

Public relations is viewed here as an organizational activity whose purpose is to provide relevant information assisting policy makers and practitioners in all phases of decision making. From this perspective, PR plays an instrumental role in *creating* a shared vision among all organizational stakeholders, *designing* a plan of action, and *evaluating* the organization's progress toward reaching its agreed-on goals.

SOCIAL SCIENTIFIC SURVEYS

In examining the ways in which one can use tools to collect, analyze, and share relevant decision-oriented information, the PR specialist should look at social scientific surveys as a valuable tool. Surveys, like other scientific and technical tools, can be well or poorly made and can be used in appropriate or inappropriate ways. In their widely referenced book, Bradburn and Sudman (1988) discuss a wide range of survey uses and provide excellent examples of appropriate, inappropriate, and questionable usage. Conducting a survey prior to making certain administrative decisions may improve the process and outcomes of those decisions. For example, restructuring, adjusting to new state mandates, and determining whether to keep a long-standing program are difficult decisions that should be based on accurate information. In conducting surveys, the identification of key stakeholders helps to determine the population for a study. For example, the planning group considering year-round schooling might want to know the preferences of students, parents, teachers, voters in the district and stakeholders who are affected if a year-round school calendar is adopted.

When researchers and policy analysts introduce the topic of social scientific surveys, two questions naturally arise. The first is: What is the difference between a *survey* and a *poll?* Some authors (e.g., Bradburn & Sudman, 1988) treat these two terms as being interchangeable; differences usually relate to application. For example, polling involves surveying the public. Education researchers and practicing administrators typically use the term *survey*, or they use yet another synonym, *questionnaire*.

The second question that arises is, What is the difference between a *social scientific survey* and a *probability sampling survey?* Put briefly, these two terms are also interchangeable. Social scientific surveys use probability sampling to ensure that the sample is an accurate representation of the population to which the survey researcher wishes to generalize (Babbie, 1990). A *margin of error* (an essential feature of social scientific surveys) can be constructed *only* when a true probability sampling plan is implemented (O'Shea, 1992; Williams, 1978). There are several sources that provide detailed information about basic survey operations; see, for example, McNamara (1994b).

Sampling Issues

Most often it is not necessary to survey an entire population to get an accurate measure of opinions because a scientific random sample may produce results very close to those obtained from an entire population. This is because a scientific random sample, by definition, provides an equal chance that every individual in a population will be chosen (Krathwohl, 1998). A true random sample is free of bias or predetermined purpose that would skew the results. It is far different from the case where only people who happen to be at a particular place (e.g., the mall or even an open forum held at one of the schools) are asked to complete a survey. Random samples are systematically selected through a computer or a table of random numbers that matches an individual in the population with a selected number. Often a simple random sample is sufficient to produce the desired information. However, if the administrator seeks to produce information about subgroups, a stratified random sample may be more appropriate. This technique produces separate samples of proportional size so that the subgroups are representative of the whole population. As an example, a stratified random sample is the appropriate choice if a planning committee wants to compare the preferences of stakeholder groups (e.g., parents versus nonparent taxpayers or community residents of lower socioeconomic status versus the rest of the community). To ensure adequate statistical power (i.e., the ability of the survey to detect true preference differences), at least 100 randomly chosen survey respondents are recommended for each stakeholder group.[1]

If the planning committee wishes to compare the preferences of two or more stakeholder groups using formal statistical tests (e.g., a *t*-test of proportions from two independent groups or an *F*-test of proportions from two or more independent groups entered into an analysis of variance model), then the sample sizes should be based on sample size formulas used in hypothesis-testing designs to ensure adequate statistical power. Differences in the rules between formulas used elsewhere to determine sample size and those used in hypothesis testing can be found in research method books (e.g., McNamara, 1994b).

If a population is small (e.g., 100 or 200), random sampling may not always be a good choice. For example, a principal surveying the parents of fifth-grade students should include all of them. When all individuals in a group are included, you have a population (see Table 12–1 for examples of the differences between samples and populations). With small populations, scientific random sampling excludes a relatively small number of people. Any cost savings associated with using random sampling (e.g., as a result of having to send out fewer surveys) may be outweighed by the ill feeling of those individuals who were not included. Stratified random sampling can be viewed as a series of simple random sampling designs with each person in the population appearing on only one list.[2]

In a policy preference survey of members in each of several stakeholder groups, some of the names will appear on more than one list. For example, a teacher may also be a parent. This poses no real problem, however; if a teacher's name was selected from the population list of

TABLE 12–1

Examples of Populations and Samples

Category	Examples
Population	All parents of students in a school; all parents of students in a grade within a school; all adult residents in a school district
Random sample	Every third parent from an alphabetized list of all parents in a school district; 20% of the parents from a middle school selected through a random drawing
Stratified random sample	Every third male parent and every third female parent from an alphabetized list of all parents in a school district; 10% of parents in each of three income categories (high, average, low) selected through a random drawing
Nonrandom sample	Every individual who physically visits a school and completes a survey there; parents who actually file a complaint with a school official

---

[1]The specific reason for recommending at least 100 respondents in each stakeholder group is to ensure that the survey sampling design and the corresponding test statistics are able to detect real and meaningful group differences. For a brief overview of statistical power and its sampling requirements, see McNamara (1991, 1994b, chap. 3).

[2]On the use of stratified sampling in policy preference surveys, see McNamara (1994b). For an easy-to-read treatment of all essential features of stratified random sampling, see Sheaffer, Mendenhall, and Ott (2006, chap. 5).

teachers, the response requested would be from a teacher's perspective. If the teacher's name was also selected from a population list of parents, the parent's viewpoint would be requested.

In situations where sampling is a preferred approach, the researcher must determine a reasonable margin of error, as well as a reasonable level of confidence. The margin of error is a measure of how closely the information obtained from a sample represents the entire population. The level of confidence addresses the fact that in a few cases it is possible that the results are not as close to the population as the margin of error adopted. If the results of a survey indicate that 80% of the parents are in favor of the new plan, the margin of error indicates how close the percentage of those actually in favor of the plan is to exactly 80% of the population. Specifically, a margin of error of plus or minus 5 percentage points means that the 80% result is an estimate that 75 to 85% would favor the plan if the whole population was surveyed. In many cases, this is close enough, but if there is a need to be more exact, then a smaller margin of error needs to be set (e.g., a margin of error of plus or minus 2 percentage points means that with an 80% result, the estimate ranges from 78 to 82%).

The level of confidence is typically stated in terms of *error probability*. For example, if the researcher sets the probability of sample data being in error at .05, he or she is accepting the fact that there are 5 chances in 100 that the results obtained from the sample are not accurate (defined by the margin of error) for the entire population. This is also referred to as a 95% confidence level. Although not a universal standard and not something that should be accepted lightly or without thoughtful consideration, 95% is a commonly used confidence level. Many researchers would say that 95% allows enough confidence that the results obtained are very close to the results that would have been obtained if everyone in the population had been asked, and therefore, it is acceptable for purposes of administrative decision making. To put it another way, a 95% confidence level indicates that you would obtain the 80% result in less than 5 out of 100 samples if the population was more than 85% in favor or less than 75% in favor.

Return Rates

Another important aspect of using surveys to collect data is the return rate. The size of your sample is important, but the return rate of your survey is even more crucial in the interpretation of the results. Although the size of the population can make some differences for any large population, a sample of 384 will be sufficient to obtain a .05 level of confidence with a 5% margin of error. However, it is the return rate that is used to estimate how much the results can be generalized (i.e., used to interpret what the population response would have been had the entire population been surveyed). Private businesses often are willing to make decisions based on surveys with relatively low return rates (e.g., 20% or less) because the risk does not involve a public interest. However, the type of decisions made in the private sector (e.g., marketing decisions) are quite different from those that educational administrators make that involve the expenditure of public funds and, more importantly, influence the future of students.

When an educational decision is made based on survey data, the administrator should remember that the information collected provides no insights about those who did not respond. Therefore, with a 40% response rate, no conclusion can be made about the other 60%. If information about nonrespondents is needed, follow-up studies may be necessary.

However, it is less expensive to properly design surveys to enhance return rates. Educators often seek return rates of 60–80% or more so that the known outweighs the unknown. Schools have an advantage over other groups doing surveys if they include information indicating that it is important to get input from *all* citizens. However, it does need to be emphasized that even those without children need to give input on certain issues. Most people will respond to a short survey (something that takes five minutes or less) if it is from the schools because many people do care about children or at least the tax dollars needed to support them. The survey's clarity, length, design, and interest that it holds for the respondents, as well as the method of implementation, can greatly impact the return rate.

In addition to the practical considerations of aggravating people, there are ethical considerations involved in survey research. Since ethical concerns are sometimes not considered to be part of scientific methods, researchers and practitioners look to another set of guidelines. These guidelines are given in the *Code of Professional Ethics and Practices* published by the American Association of Public Opinion Research (AAPOR), an interdisciplinary association of both academic and commercial survey researchers.[3]

Method of Implementation

There are four survey methods used to collect data: (a) the face-to-face interview, (b) the written form that is dropped off and picked up later or the mailed questionnaire, (c) the telephone interview, and (d) the Internet or e-mail survey. Each has strengths and weaknesses, which should be considered. The wording of questions is important in all four methods.

There are strengths associated with face-to-face interviews that other approaches lack. As an example, clarifying questions can be asked when the information being considered is complex or detailed. In addition, this method typically produces a high return rate, which, as noted, is very important. However, the face-to-face interview often has serious limitations and problems associated with it. Consider some of the more prevalent concerns:

- ◆ Unless the interviewer is properly trained, face-to-face interviews may produce unreliable data. An inadequately prepared interviewer may behave inconsistently. For example, the interviewer's nonverbal behaviors or verbal inflections may be uneven across the interview—a condition that could result in varying levels of influence on the respondents. Put another way, inconsistencies in the questions or interviewer behavior are very likely to produce reliability problems for quantitative data.
- ◆ Validity (i.e., accuracy) is also a potential concern with face-to-face interviews. Specifically, interviewees often feel compelled to give socially acceptable responses (or politically correct responses). When the interviewer and interviewee know each other, the interviewee may be reluctant to provide any answer that he or she believes will offend or anger the interviewer. For example, some citizens may tell an administrator that they support a tax referendum for a new school building when they do not.
- ◆ The environment in which data are collected may influence answers. For example, an interviewer may conduct the session in the interviewee's home. A noisy or messy

---

[3]A reprint of the AAPOR code can be found in Babbie (1990). On the use of ethical guidelines for survey research in educational organizations, see also McNamara (1994b).

environment may influence the tone of the communication (e.g., influence eye contact or candidness). In a true random sample, some respondents may reside in geographic areas where the crime rate is high or security restricts access; consequently, interviewers may be reluctant or unable to interview everyone in the sample.

A written form dropped off and picked up by the researcher also requires communication skills. For example, the respondent may ask questions about the survey or the meaning of some of the items on the survey. Therefore, it has some of the disadvantages of face-to-face interviews, but to a lesser degree.

The mailed questionnaire is very popular largely because it is time efficient. A big advantage of this method is candidness, especially if anonymity is ensured. In addition, all individuals in the population or sample probably can be reached via mail, and this option is relatively inexpensive. The technique, however, has three noteworthy potential problems:

1. The technique tends to have the lowest return rate among primary survey methods.
2. A person other than the intended respondent could fill out the questionnaire and return it.
3. Pressure groups may try to influence respondents.

There are some things that can be done to increase the return rate. The most basic concept is to keep it short and simple. Other specific strategies can be found in most basic survey research texts.

The e-mail survey is a variation of the mailed questionnaire. It has become increasingly popular because of its low cost and relative speed. Because anonymity is harder to ensure, some members of the population or sample refuse to respond, or they give less than honest answers. In certain school districts, a significant portion of the population, those without e-mail addresses, may be automatically excluded if this technique is used. As the volume of e-mail increases, many individuals quickly sort incoming communications or have systems that sort them, and more e-mails are treated as spam or placed in junk files. Thus, a survey could be discarded without the interviewee even seeing it.

The telephone interview is another inexpensive way to collect data in a relatively short time, especially if all the calls are toll-free or made with a special long-distance line. This option, however, also has several limitations.

- Some residents may have unlisted telephone numbers, making them ineligible to participate.
- Some residents may not have a telephone, or they may have only a cell phone and no land line that a researcher can access.
- Some residents may hang up immediately after receiving an interview call because of their attitude toward telemarketing.

Training is a key variable for success with telephone interviews. Such preparation helps ensure interviewer consistency.

Survey Question Development

Incorrectly wording survey questions can waste time and effort. For example, answers to poorly worded questions are generally unusable. Designing a survey question may seem like a simple task, but it is not. Often the question does not ask what is intended, or the question is ambiguous. Consider, for example, the *double-barreled question*—a question that asks two things at the same time: "Do you favor year-round schools and longer school days?" The respondent may be confused if he or she agrees with one part of the question, but not the other.

There are several other pitfalls to be avoided. One of the most common is the *ambiguous* or *unclear question*. Here a problem results because the researcher and respondent are using different frames of reference. For example, a respondent may not understand a question that reads: "Is the principal doing a good job?" This question could be interpreted in many different ways because performance criteria are not identified.

Another concern is the *esoteric question*. This problem results from using words or concepts not understood by some or all of the respondents. For example, one superintendent surveyed parents about their support for year-round school calendars, but never described or defined the concept. Most parents simply failed to respond to the survey. Because education surveys are intended to obtain accurate data for the entire community, great care should be given to drafting questions in language that can be understood across social, economic, and cultural groups.

Response options also are another important consideration. A principal, for example, distributed a survey to parents asking "How long have you lived in this district?" A blank space was provided for the answer, but neither instructions nor response choices were listed. Consequently, the respondents answered in many different ways, ranging from exact quantitative data to very general statements (e.g., "a very long time"). As a result, the principal was unable to tabulate the answers. This principal should have provided a finite number of response choices (e.g., 1 year or less, 2 to 5 years, and 6 or more years). When establishing response choices, it is essential to consider the type of information needed. Also, the options need to be clear. An example of unclear choices would be this: from 0 to 10 years and 10 or more years. A person having lived in the district for 10 years could select either option.

Researchers obviously cannot respond to clarification questions raised by respondents using a written survey. For this reason, these instruments usually contain instructions and clarifying information, such as definitions of key terms. But such additions to a survey can cause problems. For example, clarifying information suggesting that a proposed program will result in cost savings may strongly influence the level of support for the program. For this reason, definitions and clarifications should be as neutral and accurate as possible.

Asking leading questions is another potential problem. These are questions designed to encourage the respondent to give the researcher answers he or she prefers. Most people resent being manipulated; therefore, even the mere suggestion of manipulation may result in a loss of trust and unreliable responses.

Conducting pilot studies—collecting data from a group of individuals who are similar to the targeted population—can be very helpful in survey research. Such studies, for instance, may reveal if certain survey questions are leading, ambiguous, or double-barreled. A pilot study also may uncover questions or wording that is or may be potentially offensive. Conversely, results from these studies may reveal the need to include additional questions in the survey before it is used with the targeted population. The effectiveness of a pilot study depends largely on whether the researcher selects a group of respondents who are reasonably similar to the targeted population. If a researcher's ultimate goal is to poll taxpayers in a school district, he or she must use a group of respondents in the pilot study who possess characteristics (e.g., income level, political persuasion, education level) representative of those taxpayers.

Administrators planning to use surveys should also consider the following:

◆ Respondents often believe that the researcher has an implied obligation to share the outcomes of the survey with them. For this reason, the researcher should inform participants regarding this matter at the time that their participation is requested. The AAPOR has set both ethical guidelines and scientific standards for reporting survey research findings. In addition to reporting the margin of error, seven other items should appear in a publication reporting survey results: *sample size, sponsor, response rate, dates when the data were collected, an accurate definition of the population, how respondents were contacted,* and *the precise wording of questions used in the survey.* See Babbie (1990) and McNamara (1994b) for more complete information about these topics.

◆ Because information gathered by public schools is almost always in the public domain, consideration should be given to how data will be analyzed and reported before they are collected.

◆ Survey instruments should be user-friendly. That is, they should be concise, clearly worded in language that the respondents can comprehend, and printed at a level of quality allowing respondents to read them without difficulty. Many respondents will elect not to complete a survey if it requires more than 10 minutes of their time or if it requires special effort.

◆ The purpose and importance of a survey need to be explained. In the case of education, such information often is a deciding factor in determining if a person will respond. If the project is quite large, purpose and importance can be conveyed to the entire population through press releases or public service announcements.

◆ Providing an envelope with postage (or a one-page fold-over form with postage) can be a determining factor in getting a respondent to complete and return a survey. Consequently, such return envelopes should be used in direct-mail surveys.

◆ Researchers should include an introductory letter to the survey that (a) states the purpose and importance of the study, (b) describes the conditions of anonymity (it is almost always preferable to provide anonymity unless there are ethical reasons not to do so), (c) explains how the results will be used, and (d) expresses appreciation for the respondent's cooperation.

QUALITATIVE RESEARCH STRATEGIES

There are numerous approaches to qualitative research, but this chapter will address two case studies and focus groups that may have the most practical use for school administrators:

Case studies and focus groups, both of which are usually conducted using open-ended interviews with individuals or groups, are also often used as an initial step in the design of a standardized instrument or a custom-made questionnaire to be used later in a social scientific survey. The use of focus groups, one of the prevalent methods for this activity, is explained in a number of research methodology books (e.g., Morgan, 1997; Stewart & Shamdasani, 1990).

Focus Groups

Janesick (2004) defines a focus group as "a group interview with a trained moderator, a specific set of questions, and a disciplined approach to studying ideas in a group context. The data from the focus group consist of the typed transcript of the group interaction" (p. 80). Focus groups, like all techniques, have strengths and weaknesses. People sometimes act differently and say different things in groups than when interviewed individually. This is not necessarily bad or good, just different. Sometimes the group interaction provides data and ideas that would not have come from observation or individual interviews, and other times individuals will withhold or modify what they would say. The researcher can observe how individuals interact, as well as analyzing the transcripts of what was said. A strength of focus groups is that researchers can be less obtrusive and allow the participants to interact about a topic, thereby reducing researcher bias effects.

In organizing the actual focus group sessions, the administrator needs to pay careful attention to details. Recording equipment must be checked to ensure it is working properly and to determine how well the sound is recorded from where each participant will sit. Extra batteries, tapes, and possibly a backup recording machine should be available in case something goes wrong. Many times focus group data are completely lost due to mechanical difficulties. The presence of an assistant to handle the recording or deal with other distractions can be of great help. Another area of concern for the administrator is making sure a sufficient number of people are present at the focus group in order to have the type of interaction that is sought. If a group of 6 to 8 people is desired, it is often a good idea to invite 7 to 9 or 10, especially if they are busy professionals. It is a good practice to send letters verifying the date, time, location, and so on and then make a reminder telephone call a day or two prior to the session.

The moderator of the session needs to have some skill working with people so as to get the quiet participants to express themselves and not allow the vocal participants to dominate. Another difficult task for the moderator is to lead the discussion in a way that obtains useful data without overly influencing the discussion. Even a simple nodding of the head with a big smile or a comment of approval such as "that is exactly what I think" or "fantastic" (or, conversely, a comment of disapproval) can greatly change the type of data some groups will provide. The moderator must be prepared and should have thought out what types of probes he or she may want to use (or not use) to keep the conversation going.

Once the focus group is done and the data are transcribed, the analysis can proceed in a manner similar to phases 2 through 4, described below in the section on case studies. Where emergent themes are identified, the participants are asked if the themes make sense to them and then a written report is prepared for use in making organizational decisions.

Case Studies

Using the first two concepts of Simon's (1977) decision model, a case study focusing on collaboration between schools and universities is developed here to demonstrate how data can be collected, analyzed, and reported. The two concepts are an *intelligence activity*, which focuses on problem-defining tasks, and a *design activity*, which focuses on problem-solving tasks.

In keeping with the rich historical overview provided by Lancy (1993), most social science researchers and program evaluators acknowledge the case study to be an integral part of the qualitative research tradition. Along with Stenhouse (1985) and Patton (2002), Lancy argues that case studies conducted in educational research share a common purpose: They all address directly the improvement of practice. Accordingly, case studies in education are designed to influence important educational policy decisions.

Yin (1984) suggests that the case study has at least four applications:

1. *Explaining* relationships in interventions that are too complex for survey or experimental strategies,
2. *Describing* the real-life context in which an intervention has occurred,
3. *Creating* a rich illustration or journalistic account of an intervention, and
4. *Exploring* situations where a promising intervention has no clear, single inventory of outcomes.

Setting Up the Case Study.   Over the past decade, school and university collaborative arrangements have been undertaken as a means to bridge the gap between theory and practice, as well as the gap between public schools and teacher training. Assume that education school professors and public school practitioners in a single district have recently agreed to conduct joint research and development projects. Also assume that the university collaborators were asked explicitly by their school district colleagues to take the lead in two areas: *designing* the organizational governance structure for the partnership and *identifying* promising cooperative research and development projects.

One way the university collaborators can be responsive, but not prescriptive, is to use the case study as a decision tool to uncover *how* school district practitioners partners would prefer to interact with key players in the collaborative and *what* real-world problems these school partners would like to research together.

In the case study offered below, the superintendent was chosen to be the school partner whose views were to be collected, analyzed, and ultimately shared with those having the responsibility for shaping a productive partnership. Obviously, other school partner case study efforts could be (and more than likely would be) conducted following the four-phase strategy elaborated below. Put briefly, these phases are collecting the data, analyzing the data, verifying the findings, and sharing the report.

Using the Case Study in Decision Making.
Phase 1: Collecting the Data. The collaborating school district superintendent was interviewed on a Friday morning. The interview started at 9:15 and was concluded at 10:15. A semistructured instrument was used, containing a few general questions designed to elicit the superintendent's perspectives on school and university collaboration in her school district. What follows is a transcript of the interview.

Question: What role do you (as superintendent) play in school-university collaboration in your district?

First, I want to make it clear that any collaboration between the school and university must be a good fit with our district's mission. I want to assure you that *all* of our students receive the best education—not just a select few.

Question: How do you interact with key players in the collaboration? What communication strategies do you use?

My role involves setting up communication channels that are formal. For example, it is my understanding that there is a subgroup—namely, the Administration Council (10 key players in our collaborative)—that is cochaired by my assistant superintendent for instruction. He informs me about the goings-on of the collaborative, and I in turn keep the school board updated.

Question: How do you do this—communicate with the board, that is?

I brought this idea with me from my last superintendency in [another city]. I personally write a formal update of issues to be shared with the board in a weekly written report called *Board Notes*. Board notes are separated into two categories. One includes ongoing activities that the board needs to know about—such as details about what is happening at our partnership middle school. The other focuses on separate issues that require board action. I have a senior administrative staff member who helps me on this. This is my way of informing *all* board members. In other words, *no* single board member receives information that is not provided to other board members. This is a kind of one-on-one, almost face-to-face communication strategy. It avoids the common problem that many superintendents have when some board members receive more information than others do. I also have a CONFIDENTIAL stamp that I use for information that should not go beyond their purview. This way we have a common level of understanding about confidentiality.

Question: Do you have a screening procedure for collaboration with the university?

Yes, we are now involved with another collaborative at a second partnership school (an elementary school that is operating as a professional development school). This partnership will involve a host of projects that must be screened. My assistant superintendent for instruction will be responsible for this. Again, let me say that collaboration ventures are messy, and I understand and welcome that.

Question: What do you mean by "messy"?

Any effort to change the way things have always been done is messy. If we expect innovation, then we have to be able to tolerate ambiguity, and I have a high tolerance for ambiguity. However, I know when to draw the line. If I believe that any of these programs is counter to our mission, then I put a halt to it.

Question: What are your thoughts on the university's ultimate goal—to involve other professionals from health care and human services in the collaboration?

I feel that this will take time, and I'll tell you why. There is some confusion among parents and board members about issues like condom distribution. That's the bottom line. Sadly enough, whenever parents hear about health services coming into the school, they believe that their morals will be compromised. This is unfortunate because our goal is to have students coming to school ready to learn, and they can't do this when they aren't healthy—physically or mentally healthy. In my last superintendency, we had a health center located on our high school campus. It worked beautifully. The students who used it were for the most part—and I mean about 95%—students that had stomachaches, sore throats, toothaches, and so on. Normally, they would stay home for at least a day, and in the case of sore throats, they'd be out for a week if an infection occurred. This way, with a health center, they came to school knowing they'd get help. They'd miss only an hour or so of school. Schools need to take the position that a health center facilitates bringing service to where the customer is. We can serve kids best by keeping them in school. This is why stores like Randall's have film developing and flower delivery services located right in the store. It's good business!

Question: Do you see moving toward full-service schools anytime soon?

This will take time. We need to work on our constituency. Educate them. Get them to understand the need. They must understand that schools are not insular. [The city where I previously had a superintendency] already has networks with a variety of other groups. I realize, though, that this community is conservative and will reject this move. We need to build trust, explain that only a small number of cases deal with the issues they fear most.

Question: Do you have any other concerns that you want to discuss about the superintendent's role in collaboration?

Yes. The district and the university need to get together and sit down and say we won't have things done the way they're being done in the language arts area. Our students deserve a better program—not one where reading and writing and grammar are separated into different classes. I see this as urgent and critical. It's a travesty that these subjects are taught separately. We must put a stop to it. This idea of separate subjects is one of the keenest instructional issues I've had to face.

Question: Why is it so difficult to change? Can't you just demand a change?

Again, here is something that will take time and training. I was shocked at the initial response I received when I proposed an instructional change with teachers. One teacher actually said, "We see ourselves as grammarians, not as remedial teachers." They confuse reading classes with remediation—a carryover from the past. We are giving one more year to allow teachers to adjust to the idea of teaching in another way. We'll provide training. We'll seek a waiver for certification problems, and we'll provide a safety net for teachers. But change they must!

Question: Do you see collaboration with the university as helping with this?

Yes. Together maybe we can change teacher attitudes. We need to sit down together—all of us—[this city], the university, *and* [another major city in the region that also has its own independent school district]. We need to show teachers and principals evidence that these areas—reading, writing, literature, grammar—are interdependent. They must be taught together, not in unrelated packages. We want our schools to produce clear thinkers, and one way to do this is to provide students with more than we presently offer. This is our challenge. [End of the formal interview.]

Phase 2: Analyzing the Data. In analyzing the data from the superintendent's interview, the case study researcher uncovered six emergent themes that help clarify how the superintendent views her role in school and university collaborations:

1. *Promoting the district's mission.* The superintendent is clear about the necessity for a good fit between university goals and the mission of the district. As superintendent, she believes her role is to ensure that the district's mission is the driving force behind collaborative activities.

2. *Respecting community values.* The superintendent respects the values and beliefs of all stakeholders in her community. She understands that community values cannot be compromised. Implementing collaborative programs involving health care and human services in the schools will work *only if* the community believes that the effort is meaningful.

3. *Communicating with the school board.* The superintendent's role includes following an organized strategy for informing board members about collaborative activities. In addition to meeting with them monthly, she sends each board member a weekly copy of the *Board Notes*.

4. *Defining problems.* The superintendent's role as problem definer is reflected in her description of the instructional changes that she hopes to implement. Although she welcomes input from university personnel, it is clear that she will *not* allow them to dictate what changes are necessary in district classrooms.

5. *Empowering key players.* The superintendent's role in collaboration includes sharing power with her assistant superintendent for instruction, administrative council members, principals, and teachers. In accordance with this role, the superintendent promotes staff development and other workshops for training teachers. Her goal is to encourage teachers to assume ownership and leadership in efforts toward change. She is sensitive and responsive to their concerns.

6. *Reaping benefits.* The superintendent sees school and university collaboration as a way to effect positive change in teaching and learning in her district. For example, she suggests that a collaborative effort is an excellent way to solve the school district's instructional problem regarding the need to integrate reading, literature, writing, and language arts. It is also of interest to note that she believes collaboration efforts can involve several school districts working together with the university to solve problems of mutual interest. For example, in the interview she suggests that both her school district and the other major school district in the region might join with the university to work on a curriculum project devoted to integrating instruction in reading, literature, writing, and language arts.

Reanalysis of these six themes indicates that they are consistent with the literature on successful collaboration. Most important among these themes is the superintendent's insistence that school-university collaboration be based on a shared vision of the outcomes to be produced by their joint efforts.

Phase 3: Verifying the Findings. Once the initial draft of the case study report is prepared, the next step is to share this written record with the superintendent, who should verify the accuracy of both the interview text and the themes that were uncovered in the analysis of the data.[4] Also to be accomplished in this are two important steps. First, the superintendent

---

[4]In naturalistic inquiries, the verification activities described here are seen as "carrying out a member check." The purpose of a member check is not only to test for factual and interpretative accuracy, but also to provide evidence of credibility (a criterion of quality research analogous to internal validity in conventional quantitative studies such as scientific surveys). On member checks, see especially Lincoln and Guba (1985, chap. 11) and Erlandson, Harris, Skipper, and Allen (1993, chap. 7).

and the case study researcher should discuss any special circumstances (ethical and legal issues) that might require revision before the report is shared in a public meeting.[5] Second, once the case study report is revised and meets with the approval of both the university researcher and the school district superintendent, the researcher should exercise professional courtesy and formally request the superintendent's permission to go public with the final draft of the report. Going public at this point means sharing the case study report with school district and university collaborators.

Phase 4: Sharing the Report. When the case study is used as a decision tool, it is essential that the report be written and shared with the intended audience. In many circumstances, the format used to report case study results can vary. For example, Merriam (1997) suggests that one might consider executive summaries or specialized condensations. Yin (1984) offers another suggestion: Replace the narrative with a set of open-ended questions and answers drawn from the data.

For this case study on the superintendent's position regarding school-university collaboration, the report probably should remain in the format presented here. Accordingly, the first part of the report is in question-and-answer form (using the actual semistructured questions raised in the interview), and the second part provides brief analytic summaries of themes uncovered in data analysis. To maximize the value of this information in a planning work session, the case study report should be distributed to work session participants about a week prior to the actual session. Moreover, having the superintendent present as a participant in the session is advantageous.

Essential Characteristics of a Case Study.   The unique value of the case study as a decision tool can be recognized by reflecting on its essential characteristics. Merriam (1997) has pointed out four properties of case studies that are especially important:

1. *They are particularistic.* This implies that case studies focus on a particular situation, event, program, individual, or group. They can suggest to the reader what to do or what not to do. They can concentrate on a specific instance, but illuminate a general problem or outcome.
2. *They are descriptive.* This implies that case studies yield a rich description of the event or entity being investigated. They can illustrate the complexities of a situation, identify differences in opinion on an issue, and suggest how these differences might influence the actual decision reached. Most importantly, they can describe the views of a wide array of organizational stakeholders.
3. *They are heuristic.* This implies that case studies extend the reader's understanding of the issue or entity selected for inquiry. Accordingly, they can explain the reason for a problem, lead to the discovery of new relationships, verify (or negate) an informed speculation, and most importantly, explain why an innovative program worked or failed to work.

---

[5]See especially the treatment of the issues of validity, reliability, and ethics in qualitative case study research in Merriam (1997, chap. 10).

4. *They are inductive.* This implies that case studies rely on inductive reasoning. As such, they begin with the collection of data (empirical observations of interest) and then identify theoretical categories and patterns (trends or propositions) from relationships uncovered in data analysis.

Two additional points deserve mention. First, the case study does not claim any particular method for either data collection or data analysis. However, qualitative methods are most often chosen in conducting case studies because researchers or policy analysts are primarily interested in insight, discovery, and interpretation, rather than in testing hypotheses or estimating parameters. Second, it should be kept in mind that the case study is just one of many qualitative decision tools that can be used to inform administrative decision making.

SUMMARY

Three essential ideas were advanced in this chapter. First, both the social scientific survey (a quantitative method) and the case study (a qualitative method) can serve as decision tools for administrative decision making. Second, collecting data and then analyzing them are necessary activities, but not sufficient in themselves to inform decision making. These two essential functions must be followed by a formal effort to prepare and share a written report that effectively communicates the findings of the inquiry to the intended audience. Third, the decision-making tools discussed in this chapter can be used by administrators to create a shared vision, design a plan of action, and evaluate progress toward agreed-on goals.

Administrators interested in taking the lead in the use of modern decision tools in districts and schools should heed the words of Machiavelli (1950) in *The Prince*.

There is nothing more difficult to carry out, nor more doubtful of success, nor more dangerous to handle that to initiate a new order of things. For the reformer has enemies in all those who profit by the old order, and only lukewarm defenders in all those who would profit under new order. (p. 21)

QUESTIONS AND SUGGESTED ACTIVITIES

CASE STUDY

1. You were just hired last month as principal of the John F. Kennedy Elementary School. A local state university that has an excellent record of collaborating with school districts is located just 20 minutes from your school. Given the problems described in the case study, Jane West, the director of communication, has expressed an interest in having you and the field studies research group from the local university conduct a needs assessment for the district.

    You meet with Dr. West and learn that the needs assessment must answer two policy questions: What percentage of the families with school-age children residing within the Kennedy attendance boundaries are interested in participating in a year-round school program? Do the families express a preference for a type of year-round calendar (e.g., single track or multiple track)? In addition, Dr. West lets you know that she is agreeable to using both a social scientific survey and a set of case studies to explore these two policy questions in detail.

With this information in hand, you agree to prepare a two-page needs assessment proposal elaborating a specific research plan for the Lancaster School District and forward it to Dr. West. Prepare the proposal. You may include some draft questions (as an appendix) and the rationale for each question that you think could provide useful data for your decisions.

2. Was Dr. West properly prepared for the meeting with parents? Why or why not?
3. Why did so many parents elect not to fill out the survey?
4. Invite an educational research methods professor to join one of your PR classes. Prior to the professor's visit, each student should develop at least one question to ask the professor about collecting, analyzing, and reporting data for a district or school.
5. What are some common errors that can be made in constructing questions for a survey?
6. What is a focus group? What are the purposes of a focus group?
7. What are some of the advantages and disadvantages of conducting face-to-face interviews?
8. Should a researcher always convey the purposes and importance of a study to potential respondents? Why or why not?
9. What is the basic difference between quantitative and qualitative data?

SUGGESTED READINGS

Bradburn, N. M., & Sudman, S. (1988). *Polls and surveys: Understanding what they tell us*. San Francisco: Jossey-Bass.

Carbonaro, M., & Bainbridge, J. (2000). Design and development of a process for Web-based survey research. *Alberta Journal of Educational Research, 46*(4), 392–394.

Jacobs, L. R., & Shapiro, R. Y. (1996). Toward the integrated study of political communications, public opinion, and the policy-making process. *PS: Political Science & Politics, 29*(1), 10–13.

Jaeger, R. M. (1984). *Sampling in education and the social sciences*. New York: Longman.

Krejcie, R. V., & Morgan, D. A. (1970). Determining sample size for research activity. *Educational & Psychological Measurement, 30*(6), 607–610.

McNamara, J. F. (1994). *Surveys and experiments in education research*. Lancaster, PA: Technomic.

McNamara, J. F. (1997). Parental views on the biggest problems facing public schools: National versus local findings. *International Journal of Educational Reform, 6*(3), 377–389.

Merriam, S. B. (1997). *Qualitative research and case study applications in education* (revised and expanded from *Case study research in education*). San Francisco: Jossey-Bass.

Newman, I., & Benz, C. R. (1998). *Qualitative-quantitative research methodology: Exploring the interactive continuum*. Carbondale: Southern Illinois University Press.

Tacheny, S. A. (1997). Polls are useful: Yes, no, or maybe? *Educational Leadership, 54*(5), 49–51.

REFERENCES

Austin, E. W., & Pinkleton, B. E. (2001). *Strategic public relations management: Planning and managing effective communication programs*. Mahwah, NJ: Lawrence Erlbaum.

Babbie, E. (1990). *Survey research methods* (2nd ed.). Belmont, CA: Wadsworth.

Bradburn, N. M., & Sudman, S. (1988). *Polls and surveys: Understanding what they tell us*. San Francisco: Jossey-Bass.

Erlandson, D. A., Harris, E. L., Skipper, B. L., & Allen, S. D. (1993). *Doing naturalistic inquiry: A guide to methods*. Newbury Park, CA: Sage.

Janesick, V. J. (2004). *"Stretching" exercises for qualitative researchers* (2nd ed.). Thousand Oaks, CA: Sage.

Jones, R. A., & Beck, S. E. (1996). *Decision making in nursing*. Albany, NY: Delmar.

Krathwohl, D. R. (1998). *Methods of educational and social science research: An integrated approach* (2nd ed.). New York: Longman.

Lancy, D. F. (1993). *Qualitative research in education: An introduction to the major traditions*. New York: Longman.

Lincoln, Y. S., & Guba, E. G. (1985). *Naturalistic inquiry*. Newbury Park, CA: Sage.

Machiavelli, N. (1950). *The prince and the discourses* (L. Ricci, trans.). New York: Random House.

McNamara, J. F. (1991). Statistical power in educational research. *National Forum of Applied Educational Research Journal, 3*(2), 23–26.

McNamara, J. F. (1993b). Administrative decision making: Part one. *International Journal of Educational Reform, 2*(4), 465–474.

McNamara, J. F. (1994a). Administrative decision making: Part two. *International Journal of Educational Reform, 3*(1), 113–121.

McNamara, J. F. (1994b). *Surveys and experiments in education research*. Lancaster, PA: Technomic.

McNamara, J. F., & Chisolm, G. B. (1988). The technical tools of decision making. In N. J. Boyan (Ed.), *Handbook of research on educational administration* (pp. 525–567). New York: Longman.

Merriam, S. B. (1997). *Qualitative research and case study applications in education* (revised and expanded from *Case study research in education*). San Francisco: Jossey-Bass.

Morgan, D. L. (1997). *Focus groups as qualitative research* (2nd ed.). Thousand Oaks, CA: Sage.

O'Shea, D. W. (1992). Survey design. In M. C. Alkin (Ed.), *Encyclopedia of educational research* (6th ed., pp. 1323–1331). New York: Macmillan.

Patton, M. Q. (2002). *Qualitative research and evaluation methods* (3rd ed.). Thousand Oaks, CA: Sage.

Sheaffer, R. L., Mendenhall, W., & Ott, L. (2006). *Elementary survey sampling* (6th ed.). Florence, KY: Brooks/Cole.

Simon, H. A. (1977). *The new science of management decision* (rev. ed.). Englewood Cliffs, NJ: Prentice Hall.

Stenhouse, L. (1985). A note on case study and educational practice. In R. G. Burgess (Ed.), *Field methods in the study of education* (pp. 263–271). London: Falmer Press.

Stewart, D. W., & Shamdasani, P. N. (1990). *Focus groups: Theory and practice*. Newbury Park, CA: Sage.

Williams, B. (1978). *A sampler on sampling*. New York: Wiley.

Yin, R. K. (1984). *Case study research: Design and methods*. Newbury Park, CA: Sage.

CHAPTER 13

Developing and Executing a Successful Funding Campaign

Glenn Graham
Gordon Wise

CASE STUDY: LEARNING FROM THE MARKET

Residents of a suburban school district defeated a $10.5 million bond issue by a vote of 64% against, 36% for. The bond had included the following components:

♦ An addition to the present middle school, which would permit all sixth, seventh, and eighth graders to attend one facility;
♦ The removal of asbestos from the elementary schools and the middle school;
♦ The addition of locker and training rooms for boys and girls at the high school;
♦ The remodeling of the elementary schools to add classrooms and increase energy conservation;
♦ The addition of a gymnasium/multipurpose room at the high school; and
♦ The addition of instructional facilities—library/media center, art room, music room, science labs—at the high school.

Before putting any further bond issues on the ballot, the school board decided to conduct a market survey and use the results to guide a new campaign. A survey instrument was developed, and a sample of 300 households was chosen for door-to-door interviews. The survey question and results are shown in Table 13–1.

When district staff projected the vote for different combinations of the six bond components, they came up with the figures shown in Table 13–2.

TABLE 13–1
Survey Question and Results

Which of the components from the previous bond campaign did you consider *Indispensable, Very Important, Somewhat Important,* or *Not Important?**

Component	Indispensable	Very Important	Somewhat Important	Not Important
Addition to middle school	18	35	32	15
Asbestos removal	59	23	10	7
Locker and training rooms	7	25	42	26
Remodeling elementary schools	22	43	28	7
Gym/multipurpose room	3	13	36	48
Additional instructional facilities	14	38	32	15

All numbers are percentages; lines two and six total only 99 percent due to the rounding of the percentages.

In analyzing the results, the district found that the top five factors encouraging a positive vote were as follows:

1. Explain *why* money is needed and *how* it will be spent.
2. Allow elementary schoolchildren to attend a neighborhood school.
3. Eliminate overcrowding at the elementary schools.

4. Prepare for growth in enrollment.

5. Avoid cost increases that will accompany a wait-and-see stance.

Analysis also revealed that the top five factors encouraging a negative vote were these:

1. Building now will increase property taxes.

2. The information from the last campaign was not sufficient.

3. New industrial property has been tax-abated.

4. Renovation of the board of education building last year was unnecessary.

5. The operation of new or expanded schools is bound to increase property taxes.

TABLE 13–2
Projecting the Vote

Component Combinations	Cost ($ million)	% For
All six components as before	10.5	28.6
Build new middle school	6.5	36.3
Build new middle school and remove asbestos	7.8	37.9
Remodel elementary schools, build addition to middle school, and remove asbestos	5.3	40.6
Remodel elementary schools and build addition to middle school	4.0	39.7

One of the most critical tests of public relations (PR) activities conducted by and for public schools comes at those inevitable times when the schools must turn to the community of voters for financial support. In most of the United States, the level of state financial support has failed to keep pace with increases in the cost of public education. In recent years, many states have made substantial cuts in financial support. Increasingly costly and rigorous mandates for programs and facilities are commonly thrust on schools, typically without accompanying budgets to fund them.

All this leads to more frequent trips by the schools to the public funding well. In most states, such a trip is successful *only* if the voters in the district approve some form of tax levy or bond issue. It is in this all-too-common and frequently dreary scenario that PR activities (both long term and short term) are vital.

Let it be said up front that a school district that reaches for its PR tools only at times when a funding referendum approaches is not worthy of the support of its community. A basic theme of this entire book, and certainly of this chapter, is that an effective PR effort must be *ongoing*. The promotion and PR efforts undertaken during funding campaigns will ideally reinforce, support, and supplement the regular links already in place between the community and the schools.

MARKETING VERSUS SELLING

The ongoing PR effort, including those activities used during funding campaigns, should be an integral part of a broader marketing commitment of the schools. In the past (and, sadly, too often at present), schools have tended toward a more traditional selling approach in their promotional efforts, which may include some nod toward the PR area.

Schools that are the most successful at funding campaigns are also the most successful at discerning the differences between marketing and selling approaches. When "selling," the attempt is to "get rid of what one has"—for example, the grocer who has a surplus of produce needs to "sell" it to the buyer to get it off his or her hands. "Marketing" is having what one "knows one can get rid of."

This distinction may sound overly simple, but the difference is profound. In the former (selling) posture, the focus is on the *product* (the program, the curriculum, the levy campaign) in an effort to convince the *market* (students, parents, voters) that they must accept or vote for that product. In the latter (marketing) posture, the focus is on the market. Here the primary efforts are devoted to determining what constitutes "value" to that market: What are its needs, wants, and desires? What perceptions and expectations does that market have? Then—and only then—does the school district that practices a marketing approach attempt to put together its product. This revised focus allows the astute marketer to combine the resources he or she controls into a bundle of satisfactions that has the best chance of gaining acceptance from the market.

THE FOUR P'S OF MARKETING

The marketing tools used by a school district are very similar to the marketing tools used by a business firm. They include the following:

1. The *product*, or the "bundle of satisfactions" developed from the resources the organization controls.
2. The *price*, or the sacrifice of resources required to access that bundle of satisfactions. This may be found in fees and taxes, but also in time, effort, and energy provided to the school district by the person who chaperones the band bus or the prom or who serves at a PTA function.
3. The *promotion*, or the application of both personal and nonpersonal efforts to expand awareness, interest, and support for the product. This area of marketing encompasses the PR effort.
4. The *place* (physical distribution), or the actual delivery of the bundle of satisfactions. Schools find "place" activities in such areas as boundaries, districts, bus routes, and the grouping of students or classes. (Should the sixth grade be in the elementary school or in the middle/junior high school?)

The successful ongoing marketing program of a school uses these tools in appropriate and often-changing proportions to develop and direct its *controllable* marketing efforts in response to those *uncontrollable* variables it must confront. Included in those uncontrollables are such things as changing populations and demographics; the emergence of "competitors" (private schooling, home schooling, and open enrollment, as well as anything that competes for the time and resources the school would normally attract from its students, parents, and taxpayers); and the wide range of environmental variables (economic, sociocultural, legal–public policy) that can thwart the objectives of the schools. (The authors have treated this subject in greater depth in a specialized article addressing the need for school administrators to adopt an ongoing total marketing approach. See Graham and Wise, 1990.)

THE SCOUTING REPORT AND GAME PLAN

Consider approaching a campaign for a school tax levy or bond issue as a coach approaches an upcoming game. You scout the opposition, ascertain its strengths and weaknesses, and from this scouting report, develop a game plan to achieve victory.

Preparing the Market Report

The "scouting report" here is a survey of the market—the voting-age population of the school district. The market survey method that works best is the door-to-door, structured, personal interview. This format is preferred over mail or telephone surveys for several reasons:

1. With mail surveys, one risks hearing primarily extreme positions and not those in the middle, yet those in the middle are often critical to the campaign's success.
2. The response rate of mail surveys is notoriously low—usually about 20%.
3. With both mail and telephone surveys, it is much more difficult to tell if respondents are being honest.
4. Many people react negatively to telephone surveys, and this disposition might translate into a negative vote.

In a structured interview, all questions are predetermined; the interviewer merely reads them and records interviewee responses. Because the campaign strategies and tactics—that is, the game plan—depend on the information obtained from these interviews, they must be carefully planned.

Initially, a school district committee consisting of school administrators and board members should meet to determine components of the interview. This committee might ask itself: Are specific school programs to be evaluated? Are attitudes to be evaluated? What are the issues that influence people to vote "Yes" or "No"? What demographics should be obtained?

Following this process, three or four focus groups should be convened from a cross section of the voting-age population of the school district. In order to gather input from all segments of the community, the composition of the focus groups should be at least as diverse as that of the community. The authors typically provide the following checklist to clients to assist them in creating the greatest possible diversity in the focus groups: Each focus group should have from 8 to 12 people. Included in the total composition of all groups should be representatives from

- ◆ Both genders
- ◆ All age groups (high school students through senior adults)
- ◆ Clergy
- ◆ Service providers (e.g., barbers and hairdressers)
- ◆ School personnel (staff, teachers, administration)
- ◆ Professionals (attorneys, doctors, dentists)
- ◆ School critics (we need to hear from this side of the issue)
- ◆ The various geographic regions of the school district
- ◆ Racial/ethnic groups
- ◆ Politicians
- ◆ Realtors
- ◆ People who do and do not have children in school

In recruiting focus group members, it is critical to issue invitations in person or by telephone. *Do not* simply send a letter to prospective participants. They should be invited to come and share not only their perceptions, concerns, issues, and so forth, but also those of the people with whom they have contact. Persons who commit to participate should be given the dates and times of the focus group sessions and then be allowed to choose a session convenient to them. A follow-up letter of confirmation should be sent, followed by a reminder phone call the day before the focus group session. (Always remember to send a thank-you note following their participation.)

There should be two focus group leaders to take notes and keep the discussion going (Wise & Graham, 1993; Wise, Graham, & McCammon, 1994). Encourage honest, open dialogue; no tape recorders or video recorders should be used. With two people taking notes, not much will be missed. Some focus group questions might include the following: What are the strengths and weaknesses of the schools in this district? Why was the operating levy defeated in the last election? What reasons do people give for being for or against the upcoming levy? An hour to an hour and a half of open-ended discussion should generate many positive and negative concerns from focus group members. This input provides the basic ingredients for the structured interview.

The structured interview should utilize forced-choice items: The interviewer reads a statement to which the interviewee responds according to a scale, such as strongly agree, agree, neutral, disagree, or strongly disagree. This type of response mode is good for obtaining attitudes toward the schools and school programs. In the next section of this chapter, there is a discussion of how two other types of forced-choice items are used to deal with positive and negative perceptions.

Once the first draft of the interview guide has been prepared, it should be shared with the school committee for possible revisions. The next step is to select about 10 people to field-test the interview. These persons should be handed the instrument so that they have an opportunity to discuss the questions and to ensure that the content is clear and unbiased. The final version of the interview guide evolves from this process. An interview should take about 15 to 20 minutes, and it is always advisable to field-test the instrument before actually doing the survey. Before administering the survey, interviewers need to be trained so they are thoroughly familiar with it.

It is critical that interviewers understand their role is reaching into the community for information. The following "ten commandments" for interviewers should be considered as guidelines:

1. Go to neighborhoods where you are not known. Do not interview friends, relatives, or acquaintances.

2. Read through the survey questions several times until you are thoroughly familiar with them. Do a few practice interviews before starting with the real ones.

3. Do not discuss the results of your interviews with anyone except those analyzing the results. If word gets out about what was said or who said it, the credibility of the survey is compromised.

4. Be courteous. The respondents will view you as an extension of the schools. Your actions could possibly affect how someone will vote.

5. Do not express agreement or disagreement with the respondents' answers. Assure them there are no right or wrong answers; your only function is to record their answers.

6. Do not campaign. If a respondent is negative, so be it. Do not try to change his or her mind during the interview. The campaign comes later.

7. Avoid nonverbal and body language cues. Do not smile when they say something you like and frown when they say something you don't. Be pleasant and noncommittal.

8. If someone refuses to be interviewed, be gracious and do not plead. Thank the person and leave. If someone is hesitant, explain the importance of the survey and ensure anonymity. If suspicious, suggest he or she call the police and verify your legitimacy.

9. Keep a count of the number of refusals. These may be indicative of a negative attitude toward the bond or levy.

10. Be sure to record the demographic data on your sample. Those who analyze the survey data not only want to tabulate the percentage of responses to each question, but also need to be able to cross-tabulate answers by demographics: Do men and women respond differently? Are there differences depending on age? Do registered voters differ from those who are unregistered? Are there differences between high- and low-income neighborhoods?

The names of the interviewers should be given to the local police department, and interviewers should wear an identification badge when collecting data. Should anyone be concerned about the survey, the interviewer can suggest that the police be called for verification. This will help the interviewer access people who might otherwise refuse to be interviewed.

Interviewees should be selected as randomly as possible. One approach is the stratified random sample. This can be done by dividing the school district into voting blocks (precincts or townships). Using results from the last two or three school votes—for example, board elections or referenda—determine what proportion of the total vote came from each voting block. If, for example, 4% of the vote came from precinct 1A, then 4% of the sample should come from 1A. Next, number all the streets and roads in *each* precinct, starting at 1 each time. Using a table of random numbers (which can be found in most statistics texts or can be computer-generated), select the streets and roads for your sample. Each time the street number comes up in the table, select one residence from it. A residence can be a house, apartment, or mobile home. For example, if Plum Street is number 15 on the list, and 15 occurs in the random number table, then pick a residence on Plum Street; should 15 occur again, pick a second residence. Which *specific* residence is picked is up to the interviewer, for if no one is at home at one location or if a person refuses to be interviewed, the interviewer can go to another residence on the same street. If no interview can be obtained on the street selected, the interviewer should go to the next closest street.

The size of the sample to be interviewed depends on the population of the school district and the amount of error with which the district is comfortable. Typically, in school districts of 5,000 to 100,000, sample sizes will range from about 300 to 400 people, for an error rate of plus or minus 5%.

Identifying and Dealing with Positive and Negative Perceptions

Identifying the Issues That Influence a Vote.   Using the focus groups as the source, an administrator can identify the issues that potentially have a positive influence (encourage a vote for the levy or bond) or a negative influence (encourage a vote against the levy or bond). These issues are incorporated into the market survey by means of a statement such as this:

> In any levy (bond) election, there are certain issues that may influence you to vote for it, some issues that may influence you to vote against it, and some issues that would have no influence on how you vote. For each of the following, please tell me if it would
>
> 1. Influence you to *vote for* the levy (bond).
> 2. Have *no influence* on how you would vote.
> 3. Influence you to *vote against* the levy (bond).

The interviewee is then handed a sheet with the preceding response options, and each of the issues is read. Once the list of issues has been covered, each issue can be classified as positive, negative, or a nonissue. But if the administrator stopped at this point, he or she would miss a crucial piece of the information—that is, the *relative strength* of each issue. Which issues will have the *most influence* on positive or negative votes? After the list of issues has had its initial reading, the interviewer proceeds to give these directions:

> I am going to show you the issues from this list that you picked as influencing you to vote for the levy (bond). Of these issues, which is the *single most important* in influencing you to vote for the levy (bond). [Pause] Which is the *second most important?* [Pause] Which is the *third most important?* [Pause] Now I'm going to show you those issues you picked as influencing you to vote against the levy (bond). Of these issues, which is the *single most important* in influencing you to vote against the levy (bond). [Pause] Which is the *second most important?* [Pause] Which is the *third most important?*

Weight each of the ranks, giving 3 points to issues ranked "most important," 2 points to "second most important," and 1 point to "third most important." Total the points for the positive issues and for the negative issues. From these, the top five or six of each of the positive and negative issues become the issues that should drive the campaign.

Dealing with the Positive and Negative Issues.   In the words of an old song, you must now "accentuate the positive" and "eliminate the negative." To eliminate the negative does not mean to ignore the negative issues and hope they will go away. Those issues influencing a "No" vote need to be explained carefully and honestly in order to weaken their impact. For example, although people do not want to pay more taxes, they typically like increased property values. By emphasizing a nexus between the quality of schools and increased property values, the impact of the tax increase may appear less severe.

The lists of top issues should serve as a screen for any campaign materials, whether they are ads, brochures, or letters to the editor. After all, these are the issues that community members have said will influence their vote; therefore, all campaign materials should focus on these. If at least one of the top positive or top negative issues is not addressed, then that campaign material should not be used.

Projecting the Election Outcome

Many school systems have run campaigns based on a false optimism that is trampled by harsh reality on Election Day. Afterward district leaders will hear comments from the campaign committee such as "But they told us they'd vote for it!" The problem may have been that the questions were asked in the wrong way. Take the question "Will you vote for or against the levy (bond)?" This question requires a socially acceptable answer; most people will not admit that they intend to vote against the schools. Therefore, a question designed to help project the voting outcome must allow the respondent to say "No" in a socially acceptable way. The question could have been phrased as follows:

If an election were held today, and you were asked to vote on a 5 million levy to increase property taxes to support operating expenses of our school district, how would you most likely vote:

1. I would *certainly vote for* the levy.
2. I would *almost certainly vote for* the levy.
3. I would *probably vote for* the levy.
4. I am *uncertain* as to how I would vote.
5. I would *probably vote against* the levy.
6. I would *almost certainly vote against* the levy.
7. I would *certainly vote against* the levy.

People who respond that they will "certainly vote for" have put themselves on the line, and in most cases, they will be supportive. In projecting the vote, 90% of those who give this response can be believed. If they choose the "almost certainly vote for" option, they are hedging a bit; 60 or 70% of these responses can be believed. (If more than 30% of those asked to be interviewed refuse to do so, use the 60% value.)

Those who respond "probably vote for" will probably vote against. This is one of the socially acceptable "No" options. Such persons have passed over two more positive options to give this response. When projecting the vote, 30 or 40% of these respondents can be expected to vote for the tax. (Use the lower percentage if more than 30% have refused to be interviewed.) Those who are "uncertain" really aren't uncertain; they will almost certainly vote "no." When projecting this vote, only 10 or 20% of these respondents can be expected to vote for the tax. Obviously those who say they will vote against are to be believed.

The projection of those voting for is found by adding the following: (1) 0.90 times the number of people responding "certainly vote for"; (2) 0.60 or 0.70 times the number responding "almost certainly vote for"; (3) 0.30 or 0.40 times the number responding "probably vote for"; and (4) 0.10 or 0.20 times the number responding "uncertain." This sum is then divided by the total number of all responses to give the proportion projected as positive votes (Graham, Wise, & Bachman, 1990; Wise et al., 1994).

Although there is no highly scientific or mathematical defense for the percentages used, experience provides support for their validity. The procedure rarely projects less than 30% voting for, which is consistent with election results. Also, in those elections where little or no campaign was conducted, the voting outcome of each election has been plus or minus 5 percentage points of the prediction.

Since a good campaign can easily turn on 10% of the voters in the middle, any projection of 40% or more means the bond (levy) has a good chance of passing; a projection of 35 to 39% means there is a moderate chance; 30 to 34% connotes a high risk; and anything less means the bond (levy) has almost no chance of passing (Graham et al., 1990; Wise et al., 1994). If the last projection occurs, this does not mean that the bond or levy should be taken off the ballot. It is quite common for a bond or levy to fail several times before passing. The issues simply need to be thoroughly debated before some voters are convinced of the need.

Funding the Market Survey

Although a school board can fund the market survey, there are times when it might not be politically expedient to do so. Some opponents may charge, "If they can afford to spend the money for the survey, they don't need more money for the schools!" This argument is commonly presented in focus groups. Where such sentiment exists, administrators may want to look to outside sources to fund the market survey. The following sources may be especially helpful in this regard:

1. Individuals or groups of individuals—private citizens who see the importance of the initiative may be willing to contribute to or fund the survey entirely.
2. Chambers of commerce—many local chambers have education subcommittees and support education, so they may be willing to underwrite the project.
3. Local business and industry—schools throughout the country are establishing business advisory councils. These groups often are willing to fund special projects.
4. Education-supporting organizations—these groups may offer grants that can fund the survey.

The bottom line—do not be afraid to ask.

Developing a Plan and Strategies for the Campaign

A funding campaign is brought closer to success through thorough, timely planning. A marketing plan that identifies appropriate strategies, tactics, and timetables should be employed. The plan ought to do the following:

1. Identify the objective (e.g., figure out the proportion of votes needed for passage of a school levy);
2. Identify strategy options (i.e., determine the range of possible strategies, such as running a positive versus a negative campaign or relying on personal contact instead of the media);
3. Evaluate all strategy options (i.e., determine the costs, feasibility, strengths, and weaknesses of each option);
4. Develop tactics to support the chosen strategy (e.g., identify who will do what and how things are to get done);
5. Develop a timetable for the campaign (i.e., decide the sequence of tasks and the time parameters for each task to ensure that they get done on schedule); and
6. Develop a campaign budget (i.e., identify activities, revenues, and expenditures associated with the campaign).

Organizing Public Relations for the Campaign

Campaign Leadership: The Organizational Chart.   Many school tax issues fail because administrators did not plan properly. The campaign organization should be in place and functioning four to six months before the election. Figure 13–1 shows a suggested organizational chart for this task.

The steering committee provides direction for all aspects of the campaign. It comprises the campaign cochairs; the treasurer; the consultant(s), if any; the four division chairs; and representatives from the school board, school administration, school teachers and staff, students and parents, and local media. Having representation from the local media might not be readily accepted; however, a campaign should have nothing to hide. Keeping a media representative informed can actually be beneficial. In some instances, reporters may decline to serve in this capacity. Representatives of the clergy also can be helpful. Church bulletins, newsletters, and sermons provide additional avenues for the campaign message.

The steering committee should meet biweekly at the outset and weekly during the final two months of the campaign. A lunch or dinner meeting (the pay-your-own-expenses type) works well.

Having a steering committee at the top of the organizational structure for a levy campaign is recommended regardless of the size of the community or school district. However, for smaller or more rural districts, there may be substantial differences in the organizational structure. The manufacturing division simply may not exist—or it may be replaced by an agricultural division. The business/professional division may be structured differently to reflect the community's business and professional segment. For example, representatives from service clubs may replace business representatives. Regardless of the size of the community,

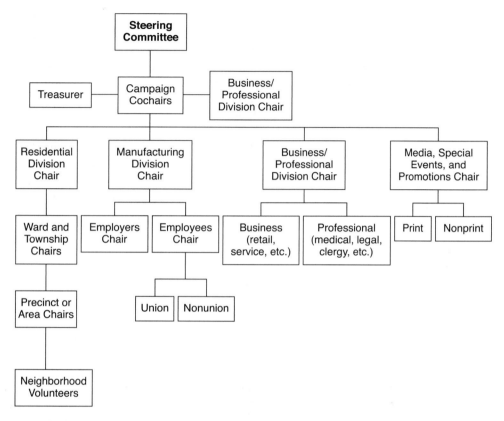

FIGURE 13–1

Organizational Chart for Funding Campaign Leadership

efforts should be made to include some professionals (e.g., physicians, dentists, lawyers) on the steering committee.

The *campaign cochairs* are responsible for the day-to-day direction of the campaign. They need to be dedicated, competent, and credible, but most importantly, they must have the time and schedule flexibility to involve themselves in

◆ Recruiting chairs for other committees,
◆ Recruiting and training volunteers,
◆ Developing a campaign theme and slogan,
◆ Approving all media copy,
◆ Scheduling ads and promotional events,
◆ Chairing the steering committee, and
◆ Speaking at public and organization meetings.

Because of the time requirements, politicians, company presidents, and media and sports celebrities—individuals who have demanding schedules—may not be good choices to cochair the campaign. They may, however, be called on to endorse the campaign.

The *treasurer* should record all financial transactions and expenditures, sign all checks for the campaign organization, and complete all forms and reports mandated by state law. This fiduciary responsibility is often overlooked.

Campaign consultants can provide valuable experience and direction in situations where administrators have had little experience with funding campaigns. Because there are both political and economic dimensions to employing consultants, school officials should always carefully check references, the quality of previous work, and consultant philosophy before retaining these resource people.

The *residential division chair* is, after the campaign cochairs, the most important person in a campaign. This individual is primarily responsible for recruiting, training, and motivating the volunteers who

- Identify positive voters and get them registered;
- Arrange for absentee ballots to be sent to those identified as positive who will not be in town on Election Day;
- Deliver, through personal contact, campaign literature to as many households as possible; and
- Cover the polls on Election Day, make phone calls to remind those identified as positive to vote, and provide assistance such as babysitting and transportation to get the positive voters to the polls.

The individual who chairs this division must be well connected throughout the school district and have excellent organizational and interpersonal skills.

The *manufacturing division chair* interacts with two groups: employers and employees. This position requires an individual with accomplished negotiating skills because obtaining the endorsements and financial support of both groups can be a delicate matter.

The *business/professional division chair* has responsibilities similar to those assigned to the chair of the manufacturing division.

The *media, special events, and promotions division chair* must handle all advertising, letters to the editor, endorsements, videotapes, parades, and other promotional activities.

School Principals.   The campaign does not need to be left in the lap of the superintendent. There are major tasks that the principals can perform. This list is not meant to be exhaustive (although it could be exhausting!).

- Recruit members to serve as campaign volunteers;
- Arrange for school open houses and tours;
- Be a member of a "speakers bureau";
- Provide names of parents who would be positive voters;
- Write newspaper articles about school events and major accomplishments;
- Find parents to write letters to the editor;
- Provide lists of past graduates who are in college or the military and who would be positive voters, but who need to be sent an absentee ballot; and
- Get senior adults into the schools through Grandparents Day; opportunities to read to or be read to by students; and free admissions to school plays, concerts, and athletic events. Each of these items is expanded in the following sections of this chapter.

The Volunteer Army. Several hundred volunteers may be needed to support the campaign. Clearly, the residential division chair cannot contact all these people, but he or she can organize and manage the process. One method is known as the pyramid system. First, ward and township chairs are recruited by the residential and campaign chairs. The ward and township chairs are expected to recruit precinct or area chairs who assist them in recruiting volunteers.

The volunteers should be in place at least one month before the last day of voter registration. This permits time for them to canvass their assigned area to locate positive voters and register them if necessary. Each volunteer should be assigned 10 to 12 residences in his or her neighborhood. Assigning more may make recruitment difficult; however, some volunteers may agree to cover more homes.

Building Potential Support Through Positive-Voter Identification

Locating and Registering Positive Voters. Volunteers should be trained to identify positive voters, and they need to know how to register them. Each volunteer should be taught to approach neighbors with basic questions such as "I'm the neighborhood volunteer for the levy (bond) campaign. Is there some information I can get for you, or are there some questions you have? What do you see as the issues?" Neighbors who make negative comments—such as "I don't see how we can afford this since we're on a fixed income," "Don't the teachers make enough money already?" and "They never told us how they spent the money from the last levy"—are likely to vote against the levy or bond. The volunteer should be taught to write down these questions or concerns and to respond by saying, "I appreciate your sharing these with me. I'll be back in a few weeks with some information to help you make a decision." The volunteer should be instructed to leave *without any further discussion or argument.* He or she should realize that the purpose of the initial contact is to find positive voters; campaigning comes later.

If the responses to the volunteer's basic questions are positive—such as "It's about time we fixed the old building for the kids," "I'm worried about losing business and industry if we don't improve our schools," and "How can I help with the campaign?"—it is likely the person will be a positive voter. If, however, the volunteer is still uncertain, he or she should ask, "Would you be willing to have a yard sign during the campaign?" Once the volunteer has determined that the person is positive, the person can then be asked, "Are you registered?" If the person is not registered, the volunteer can explain the registration procedure or perhaps actually register the person at that time (depending on registration laws).

At the training sessions, each volunteer should be given a stack of voter contact cards. These are 3-by-5-inch note cards, printed if possible, that have spaces for the name, address, ward, precinct, township, and phone number of the person contacted; the volunteer's assessment of whether that person is positive, negative, or undecided; and the questions asked or information requested. Negative comments or questions should be recorded on these cards. As the cards are completed, volunteers make a copy for themselves and return the cards to campaign headquarters, where they will be arranged by precinct or township polling place.

Following Up. Once the campaign is under way, volunteers return to their neighborhoods with promotional materials. They should make every effort to *make personal contact* with every assigned individual. Citizens who are positive need reassurance that their vote is important; those who are negative should be given additional information.

Some negative persons may have open minds and be willing to listen. Each volunteer should be challenged to convert one potentially negative voter. For each conversion, the campaign actually acquires two votes—one is removed from "against" and one is added to "for."

Getting the Positive Voters to the Polls.   In many states, a list of those who have voted must be posted at each polling place, usually by 4:30 P.M. A volunteer can be assigned to each poll site to review this list and identify which positive voters have voted. Anyone on the positive list who has not voted can then be contacted. The call should be in the nature of a friendly reminder: "Hello, this is [name] from the levy committee. I wanted to see if you have voted yet. We really need your support." Offers of babysitting and transportation can be made at this time.

ELEMENTS OF A SUCCESSFUL CAMPAIGN

Once an overall strategy is chosen, all elements of the campaign should contribute toward its implementation. Input from the market survey should be considered the "marching orders" for all phases of the campaign. Many general campaign tactics can be fine-tuned into specific activities. The list of tactics that follows is suggested only as a menu from which campaign leaders can select those that are feasible and affordable. Some of them are PR activities; others are broader forms of promotion and marketing activities. All have been campaign-tested (Graham et al., 1990; Wise et al., 1994). They are not presented in any order of importance, cost, or effectiveness.

Testimonials

Prominent people in the community can provide testimonials for the media advertising program. All that is required is a formal request. Although accustomed to communicating, some of them may prefer endorsing a prepared testimonial. This not only makes it easier for the person making the endorsement, but also gives the campaign leaders an opportunity to address the major issues by speaking through the mouths of people who command respect in the community.

One of the most successful types of testimonial is the "I've changed my mind" statement. Undecided voters may relate to such statements. These comments also suggest that becoming better informed leads to a positive position on the matter at hand.

Presentation of the Price

There is a price attached to the passage of a levy or bond issue—usually in the form of a tax increase. Voters tend to overestimate what they will have to pay, which serves only to heighten their resistance. To counteract this resistance, it is important to provide some perspective about tax increases.

An effective tool is a tax table that compares one's increase in property taxes with the present level of *taxes paid*, rather than with the current market value of his or her home. This table should be simple to interpret, but include detail so voters will be able to determine the actual tax increases for a wide range of tax amounts. The tax increase should also be broken down into cost per day. In this way, the cost is made to seem relatively small when compared with other daily expenditures. Accuracy is extremely important in constructing such a table. Input from the county auditor or treasurer will be needed to ensure that accuracy.

Such a table can be used in different ways in the campaign. Certainly, it should be included in any campaign brochure and in media advertising. These data are especially influential when accompanied by a concluding message, such as "For such a reasonable price, we must say 'Yes' to our schools."

Audiovisual Presentation

An audiovisual presentation can be an effective tool for communicating campaign issues. It can be used to present a consistent message to the community, and it provides a virtual speakers bureau for the campaign committee.

An audiovisual presentation should be produced well in advance of the campaign. Preparing the slides or videotaping the footage, plus writing and editing the narrative, is a time-consuming process that usually requires technical assistance from a media specialist. The presentation should address all issues identified through the market survey.

Once the presentation has been developed, it should be shown first to campaign chairs and volunteers to ensure they have a full understanding of its contents, to answer any questions they may have, and to correct any technical errors. Once formal approval is obtained from the campaign committee, the appropriate community groups should be made aware of the presentation's availability.

Campaign Song

Developing a campaign song is a good project for students. The task serves as a creative activity and involves them in a tangible way. The song could be recorded by the school choir and used as background for TV or radio ads. If any choir members object to participating, they should be excused. Additional opportunities to sing the song may arise if students are asked to present programs at community activities. School officials should obtain publisher approval if the song is adapted from copyrighted material.

Question of the Day

Well before the campaign begins, campaign leaders should approach newspapers, radio stations, and cable television channels to see if these media will publish or announce a daily question and answer provided by the campaign committee. If they agree to do so as a public service, no cost is involved. The same question should be distributed to all media on a given day. By arranging schedules, the most important questions may appear several times.

Campaign Brochure

A good brochure should be the centerpiece of the campaign strategy. It should be ready for distribution about three weeks before the election. It should be attractive, but not so extravagant as to cause negative reactions from voters. One should be able to read the brochure in five to seven minutes. It should include the tax table and a question-and-answer section that addresses the major positive and negative issues. State laws differ with respect to funding campaign materials; some states prohibit the use of public funds to support a referendum position.

Newspaper Coverage

The local newspaper offers several avenues for carrying the campaign message. Consider using the following:

- ◆ *General coverage.* Most newspapers cover school district news on a regular basis. Some even assign a full-time reporter to this duty. If school district officials have a good relationship with the education reporter or the editor, then the newspaper is likely to provide coverage.
- ◆ *Letters to the editor.* During the campaign, there should be a sequence of letters to the editor, from different constituencies, addressing key questions and emphasizing the benefits that the levy or bond issue will provide. Some of them may be unsolicited, but a contingency plan is advisable. Campaign leaders should designate respected persons in the community to write letters to the editor. Designated members of the campaign committee also should be prepared to respond to negative letters immediately, especially when they contain false or erroneous information.
- ◆ *Editorial endorsements.* Editorial endorsements are a powerful weapon in a campaign. Campaign leaders should provide the editor with information that facilitates a correct and objective opinion.
- ◆ *School page.* In many communities, the newspaper has a section devoted to student activities and student opinions. This feature presents another opportunity to publicize campaign issues. Students can be very persuasive when it comes to extolling the benefits they will derive from the levy passage.
- ◆ *Question of the day.* Mentioned earlier, this feature in a newspaper keeps the issues before the public on a regular basis during the campaign.
- ◆ *Paid advertising.* Postelection surveys have shown that paid advertising in newspapers is effective in influencing voters (Wise, Graham, & Bachman, 1986). A common type of paid advertising is an endorsement from business and civic leaders in the community. Another approach is to ask businesses to include a "slug" in their own ads near election time—for example, the slug "Vote yes for our school's future" could be added to an existing ad.

Radio and Television Coverage

Call-In Programs.   Call-in programs on local radio stations and community cable television channels are another outlet for getting across the campaign message. These programs should present panel members who are well informed about the campaign issues, including school board members, campaign leaders, and school administrators. Teachers, students, and parents also should be considered. Songs or promotional tapes can be infused if the medium permits. To ensure that important issues are addressed, having designated persons raise specific questions is an effective technique. If possible, school officials should reserve the right to screen out questions that are irrelevant or inappropriate. It is best to schedule call-in programs toward the end of the campaign, when specific issues need to be clarified.

Special Programming.   Local radio and television stations may be willing to carry special programs that have been prepared in advance on audiotape or videotape. One program might introduce campaign leaders to the community; another might discuss the vital issues in the campaign; still another might focus solely on economic issues.

Public Service Announcements.   Many cable television operations have a "weather screen" channel, which, in addition to reporting the weather, carries other short messages. The campaign committee should investigate this option as a way to air, at no cost, public service announcements.

Paid Advertising.   Buying television time is expensive. If a decision is made to use it, graphics, sound, and narration should be of high quality. The ad copy should highlight the issues identified in any earlier market analysis. If there is a campaign song, it might be used as a lead-in or conclusion for the ad. Radio ads are usually less expensive and require only audio presentations.

Town Hall Meetings

The town hall meeting has long been a fixture of American politics and society. We have addressed it as one of the "elements in a successful campaign" in earlier editions of this book. Unfortunately, the pace of activities of the twenty-first-century American, the precipitous decline in the proportion of households with children in public schools (or in any form of school), and the overall decline in public interest in schools have rendered the "old-fashioned" town hall meeting a near-fatal blow.

If campaign leaders choose to have some form of town meeting, they must consider "drawing a crowd" to be their most serious hurdle. Our 25 years of experience have convinced us that only select circumstances can create the setting for a well-attended town hall meeting. Those circumstances include a campaign that must address issues of serious controversy (e.g., where school boundaries or attendance areas are being changed, where closing schools is proposed, where radical changes are involved). Sometimes the use of a highly popular and visible community supporter as host/hostess/moderator will aid in stimulating attendance.

Where any such attempt is made, the event must be given as much publicity as possible. Where a public access television channel is available, the event can be transmitted live and/or taped for repeated rebroadcast.

In recent years, we have favored the use of a live television call-in program on election eve (discussed under "Radio and Television Coverage") as a substitute for the traditional town hall meeting. This approach reverses the pattern, and instead of requiring the public to come to the town hall, it allows the campaign to reach out and "come to" the public. Again, heavy promotion of the call-in program is required, and this may mean using some campaign funds designated for advertising. Another variation of the concept of the town hall meeting is addressed in the following section, "School Tour and Model Display."

A town hall meeting provides an open forum for anyone to ask questions about the levy or bond issue. Board members, administrators, and campaign leaders should be there to answer questions, to reaffirm the positive benefits to be derived from the levy, and to refute any misinformation being circulated. Such a meeting offers a way to neutralize any "We haven't been given all the facts" criticism. As with call-in programs, it is useful to have "plants" who ask questions that the campaign committee wants to address publicly. Be sure to invite the media to cover the meeting, since their reports will reach those who were not in attendance.

School Tour and Model Display

Those who have recently been inside a school building are more likely to be positive voters (Wise et al., 1986). Thus, giving the public an opportunity to see a model of the proposed new facility or the school renovation project is beneficial. Architects can provide such a model, and they can prepare a floor plan showing the number and size of rooms. A model and floor plan become even more meaningful when citizens are able to tour present buildings. At the conclusion of these tours, campaign materials may be distributed. Parent organizations and students can play a key role in conducting tours and distributing information.

The authors have identified a variation on efforts to increase attendance at school open-house events. Our research continues to confirm the importance of having persons exposed to public school buildings as frequently as possible. Such exposure nearly always correlates with a greater willingness to support school funding issues. Following is a foolproof tactic for dramatically increasing adult attendance at the school open house. Such attendance is vital when the building, renovation, or repair of facilities is an important part of the purpose for requesting added school funding.

The tactic involves a contest among classrooms in the elementary schools (and perhaps middle schools) in the district. Students are informed that the class or classroom whose students produce the greatest number of adults at the open house will be declared "school champion" and will receive a bonus (class pizza party, trophy, etc.). The key is to create such a spirit of competition that students will invite or compel parents, grandparents, aunts and uncles, neighbors—*anybody*—to attend the open house so that their class will get credit for that attendance.

When persons arrive at the school, they are each given a map of the building that identifies numerous places to visit. In order for an adult's visit to be counted for a student's class, his or her map must be stamped at each location in the building designated for a visit. At each of these locations, a student will greet the visiting adults and point out what happens at that location—with careful reference to any deficiencies in space, inadequate equipment, or whatever limitations are present. The visitors' maps will receive the required stamp, and then they will be escorted to the next stop on the tour of the facility.

We have seen increases of 500–1000% in attendance at school open-house events where this tactic has been used, with staff who realize the importance of exposing community members to school facilities providing the coordination so essential to its success. Don't try this unless you are serious and can expect full cooperation from staff. Properly promoted among students (particularly in the elementary grades) and properly planned and coordinated, it can bring huge crowds into the schools.

Main Street Projects

Letters to Employees.   Often business leaders are willing to send a letter to their employees discussing the merits of the levy or bond issues. This may include highlighting positive effects on the local economy. Another possible action is to request permission to place campaign posters on a company's bulletin boards.

Statement Stuffers.   Banks and utility companies often include stuffers on a variety of topics as a public service in their monthly statements. Officials at these companies may be willing to include a stuffer on the levy or bond issue. If so, the stuffer should be prepared well in advance and designed to fit the company's mailing envelope.

Information Table.   Businesses or firms in public buildings may be willing to have a table tent displaying campaign materials. If so, someone on the campaign committee should be assigned to keep the table supplied with materials.

Student Projects

Windshield Washing.   A unique way to involve students in a campaign is to ask service station operators to allow students to wash customers' windshields for free. After cleaning a windshield, the student would give the driver a card that says "We are pleased to clean your windshield. We hope you can see your way clear to vote YES on _____." The action may win more than a smile.

Parades.   If weather permits, a parade may be scheduled on the Saturday before the election. It might include the high school band, drill teams, and student groups who hand out campaign brochures to people along the parade route. It could conclude downtown where the campaign chairs and other supporters can ask citizens to vote "Yes."

Menugrams

Many schools distribute a weekly lunch menu, which ends up being posted on refrigerator doors. In many homes, the menu is the most frequently referred to piece of literature the school publishes. Reserve space on the menugram for a brief message about the levy campaign that urges parents to vote "Yes" on Election Day.

Lapel Badges

A distinctive lapel badge or pin carrying the campaign logo or slogan can be worn by campaign workers as they make their rounds in the neighborhoods. Many companies make these pins with only a short lead time. Ordering in large quantities keeps the unit cost low.

Announcements at Athletic Events

Campaign information or inserts can be included in the printed programs for athletic events. Many schools now have electronic scoreboards that can carry messages as well as the team scores. This technology can be used to present a brief message to a large audience. Another approach is to have campaign workers hand out brochures as people come through the gates.

PLANNING CALENDAR FOR SUCCESSFUL CAMPAIGNS

There is no such thing as a "perfect" calendar for conducting a campaign. Presented here is a model that the authors have used with success. To achieve the desired outcome, the campaign must allow sufficient time to prepare and put into place the many variables that such a campaign involves.

Election Day Minus

Eight Months.   Plan for any market analysis to determine campaign issues and community perceptions, for focus groups to surface possible issues, and for the development of a research design for gathering data. Begin fund-raising efforts to finance the campaign.

Six Months.   Conduct market analysis via survey research, focus groups, and so on.

Four Months.   Recruit and develop campaign organization leadership; fill key chair slots, with the emphasis on residential campaign leadership. This becomes the campaign's "steering committee."

Three Months.   Plan overall strategies based on the market analysis; decide whether adequate human resources exist for a "search" for positive/unregistered voters; contact the media to be used during campaign; determine the prices and availability of the most desirable media; recruit campaign workers for personal-contact efforts. The campaign "steering committee" should begin to meet weekly.

Two Months.   Conduct neighborhood searches for positive/unregistered voters (if this strategy is used); prepare materials to be used in the campaign (question-and-answer brochure, video presentation, rough drafts of media advertising).

One Month.   Begin neighborhood calling and campaigning—the "trenches" are now active and will remain so through Election Day.

Three Weeks.   The "bells and whistles" of an organized campaign begin; media advertising begins and builds to Election Day; a formal campaign "kickoff" takes place; any special efforts and events (parade, call-in program via television or radio, etc.) are off and running; the question (and answer) of the day begins to run in the newspaper and/or on the radio; the "letters to the editor" effort begins in earnest.

Note: Flexibility must have high priority from here on in the campaign. Additional issues may emerge almost without warning; uncontrollable events may demand shifts in emphasis on campaign issues gathered from the market analysis; note that such events may be positive as well as negative, so be prepared to ride any late-breaking positive event or issue, as well as to counter any such event or issues that may hurt the campaign. Daily contact among campaign leaders by phone or e-mail is a necessity, with the likelihood of personal meetings during this time increasing. Campaign leadership is virtually on a 24/7 alert.

Two Weeks.   Determine who will check the polls on Election Day to make sure that known positive voters get to the polls; determine who will call members of this group who have not voted by 4:30 P.M. and offer babysitting and so on; neighborhood canvassing is now in full swing and continues through the late afternoon hours of Election Day.

Final Two–Three Days.   If manpower is sufficient, a round of telephone calls is made to those previously identified as positive voters; intensified door-to-door calling continues; the heaviest use of media advertising comes here.

Election Day

Telephone contact is made as needed to follow up with identified positive voters after checking the names of those who have voted by late afternoon; Election Day itself remains a good time for door-to-door calling until at least mid-afternoon.

Day(s) Following the Election

If the campaign is successful, "thank-you" letters, telephone calls, and media ads are used; if the campaign fails, a "thank-you" to supporters should be combined with efforts to lay the groundwork for the next campaign—we suggest a letter to the editor from the superintendent thanking those who worked and those who supported the effort and promising to do a better job of explaining the need to those who did not support the campaign just completed.

POTENTIAL PITFALLS OR MISTAKES

There is no sure thing in funding campaigns. The activities presented here are campaign proven, but since no two situations are identical, *victory can never be guaranteed.* However, some pitfalls can generally be identified and overcome by timely and adequate planning, funding, and volunteer effort. The most serious campaign pitfalls include the following:

◆ A late start in getting (or no attempt to get) input from the market or the scouting report. With no time to gain input, the campaign leadership inevitably ends up "flying blind" in developing campaign strategy tactics. "Thinking" what the community wants is not the same as "knowing."

◆ A lack of campaign workers. Troops in the trenches are at the heart of a successful campaign. Without them, victory is difficult.

◆ A campaign organization comprising only the elite of the community. A grassroots campaign team will generally create the best image, deliver the most credible message, and turn out the hardest-working volunteers. Those promoting the campaign should be representative of the community.

◆ The presence of organized opposition. Ignoring such opponents may be very costly. They give "No" voters an excuse to legitimize their vote. Try to understand their concerns and prepare answers well in advance.

◆ Division on the school board. When school board members disagree, they transmit mixed messages. Their split vote conveys their lack of agreement and provides another excuse for a "No" voter.

◆ Asking "Yes"/"No" questions on a survey. Many campaigns will do a mail or telephone survey to gauge the vote on the levy or bond. The question asked will be something like "Can we count on your support?" or "How will you vote?" Providing only a "Yes"/"No" alternative will result in a spuriously high proportion giving the socially acceptable "Yes" response. (See the section in this chapter on "Projecting the Election Outcome.")

◆ Conducting open voter registrations. We have found through our community surveys that at least 60% of those not registered to vote will vote "No" on school issues. (See the section in this chapter on "Building Potential Support Through Positive-Voter Identification.")

◆ Putting the issue on a special election ballot rather than a general election ballot. While we can't speak for all states, in Ohio, since 1984 when special election legislation was passed, the mean and median passing percentages were less than 33% in special elections (Ohio Department of Education, 1984–2005).[1]

◆ Having more than one tax issue on the ballot. Typically, with several tax issues on the ballot, few pass, especially those asking for new money.

More information on these "fatal flaws" can be found in an article we wrote for the *Journal of School Public Relations* (Graham & Wise, 2002).

Other specific negatives usually encountered in a local campaign include

◆ Perceptions that teachers and administrators are too highly compensated;
◆ Perceptions that the district has too many frills;

---

[1]Reports from 1984 to 2005 are listed separately in the Reference list.

- ◆ Negative feelings associated with the closing of a treasured school building or consolidation of schools;
- ◆ Past abuse, scandals, or perceived sins of earlier school boards, superintendents, or other employees;
- ◆ Negative feelings about a recent teachers' strike; and
- ◆ A superintendent whose residence is outside the school district.

USING THE WORLD WIDE WEB

The *Yahoo!* and *Google* search engines are quite useful for locating sources on the Web that relate to school levies and bonds. Their addresses are http://www.yahoo.com and http://www.google.com, respectively. Once either search engine is reached, search for "school levies," "school levy campaigns," "passing school bond issues," and "passing school levies." When we did this in 1996, about 500 "school levies" sources were found on Yahoo!. As of October 2005, 64,300 sites were available on Yahoo! and 39,300 on Google! There were over 300 "school levy campaigns" sites on Yahoo! and over 200 sites on Google. You can find everything from newspaper articles to local school Web sites and campaign committee Web sites. Our suggestion is to get on and enjoy the ride; the exploration is fun and quite informative.

SUMMARY

The point has been made earlier, but it bears repeating here for additional emphasis: Public relations *must* be a continuing effort. It must *not* be used just before a levy or bond issue campaign. Much of the content of this book is directed toward the application of PR concepts and tools on a continuing basis.

This chapter has focused on one critical element of school administration: funding levies. Suggestions for planning and executing a successful campaign were provided. Experienced administrators will attest that this political responsibility is among the most challenging they face.

QUESTIONS AND SUGGESTED ACTIVITIES

| CASE STUDY |

1. Which combination of components would you put on the ballot? Explain.
2. Design the strategies and tactics you would use in the campaign.
3. Prepare five ads to be used for television, radio, and print.
4. Prepare 10 "questions of the day" to be used in a brochure and in the newspaper.

5. Prepare three letters to the editor addressing the positive and negative issues that were identified.

6. Prepare an outline of the scenes and write a script for a videotape presentation.

7. What is the difference between marketing and selling?

8. Is it possible to project the outcome of a bond election? If so, how?

9. What are the potential funding sources for a bond campaign?

10. How can positive voters be identified?

SUGGESTED READINGS

Bane, V., & Pride, K. (1993). The $325 million bargain. *American School Board Journal, 180*(10), 24–28.

Bauscher, R. H. (1994). School board election steps for winning at the polls. *Educational Facility Planner, 32*(1), 16–17.

Bohrer, S. D. (2000). Gaining rural community support for a bond issue: A superintendent's experience. In S. Dewees, & P. C. Hammer (Eds.), *Improving rural school facilities: Design, construction, finance, and public support* (pp. 71–83). Charleston, WV: Appalacia Educational Laboratory.

Boschee, F., & Holt, C. R. (1999). *School board success: A strategy for building America's schools.* Lancaster, PA: Technomic.

Cannon, G., & Cannon, P. (1997). Tax strategies. *American School Board Journal, 185*(5), 35–36.

Carter, M. A. (1995). How to blow a bond issue—or not, if you'd prefer. *Clearing House, 69*(5), 289–292.

Fielder, D. J. (1995). A bond for the record books. *American School Board Journal, 182*(10), 35–37.

Flanigan, J. L. (1995). Pre-planning the next bond referendum. *Educational Planning, 10*(1), 27–34.

Fowler, F. J., Jr. (1993). *Survey research methods* (2nd ed.). Thousand Oaks, CA: Sage.

Friedenberg, R. V. (1994). Winning school-levy campaigns. *Education Week, 14*, 32–34.

Graves, J. J. (1998). *Winning the referendum battle in education.* Springfield: Illinois Association of School Boards.

Grier, T. B. (1994). Speak right up. *American School Board Journal, 181*(11), 48–49.

Kastory, R. C., & Harrington, S. J. (1996). Voter perceptions are key to passing a school bond. *Educational Research Quarterly, 20*(1), 49–58.

Kotler, P., & Andreasen, A. (1991). *Strategic marketing for nonprofit organizations* (4th ed.). Upper Saddle River, NJ: Prentice Hall.

Lifto, D. E. (2001). Lessons from the bond battlefield. *American School Board Journal, 188*(11), 50–51, 56.

Lindstom, D. (1994). Bond tip: Let's go to the videotape. *American School Board Journal, 181*(7), 33–34.

Mathison, T. R. (1998). Successful bond elections. *School Business Affairs, 64*(1), 30–33.

Morrison, G. (2000). Raising money, winning votes. *American School & University, 73*(3), 402–405.

Mulkey, J. R. (1993). Marketing your schools. *Executive Educator, 15*(7), 32–33.

North Carolina Department of Public Instruction. (1998). *Planning successful bond campaigns.* Raleigh: Author.

Simpson, J. B. (1993). The 81-cent solution. *American School Board Journal, 180*(10), 28–30.

Walker, P. A. (1996). Passing a bond referendum starts here. *School Business Affairs, 62*(9), 32–35.

REFERENCES

Graham, G. T., & Wise, G. L. (1990). Marketing for the school administrator: Tracking the variables that ruin the best-laid plans. *Record in Educational Administration & Supervision, 11*(1), 64–69.

Graham, G. T., & Wise, G. L. (2002). Avoiding fatal flaws in planning and executing school funding campaigns. *Journal of School Public Relations, 23*(4), 249–266.

Graham, G. T., Wise, G. L., & Bachman, D. L. (1990). *Successful strategies for marketing levies* (Fastback #310). Bloomington, IN: Phi Delta Kappa.

Ohio Department of Education, Office of School Finance. (1984). *Results of elections.* Columbus, OH: Author.

Ohio Department of Education, Office of School Finance. (1985). *Results of elections.* Columbus, OH: Author.

Ohio Department of Education, Office of School Finance. (1986). *Results of elections.* Columbus, OH: Author.

Ohio Department of Education, Office of School Finance. (1987). *Results of elections.* Columbus, OH: Author.

Ohio Department of Education, Office of School Finance. (1988). *Results of elections.* Columbus, OH: Author.

Ohio Department of Education, Office of School Finance. (1989). *Results of elections.* Columbus, OH: Author.

Ohio Department of Education, Office of School Finance. (1990). *Results of elections.* Columbus, OH: Author.

Ohio Department of Education, Office of School Finance. (1991). *Results of elections.* Columbus, OH: Author.

Ohio Department of Education, Office of School Finance. (1992). *Results of elections.* Columbus, OH: Author.

Ohio Department of Education, Office of School Finance. (1993). *Results of elections.* Columbus, OH: Author.

Ohio Department of Education, Office of School Finance. (1994). *Results of elections.* Columbus, OH: Author.

Ohio Department of Education, Office of School Finance. (1995). *Results of elections.* Columbus, OH: Author.

Ohio Department of Education, Office of School Finance. (1996). *Results of elections.* Columbus, OH: Author.

Ohio Department of Education, Office of School Finance. (1997). *Results of elections.* Columbus, OH: Author.

Ohio Department of Education, Office of School Finance. (1998). *Results of elections.* Columbus, OH: Author.

Ohio Department of Education, Office of School Finance. (1999). *Results of elections.* Columbus, OH: Author.

Ohio Department of Education, Office of School Finance. (2000). *Results of elections.* Columbus, OH: Author.

Ohio Department of Education, Office of School Finance. (2001). *Results of elections.* Columbus, OH: Author.

Ohio Department of Education, Office of School Finance. (2002). *Results of elections.* Columbus, OH: Author.

Ohio Department of Education, Office of School Finance. (2003). *Results of elections.* Columbus, OH: Author.

Ohio Department of Education, Office of School Finance. (2004). *Results of elections*. Columbus, OH: Author.

Ohio Department of Education, Office of School Finance. (2005). *Results of elections*. Columbus, OH: Author.

Wise, G. L., & Graham, G. T. (1993). Using the "scouting report" in a market-centered development of policy and programs for the schools. *Record in Educational Administration & Supervision*, *14*(1), 54–56.

Wise, G. L., Graham, G. T., & Bachman, D. L. (1986). *Marketing levies and bond issues for public schools* (Monograph No. 7). Dayton, OH: Wright State University.

Wise, G. L., Graham, G. T., & McCammon, C. L. (1994). *Marketing—not selling—the successful levy campaign*. Columbus: Ohio School Boards Association.

CHAPTER **14**

Responding to Crisis

Theodore J. Kowalski

CASE STUDY: SUICIDE AT MCKINLEY MIDDLE SCHOOL

As usual, Principal Beth Rodriguez arrived at McKinley Middle School at about 7:15 A.M. She was startled to find three police cruisers and an ambulance, all with their lights flashing, parked in front of the building. Perhaps someone had come to work early and activated the security alarm by accident, maybe there had been a break-in, or perhaps vandals had damaged the school. As she moved quickly to the main entrance, Principal Rodriguez heard the sound of sirens in the distance. In her office, she found Pasha and Mary, the building custodians, talking with Detective Mario Mangioni. As the principal approached the three individuals, she immediately noticed the concerned look on their faces.

Taking Mrs. Rodriguez into her inner office, Detective Mangioni told her that the custodians had called 911 about 6:00 A.M. after finding the body of Bill Block, a science teacher, hanging from one of the rafters in the gymnasium. Block was one of the school's best and most popular teachers. The detective then added that his initial investigation indicated suicide because there was no evidence of murder. Although they would have to wait for the coroner's report to determine the actual time of death, the detective said it appeared that the teacher committed suicide about five to six hours earlier.

Obviously shaken by the tragic news, Principal Rodriguez found it difficult to concentrate. Students and teachers would be arriving shortly, however, and she had to decide how to handle the situation. Though she was an experienced principal, she had never experienced a death at school, nor had she ever contemplated having to deal with a faculty member's suicide. As she struggled to collect her thoughts, she tried to remember where she had filed the school's crisis plan. Unfortunately, her secretary had not yet arrived at work.

As Mrs. Rodriguez began to get her emotions under control, she realized it was now 7:45 A.M. and the first student buses would be arriving in 10 minutes. Under normal procedure, students congregated in either the commons area or the media center to wait for the first bell at 8:12 A.M. At that point, students had seven minutes to get to their homerooms. Panicked, the principal rushed to the bus unloading zone. By this time, many of the teachers had arrived, but the police would not allow them to enter the building. Not informed of the situation, they stood in front of the building in small groups. Looking through the glass entry doors, they could see the principal and detective talking to each other.

Nodding his head toward the doors, the detective said, "They are going to bring the body out any moment now. I think it is best to try to do that before the students arrive. You need to decide what you're going to tell the teachers. In addition, you need to determine what you're going to do with the students when they get here. Several officers are remaining on the premise to seal the area where the death occurred. I understand that Mr. Block was not married and that he has no family in the local community. I will take care of notifying his closest relative. One other thing, the media are going to find out about this very shortly, so you need to be prepared to deal with reporters. If you need me, I'll be at the morgue."

The principal's head was spinning. She reached into her pocket and took out her cellphone. She called the superintendent's office hoping that he would have advice. There was no answer.

In a crisis situation, individuals almost always find it difficult to think clearly. Yet school administrators realize they must make decisions decisively and quickly in an effort to protect the welfare of several hundred or even several thousand people. In addition, they have to communicate effectively during this stressful period. These realities are illustrated by the situation confronting the McKinley Middle School principal.

When confronted with a crisis, experienced principals have found that preparation and practice are essential. In the context of an information-based society, with dozens of cable news channels seeking stories to fill air time, even crisis situations in remote areas are likely to get national media coverage. In many past situations, unprepared administrators have caused what noted safety expert Kenneth Trump calls "a crisis after the crisis" (Kowalski, 2005b). That is, their lack of preparedness and ineffective communication result in a personal disaster after the public judges they are incompetent.

This chapter explores the connections between school public relations (PR) and crisis management. First, the process of crisis planning is explained; both process and plan content are addressed. Then focused attention is given to communication; recommended procedures are detailed for action before, during, and after a crisis.

CRISIS PLANNING

Crisis planning and management have become highly visible responsibilities for district and school administrators. Planning is intended to prevent possible crises and to provide guidelines for crises that do occur. Unfortunately, effective preparation requires more than just finding a generic plan because each district and each school in a district have contextual variables requiring specific attention. The purpose here is to examine the basic processes that are deemed essential to school safety and security (see Figure 14–1).

Defining a Crisis

Merriam-Webster's Collegiate Dictionary (1993) defines *crisis* as a "turning point for better or worse," a "decisive moment," or a "crucial time" and goes on to reveal that crisis is a "situation that has reached a critical phase." Poland and McCormick (1999) describe a crisis as a "temporary breakdown of coping" (p. 6) surrounded by anger, anxiety, and grief. In the context of the typical school, however, crisis may be defined in different ways, and therefore, it is imperative that principals identify levels of crises and provide defining characteristics for them (Trump, 1998).

Crises range in scope and intensity; for example, they can affect only one person or an entire community. They can occur before, during, or after school and, in some instances, even away from the school campus (e.g., a fatal bus accident) (U.S. Department of Education, 2003). They are typically unpredictable, and their cumulative effect on a district or school depends largely on the quantity and quality of management provided by administrators and other staff members (Fink, 1986). In this vein, being prepared to deal with disasters is imperative. In the aftermath of highly publicized murders occurring in schools over the past two decades, states have required local school systems to develop crisis plans. Mandates, however, ensure neither the quality of a plan nor its appropriate implementation. As illustrated in the case study of the middle school, the principal knew she had

FIGURE 14–1
Crisis-Planning Process

a plan, but did not know what it contained in relation to a death at school, and she needed it, but she did not know where it was.

The range of situations that qualify as a crisis in a school is larger than most educators might expect. Violent acts or threats are most readily recognized; however, natural disasters, such as fires, tornadoes, hurricanes, snowstorms, and earthquakes, also are cogent. Examples of other pertinent situations include accidental deaths, suicides, chemical spills, accidents, structural failures in the facility (collapsed wall or roof), and acts of terrorism.

Determining the Scope of the Planning Process

School crisis planning has two components: content and process. In May 2003, the U.S. Department of Education issued a model document to help administrators and other educators

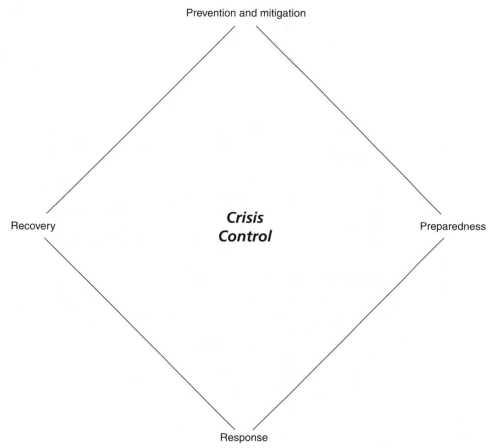

FIGURE 14–2
Stages of Crisis Control

develop individual crisis plans for schools. *Practical Information on Crisis Planning: A Guide for Schools and Communities* explains that effective planning is a continuous cycle that has four stages (also see Figure 14–2).

1. *Prevention and mitigation.* This stage has three parts: a safety audit of the school, identification of local resources/agencies (and their plans), and an analysis of traffic patterns that may be pertinent to emergencies. In addition, administrators should attempt to coordinate information with local businesses and government agencies.

2. *Preparedness.* In this phase, administrators develop site plans that will be available to first responders. These plans include floor plans, building elevations, and information about entryways, windows, utilities, communication/alarm systems, and control panels. Plans for communicating during a crisis and for conducting drills are also addressed at this phase.

3. *Response*. This phase should address issues such as locating and equipping a command center; identifying evacuation routes; disseminating crisis-planning information to relevant stakeholders; determining how reporters, parents, and spectators will be managed; and maintaining the security of the school site during a crisis.

4. *Recovery*. This phase should detail strategies for returning the school to normal operations. Provisions for aftercare services by psychologists, counselors, and other health providers need to be included.

By conceptualizing crisis management plans as living documents, administrators create a climate in which there are continuous efforts to update and improve them (Clarksean & Pelton, 2002).

In conjunction with planning, principals have to consider roles and responsibilities. Foremost in this regard is assembling a school crisis team that is "responsible for developing a plan and coordinating activities during an actual crisis" (Quinn, 2002, p. 6). In addition, the team coordinates the distribution of the plan and oversees simulations to ensure that employees and students follow the plan correctly (Rettig, 1999).

Appointing the School Crisis Team

The principal is responsible for appointing team members, and in fulfilling this responsibility, he or she should be guided by the following criteria:

♦ Effective communication skills,
♦ Stress tolerance,
♦ Interest in and availability to serve,
♦ Pertinent knowledge/skills, and
♦ Respect in the school and community.

Typically, the principal chairs the committee and appoints an assistant principal as the assistant chair. Other employees commonly appointed include security personnel, custodians, the school nurse, counselors, a coach or athletic trainer, and several other teachers (Quinn, 2002). Once appointed, committee members are assigned to the following roles:

♦ *Vice-chair*. Usually an assistant principal, this person assumes responsibility for crisis management if the principal is not present.
♦ *First-responder coordinator*. This person meets all first-responder personnel and directs them to the crisis area (e.g., provides maps, floor plans).
♦ *First-aid responders*. These individuals must be trained in first-aid techniques. They render emergency medical assistance until emergency personnel arrive. If no certified first-aid providers are employed at the school, the principal should select an employee to receive this training.
♦ *Sweep-team coordinators*. These individuals are the last ones out of the building when an evacuation is ordered. They check the hallways, restrooms, and other nonclassroom areas both to determine if all persons have left the facility and to determine if suspicious items (e.g., unusual-looking packages) are in the building.
♦ *Communication coordinator*. Though some writers (e.g., Quinn, 2002) recommend separating the coordination of internal and external communication, having one

CHAPTER 14 ■ Responding to Crisis   **343**

person coordinate both functions is likely to produce a more consistent and controllable situation. The communication coordinator works directly with the principal and a district communication coordinator (e.g., PR director). In small districts and schools, a principal may not have access to an employee who has the requisite skills; in these situations, the principal should make arrangements for the appointee to acquire the requisite training.

◆ *Staff liaison.* This person communicates with school employees about the committee's activities and seeks concerns that need to be shared with other committee members.

◆ *Student liaison.* This person performs the same duties as the staff liaison, but his or her target audience is the student body.

◆ *Parent liaison.* This person performs the same duties as other liaisons, but this particular role is typically more difficult and complex, since parents are not at the school on a regular basis.

In addition to its regular meetings, the school crisis team should conduct at least one open forum regarding crisis planning each year. The purpose is to allow all stakeholders an opportunity to voice concerns or offer suggestions for improving the current plan and procedures.

Conducting a Safety and Security Audit

According to Trump (1998), a safety and security audit provides information about existing conditions that constitute vulnerabilities and risks. Gillens (2005) divides this process into the following tasks:

◆ Policy analysis (e.g., assess policies and regulations that pertain to school safety and security);

◆ Critical infrastructure and asset identification (e.g., assess a school's information protection framework and analyze the effectiveness of these protective measures);

◆ Critical infrastructure continuity and contingency planning (e.g., assess current provisions for procuring services that protect against major disruptions to normal operations); and

◆ Physical infrastructure analysis (e.g., assess physical security and controls as a first line of defense for both the facility and the site).

In addition, Trump (1998) recommends that assessments include an analysis of discipline data, especially of incidents involving crimes, and related information obtained from employees (via survey or interviews).

Several states have developed safety audit programs that are made available to school districts (Brickman, Jones, & Groom, 2004). Trump (1998) cautions, however, that checklists or prepackaged programs may present several problems. As examples, they may not include all relevant subjects, and they may be used by individuals who are not qualified to make the necessary assessment decisions.

The safety and security audit needs to be completed prior to drafting the crisis plan because assessments and evaluations are essential to determining how risk and crises should be managed. The written report that results from an audit also has symbolic significance; it informs employees, students, and the public that school officials are paying attention to school safety and security issues (Kowalski, 2002).

Constructing the Plan

After the safety and security audit is completed, the crisis team moves forward to put together the crisis plan. By this point, the committee should have completed three important tasks:

1. Identifying potential crisis situations,
2. Defining each potential crisis by describing qualifying characteristics, and
3. Assigning roles to the members of the crisis team.

First and foremost, administrators should realize that they are expected to provide the leadership necessary to construct a crisis management plan (Duke, 2002). In addressing this task, they need to create a collaborative environment in which school personnel can work with representatives of various government agencies and services (e.g., police departments, local hospitals). Further, once this environment is established, they need to facilitate the efforts of the participants.

As noted earlier, simply finding and then adopting a crisis plan developed by another school or developing a generic plan for all schools in a district is not prudent. To be effective, a plan should be written to meet the specific needs of a school—needs that are determined by both the school's physical environment and its population (employees, students, visitors) (Trump, 1998).

A comprehensive plan should include preventive and mitigating measures, as noted above. Such information is intended to guide employee decisions that may prevent a crisis. Too often, a crisis plan is seen solely as a management plan; that is, its sole intent is to provide directions for dealing with a crisis.

According to the U.S. Department of Education (2003), a number of steps should be taken to create a positive planning context:

- Identify and involve all relevant stakeholders (i.e., individuals who are concerned about safety and security and individuals who are likely to be involved if there is a crisis) in the planning process.
- Consider existing plans and information (e.g., current crisis plans developed by the local fire department and police department).
- Identify the crises the plan will address.
- Define roles and responsibilities. Although this information may be known by the members of the school crisis team, it will not be known by others if it is not in the plan.
- Develop communication processes for all relevant publics and explain how they should be implemented.
- Obtain necessary equipment and supplies.
- Prepare to respond to a crisis immediately (e.g., making evacuation, lockdown, and relocation decisions).
- Develop and collect maps, floor plans, and other pertinent facility/site information.

◆ Develop accountability procedures (how school officials will account for students during a crisis) and student release procedures (how students will be released from school).

In addition to writing a crisis plan, school officials must take steps that help ensure the plan's success (Thompson, 2004). Trump (1998) proposes the following actions:

◆ Identify an area of the school that will serve as the command center. Applicable criteria for selecting this area include security, accessibility, size, and the appropriateness of the environment to accommodate the material that must be stored there.
◆ Appoint alternates to assume responsibilities for key roles in the event that one or more committee members are absent during an actual crisis.
◆ Determine responsibilities for school employees who are not team members.
◆ Establish emergency codes to be used when communicating during a crisis.
◆ Make pertinent data such as floor plans and utility information available in a safe location.
◆ Identify resource people, additional information needed, and backup communication equipment.

Preparing Employees to Implement the Plan

Implementation requires communicating the plan's content to stakeholders and then conducting simulations so that implementation can be practiced (Smiar, 1992). The structure and appearance of the plan can discourage employees from reading it. For example, presenting them with an unattractive, complicated, and lengthy document is not a good idea. Instead, superintendents and principals should index the content, avoid esoteric terms, and consider providing a simple-to-use digest for all employees (Jones & Paterson, 1992).

Principals who have had firsthand experience with a crisis (e.g., Baker, 2005) emphasize that it is critical for faculty and staff to know a plan's content and to have the requisite skills to implement the plan. Since crisis plans should be revised annually, practice through drills should occur periodically and always after major elements have been altered.

Dealing with the aftermath of a crisis is perhaps the most ignored element of crisis management. Once the crisis is under control, licensed mental health workers, counselors, social workers, and clergy may be able to make important contributions. Aftercare needs depend on the nature of the crisis. For example, the death of a student or faculty member (as in the case at the beginning of this chapter) may require some individuals to be taken to an area where they can receive the required assistance. Drills and simulations should include aftercare procedures detailed in the plan.

Evaluating the Plan

To be effective, crisis plans should be treated as living documents; that is, they should be revised to meet changing school and community needs. Consequently, the evaluation of a plan should be both summative and formative. The summative component determines whether the plan achieved its objectives; the formative component determines whether changes and improvements are necessary for the next school year.

One important element of the formative process is an annual safety and security audit. This inspection should identify new concerns, such as the need for new security measures prompted by the failure of current systems. Having legal counsel review the crisis plan for liability and privacy issues is another suggested action (Jones & Paterson, 1992). Once the formative and summative portions of the evaluation process are completed, the school crisis team should use the outcomes to consider revisions to the school crisis plan.

CRISIS COMMUNICATION

Administrators who have experienced a school crisis usually comment that reporters and parents arrived at the school more quickly than they had anticipated. In this information age, there is little lag time between an incident and public disclosure. Therefore, it is not surprising that school safety expert Kenneth Trump identifies communication as a

> ". . . thorn in the side of school officials in a crisis situation." Relevant problems include the mechanical aspects of communication, such as overloading of telephone systems, having non-functioning public address systems, or having too few or poor quality two-way radios. Emergency notification of parents, internal staff communications, and media aspects of communication often represent the "crisis after the crisis" for school leaders. (Kowalski, 2005b, p. 48)

Consequently, PR in general and communication specifically are integral to crisis management. The topic is discussed here in relation to conditions before, during, and after a crisis.

Precrisis Tasks

Given the frenzy that surrounds the first hour after a crisis, principals perform more effectively when they are prepared to initiate a communication program that can reach several different audiences. This is true both because pressure surrounds a crisis and because most administrators have not studied communication formally (Kowalski, 2005a). For example, many practitioners are unprepared to deal with reporters, and they do not understand that silence on their part usually intensifies media scrutiny (Kowalski, 2005b). Therefore, the following basic tasks should be addressed as part of the overall crisis-planning process:

♦ *Have a communication plan.* Ideally, school districts should have both district and individual communication plans, and the content in the two documents should be coordinated.
♦ *Designate a media spokesperson(s).* Designating only one spokesperson to communicate during a crisis is considered the ideal because this alternative reduces the likelihood of conflicting messages reaching the public. In larger school districts, however, it may be more practical to have a district coordinator and a spokesperson in each school. A spokesperson should be comfortable with reporters and knowledgeable about the organization. He or she should be credible, project confidence, have a calm demeanor, and have good communication skills.
♦ *Identify key stakeholders.* When potential crises are identified in the school plan, audiences that need to learn about each situation should be listed. For elementary

and secondary schools, these audiences typically include government agencies (police, fire, emergency services), school district administration (e.g., the superintendent, school board members), school employees, students, parents, other community members, and the media.

◆ *Anticipate difficult questions.* The principal, communication coordinator, and other members of the school crisis team should identify possible difficult questions so that they can consider appropriate ways to respond to them.

◆ *Determine policy for employees and students providing information.* Reporters will usually seek interviews with employees and students who are on the school campus. Policy should instruct persons in both groups as to how they should respond to interview requests.

◆ *Acquire necessary equipment and supplies.* There are two types of equipment and supplies necessary for communicating during a crisis: items that are part of the normal school environment (i.e., those that are used for daily operations) and items that are reserved for use in a crisis. Examples of the former include telephones, internal communication systems, fax machines, and alarm systems. The latter includes items that are stored in the command center and can be used either to augment normal systems or to supplant normal systems if they are inoperable. Examples of these items include cell phones, a bullhorn, two-way radios, and a "hot line" that is activated so that parents or other parties have a contact point with school officials. As a general rule, school officials should try to use several modes of communication to reach both internal and external audiences.

◆ *Verify the compatibility of school communication devices.* Cell phones and two-way radios, for example, have limited value if they cannot be used to reach first responders.

◆ *Establish a database containing pertinent information.* As an example, a fact sheet providing statistical information about the district and school is useful to first responders and reporters.

◆ *Establish communication pathways (protocols).* Telephone or e-mail trees should be established in order to reach the community and especially parents (U.S. Department of Education, 2003).

◆ *Make sure that spokespersons receive adequate training.* In districts where a communication spokesperson is designated in each school, and even if that spokesperson is the principal, the superintendent should ensure that the appointees receive proper training.

When asked how a communication coordinator or spokesperson can become prepared to communicate during a crisis, Brian Woodland, a highly experienced PR practitioner, responded that preparedness first depends on individual knowledge and skills. Second, it depends on having "a crisis plan, strong relationships with the media, a voice at the decision-making table in the district, effective vehicles to communicate with parents and students, and a clear understanding of the role of media" (Kowalski, 2002, p. 181).

Communicating During the Crisis

The most common communication mistake administrators make during a crisis is not recognizing or accepting the need to work effectively with reporters (Kowalski, 2005b). However, communication responsibilities are broader than media relations. Actually, the first duties involve people in the school, and this is why the school crisis plan should include notification procedures for faculty and staff.

Typically, voice commands are the best and most efficient way to notify building occupants that a crisis has or may occur. Codes, such as the following ones, inform employees of the nature of the crisis and direct them to take prescribed actions:

- ◆ Code yellow: Lock down classrooms; an unauthorized person is in the building.
- ◆ Code blue: A catastrophic medical event is occurring in the building.
- ◆ Code red: A weather-related event is imminent; move to your assigned safe area.
- ◆ Code purple: Evacuate the building and proceed to a designated student holding area.
- ◆ Code green: A general all clear; return to your classroom.

The school crisis plan should detail actions that should be taken once persons inside the school have been notified of the event. For example, when "code yellow" is sounded, teachers usually are instructed to have their students get on the floor and crawl toward the outside wall of the building, to lock the classroom door, to cover the window in the door, and to position students so that they are not visible to persons outside the building. In addition to detailing how school personnel should act, the plan should provide policy and procedures concerning communication. In the situation presented in the case at the beginning of the chapter, for example, a principal would not reveal the probable or actual cause of death (suicide) unless the cause was verified and the deceased's family agreed to releasing the information (Poland & Poland, 2004).

After school employees are notified, measures should be taken to communicate with parents and the media. Communication at this point should be shaped by the following guidelines:

- ◆ Try to get as many facts as possible before communicating.
- ◆ Use common terminology across the school district (U.S. Department of Education, 2003).
- ◆ Provide open and honest communication (Warner, 1994).
- ◆ Develop messages you want the public to receive and be consistent in delivering them.
- ◆ Avoid answering hypothetical questions by speculating; rely on the facts you have accumulated.
- ◆ The content of press releases should be cleared with the school crisis team leader and communication coordinator. School officials should not disclose the names of students and employees unless legal approval to do so has been granted (Fiore, 2002).
- ◆ Inform student's families of the actions being taken (U.S. Department of Education, 2003).
- ◆ Try to be proactive; for example, do not remain silent if the media have not contacted the principal or communication coordinator.
- ◆ Provide guidance to the public when appropriate.
- ◆ Activate a crisis hotline so that persons can contact school officials.
- ◆ Communicate both facts and messages.
- ◆ Do not be evasive; respond to media inquiries in a timely manner, never say "no comment," and do not try to hide bad news.
- ◆ Respond to rumors immediately.
- ◆ Issue press releases when appropriate (Kowalski, 2002).
- ◆ Focus on what is being done to deal with the situation.

- ◆ Keep staff informed. Faculty and other employees who are assigned to manage students during a crisis should be kept aware of developments (Heath & Sheen, 2005).
- ◆ A log of media inquiries, responses, and press releases should be maintained by the communication coordinator or spokesperson (U.S. Department of Education, 2003).
- ◆ Never get angry when communicating.

School administrators may be uncertain as to what they should do with respect to making a school crisis plan available to the public. For example, would wide dissemination be detrimental to safety and security? Discussing the need to inform stakeholders of the crisis plan, Kenneth Trump suggested that school officials

> should not put their crisis plans on the Web site or distribute copies at school bake sales. But they should be communicating with parents via school newsletters, their Web site, the media, and other mechanisms about school safety before an actual crisis occurs. Parent workshops, professional staff development, school safety assessments, working with public safety partners, conducting tabletop exercises of emergency plans, involving students in school safety planning, and numerous other strategies can be employed to help communicate the priority of school safety issues to a school community. (Kowalski, 2005b, p. 54)

Communicating After the Crisis

Media coverage does not end when a crisis is brought under control. Administrators should anticipate that reporters will analyze causes and management and will ask questions about preventive measures that have been taken. Therefore, the communication coordinator or spokesperson should be prepared to detail what school officials have done to bring the school back to normal operations.

Among the actions that administrators can take or encourage others to take in the aftermath of a crisis, the following are especially cogent with respect to communication:

- ◆ Monitor how employees and students are doing and be prepared to summarize this information.
- ◆ Identify what was done to bring the school site and facility back to normal operation.
- ◆ Develop a list of follow-up procedures that were implemented and aftercare services that were available and provided.
- ◆ Provide debriefings for employees and students.
- ◆ Plan to acknowledge the anniversary of the crisis.
- ◆ Assure the public that school officials have analyzed the cause and management of the crisis.
- ◆ Describe lessons learned from the crisis and detail how this knowledge has improved prevention and planning. (U.S. Department of Education, 2003)

SUMMARY

Credibility, trust, and competence help determine if a school administrator is successful in managing a disaster. Credibility stems from being prepared, letting stakeholders know you are prepared, and helping others to become prepared. Trust emanates from open and continuous communication with relevant publics, both inside and outside the school. And competence comes from acquiring knowledge and applying it so that the requisite skills are mastered.

This chapter provided an overview of crisis planning as it relates primarily to individual schools. Special attention was given to planning, managing, and communicating. As you reflect on the chapter's content, consider what has been done or not done in your school, district, and community to ensure that school employees are prepared. In fact, schools remain vulnerable to crises partly because they are large facilities with modest security provisions. Experiences since 1990 have exhibited quite clearly that disaster can strike anywhere and at any time, and when it does, the public expects school administrators to protect students and employees.

QUESTIONS AND SUGGESTED ACTIVITIES

CASE STUDY

1. What questions about the teacher's death are reporters likely to ask Principal Rodriguez?
2. Should the principal tell the faculty, students, and media how the teacher died? Why or why not?
3. What could have been done to better prepare the principal and other employees to deal with the teacher's death?
4. Who should communicate with reporters when they arrive at the school?
5. If you were the principal, what would you do with the children when they arrive on the buses?
6. If you were the principal, what would you tell the school employees and how would you communicate with them?
7. Should students' parents be notified about the death? Why or why not?

CHAPTER

8. Who should serve on a school crisis committee?
9. What is a command center? Where should it be located?
10. What information should first responders receive about the crisis plan?
11. Is it a good idea to coordinate planning with first responders? Why or why not?
12. Who should communicate with the media, parents, and other members of the community in the event of a crisis?
13. The chapter content refers to a crisis plan as a living document. What does this mean?

SUGGESTED READINGS

Baker, D. E. (2005). Lockdown! *Principal Leadership*, 6(2), 8–9.

Brickman, H. K., Jones, S. E., & Groom, S. E. (2004). Evolving school-crisis management since 9/11. *Education Digest*, 69(9), 29–35.

Brock, S. E., & Cowan, K. (2004). Preparing to help students after a crisis. *Education Digest*, 69(6), 34–40.

Eastridge, H. (1999). The do's and don'ts of coping with crises. *School Administrator*, 56(6), 31–32.

Kowalski, T. J. (2005b). Revisiting communication during a crisis: Insights from Kenneth Trump. *Journal of School Public Relations, 26*(1), 47–55.

Richtig, R., & Hornak, N. J. (2002). 12 lessons from school crises. *Principal Leadership, 3*(4), 35–37.

Sharp, H. M. (2005). After the fact. *Principal Leadership, 5*(5), 39–41.

Stephens, R. D. (1998). Ten steps to safer schools. *American School Board Journals, 185*(3), 30–33.

Summers, R. (2005). When bad things happen to good schools: Managing communications in a crisis. *Momentum, 36*(2), 11–15.

Trump, K. S. (1998). *Practical school security: Basic guidelines for safe and secure schools.* Thousand Oaks, CA: Corwin Press.

U.S. Department of Education (2003). *Practical information on crisis planning: A guide for schools and communities.* Washington, DC: U.S. Department of Education, Office of Safe and Drug-Free Schools.

REFERENCES

Baker, D. E. (2005). Lockdown! *Principal Leadership, 6*(2), 8–9.

Brickman, H. K., Jones, S. E., & Groom, S. E. (2004). Evolving school-crisis management since 9/11. *Education Digest, 69*(9), 29–35.

Clarksean, L., & Pelton, M. H. (2002). Safe schools: A reality check. *Leadership, 32*(1), 32–35.

Duke, D. L. (2002). *Creating safe schools for all children.* Boston: Allyn & Bacon.

Fink, S. (1986). *Crisis management.* New York: American Management Association.

Fiore, D. J. (2002). *School community relations.* Larchmont, NY: Eye on Education.

Gillens, H. (2005). Assessing safety. *American School & University, 77*(11), 30–33.

Heath, M. A., & Sheen, D. (2005). *School-based crisis intervention: Preparing all personnel to assist.* New York: Guilford Press.

Jones, M., & Paterson, L. (1992). *Preventing chaos in times of crisis: A guide for school administrators.* Los Alamitos, CA: Southwest Regional Lab.

Kowalski, T. J. (2002). Working with the media during a crisis situation. *Journal of School Public Relations, 23*(3), 178–186.

Kowalski, T. J. (2005a). Evolution of the school superintendent as communicator. *Communication Education, 54*(2), 101–117.

Kowalski, T. J. (2005b). Revisiting communication during a crisis: Insights from Kenneth Trump. *Journal of School Public Relations, 26*(1), 47–55.

Merriam-Webster's collegiate dictionary (10th ed.). (1993). Springfield, MA: Merriam-Webster.

Poland, S. J., & McCormick, J. (1999). *Coping with crisis: Lessons learned, a resource guide for schools, parents, and communities.* Longmont, CO: Sopris West.

Poland, S. J., & Poland, D. (2004). Dealing with death at school. *Principal Leadership, 4*(8), 8–12.

Quinn, T. (2002). The inevitable school crisis: Are you ready? *Principal, 81*(5), 6–8.

Rettig, M. A. (1999). Seven steps to schoolwide safety. *Principal, 71*(9), 10–13.

Smiar, N. P. (1992). Cool heads: Crisis management for administrators. *Child Welfare, 71*(2), 147–156.

Thompson, R. (2004). *Crisis intervention and crisis management: Strategies that work in schools and communities.* New York: Brunner-Routledge.

Trump, K. S. (1998). *Practical school security: Basic guidelines for safe and secure schools.* Thousand Oaks, CA: Corwin Press.

U.S. Department of Education. (2003). *Practical information on crisis planning: A guide for schools and communities.* Washington, DC: U.S. Department of Education, Office of Safe and Drug-Free Schools.

Warner, C. (1994). *Promoting your school: Going beyond PR.* Thousand Oaks, CA: Corwin Press.

CHAPTER

15

Evaluating Public Relations Programs

Doug Newsom

CASE STUDY: EVALUATING THE IDENTIFICATION/BRANDING EFFORTS OF A "BEDROOM" CITY'S INDEPENDENT SCHOOL DISTRICT

What parents think about school districts is a major consideration in determining where to live, and it may even be a deciding factor in whether or not a family accepts job opportunities that involve a move. The identification and recognition of a school district are especially important when a medium-sized district is nestled between two large cities and surrounded by small cities and towns in a large metroplex.

The community considered here is a medium-sized city that is a college town, too, but home mostly to commuters. The city is framed by major interstate highways and has a nationally known theme park and two sports arenas, all of which attract visitors. Although the city has a number of scattered shopping centers, it never has had a recognizable "downtown."

The school district has reached out to the community and made special efforts to include a diversified cultural mix that, though predominately white, has large numbers of Asians, Hispanics, and African Americans—most of whom are professionals. The district has established and maintained ties to the state university located in its heart.

The district's efforts to establish relationships with its various publics, including those most important to it, such as personnel, parents, and community leaders, are all examined in ongoing ways. Programs are evaluated and adjusted. This formative research helps the school district set and adjust its goals on a continuing basis. While that effort measures year-to-year progress and identifies problems, the school district decided that it needed summative research to determine the impact its efforts and its policies were having.

Because employees are always the organization's most important public, the most credible to outsiders, and the most reflective of the organization to the community, the school district decided to initiate its research with the district's teaching and nonteaching employees. Its intent was to discover their perceptions of the district and to identify their concerns.

The school district approached the university for some research assistance and contracted with a professor to handle a thorough look at its reputation, starting with employees. The research involved all employees, teachers, and nonteaching staff. The approach used included focus groups, interviews, and surveys. Because employee identification is critical to reputation, the summative evaluation with employees was designed to see how they viewed the school district and what they reflected to external stakeholders. The intent was to determine how employees thought the district was identified by its various constituencies with whom they had contacts. An effort was made to see what associations were made with the district as a result of its branding efforts.

Some questions the administration had that initiated the research would have to be revisited when the research results were in:

♦ Does the district's administration have a clear view of how employees view the goals and objectives of the district?
♦ What impediments to reputation do employees experience?

- ◆ What problems do employees experience with internal and external constituencies that affect perceptions of the district by other stakeholders?
- ◆ How significant is branding to reputation?
- ◆ Does summative research need to be done annually or at other intervals, such as every three years, every five years?
- ◆ What effect do changes in the district's demographics have on the brand, if any?
- ◆ What effect does news about the community itself have on the brand?
- ◆ If community news is positive (i.e., new businesses, lower crime statistics, etc.), does that "polish" the brand?
- ◆ If community news is negative (i.e., plant closings, crime up, etc.), does that "tarnish" the brand, regardless of the district's accomplishments?
- ◆ If either is the case, what is the district's public relations (PR) opportunity?
- ◆ Can summative research discover community news effects?

Establishing a starting point for the summative research about the district's reputation was based on the public that most affects reputation. The interface of employees with other stakeholders, especially those in the community, was seen as critical, so that is where the research was initiated.

Starting with employees, two categories were created: teaching and nonteaching. Focus groups were used with each, choosing participants from all levels of schools with representation throughout the district. Concerns and compliments emerged from the discussions. The compliments were almost exclusively for the district and not for the individual schools.

Concerns among the teachers were about communication at the principal level and discipline issues. Other major issues were the availability of classroom materials and the unevenness of their quality across the district. Another major issue was the relevance of teaching matter to the state tests on which the teachers knew they, as well as their schools, would be ranked. The teachers were frustrated that they had no input into the state tests.

Like the teachers, the nonteaching staff saw communication at the supervisory level as a major concern in that instructions were not only unclear, but also inconsistent. Miscommunication often kept them from completing projects, they said, and had some major impacts on certain departments. Also, they felt that they did not get good feedback that would help them improve their work or do something different. Some felt that regulations were not communicated in such a way that staff were aware of how these would be interpreted by management.

Nonteaching staff also felt they were not always valued and that their advancement was blocked. The focus group members did not agree on the best way to reward or punish, and some said that perceptions of fairness were an issue and often created mistrust.

The focus groups' information provided content for questions used in surveys given to all employees in both groups. The surveys put some of the focus group information into perspective because both surveys used a summated rating scale from strongly agree to strongly disagree. Both surveys included open-ended questions at the end. These could be evaluated with content analysis. Also, some multiple-choice responses allowed respondents to indicate how they felt about their career/job choice.

The focus groups and the follow-up survey, intended to discover the concerns of all employees, identified significant issues that could affect how employees, as insiders, would represent their view of the quality of the school district. Both teaching and non-teaching staff felt that management and communication at the district level were good, but uneven at individual schools.

The district's new intranet system was valued as a more open and faster communication channel, with announcements by the PR person having a higher readership and value than the comments from the chief administrator. Communication at the school level was viewed as uneven, with e-mails being more political than useful. Meetings were an effective tool at some schools, but not at those where hierarchy seemed to stifle input.

Both sets of employees felt that changing demographics in the community were difficult to cope with, and the mix of cultures, was a challenge, as were increasing numbers of students with special needs. Lack of support from parents, attributed to their work demands, made partnerships weak with that major constituency, something felt equally by teaching and nonteaching staff. A lack of good connections with parents also affected discipline problems, as did the lack of facilities for handling students with severe discipline problems. Unclear expectations and consequences of independent decisions created so much uncertainty that handling problems with students was uneven and unpredictable.

One good result of the research was that both teaching and nonteaching staff agreed that helping students be successful was the district's most important mission and a value they held strongly.

As might be imagined, reporting research results that can be seen as negative often has unfortunate results. Although the district itself got good marks for establishing common values and communicating well, management at the individual unit levels needed improvement, as did communication.

All constituencies of today's schools are increasing their demands for accountability, responsibility, and credibility. Keeping ahead of these expectations means that PR research is essential. Summative research can reveal if the branding's reflection of the mission statement is accurate and if communication of positioning strategies is working. Because employees often are the "image" of the organization to other stakeholders, each summative evaluation has to start with them. They have to buy into the mission statement and accept the positioning of the district.

SUMMATIVE EVALUATION OF MISSION AND POSITIONING STRATEGIES

Although a mission statement should be the focus for an organization's activities, the statement itself does not define how an organization wants to be seen by all its publics/stakeholders. That is the purpose of a positioning strategy, which is also expressed as a statement and drawn from an interpretation of the mission statement. Branding reflects and reinforces both. Branding means being sure that all communication speaks with one voice and that policies reinforce these statements in all of the relationships with a variety of stakeholders. Such a process not only validates the mission statement and administrative positioning, but also gives some evidence of the effectiveness of the organization in communicating its self-image.

SIGNIFICANCE AND USE OF EVALUATION

The way publics see the organization living up to its self-defined role is critical to the financial and moral support the organization gets. Evaluating public perceptions of how well the organization has achieved its goals and objectives—inspired by its mission statement and focused by its positioning strategy—is as important as documenting its achievements. Many accrediting reviews, such as those required by state departments of education, attest to this in that they ask for the opinions of both internal and external publics, as well as hard evidence on such matters as promotion and testing results at the lower levels and retention and graduation statistics. Summative data give quantitative evidence that validates actions, communication, and policies.

One use of summative evaluations is living up to schools' social responsibility by providing information related to accountability. Although public schools don't have stockholders, they do have stakeholders, which include all of their publics (Hendrix, 2004, chap. 2). Private schools have direct and indirect investors, indirect investors being those who may offer "gifts in kind," such as landscaping. Knowing what they got for their investment is important.

Another use of summative evaluation is internal. Evaluations give valuable advice to management regarding ways that communication and information management can be improved within the organization. Summative evaluations are a form of "report card," and as such, administrators should discuss their relevance with the district's PR specialist.

Reporting

Communicating the results of summative evaluations helps administrators and overseers, such as school boards, understand what the needs, concerns, and successes are. Also, it gives confidence to students, teachers, and parents who are investing time and energy. Evaluations also give authority to the official reporting requirements of all institutions. Such factors as dropout rates, drug abuse cases, and harassment situations all must be assessed and the results reported. On a more positive note, administrators who have invested heavily in computer equipment may be able to report increased research skills and an interest in fact-finding on the part of students.

School administrators must justify their actions to a plethora of oversight groups, from regulatory and accrediting agencies to special-interest groups. Monitoring and evaluating on a regular basis offer credible benchmarks for progress made and justify actions taken. Monitoring and evaluating activities also provide opportunities to communicate an organization's effectiveness to different constituencies. Survey results often generate responses from publics and influence opinions.

Counseling Decision Makers

Advice or counsel is a reasoned recommendation based on sound evidence, not necessarily experience. Counseling is a primary PR function for strategic decision making, and it is not an "I think" process. Acceptable evidence must come from ongoing monitoring and evaluation. Counseling is most critical, of course, when there is a crisis. Crisis counseling, sometimes called "reputation management," is often needed when a reputation can no longer be "managed" because of prior action or inaction. However, sound counsel can come from evidence of how priority, and sometimes nonpriority, publics[1] are likely to respond.

Evaluation often provides the critical evidence needed in emotional decisions, such as whether to allow students who are not getting a diploma to sit with a graduating class. One incident that got national attention involved a mainstreamed student with a disability who still had more work to do to complete his graduation requirements, but who wanted to sit with his class at commencement. Evaluations can help with such situations by monitoring the percentage of a class that is unlikely to graduate, especially if the reason involves a disability. If this is done, decisions can be made and communicated early enough to avert or at least reduce the impact of a crisis situation.

Fleshing Out Problem Areas with Research.   Three basic informal measurement methods are available: unobtrusive measures, audits, and publicity analysis. Secondary research can be formal or informal (Newsom, Turk, & Kruckeberg, 2007, chap. 4, Table 4.2).

Unobtrusive measures are observations that do not intrude on the process of gathering data—for example, color-coding tickets to a performance or lecture so you can see which publics are most responsive to that offering. Sometimes this helps determine whether it is worth doing again. Such measures are indicators, but not very reliable ones. A ticket intended for one person representing a particular public might be given to and used by someone else.

Audits are more structured and reliable, especially if they incorporate some formal research methods as part of the examination. Public relations audits are not financial audits, but communication audits. What they have in common with financial audits is an examination of process.

Publicity analysis is collecting everything that is said and/or written about the organization, whether the source for the information is the school district or another source (Wimmer & Dominick, 2005). Much of that information is on the Internet. Some of it is in formal news outlets with a Web presence where published or broadcast news and opinions are found, but often it is in other expressions of opinion such as blogs (Web logs) or alternate Web sites that imitate or mimic their object's own site in name. Evaluating other research for its validity and application is critical (Newsom & Haynes, 2005, chap. 5). Although informal reviews of publicity can be informative, serious evaluation involves content analysis, a formal research process. Content analysis (Berelson, 1953) is essential in discovering what is being said or written about an organization in a structured way that puts the information in context and gives some quantitative evidence for decisions.

---

[1]Priority publics for public schools typically include parents, local government officials, and other local resident taxpayers.

TABLE 15–1

Advantages and Disadvantages of Formal Research

	Qualitative	
Method	Advantages	Disadvantages
Focus groups	1. Provide quick and less expensive feedback than do other methods. 2. Flexible in design and format. 3. Offer some insight into behavior by offering answers to "why."	1. Are misused, often represented as offering conclusive evidence. 2. Can be mishandled by the moderator so that opinions are influenced and some opinions are not expressed. 3. Are not always representative of the research universe.
Panels	1. Have some of the same advantages as focus groups. 2. May be chosen to represent a specific population.	1. Have some of the same disadvantages as focus groups. 2. Can "learn" problems of the organization over time and then fail to be preventative.
In-depth interviews	1. Allow follow-up on new lines of inquiry. 2. Offer detailed responses. 3. Permit broader, more comprehensive questions.	1. Are difficult to transcribe and code for content analysis. 2. May allow the interviewer to influence responses. 3. Often include extraneous information in the responses.
Historiographies, case studies, diaries	1. Give insight into situations. 2. Suggest further research opportunities. 3. Provide detail that offers perspective to facts.	1. Are difficult to generalize from. 2. Often lack the rigor of scientific methods. 3. Are time consuming and often require searching for data that are then selectively presented.
Content analysis	1. Shows what appeared, where, how often, and in what context. 2. Permits comparison with other data, especially about publics. 3. Its useful in tracking trends and monitoring change.	1. Its costly and time consuming. 2. Provides no information about audience impact. 3. Does not include critical information that is not in the news media.
Survey research	1. Its flexible in use. 2. Can be administered in various ways. 3. Capitalizes on the desire to express opinions.	1. May not result in truthful answers, either because respondents don't remember or because they are conscious of the socially expected response. 2. Doesn't allow for expression of in-depth feelings. 3. Often asks the wrong questions of the wrong people in the wrong way.

Source: Adapted from Newsom, Turk, & Kruckeberg, 2007, chap. 4. Copyright 2007 by Wadsworth/Thompson Learning. Reprinted with permission of Wadsworth/ITP.

Secondary research involves gathering and studying existing information—such as comparative data for other school systems; looking at communication policies, plans, and procedures; and collecting whatever information is available on branding for schools and universities that are heavily involved in this sort of identification and measuring its relative success. Much of these data are the result of formal research.

Formal research methods may be qualitative or quantitative. Qualitative measures include the use of focus groups and panels; in-depth interviews that are fairly self-explanatory; and case studies, diaries, and historiography. Quantitative techniques are varied, but the most commonly used in educational PR are content analysis and surveys. Whether the method used is qualitative or quantitative, researcher bias is always an issue. For the advantages and disadvantages of various types of research, see Table 15–1.

Technology and Survey Research

Much survey research can be accomplished online by posting the survey site in an e-mail and often using a list serve as the database and means of distribution.

While convenient and economical, this method has its drawbacks. Delivery is uncertain. E-mail addresses change rather frequently, and many respondents whose information would be helpful have opted out of list serves. Others who get the survey simply delete it immediately. Some may click on it, but not respond when they find out how long the survey may take. Of course, potential respondents can throw away questionnaires, too, but they may complete them, since they can go back to a hard copy if interrupted. Staying online at a single site for a long period of time tests the patience of even the most committed members of the public. As a result, respondents who do complete the electronic questionnaire may be even less representative of the intended public than if other methods are used.

Electronic questionnaires that come in a list serve are more likely to get a response from individuals who don't want their answer traced to them, as an e-mail is likely to do. That can be avoided if the respondents to a personal e-mail simply go to the survey site by clicking on to it, but some suspicious respondents may not trust the anonymity of their response. Another element that arouses their suspicion is the ability to click on the survey response to receive a copy of the results. That's almost asking for the respondent to opt out. More attractive is a promise to post the results at a special Web address, although tech-savvy respondents know that by going to that site they will provide information that will identify them.

All sorts of evaluative research, especially summative explorations that probe opinions, are more likely to prove difficult to get when the source seeking the information has gone through some difficult or controversial situations.

ETHICAL, LEGAL, CULTURAL, AND ECONOMIC RAMIFICATIONS OF MEASURING

Ethical and Legal Issues

Ethical and legal problems can occur during the research process. Ethical issues include honesty in the gathering of data and in the consideration of subjects—not adversely affecting subjects or misrepresenting to them who wants to know what and why.

Confidentiality must be preserved, if that is a factor, and there must be no misrepresentation of the results, or "cooking the data," which can occur with both qualitative and quantitative measurements. These are concerns whether the research is being done in-house or by a vendor. When the research is bought from an outside contractor, it is imperative that the PR director or the coordinating administrator understand the methodology well enough to judge its validity and to determine if the conclusions drawn are legitimate.

Breaches of confidentiality can harm respondents and invite legal problems. For example, people identified in focus groups or through survey responses may be fired or transferred as a result of disclosure of their identities. It is also important to be sure that in reporting results, such as candid responses to an audit question, respondents are not damaged in a way that might produce a libel suit.

The accumulation and storage of data can create both ethical and legal problems, so research results must be protected. If results are shared in industry, trade, or professional publications, the name of the organization, as well as the names of all respondents, must be masked unless specific, written permission for disclosure is given.

Cultural Considerations in Research

Cultural awareness includes remembering that not everyone living in the United States is a citizen. Citizens of other nations living here have a considerable impact on school populations. In certain parts of the country, there are high concentrations of citizens from other countries who are working in multinational companies or in companies that need their skills or expertise. Their children attend local schools. Many ordinary processes taken for granted are unfamiliar and perhaps even seen as invasive by other cultures. Schools involved in research must be aware of this or risk alienating some of their students and their families.

Beyond that, some minority populations among U.S. citizens have a different worldview from the majority population and certainly from each other. What is accepted by one culture is not necessarily accepted by another. The biggest risk in doing research in the multinational, multiethnic population that exists in this country today is assuming too much. Although it always is true that there is no homogeneity among publics, this especially needs to be considered in doing research among a mix of cultures (Duncan, 2002, chap. 19).

Cultural sensitivity means researchers must remember to pretest survey methodology and questions with all diverse publics. Given today's religious and ethnic diversity, some questions we might take for granted are considered invasive and even threatening. Words have different interpretations depending on a respondent's familiarity with American English. Always there is some risk that a survey questionnaire sent to a child's parent will be completed by an individual who does not have a very good command of the English language. Often the child has to translate the questions for the parent. Strict translations are rarely accurate because vocabularies are incongruous across languages. Even professional translators often must search for the best word to convey meaning and intent. Relying on a young child or even an adolescent with a limited vocabulary to translate survey questions is obviously a precarious decision.

Budgeting for Research

Research always has an associated cost, and an administrator needs to plan for this in developing a budget. Look at each activity or goal for the year and determine what sort of research is indicated for each. Depending on district or school needs, it may be that most of the research can be done internally, but this does not mean that costs are not involved. The researcher may require released time, and personnel costs may need to be increased. Also, cost increases for supplies, copying, printing, distributing, and so forth are likely. As a general rule, approximately 10% of a project's budget should be allocated to research and evaluation costs.

Research is an investment, not a luxury. High-visibility projects often require external evaluators, largely for credibility reasons. However, time is another consideration; often a consultant can complete the research more quickly than an internal team. Last, external reports provide a degree of protection for a superintendent or principal, especially if the results are not welcome by the school board and public. Often people blame the messenger for negative news.

Remember that monitoring all publics all the time in great detail is generally not cost effective for a school district. Administrators create the problem of scarce resources, so they must be selective in making financial decisions. However, a communication audit should be done once a year for each high-priority public, just as audits are done for other aspects of the institution. Such communication audits produce longitudinal documentation for decision making. An audit of nonpriority publics on a revolving basis can then be budgeted.

Commissioning Research

Although much ongoing research and even some special project research, such as for a single campaign, may be handled internally by staff, summative research is often commissioned. There are several reasons for considering getting outside help. First is the time consumed because most employees already are working at maximum capacity and seldom can be freed from other responsibilities to handle an involved research project. Another consideration is that the school or district may not have the computer programs, capacity, or expertise required. Yet another consideration is the credibility that outside evaluation brings because of its perceived objectivity.

If commissioning research is a possibility, proposals need to be sent to possible suppliers early enough to give the one chosen time to get familiar with the project, the participants, and the available information. Budget is often raised as an issue in getting an outside evaluation, but research costs, whether done internally or externally, and that should be reflected in any school/district budget.

Additional considerations are the expertise of the organization doing the research and the commitment of confidentiality. The person or committee making the decision after proposals are submitted needs to be familiar enough with research techniques to evaluate the proposals. The lowest in cost is not always the best. Those choosing the organization that will be commissioned must understand exactly what the proposal includes and whether or not that is what is needed. Also, since the school/district knows its stakeholders better than any outsider, the approach to these groups by the research firm has to be sensitive to the attitudes of those stakeholders so no one will be offended in the process. Confidentiality is important both in gathering the information and in processing it. Some districts may have committees in place to consider such proposals in order to assure confidentiality and protect individuals.

When the research is completed, the person or committee who chose the research firm should consider the results, methodology, and process to be sure the final report measures up to expectations. Usually, a summative research project is divided into pieces, as illustrated in the case study. Segmenting summative research and tying it to problem areas provide a good approach. Elements identified as less than satisfactory in the first stage of the project can be corrected before evaluation in the subsequent stages.

Yet another concern is who owns the raw data compiled by the research firm. This has to be determined at the outset. If the school or district wants to retain the raw data, then responsibility for protecting it lies with those who commissioned it. Often the contract with the research firm allows the firm to keep raw data and copies of its report. How the firm uses either raw data or the final report should be stipulated in the contract. In some situations, such as in this chapter's case study, when a professor is commissioned to do the research, the professor may expect that he or she can use the data in relation to teaching, research, and publication. Moreover, research firms may wish to show the project to prospective clients or to enter the report in professional competitions. Therefore, use restrictions should be stipulated when the contract is negotiated.

What Research Reveals: Collective Perceptions

Reputations of the "best schools" often are purely opinion based. A system must be developed, therefore, to measure how publics, especially priority publics, are perceiving the institution. That is the special asset of summative evaluations.

Collective perceptions of an organization by its publics are based on what it says and what it does. These collective perceptions constitute the organization's image. If all these fit together, then public perception is fairly close to reality. The reason for that congruity is simple. What the organization says is consistent with what it does and fits with the mission statement that has given people some expectations of what it should be. When this is true for most of the organization's publics, the image of the institution or organization is generally clear and accurate. That image may not fit a new positioning strategy statement. Also, it may not match what the goals are for the organization—but the image will be clear and measurable. If an organization wants to change the image to reflect a new positioning or new goal, it will be relatively easy to see when the image begins to change.

If an organization has an image that is not clearly defined, it may indicate two problems. One is that the organization is not communicating very well with its publics. Another is that what it is saying does not match what it is doing or what various publics are experiencing in their relationships with the institution. When that happens, a problem profile for an organization may begin to appear.

A problem profile results when different priority publics hold very different views of the organization. The solution is to discover through research where the discrepancies are and correct them through communication or policy changes that are then clearly communicated.

Anticipating responses from all publics, especially priority publics, is key to evaluating and monitoring the climate of public opinion, another responsibility of the PR officer. Yet this cannot be done effectively unless the officer has good evidence of the perceptions of relevant publics about the organization. The PR practitioner (or anyone else in the institution) cannot create an image for the institution. But the PR officer can be effective in improving the way publics perceive an organization, a goal achieved only by monitoring public opinion, which is always in flux and highly sensitive to events and experiences.

Sound program evaluations tell an organization how it is seen by different publics, thus supporting the identification and analysis of shortcomings. These evaluations are especially critical when building a precrisis constituency. They also help to determine the persuasive level at which continuing campaigns are functioning.

Determining Strategy According to the Persuasion Process

Summative evaluations can also be used to estimate the level at which new campaigns should be launched to be successful. When a campaign is over, a sound evaluation indicates what succeeded with whom and why, as well as the quality and depth of the residue of goodwill that is left for the future.

An organization seldom has only one campaign going on at once. Although there may be something that is a priority, such as a school district's bond drive, there may also be a campaign to get new computers in the classrooms—a co-op program with a local grocery store chain or other retail outlet. It may be a direct fund-raising campaign.

The typology of campaigns mirrors the six steps of the persuasion process: presenting, attending, comprehending, yielding, retaining, and acting. Therefore, it is critical to know at which persuasive level priority publics are before structuring a campaign.

A campaign to create awareness, the first level of the persuasion process, may be required if priority publics are not aware of the issue, problem, or need. Whatever it may be, the focal point must be presented to them. Monitoring and evaluation processes can identify this for each public. However, since awareness campaigns are perhaps the most expensive to launch and maintain, resources can be saved if the priority publics for the campaign are already aware of the problem, but are not really paying attention to it—perhaps because they are not convinced it is important.

A campaign to convey information, the second level of the persuasion process, is totally different in structure from an awareness campaign, both in using media and in crafting messages. A message has to be strong enough to gain their attention. Monitoring and evaluation of publics help indicate where to start.

Suppose the knowledge of an issue among priority publics is such that there is no need to get their attention or to inform them about its significance. This does not necessarily mean the publics understand what they can do about the issue or, more importantly, what the educational organization wants them to do about it. Thus, the campaign should be structured to gain the publics' comprehension, the third level of persuasion.

Yielding is the next level. Pitched at this level of the persuasion process, a campaign is likely to emphasize shared values as a way of getting compliance or participation. Such a campaign is a facilitating effort aimed at getting priority publics to act on whatever it is that they already have accepted and are ready to do. Say that a school's library was damaged by fire, and the extent of the damage is widely known and understood; many constituencies may help rebuild the collection, if only they are told specifically how they can help.

Publics must be encouraged to retain a desirable position, especially if they have been encouraged to do something new. Suppose, for example, that the library situation attracts some local bookstores that never paid any attention to the school before. It is easy to write off the bookstores as "one-timers" and be grateful for that. It is even better to change the bookstore owners' or managers' attitudes or behavior and convert them to regular contributors of one kind or another.

Priority publics may already be at the persuasive level of acting. But what they do now may not be exactly what is desired. If so, a campaign to modify behavior is needed. A school district might find new "adopt-a-school" or other partnership opportunities from those who help with the problem. The ongoing campaigns of an organization are likely to be at all these different levels, depending on the issue or need, the priority publics, and their level of understanding.

Determining the Level of Success

All campaigns should have specific purposes derived from goals and objectives that are the tangible expressions of the mission statement and positioning. But evaluating a campaign is more than determining whether the purpose was achieved. A capital fund-raising campaign can meet its goal and leave a path littered with hostile publics who not only will never help again, but also will make negative comments about the organization every chance they get.

Evaluations should examine two outcomes: (a) what the organization did and how much it cost to do it and (b) what the results were for each effort, tangible and intangible. First, the focus is on determining the actual productivity involved in the campaign and the real costs of each effort. Then the cost effectiveness of the various efforts is determined. Sometimes carefully contrived formulas are used to figure out something like the dollar equivalent of publicity if the same space or time had been bought. That sort of fiction is not very useful. What you want to know is who saw it and what they thought about it. Or if a campaign has focused on the introduction of a new core curriculum, for instance, no matter how much meeting time it took or how many publications were produced, the bottom line is whether students and teachers understand it and see it as an improvement. It is also important to know whether other evaluators, such as accrediting groups and professional associations, say good things about the school for making the change.

Glorious campaigns have introduced dismal failures. The commercial marketplace makes quick assessments, but the marketplace of ideas sometimes takes a little longer. Evaluations must judge results and offer predictive information for planning.

SUMMARY

Evaluating PR activities is essential to sustaining support, so research by school PR practitioners is critical for schools to be credible, accountable, and responsible to all their constituencies. The primary role of the PR professional is to offer counsel in strategic planning that offers measurable results. Summative research provides necessary information for adjusting policies and meeting the expectations of the publics so there is a solid support constituency in the event of a crisis. Summative research helps to get an idea of what the institutional image is, how well its branding is being accepted, and how faithful that identification is to the mission and positioning. Knowing a school or a district's reputation is essential to management, politically and economically.

The most useful research tools for gathering new information for summative research are focus groups and surveys. For discovering what perceptions of the various publics are, the most useful tool is content analysis, which finds out what others have said and written.

When summative evaluation is used for strategic moves such as campaigns, it is important to determine what strategy should be used based on where targeted publics are on the six levels of the persuasion process: presenting or making people aware, attending or giving them information to which they will pay attention, comprehending or understanding the message, yielding or accepting, retaining the position, and acting on the persuasive message. Finally, the level of success has to be evaluated from the position of how all publics have reacted to the campaign. Summative evaluation also tells how the school or school district ranks with others and gives important comparative data.

QUESTIONS AND SUGGESTED ACTIVITIES

CASE STUDY

1. Name and explain the types of evaluation used in this case and their relative effectiveness.
2. What do the findings suggest to management in terms of the school district's reputation?
3. How significant are the problems employees encounter to their reflection of the district to other stakeholders?
4. How can employee perceptions be checked against those of other stakeholders (i.e., Do other stakeholders see the same issues that employees do?)?
5. How could communication channels within the district be improved?
6. What other types of research tools might provide more feedback on an ongoing basis so that summative findings could be improved?

CHAPTER

7. Identify the major considerations in implementing summative research.
8. Choose an issue that creates an opportunity to institute a new policy, and determine what research needs to be done to see the policy through to a successful endorsement.

9. What is the role of summative PR research in (a) guiding policy evaluations, (b) suggesting policy and program changes, (c) suggesting campaigns, and (d) providing comparative data.

10. What are the primary obstacles to evaluating reputation (opinions) and policy/programs (facts) through summative research?

11. How much do employees reflect and thus affect the school district's reputation to other stakeholders?

12. How can addressing employee concerns with policy and management initiatives impact reputation?

13. What occurs when positioning by the district is not seen as realistic by employees, teachers, and nonteaching staff?

14. How can branding affect and reflect reputation?

SUGGESTED READINGS

Babbie, E. (2005). *The practice of social research.* Belmont, CA: Wadsworth/ITP.

Barzun, J., & Graff, H. F. (2004). *Modern researchers.* Belmont, CA: Wadsworth/ITP.

Broom, G. M. (2005). *Effective public relations.* Upper Saddle River, NJ: Prentice Hall.

Center, A. H., & Jackson, P. (2002). *Public relations practices, managerial case studies and problems.* Upper Saddle River, NJ: Prentice Hall.

Culbertson, H. M., Jeffers, D. W., Stone, D. B., & Terrell, M. (1993). *Social, political, and economic contexts in public relations: Theory and cases.* Hillsdale, NJ: Erlbaum.

Newsom, D., Turk, J. V., & Kruckeberg, D. (2007). *This is PR: The realities of public relations* (9th ed.). Belmont, CA: Wadsworth/Thompson Learning.

Stacks, D. W. (2002). *Primer of public relations research.* New York: Guilford Press.

Stewart, T. D. (2002). *Principles of research in communication.* Boston: Allyn & Bacon.

Strauss, A. L., & Corbin, J. M. (1998). *Basics of qualitative research.* Thousand Oaks, CA: Sage.

Wilcox, D. L., & Cameron, G. T. (2006). *Public relations strategies and tactics.* Boston: Allyn & Bacon.

REFERENCES

Berelson, B. (1953). Content analysis in communication research. In B. Berelson & M. Janowitz (Eds.), *Reader in public opinion and communication.* Glencoe, IL: Free Press.

Duncan, T. (2002). *IMC: Using advertising and promotion to build brands.* New York: McGraw-Hill.

Hendrix, J. A. (2004). *Public relations cases.* Belmont, CA: Wadsworth/ITP.

Newsom, D., & Haynes, J. (2005). *Public relations writing: Form & style.* Belmont, CA: Wadsworth/ITP.

Newsom, D., Turk, J. V., & Kruckeberg, D. (2007). *This is PR: The realities of public relations.* Belmont, CA: Wadsworth/Thompson Learning.

Wimmer, R. D., & Dominick, J. R. (2005). *Mass media research: An introduction* (8th ed.). Belmont, CA: Wadsworth/ITP.

Index

profile and database
development, 222–225
staffing, 169–170
Diversity
and collaborative groups, 118, 119
and conflict resolution, 153–154
and eye contact, 144–145
multicultural perspectives,
deploying, 252–253
and nonverbal communication, 142
and parent involvement, 255, 256
and personal space, 146
of population, 131–132
and PR, 174
and public opinion, 45
and reflective listening, 138
and research considerations, 360
in schools, 18, 34, 36–37, 40–41, 255
and vision development, 117
Doctrine of sovereign immunity, 79
Double-loop learning, 110
Dress, and nonverbal
communication, 147
Drolet, B., 148, 149, 150, 151
Dropouts, school. *See* graduation rates
Du Four, R., 113
Duan-Barnett, N. J., 50

Eaker, R., 113
Easton, D., 108, 109
Economic underclass, 37
Education
improving, 14
planning in, 215–219
Education Consolidation and
Improvement Act, 61
Educational Leadership Constituent
Council (ELCC), 134
Educational public relations. *See* school
public relations
Educational Testing Service
(ETS), 56, 57
Electronic media reporters
radio, 284
television, 283–283
Web-based outlets, 285
Electronic newsletters, 176
Elementary and Secondary Education
Act (ESEA), 54, 66
E-mail survey, 297–298
Emotions, expression of, 142
Engagement, 256–257
Engagement plan, 258, 259f
English-language learners, 41
Enrollment, school, demographics of, 41
Entrepreneurial schools, 191
Environmental scanning, 10
Environmental space, 146–147
Equal Access Act, 85
Equal opportunity movement, 60–61

Emblems, 146
English, Fenwick, 220
Environmental space, 146–147
Epstein, J. L., 257
Error proability, 296
Establishment Clause, 84, 85, 86
Ethics, 88
and public relations, 90–91
and research, 359–360
in school administration, 89–90
Etzioni, A., 219–220
Evaluation, 15
of PR plan, 239
Evaluation, PR programs
case study of, 353–355
ethical, legal, cultural, and economic
ramifications, 359–364
significance and use of, 356–359
summative evaluation of mission and
positioning strategies, 255–356
Excellence in education
movement, 62–63
Expression, freedom of. *See* First
Amendment rights
External publics, 250
Eye contact, 144–145

Face-to-face interviews, 297–298
Facial expression, 143
Faculty
role in school-level PR, 173
Fair-use doctrine, 87
Families, changing structure
of, 36–38, 255
Family Educational Rights and Privacy
Act (FERPA), 83–84, 176
Family hygiene, 256
Fatherhood, and changing families, 38
Federal Bureau of Investigation (FBI), 176
Feedback
summative, 108
supportive, 139
Feedback loops, 108
Feedback mechanisms, 111
FileMaker Pro™, 223
First Amendment
rights, 80, 81–82, 84, 86
First World Assembly of Public
Relations Associations, 10
Fiscal requirements, 234
*Fleischfresser v. Directors of School
District 200*, 86
Flemming, T., 109
Focus groups, 9, 300, 301
and data analysis, 224, 225–226
Follett, M. P., 107
Formal research, 357–358
Forming group stage, 118
For-profit schools. *See* entrepreneurial
schools

Forums, 67
Free-lunch programs, 36
FrontPage®, 223
Frye, E. T., 249
F-tests, 295
Fullan, M. G., 147
Funding
of market surveys319
and the PR plan, 234
of private schools, 192–193
Funding campaigns, 312
case study of, 311–312
four P's of marketing, 313–314
marketing versus selling, 313
pitfalls/mistakes, 331–333
scouting report and game
plan, 314–324
successful campaign, calendar
for, 330–331
successful campaign,
elements of, 324–330
and the Word Wide Web, 333
Fusarelli, L., 257

Gallagher, D., 218
Gallup Poll, 54, 56
Gates Foundation, 43
Gender
and eye contact, 144–145
and personal space, 146
General systems theory/model,
107–108, 108f
Gestures, 146
Getzels, J., 109
Gillens, H., 343
Glass, T., 31
Goal-free planning, 216
Goals, 14–16
and media relation plans, 270
and PR plans, 231–233
and vision development, 116
Golen, S., 135
Gonring, M. P., 268
*Good News Club v. Molford Central
School District*, 85
Goodwill, establishing, 15
Google search engine, 333
Gordon, J. C., 9
Government
immunity of, 79
and school policies, 60–61
and societal change, 34–35
governmental immunity, 79
Graduation rates, 17–18, 37, 41–42, 64
Graham, G., 310
Gregersen, H. B., 215
Griffiths, D., 111
Groups
and collaborative visioning, 117–121
and conflict, 121